Studies of psychosocial risk

Studies of psychosocial risk: the power of longitudinal data

Edited by
MICHAEL RUTTER
MRC Child Psychiatry Unit
Institute of Psychiatry, London

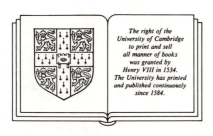

The right of the
University of Cambridge
to print and sell
all manner of books
was granted by
Henry VIII in 1534.
The University has printed
and published continuously
since 1584.

Cambridge University Press
Cambridge
New York   New Rochelle   Melbourne   Sydney

Published by the Press Syndicate of the University of Cambridge
The Pitt Building, Trumpington Street, Cambridge CB2 1RP
32 East 57th Street, New York, NY 10022, USA
10 Stamford Road, Oakleigh, Melbourne 3166, Australia

First published 1988

Printed in Great Britain by Billings, Worcester

British Library cataloguing in publication data

Studies of psychosocial risk: the power of
longitudinal data.
1. Developmental psychology. Longitudinal studies
I. Rutter, Michael
155'.0722

Library of Congress cataloguing in publication data

Studies of psychosocial risk: the power of longitudinal
data / edited by Michael Ruter.
    p. cm.
Includes index.
ISBN 0 521 35330 0
1. Developmental psychology – Longitudinal studies.
2. Antisocial personality disorders – Longitudinal studies.
3. Psychology – Research – Methodology.
I. Rutter, Michael.
BF713.5.S78   1988
150'.724 – dc 19, 88-1491 CIP

ISBN 0 521 35330 0

CE

Contents

Principal contributors

Dr L. Bergman
Department of Psychology, University of Stockholm

Professor G. Brown
Department of Social Policy and Social Science, Royal Holloway and Bedford New College, London

Dr J. Dunn
Pennsylvania State University, Department of Individual and Family Studies, College of Human Development

Dr D. Farrington
Institute of Criminology, Cambridge

Mr D. Fergusson
Christchurch Child Development Study, Department of Paediatrics, Christchurch Hospital, New Zealand

Professor N. Garmezy
Department of Psychology, University of Minnesota

Dr K. E. Grossmann
Lehrstuhl Psychologie IV, University of Regensburg

Dr D. Hay
MRC Child Psychiatry Unit, Department of Child and Adolescent Psychiatry, Institute of Psychiatry, London

Professor R. Hinde
MRC Unit on the Development and Integration of Behaviour, Cambridge University

Professor Dr A. Kalverboer
Laboratory for Experimental Clinical Psychology, Groningen

Professor I. Kolvin
Nuffield Psychology and Psychiatry Unit, Fleming Memorial Hospital, Newcastle upon Tyne

Dr D. Magnusson
Department of Psychology, University of Stockholm

Ms B. Maughan
MRC Child Psychiatry Unit, Department of Child and Adolescent Psychiatry, Institute of Psychiatry, London

Dr A. Pickles
MRC Child Psychiatry Unit, Department of Child and Adolescent Psychiatry, Institute of Psychiatry, London

Dr L. Pulkkinen
Department of Psychology, University of Jyväskylä

Dr D. Quinton
MRC Child Psychiatry Unit, Department of Child and Adolescent Psychiatry, Institute of Psychiatry, London

Professor L. Robins
Department of Psychiatry, Washington University School of Medicine

Professor M. Rutter
MRC Child Psychiatry Unit, Department of Child and Adolescent Psychiatry, Institute of Psychiatry, London

Professor R. Silbereisen
Department of Psychology, University of Giessen

Dr J. C. van der Wolf
Department of Orthopedagogics, University of Amsterdam

Dr M. Wadsworth
MRC National Survey of Health and Development, Department of Community Medicine, University College London and the Middlesex Hospital Medical School

Foreword

Understanding the biological, psychological and social structures and processes operating in individual life courses is a challenging task for scientific endeavours. Research in this field constitutes a central scientific concern in its own right. The societal importance is also obvious, in as much as knowledge about both positive and negative aspects of human development can be used to promote healthy development and prevent harmful development.

It has become increasingly evident that better knowledge about developmental processes requires a longitudinal research approach, as a complement to the more traditional cross-sectional studies. However, longitudinal research is methodologically difficult and may be characterized as a somewhat risky enterprise. The traps are numerous, with respect to the long-term consequences of even small mistakes in the early planning stages regarding funding, and with respect to the delay of gratification and publication, factors that are important in a professional science career.

Recognition of the importance of a longitudinal approach to research on individual development, the conviction that such research needs stimulation and support, and the understanding that combined efforts will yield results where the total is more than the sum of the parts were determining factors for the European Science Foundation's decision to give this type of research a high priority. The resultant outcome of the Foundation's positive assessment was the establishment in 1985 of the ESF Network on Longitudinal Research on Individual Development. Subsequent endorsements of the ESF's governing bodies suggest that the Network will continue for several years, and thus seek to meet the considerable and much broadened range of interests and expectations in this new European science endeavour.

The volume that is presented here is the first scientific outcome of the activities within the Network. Placing the concerns of the book at the top of the list of activities of the Network reflects the view that we have to start with the substantive issues as a basis for later discussions about the methodological issues involved in longitudinal studies.

The main topic of this book – risk and protection factors in psycho-social disorder – covers an area of central interest for research on individual development. It is my firm conviction, and that of my colleagues responsible for the running of this ESF Network, that the identification of substantive issues and methodological problems pertinent to this field of research will enhance more effective theoretical and empirical analyses of the important topic of individual development.

David Magnusson
Chairman,
The ESF Network on Longitudinal Studies
on Individual Development

Preface

This book had its origins in an ESF workshop held in 1987 with the purpose of discussing the ways in which longitudinal data may be used to study the mechanisms involved in the operation of risk and protective factors for disorders of psychosocial development. While it is generally accepted that longitudinal studies have huge advantages over cross-sectional inquiries for the investigation of causal processes, it is an unfortunate fact that much longitudinal research has failed fully to capitalize on those advantages. The main aim of the workshop was to consider the conceptual and methodological issues involved in making better use of longitudinal data and, in so doing, to give some examples of the successful exploitation of longitudinal research strategies. It was not anticipated that there would be any one 'right' answer on how this should be done and, in order to encourage an exploration of the pros and cons of different approaches, each topic had a 'pair' of speakers who were expected to emphasize the differences, as well as the similarities, in their perspectives. The result was a lively meeting in which participants came away with a better appreciation of the range of longitudinal research strategies and of how much can be achieved by their use.

The chapters written after the meeting were prepared specially for this volume. However, in order to retain some sense of the dialogue and exchange of ideas, the plan of paired contributions has been retained and authors were encouraged to make cross-references to other chapters where that seemed appropriate. Rutter's introductory chapter on some of the uses and pitfalls of using longitudinal data to study causal processes sets the scene for the more detailed discussion of specific issues in the chapters that follow. Garmezy responds to some of these points and provides a historical perspective on psychiatric risk research.

In the third chapter, Magnusson and Bergman use data from their pioneering Stockholm longitudinal study to consider the need to base analyses on individual *patterns* of behaviour, as well as on specified behavioural traits or attributes. Pickles extends this discussion by considering how statistical modelling may be applied to the testing of different hypotheses on longitudinal patterns. Kolvin, Miller, Fleeting and Kolvin introduce the topic of the ways in which outcomes may be influenced by protective, as well as risk, variables and of the desirability of pinpointing *when* and *how* variables operate at different points in the life span. Silbereisen and Walper go on to point out that those issues demand the delineation of the mechanisms underlying mediating and moderating effects, suggesting that a person–process–context paradigm may be helpful for this purpose.

Kalverboer focuses attention on some of the particular issues posed by the study of biological high-risk variables and, in his response, Grossmann considers whether additional perspectives may be obtained from some of the lessons learned from the study of low-risk samples. Farrington argues that the concept of cause necessarily involves the concept of change within individuals, and that causal-order questions can be examined more satisfactorily by within-subjects than between-subjects analyses. He uses delinquency data as examples for this purpose. Pulkkinen notes the many striking parallels with her own delinquency data and uses both studies to consider some possible theoretical interpretations of the findings.

Most psychosocial risk research has been concerned with either individual or family characteristics. Maughan discusses the growing body of evidence that school experiences can also serve as risk or protective factors for psychosocial and educational difficulties; van der Wolf notes that planned interventions in the school have a role in the investigation of the causal processes associated with school effects. Dunn draws attention to another often overlooked set of risk and protective factors, namely normative life events such as the birth of a sibling or starting school. Hay discusses the value of combining experimental with naturalistic research strategies for this purpose. Wadsworth takes a third relatively neglected topic, the study of intergenerational continuities and discontinuities, giving examples from the British National Survey, which has followed prospectively individuals born in 1946, many of whom are now parents of a further generation of children. Quinton responds by considering some of the conceptual and methodological issues involved in this line of inquiry, making reference to the findings from several other investigations (including his own) that have spanned the generations.

Brown uses data from his own study of both childhood experiences and current social circumstances as risk or protective factors for adult depression, to argue the need to consider indirect, as well as direct, causal paths, chains and strands. In doing so, he illustrates how longitudinal research strategies may be employed to great effect in the analysis of data that has been obtained cross-sectionally. Robins responds by contrasting prospective and retrospective approaches, going on to discuss what is known on retrospective recall.

Fergusson and Horwood take up the methodological theme in their outline of the ways in which structural equation modelling may be used to assess and circumvent measurement error in the investigation of causal processes. Bergman goes on to consider error from a range of different perspectives, noting the crucial importance of specifying the model of how key factors might operate and of how measurement error might arise. Finally, Hinde draws together many of the themes that span chapters in his discussion of some of the ways in which continuities and discontinuities in the developmental process occur.

Longitudinal research constitutes an essential research strategy for the study of normal and abnormal developmental processes. This volume reflects the many conceptual and methodological advances that have taken place, and which are still occurring, in longitudinal research. The individual chapters provide many illustrations of what can be achieved and also point the way ahead. These should be of equal interest to researchers who seek to study risk and protective factors for psychosocial disorders, and to practitioners who are interested in the process of human development in order to gain a better understanding of the nature and origins of different forms of disorder.

As editor, I have been fortunate in having a group of authors who have cheerfully and imaginatively responded to challenges on how their arguments were affected by contrary points of view as expressed by the authors of other chapters, and to suggestions on the need to clarify conceptual and methodological points. I am particularly grateful for their positive response to my chivvying on the need to meet tight deadlines; their helpfulness has made the editorial task an easy one. An especial word of thanks is needed to Helen Journeaux, and also Joy Maxwell, for their good work in checking text and references and in numerous other editorial and clerical tasks.

Michael Rutter

1 Longitudinal data in the study of causal processes: some uses and some pitfalls

Michael Rutter

Introduction

In medical research the study of causal processes is sometimes seen as a search for the one basic causal agent that serves as a necessary and sufficient factor for the genesis of some disease state. Even with infectious conditions, which probably come closest to this model, the concept constitutes an oversimplification because various factors influence the pathogenicity of the infectious agent and because marked individual differences in resistance to the pathogen must usually be taken into account (Eisenberg, 1986). Thus, with tuberculosis, it is known that resistance to the tubercle baccillus is influenced by both genetic factors and nutritional status. As demonstrated with streptococcal infections, psychosocial stressors may also help to determine whether or not an individual develops the disease (Haggerty, 1980).

In the case of mental disorders, this model of a single basic cause is much more seriously misleading. It is usual for aetiology to be multifactorially determined. Thus it is obvious that there are numerous disease processes that can lead to severe mental retardation. A necessary consequence of this fact is that any one cause will account for only a small proportion of the variance, simply because there are so many other causes. It is also the case that very few causal factors invariably lead to the psychopathological outcome. There are individual differences in susceptibility to the risk factor and also protective mechanisms may operate to reduce the risk of a pathological outcome (Rutter, 1985a; in press a).

A further crucial consideration is that the effects are rarely fixed. Whether or not a risk variable ultimately leads to a psychopathological outcome depends on what happens over time. In some cases the maladaptive outcome is dependent on the individual encountering particular situations that, in effect, activate the vulnerability produced by the risk factor. For example, the severe vulnerability to maladaptive parenting produced by an institutional rearing seems to be dependent to a large degree on the women raised in such conditions finding themselves without a supportive spouse and living in disadvantaged circumstances. In the absence of these current stressors in adult life, the institution-reared women's parenting differed little from controls in Quinton and Rutter's

1

(1988) follow-up study. It has also been shown that maladaptive outcomes are dependent on whether the early risk experiences are intensified by later maladaptive circumstances or ameliorated by later beneficial experiences. There are several examples in the literature of turning points in people's lives that have served to intensify or reduce risk effects. For example, Brown *et al.* (1986) showed that the ways in which single girls coped with an unwanted pregnancy played an important role in directing their later life trajectory. Similarly, Quinton and Rutter (1988) noted that the circumstances to which institution-reared girls went on leaving their group foster homes in their late teens could serve either to greatly improve or worsen their chances of successful functioning in early adult life. Maughan and Rutter (1986) found that the greater persistence in education of black adolescents in inner London schools enabled them to counter their earlier educational disadvantage to a considerable extent.

As long-term outcomes so frequently depend on a multiplicity of intervening events, it is rarely useful to examine causal processes in terms of a correlation between the hypothesized risk factor and the supposed pathogenic outcome (Labouvie, 1986; Rutter, 1987a). Rather, it is necessary to examine distal causal relationships in the form of chains and of linked sequences involving several different, relatively short-term effects or operations. The sheer complexity of these processes over time means that there are many hazards to be avoided in drawing inferences about causation from statistical associations. Nevertheless, provided that there is an appropriate attention to methodological issues, non-experimental studies can provide powerful tools for the testing of causal hypotheses. In most cases, however, it is highly advantageous, if not essential, to have longitudinal data.

In this chapter I review first the many advantages that stem from the availability of longitudinal data. These include (a) precision in the timing and measurement of experiences and of forms of behavioural expression; (b) the possibility of studying the process by which a risk variable leads to several different maladaptive outcomes; (c) the subdivision of disorders according to age of onset; (d) the study of change in individual subjects as a result of exposure to some risk variable; and (e) the analysis of indirect causal chain mechanisms. However, the rich potential of longitudinal analyses requires explicit statements on the underlying constructs and on the postulated causal processes. This need is discussed further in relation to some key problems and issues in using longitudinal data to tackle causal questions. These include (a) the exclusion of third variable effects (as through the study of natural experiments in which the real-life situation introduces changes over time or over place in the hypothesized risk factor or mechanism); (b) the need to differentiate risk indicators from risk mechanisms; (c) the choice of sample to highlight risk comparisons; (d) the choice of the most appropriate variable for the causal hypothesis being investigated; (e) the selection of the form of statistical analysis; and (f) the tracing of circular causal processes and of chain effects over time.

Advantages of longitudinal research strategies

Precision in timing and measurement

The most obvious advantage of longitudinal data is that frequently they allow a better delineation of the hypothesized risk factor. It has been well demonstrated that some kinds of retrospective recall are open to a variety of biases created by people's situation at the time of recall or by events and happenings during the intervening years (Chess *et al.*, 1966; Yarrow *et al.*, 1970). There is a tendency to reconstruct the timing of events and the nature of prior experiences in ways that serve to make greater sense of the person's current situation. Of course, these biases do not apply to all past events to the same degree (Robins *et al.*, 1985) and skilled interviewing can do much to reduce the biases. Nevertheless, it is always preferable to have prospective contemporaneous recordings of events as they occur rather than to have to rely on fallible later recollections.

In addition, of course, there are many variables that, by their nature, cannot be recalled. This would apply, for example, to physiological variables, many cognitive attributes, and to the details of behavioural patterns shown at an earlier age. If these are to be studied as risk factors there is no acceptable alternative to measuring them at the time, with reliance on longitudinal data to study later outcomes.

Heterogeneity of outcome

A second major advantage of longitudinal data is the opportunity to study 'escape' from the risk process. Continuities looking forwards often differ markedly from those looking backwards (Rutter *et al.*, 1983b). Thus, Quinton and Rutter (1988) showed that recurrent parenting breakdown was virtually confined to families in which one or other parent had suffered serious adversities in their own childhoods. However, prospective study of individuals suffering such severe adversities showed that only a minority exhibited later parenting breakdown. An adequate understanding of the causal process requires not only information on the likelihood that a deviant outcome *B* will have been preceded by the risk factor *A*, but also the frequency with which factor *A* is followed by outcome *B*. Longitudinal data are necessary for the investigator to grasp both ends of this stick.

The third advantage deals with a related point, namely the opportunity to study the heterogeneity of abnormal outcomes. If causal processes are tackled by means of a search for risk factors for a single pathological outcome, there is a danger of assuming that the risk is specific for that outcome when in fact the risks may apply to a much broader range of sequelae. For example, parents who abuse or neglect their children have often experienced abuse or neglect in their own upbringing (Rutter and Madge, 1976; Rutter, in press b). However, longitudinal data have shown that these adverse childhood experiences lead to a much broader range of maladaptive outcomes. Similarly, investigators have noted the frequency with which childhood depression is associated with major depressive disorders in the parents and other family members (Puig-Antich, 1986). However, data on the children of depressed parents show that the depression is only one of a range of psychiatric disorders for which they have a higher risk (Weissman *et al.*, 1987). A crucial specific aspect of this heterogeneity of outcomes is the need to identify subtle, but serious, sequelae that do not constitute an as yet recognizable pattern. A good example of this is provided by Hodges and Tizard's (in press a, b) study of children who spent their first few years in residential nurseries and who were then adopted at the age of 4–7 years. The adopted children at both 8 (Tizard, B. and Hodges, 1978) and 16 years (Hodges and Tizard, in press a, b) had a generally good outcome compared with controls and a very much better outcome than the residential nursery children who had returned to their biological parents to be brought up in discordant disadvantaged families. However, the longitudinal data were important in showing that the adopted children, in spite of their different later experiences and their otherwise different behaviour in adolescence, were strikingly similar to the non-adopted residential nursery children in their patterns of peer relationships. They were less likely to confide in peers, were less likely to have a definite special friend and more likely to be indiscriminately friendly in their peer relationships. This finding would not have been apparent if there had been reliance on the retrospective study of young people with identified pathological outcomes.

Subdivision by age of onset
For certain sorts of disorder it may be important to subdivide them according to the age of onset. For example, in the Isle of Wight study (Rutter *et al.*, 1976; Rutter, 1979) the correlates of adolescent psychiatric disorder that had had an onset before the age of ten years were strikingly different from the correlates of disorder at the same age that had arisen after the age of 10. In particular, the early-onset disorders had a strong association with severe reading retardation that was not present at all in the later-onset adolescent disorders. It was only because the individuals with disorder at the age of fifteen had been studied previously at the age of ten that this distinction could be made with reliability.

Intra-individual change
Almost all research into risk and protective factors has been concerned with the study of differences between individuals or between groups,

rather than of changes over time within individuals (Labouvie, 1986). Cross-sectional investigations are necessarily concerned with the former, but longitudinal studies can be analysed in either fashion (although few have been). One of the most important advantages of longitudinal data is that they provide the opportunity of investigating changes within the individual, as distinct from group tendencies (see chapter 9). Thus it has been possible to ask whether a geographical move away from inner-city areas reduces a person's delinquent behaviour (West, 1982); whether leaving school (Elliott and Voss, 1974) or marriage (Knight *et al.*, 1977) does the same; and whether the personal experience of unemployment has effects on life satisfaction and psychological well-being (Farrington *et al.*, 1986; Feather and O'Brien, 1986; Warr and Jackson, 1985). It is important to appreciate that the causal models represented by individual differences analyses are not synonymous with those implicit in intra-individual change approaches, and in some circumstances they may lead to opposite conclusions even when derived from the same set of data (Labouvie, 1986). It is not, of course, that one model is right and the other wrong. Rather, they tackle different causal questions. The situation parallels the contrast between secular trends and individual differences (Rutter and Madge, 1976). Thus the causal explanation for *X* being out of work, while *Y* is not, may well not be the same as the causal explanation for the marked rise in unemployment in the community as a whole during the last decade. The point is that longitudinal data enable both inter-individual differences and intra-individual change to be investigated.

Causal chain analyses

It has been noted earlier that causal processes often involve complex chains of continuities and discontinuities over time (see chapters 17 and 21). One key issue, therefore, concerns the study of the extent to which sequelae do or do not persist over time. For example, the longitudinal data of Magnusson *et al.* (1986) showed a marked effect of early maturity in girls leading to a higher rate of drunkenness and heavy alcohol consumption during adolescence. Follow-up of the same girls into early adult life, however, showed that the effect of early maturity did not persist. On the other hand, the effects of early maturity on educational careers did prove lasting. The availability of longitudinal data were crucial in delineating the mechanisms that were probably involved in this contrasting pattern of persistence and non-persistence for different dependent variables. For this to be possible, it is necessary to have longitudinal data on the same individuals studied over time.

An example where longitudinal data are still needed to understand causal processes is provided by the genetic data on delinquency (Rutter and Giller, 1983; Crowe, 1983). It seems from twin data that the heritability of criminal behaviour in adult life is substantially greater than that for delinquent behaviour in childhood. However, because these data apply to different samples, it is not known whether a high heritability would also be found for delinquent behaviour in childhood that persists into adult life. Longitudinal data are needed in order to determine which varieties of childhood delinquency involve a greater genetic component.

Finally, longitudinal data are crucial for the study of intervening links in the causal chain that is made up of the various risk and protective mechanisms operating at different points in time. A striking example is provided by the study by Robins *et al.* (1977) of socio-demographic factors in heroin addiction among men who had served in the American armed forces in Vietnam. The overall correlation between such factors and addiction following return to the United States was essentially zero, but this apparently negative finding was misleading. Longitudinal data were important in showing that socio-demographic factors were significantly associated with different points in the causal process. The overall lack of association was a consequence of the fact that such factors tended to work in opposite directions at different points in time. Thus inner-city blacks were most likely to take heroin while in Vietnam, but, of those who took heroin while in the armed forces, inner-city blacks were least likely to remain addicted on their return. Sometimes, too, longitudinal data may change the interpretation placed on the causal processes stemming from early risk factors. For example, Quinton and Rutter (1988) found that disrupted parenting in infancy was a powerful predictor of adult outcome among institution-reared women. At first sight it seemed as if the adverse infancy experiences had had a direct lasting effect on adult behaviour. However, data on the intervening years showed that disrupted parenting in infancy was also a powerful predictor of adverse experiences on leaving the institution in the late teens. At least in part, the apparently persistent effects of disruptive parenting in infancy were a consequence of the further adversities in late adolescence.

The role of theory

It is clear that, if properly dealt with, longitudinal data offer the possibility of moving from statistical associations between risk factor X and maladaptive outcome Y, to the testing of possible causal mechanisms and processes. This is because the time dimension allows the assessment of *change* in behaviour as a result of exposure to some hypothesized risk variable. However, in order for longitudinal data to be used in this way it is crucial that there be some explicit notion (hypothesis or theory) about the mode of operation of the suggested risk variable. This is particularly important because much risk research deals with risk indicators that have an ambiguous relationship with a varied range of risk mechanisms (see below). For example, it is well established that the delinquency rate is higher in males than females. But is this a function of sex-associated differences in temperament (Cloninger, in press; Maziade *et al.*, 1984), or in peer group influences (Maccoby, 1986); of prenatal hormonal effects (Reinisch and Sanders, 1984); of the prenatal effects of testosterone (Olweus, 1986); of the greater frequency of educational failure in males (Yule and Rutter, 1985a); of the higher risk of neurodevelopmental impairment in males (Shafer *et al.*, 1983); or of yet other features that are more frequent in boys than girls? Or is it a direct consequence of having a Y chromosome. It is clear that the finding of a sex difference does not in itself define the mechanism. Some gender-associated features are unmodifiable but others are not, and longitudinal data may be useful in testing alternative hypotheses.

One of the potential advantages of structural equation modelling (see chapters 4, 19 and 20) is that they require the investigator to decide on the nature of the underlying theoretical construct and on the possible mechanisms by which variables may operate on one another. These analytic techniques have an important place in developmental research but they also have their drawbacks (Biddle and Marlin, 1987; Martin, 1987) and they provide no cure-all in the study of causal mechanisms. Their importance lies less in the specifics of the mathematical techniques they employ than in their reflection of a crucial movement towards a more explicit statement and testing of causal mechanisms. Such mechanisms must include consideration of the possibility of individual turning points in development as a consequence of particular experiences (such as marriage or institutional admission or higher education) or of internal biological change (as with puberty), and of effects that are contingent upon particular sequences or combinations of risk and vulnerability factors (see chapters 5 and 17). Individual differences in the outcome following exposure to risk factors may also be a function of protective mechanisms (Rutter, in press a). It should be added that causal processes need to be considered not just in individual terms but also in terms of interpersonal interactions (see chapters 8 and 21) and of the effects of broader social experiences (as in the studies of schools described in chapters 11 and 12).

Types of longitudinal studies

In arguing for the value of longitudinal data in studying the operation over time of causal chain processes, it is not suggested that it will always, or even usually, be necessary to study individuals prospectively throughout the whole time period. As Robins (1979) has pointed out, there are several different types of longitudinal studies. For some purposes, it is necessary to have data that involve true-time prospective data collection. However, although this approach has the advantage that the investigation can select the data to be obtained at each data collection point, there is the major disadvantage in the study of long-term sequelae of a very long wait before the risk outcome can be measured.

The 'catch-up' longitudinal design provides a good alternative for many purposes. This approach makes use of contemporaneously collected data that were obtained previously for a different purpose. A follow-up then allows the linking between two data points that are separated by many years. For example, this was the method pioneered by Robins (1966) in her now classic study of the adult outcome for children who had attended a child guidance clinic when young. In that case, the investigator had to rely on routine clinical case record data for the measures of childhood behaviour. Sometimes, however, it may be possible to use research data that were obtained as part of an earlier, different investigation. That was the case, for example in Quinton and Rutter's (1988) follow-up of institution-reared girls. Both the institutions and the girls had formed a part of a study by King *et al.* (1971) a decade or so earlier. By a happy coincidence, exactly the same behavioural data had been obtained in a general population study of girls of the same age, also living in inner London (Rutter, 1977; Rutter and Quinton, 1984).

A further alternative is provided by the follow-back strategy in which the outcome groups are identified at the time of the study and then linked with some contemporaneously collected data set that applied to the individuals when they were very much younger. For example, Watt (1974) and Lewine *et al.* (1980) used school records in this way to study the childhood precursors of adult schizophrenia. It will be appreciated that, of course, this approach does not provide an effective means of studying 'escape' from the risk factor. Zeitlin (1986), used the same method when studying links between psychiatric disorders in childhood that were followed by mental illness in adult life. In this case, however, the initial data were obtained from psychiatric clinic records.

Yet another alternative is afforded by the existence of registers of contemporaneously collected data on total populations. Thus the psychiatric, alcoholism, and crime registers available in Scandinavia have been employed to study the adult outcome of various high-risk child populations (Nylander, 1979; Rydelius, 1981; Almqvist, 1983; von Knorring, 1983).

Problems and issues in tackling causal questions

Exclusions of third variable effects

Whenever a statistical association is found between a risk factor A and an outcome B, it is always necessary to exclude the possibility that the link is due to the operation of some third variable C that is associated with both A and B. With cross-sectional studies there is the additional problem of determining whether B led to A rather than the other way round. With longitudinal data this possibility can usually be ruled out by means of the time relationships between variables, but the problem of excluding the effect of a third variable is equally critical. Several different methods may be used to test the hypothesis of a true causal effect from *A* to *B* (Rutter, 1981a).

The most generally applicable approach with cross-sectional data is to undertake some form of statistical analysis to partial out, or otherwise control for, the effects of possible confounding third variables. The same procedure is also necessary with analyses of longitudinal data. However, longitudinal data have the major advantage that they provide the opportunity of examining changes over time in whatever behaviour is being studied as the outcome variable. In addition, it will be possible to measure confounding variables at the point of operation of the risk factor rather than having to extrapolate backwards from data collected at the time of measurement of the outcome. This was the procedure followed in the study of Rutter *et al.* (1979) of school influences on children's behaviour and attainments (see also chapter 11). In that study, the children were first assessed initially during the year before they transferred to secondary school, then followed prospectively through to the end of their secondary schooling, with a further follow-up a year later.

There are two main problems in statistical attempts to control for the effects of possible confounding variables. The first difficulty is that it is never possible to be entirely sure that all relevant confounding variables have been included and adequately measured. The second difficulty is that when an important confounding variable distributes very differently between the groups to be compared, there are inevitable concerns that any form of statistical adjustment will fail adequately to take account of possible third variable effects. In these circumstances, it may be desirable to restrict the comparisons to subsamples that are much more closely comparable with respect to the postulated confounding variables. This was necessary, for example, in Maughan and Rutter's (1987) comparison of children's academic progress in selective and non-selective schools within a mixed school system.

Very often the combination of cross-sectional and longitudinal data may be helpful. Thus Richman *et al.* (1982) showed that the marital discord and maternal depression were associated with psychiatric disorder in three-year-old children in the families they studied. The causal hypothesis could be put to further test through longitudinal analyses by focusing on the children *without* disorder at the age of three and determining whether or not they developed psychiatric disorder during the next few years. The finding that the psychiatric risk for such children was substantially greater than for children without these risk factors provided further confirmatory evidence for the causal hypothesis. However, it needs to be appreciated that there is a possible snag in this use of longitudinal data if the sample has already had prolonged exposure to the risk variable at the first point of data collection. The point is that those individuals who have not already succumbed at the start of the study may represent an atypical subsample who have an unusually enhanced resistance to the risk factor. In so far as that is so, one would expect the longitudinal relationships to be weaker than the cross-sectional ones. It is possible that this is the explanation for that pattern in the links between puberty, hormones and sexual initiation in the study by Udry (in press) and the associations between sex hormones and self-image in the investigation by Chrousos and Nottlemann (in press).

When faced with these difficulties, epidemiologists like to search for 'natural experiments' in which nature introduces the risk variable in a quasi-random manner that approximates to the levels of control possible in laboratory experiments. Rutter *et al.* (1983a) used severe head injuries in this fashion to study the effects of brain damage on intellectual and behavioural functioning in childhood. A sample of children was obtained in which all had suffered severe injuries as a result of accidents of one kind or another. The group was subdivided into those who had experienced severe brain trauma as evidenced by injury to the skull followed by prolonged post traumatic amnesia, and those with severe limb injuries that were not accompanied by damage to the head or by loss of consciousness. A two-and-a-quarter year follow-up study enabled a comparison between these two groups to be made for the majority of children in both groups who were free of disorder at the time of the initial assessment. The finding that there was a marked increase in psychiatric disorder in the brain-damaged group but not in the orthopaedic group provided a strong indication that brain damage was likely to be a truly causal risk factor for psychiatric disorder in childhood.

Roy (1983) used the natural experimental variable of type of residential placement to study the effects of an institutional upbringing on infants whose parenting by their biological parents had broken down. She compared those placed in family foster homes and those placed in residential nurseries in terms of their behaviour between the ages of five and eight years. Having shown that the groups were closely comparable in their family background, it was possible to infer that the higher rates of inattentive and poorly modulated task and social behaviour in the institutional group were likely to have been a function of their pattern of rearing. Tizard and her colleagues (Tizard, B. and Joseph, 1970; Tizard, B. and Rees, 1974; Tizard, B. and Hodges, 1978) were able to take this type of study further through their collection of true-time prospective longitudinal data. Adopted children had higher IQs and less behavioural disturbance than children who were restored to their biological parents; and those who were adopted early had higher IQs than those who were adopted late. These differential outcomes did not seem to be a function of selective placements based on the children's prior characteristics. A slightly different 'natural experiment' undertaken to study similar causal questions was undertaken by Schiff and his colleagues (Dumaret, 1985; Schiff and Lewontin, 1986). In this case, sets of siblings born to the same mothers were subdivided into those who remained in their disadvantaged social environments, those who were abandoned and adopted early into privileged environments, and those who were raised in institutions or foster homes. The results showed that the social environment had important effects, with the adopted group fairing best.

In the natural experiments discussed so far, the 'experiment' has been based on a contrast between two broadly comparable groups of children undergoing different experiences at the same time. An alternative approach is afforded by examination of the progress of different groups of children passing through the same environment over a period of time during which that environment undergoes radical change. That was the strategy employed by Rutter *et al.* (1986) in their study of the consequences for children's school attendance and exam performance when schools that had been experiencing difficulties had new principals appointed. The schools continued to serve the same catchment area and the characteristics of the intake did not change appreciably during the period of time studied. Nevertheless, in one out of the three schools investigated, there were dramatic improvements in the children's attendance and attainment. As similar changes were not apparent in other schools serving similar areas that had not had a change of principal, it could be inferred that it was likely that the change in school functioning was responsible for the improvements in pupil progress.

It is clear that these experiments of nature inevitably lack the rigorous controls that are possible in experimental procedures in the laboratory. It is never possible to be certain that the changes that have been observed are not due to some unmeasured differentiating variable rather than the factor under investigation. Even so, different natural experiments are likely to have different patterns of advantages and limitations. Often the combined findings of different studies allow causal inferences to be drawn with some confidence. However, because in real life the changes under investigation usually involve multiple variables, it is often quite difficult to identify the key causal mechanism. In particular, there is a need to differentiate between risk indicators and risk mechanisms.

Risk indicators versus risk mechanisms

In behavioural research, it is usual for investigators to have to rely on measures that constitute only indirect representations of the latent variable that they wish to study. Sometimes it is obvious that this must be so. For example, Wing and Brown (1970) found that the progress of psychiatric patients was associated with differences in the institutional environment of the mental hospitals to which they had been admitted. One of the most effective measures of a 'poor' environment was a failure to provide patients with a personal toothbrush for their own private use. No one would suppose that the outcome of patients would be improved by an edict that from now onwards all patients must have their own toothbrushes! Rather, the lack of such a personal item as a toothbrush served as an indicator of an institutional lack of concern for the individual. Somewhat similarly, in our comparative study of twelve inner London secondary schools (Rutter *et al.*, 1979) it was found that exam results were substantially better in schools where children's work was displayed on the walls. It is, of course, not in the least bit likely that the placing of work on the walls had any direct causal influence on children's success in national examinations. Instead, we must assume that it stood as a proxy for some broader aspect of the school environment that did have a causal influence on children's functioning.

In many cases it is not as obvious as in these examples whether the measure is a risk indicator or represents a risk mechanism. Several alternative strategies are available for differentiating between the two. Bradford Hill (1977) set out a helpful list of requirements for inferring a cause–effect relationship in biological studies. He emphasized the importance of consistency across studies which used rather different samples and different research strategies. The point is that if the same variable is shown to have an association with the specified outcome in populations that differ markedly in their characteristics, it is much more likely that the measure is reflecting something close to the causal mechanism. Nevertheless, we are rarely wise to make strong inferences from a single study, however well conducted. Replication across a range of different studies is the real test in science. Statistics are no more than the poor man's guide when having to interpret the results of just one study. Of course, we are all poor men in that respect and it is right that we make heavy use of statistical procedures so long as we are aware of the inevitable limitation in the inferences that can be drawn from any study when considered in isolation.

Bradford Hill (1977) also argued that causation was much more likely when the association with the risk factor was both strong and specific. While this is undeniable, it has to be recognized that when dealing with multifactorial causation, as well as when considering contributory vulnerability factors rather than specific pathogenic agents, strong specific associations are not to be expected. Biological plausibility is another consideration. That is, is there a likely mechanism by which the causal effect could be mediated? This is the situation in which reference to experimental data and to research using animal models may be informative. Such models cannot indicate that any particular mechanism *does* operate in the human species but they can be helpful in pointing to possible processes by which effects *might* be mediated.

Perhaps, the one criterion of Bradford Hill's that is most readily applicable is the requirement of a dose–response relationship. In other words, it is argued that if a risk factor truly reflects a causal mechanism, it should follow that the higher the 'dose' (meaning an amalgam of duration and intensity of exposure as well as the severity of the risk factor), the greater the likelihood of the individual developing the specified psychopathological outcome. For example, in our prospective study of children suffering head injuries (Rutter *et al.*, 1983a) the finding that the extent of intellectual impairment went up in linear fashion with the severity of the brain damage provided powerful supporting evidence for the causal hypothesis. Nevertheless, it is important to recognize that there may be threshold effects below which there is no risk, as well as ceiling effects above which the risk does not increase. Thus in the same head injury study there was no dose–response relationship within the range of mild head injuries giving rise to post traumatic amnesia lasting less than a week.

In order to proceed further in narrowing down the likely risk mechanism, it is usually necessary in behavioural studies to find one means or another of testing contrasting hypotheses on mechanisms. The first approach is provided by between-group comparisons, with the groups chosen to be contrasted on the basis of factors representing different specific-risk mechanisms. For example, some of the early high-risk studies of schizophrenia focused on a comparison of the children of schizophrenics with children from normal samples. A variety of measures of aggression, emotional disturbance and social maladaptation were thought to represent the precursors of schizophrenia. However, several studies during the last decade that have compared children of schizophrenics with children of parents with other forms of psychiatric disorder have found little difference in the behavioural characteristics of these two contrasting high-risk groups (Rutter and Garmezy, 1983; Watt *et al.*, 1984). The between-group comparison was important in ruling out these behavioural indicators as specific mediators of the risk for schizophrenia. Rather, they represented generalized indicators of psychopathological disturbance. Similarly, comparisons of the psychiatric risk associated with parental mental disorder and the risk associated with other forms of psychosocial disturbance have found few differences with respect to the risk for the common forms of emotional and conduct disturbance in childhood (Rutter and Quinton, 1984). The implication is that the risk stems from some aspect of family disturbance associated with parental mental disorder rather than with the psychiatric condition in the parent as such. Often, it is desirable to choose contrasting high-risk samples that are similar in many features but yet different in the one hypothesized risk mechanism. For example, children whose homes were broken by parental death were compared with those whose homes were disrupted by parental divorce (Rutter, 1971) in order to differentiate the consequences of parental loss unassociated with discord from persistent discord, in which loss was just one component. A substantially higher psychiatric risk associated with parental divorce than death pointed to the greater importance of discord.

Within-group comparisons may serve the same purpose if the overall sample can be subdivided according to the hypothesized risk variable. For example, within a sample at high risk because of parental mental disorder, the children were subdivided according to whether or not they had been exposed to persistent family discord (Rutter and Quinton, 1984). The higher rate of psychiatric disorder in those experiencing discord suggested discord played a part in the mediating mechanism. Similarly, a comparison within a sample of children all of whom had experienced a separation from their parents lasting at least four weeks, of those whose separations were associated with family disorder or disruption and those where it was not (for example prolonged holidays or periods of convalescence) indicated that psychiatric risk was associated largely with the former (Rutter, 1971). Another example is provided by studies of children born following perinatal complications. Numerous studies in the past have shown rather weak associations between such complications and various abnormal outcomes (Birch and Gussow, 1970; Sameroff and Chandler, 1975). Since maladaptive outcomes were more strongly associated with social disadvantage than with perinatal complications it came to be assumed that social variables constituted the main risk mechanism. The availability in recent years of non-invasive brain-imaging techniques has cast a rather different light on the findings (Stewart, 1983; Stewart *et al.* 1987). Within a group of babies at high risk because of perinatal factors, the worst outcomes are associated with those in whom ultrasound findings have indicated intraventricular haemorrhage or periventricular anoxia. Social factors may well be important in those who have not suffered overt brain damage (or in those where the damage is of a trivial degree), but when significant brain injury has occurred, the severity of that injury is much the most powerful predictor of later cognitive impairment.

Although a surprisingly little-used research strategy, the non-replication of findings across studies may sometimes be very informative in deciding between alternative risk mechanisms (Rutter, 1974). Thus directly comparable measures, employed by the same team of investigators, were used in studies of ten-year-old children in inner London and the Isle of Wight (Rutter *et al.*, 1975a, b). Most of the risk factors found in one population were replicated in the other. However, broken homes were much more strongly associated with child psychiatric disorder in London than on the island. The implication was that broken homes as such were unlikely to constitute the key mechanism. A closer look at the causes and consequences of broken homes in the two populations supported that inference. The break-up of the family in inner London was more likely to have been preceded by discord and more likely to have been followed by further discord and disruption.

It is apparent that in most of the studies that have been cited, the supposed risk mechanisms have concerned rather broad variables. As a result, the findings, while important in pointing to the likely domain of mechanism, have not been able to delineate the specific psychological processes involved. Nevertheless, the strategies have the potential for doing just that if the appropriate concepts can be matched to the relevant choice of samples and of measures.

Choice of sample

The need for careful choice of sample in order to highlight risk comparisons, and in order to test contrasting hypotheses on mechanisms, has been emphasized. Indeed, much of the art, as well as the science, of epidemiological/longitudinal research in the investigation of risk and protective factors for psychosocial development relies on skilled sample choice. However, there are snags and pitfalls that much complicate such choices. Often, the choice of a high-risk group necessarily means that the group is atypical in respects that could be important. For example, the most popular high-risk strategy in schizophrenia research has involved study of the offspring of schizophrenic mothers (Watt *et al.*, 1984). The strategy has had a rich pay-off but, although the risk of schizophrenia in the offspring is some ten times that in the general population, it focuses on a minority (and possibly an atypical) group of schizophrenic individuals. Some nine out of ten schizophrenic patients do *not* have a schizophrenic parent (Gottesman and Shields, 1976). A further consideration is that the men who father the children of schizophrenic mothers are disproportionately likely to have antisocial or personality disorders themselves (Parnas, 1985), so that the risk variable is not as pure as one might wish.

Frequently, too, samples are deliberately chosen in order to separate two risk factors that ordinarily go together. For example, the study of adoptees was developed in order that the parental genetic background could be separated from the social parenting environment. The strategy has been an important one in showing that, for many psychiatric disorders, the main risk is associated with mental illness in the biological parent (who did not rear the child) rather than in the non-related parent who provided the rearing environment (Gottesman and Shields, 1976; McGuffin, 1984). There is no question but that this strategy provided an important step forward in genetic research. However, just because the design separated genetic from environmental effects, it necessarily underestimated the importance of gene–environment interactions. Different designs may be needed in order to test their importance (Kendler and Eaves, 1986).

Nevertheless, in spite of this problem, there is much to be said for the choice of samples that avoid the need for statistical controls to deal with closely associated confounding variables. For example, a variety of studies have shown statistical associations between higher body lead levels and lower levels of intellectual functioning (Yule and Rutter, 1985a). The interpretation of the causal inferences to be drawn from this association has been seriously bedevilled by the usual finding that both raised lead levels and lower IQ are associated with social disadvantage. It has proved quite difficult in practice adequately to separate the effects of lead from the effects of social circumstances. Accordingly, the New Zealand study (Silva *et al.*, 1985), in which lead levels were not related to socio-economic status, has an unusual importance. Much the same situation has applied to the statistical associations between serous otitis media, together with the resulting transient conductive hearing impairment, and delayed language development and impaired scholastic attainment (Paradise, 1981). As ear infections tend to be more prevalent in socially disadvantaged sections of the population, there has been uncertainty as to whether the cognitive deficits have derived from the hearing impairment or the poor social conditions. Once again, the New Zealand study (Silva *et al.*, 1982; 1986), where ear infections were not associated with social disadvantage, adds to the evidence in an important way. With both these examples, the evidence is too complex to allow any simple, unambiguous conclusion. However, the evidence from samples where confounding variables are much reduced have been important in indicating support for the hypothesis that these biological hazards may indeed carry a risk for intellectual impairment (albeit probably quite a small risk in most populations).

Age and sex differences

It has become standard in developmental research to look for age and sex differences in effects. The issues are undoubtedly important but there are many methodological problems involved both in determining the validity of age and sex differences and also in the interpretation of their meaning. For example, there has been much debate in the literature on whether the effects of brain damage in infancy are less than those that follow damage to the brain when incurred at a later age. The question seems simple enough but there have been major difficulties in ensuring that the measures at different ages are comparable, that the degree of brain damage in children of different ages has been equivalent, and in using comparable periods of follow-up (Heywood and Canavan, 1987; Goodman, 1987; Rutter, 1982). Thus, for example, in order to equate the opportunities for recovery it is desirable to have identical periods of follow-up in the age groups to be compared. On the other hand, in order that the cognitive outcome tasks to be compared are equivalent (mathematical skills as assessed at 6 years are very different from those assessed at 16 years), it is desirable that the groups to be compared are tested at the same age. For obvious reasons, these two requirements are incompatible. An assessment of the evidence, taken as a whole, suggests that there are important age differences in children's response to brain injury but that they do not add up to effects being generally 'worse' or 'better' at one age or another. A variety of different mechanisms are involved and these do not all pull in the same direction.

Somewhat similar problems are associated with the understanding of sex differences in risk effects. For quite a wide range of risk variables, boys seem to suffer more than girls (Gualtieri and Hicks, 1985; Zaslow and Hayes, 1986). Moreover, it is not just that there are sex differences in susceptibility to disorder. In addition, apparently similar behaviours seem to have different consequences in the two sexes. Thus Stevenson-Hinde and Hinde (1986) and Simpson and Stevenson-Hinde (1985) found that whereas shyness in boys was associated with negative interpersonal interactions, in girls it was associated with positive personal interchanges. Maccoby and Jacklin (1983) found that when mothers backed away from aggressive behaviour in boys this tended to have an escalating effect, whereas this was not found in girls. Robins (1986) showed that antisocial behaviour in childhood predicted adult personality disorder in both sexes, but in females only it also predicted emotional and somatizing disorders. This interesting sex difference in outcome suggests that it may be necessary to rethink our diagnostic grouping of personality disorders (Rutter, 1987c). Longitudinal data can be helpful in disentangling the mechanisms involved in these contrasting patterns that differ by sex.

Choice of variable

In longitudinal, as in cross-sectional, research, the choice of variables has important implications for findings. This is evident, for instance, in the debate about the relative importance of trait variables as against situational effects (Eysenck and Eysenck, 1980; Mischel, 1979). There is good evidence that both are important. However, the relevant point here is that different types of measure are needed for the study of one compared with the other, and also that the choice of variable will determine in part the findings on trait versus situation effects. In order to study person–environment interactions it is necessary to have measures of individual behaviour that are specifically applicable to the situations to be studied. Provided that situations can be conceptualized and classified, the investigator may well choose to pool measures of behaviour across situations within the same class. However, it would obviously be undesirable to have behavioural measures that spanned diverse situations. Conversely, if one is wanting to measure behavioural characteristics that are pervasive over situations, measurement in multiple settings would usually be required. Longitudinal data provide an important means of dealing with fluctuations in behaviour over time as well as over situations. Two points require particular emphasis in this connection. Firstly, the impression given of the strength of continuity over time depends hugely on the method of statistical analysis employed (Rutter, 1977). Thus, in a four-year prospective study of a general population sample of children, the correlation between the behaviour rating at the outset and that four years later was only .25, accounting for a mere 6% of the variance. However, that correlation reflects a twofold increase in risk, an expression of persistence that sounds greater, although in fact it is not. But, more importantly, the behaviour rating at the outset was associated with a tenfold increase in the risk of *persisting* behavioural deviance – an apparently much stronger level of continuity in spite of the fact that the analyses are all based on the same set of data. The reason is that at any one point in time about half the children are showing transient problems and about half persistent ones. Those with transient problems are a different set of children each time, but obviously the ones with persistent difficulties are the same individuals. It is also relevant that a focus on children with persisting behavioural abnormalities may often highlight risk effects, whether due to environmental or constitutional causes. For example, the psychiatric risks, for children, associated with being brought up in a family with a mentally ill parent largely applied to persistent disorders rather than transient ones (Rutter and Quinton, 1984). The degree of psychiatric risk was quite minor when based on cross-sectional analyses but much more substantial when based on longitudinal data.

A further consideration in any longitudinal study is whether to use dimensional or categorical variables, single-trait measures or behavioural composites. Several studies have shown that the findings may be much influenced by the choice made. This is not just a matter of broad measures being better than narrow ones or of factors being superior to the components of the factors. Rather it is an indication that in some circumstances the association of two behaviours may change their meaning (see chapter 3). Thus Kagan *et al.* (1987) found that their heart-rate measures (treated in dimensional terms) added nothing to the variance accounted for by their behavioural measure of inhibition. But the subgroup of children with both behavioural inhibition and a high stable heart-rate were strikingly different from the remainder. Magnusson (1987) noted the same with respect to the role of autonomic measures in relation to aggressivity. This effect does not necessarily reside, however, in the combination of physiological and behavioural measures. Magnusson (1987) found that it also applied to the combination of the two behavioural measures of restlessness and aggressivity. Similarly, Loeber (1986) found that hyperactivity was a risk factor for delinquency only when it occurred in conjunction with conduct problems, especially aggression.

Attention has already been drawn to the value of longitudinal data for the detection of unusual patterns of outcome following risk experiences. Thus studies of children exposed to physical abuse or severe parental depression have been notable for their highlighting the frequency of unusual maladaptive patterns of attachment that were not apparent on the usual methods of classifying security of attachment (Crittenden, 1985; Radke-Yarrow *et al.*, 1985; Main *et al.*, 1985). Similarly, the study by Earls *et al.*, (in press) of the offspring of alcoholic parents found that the behavioural pattern that most differentiated them from controls was the combination of emotional difficulties and conduct disturbance – a pattern that is not recognized by many of the standard systems of psychiatric classification.

The problem of ensuring comparability of measures across a wide age range has already been discussed. Nevertheless, there is a special interest in risk research in the study of continuities and discontinuities between psychopathology in children and that in adult life (Rutter, 1984a). It is very striking that these patterns differ markedly between the major groups of psychiatric disorders.

Choice of statistical analysis

Most studies of developmental continuities or linkages have relied on correlational analyses of one kind or another. These have many strengths but they also have important limitations (Rutter, 1987a). Perhaps the most basic problem is that, despite their often being interpreted as such, correlations are not a measure of the strength of association between two variables. Rather, they provide an index of the proportion of population variance explained. This is not the same thing because the size of the correlation is crucially dependent on the base rate of the independent variable. Correlations will be low when there is a very low base rate (meaning that there must be other causes of the outcome being assessed) or a very high one (meaning that there are important modifiers of effect). It is also the case that it is possible for an environmental influence to have a very substantial effect in raising the mean level of an outcome variable without it making much, if any, difference to individual variation, and hence without there being any appreciable effect on the strength of correlation. This is apparent in the role of improved nutrition on height (Tizard, J. 1975), in the effects of adoption into superior homes of infants from a severely disadvantaged background (Rutter, 1985b), and in the benefits associated with preschool intervention programmes (Ramey *et al.*, 1984).

Correlations necessarily rely on the consistency of association across the range (over time and over the distribution of the variable). In some cases, effects may be marked but yet applicable only to subgroups of the population or only to extremes on the risk variable. For these, and other reasons, Hinde and Dennis (1986) have argued that analyses based on categorization may be preferable for some purposes to correlational analyses. As already noted, correlational analyses provide data on individual differences, so that different statistical approaches are required for the study of intra-individual change (Labouvie, 1986).

A further set of problems stems from the crucial importance of taking into account the heterogeneous mixture of interactions between the variables that may influence risk outcomes (Rutter, 1983; 1987a). There are, of course, ways of testing for these interactions, but it is important to note that they may well be missed by the multiplicative interaction terms in the usual multivariate statistical packages. The chapter by Pickles gives some examples of how statistical procedures may be applied to hypotheses that involve assumptions of population heterogeneity and of interactions of various kinds.

Circular causal processes and chain effects

Longitudinal data really come into their own in the analysis of causal processes that involve feedback mechanisms, circular processes, and chain effects over time (Rutter, 1987a). Such effects may be evident over very short time periods or very long ones. For example, in an experimental study, Brunk and Hengeller (1984) showed that by the end of a 20-minute session, adults were already responding differently according to the children's behaviour at the beginning of the session. It seemed that, even in this short time, important expectancies had built up that influenced how people reacted. A rather longer term effect was evident in the circular process noted by Maccoby and Jacklin (1983), in which different behaviour shown by boys caused mothers to back away. The backing-away then, in turn, increased the likelihood that the difficult behaviour would escalate. Much longer term chain effects were evident in Quinton and Rutter's (1988) follow-up into adult life of institution-reared girls. The major protective influence leading to a good outcome was the presence in adult life of marital support from a non-deviant spouse. The likelihood of having such a spouse, however, was much influenced by whether or not the girls in late adolescence showed a tendency to plan their lives – with respect to both marital choice and work careers. The likelihood that the institution-reared girls would exhibit this planning characteristic was, in turn, shown to be associated with their having a range of positive experiences at school. No one event at any period during the course of development was decisive; rather, both risk and protective mechanisms derived from a chain of continuities and discontinuities over time that served to increase or decrease the likelihood of a maladaptive outcome (see also chapter 17).

One specific aspect of long-term effects over time is the issue of delayed sequelae. Their existence is well established in medicine as a whole. It should be noted, however, that the delay in the development of *pathology* does not necessarily mean that the initiation of the risk *process* is delayed. Indeed it is usual for that process to be set into action at the time. The apparent delay (or 'sleeper' effect as it is sometimes termed) is generally a function of our ignorance of, or inability to measure, the pathological process that takes time to lead to a maladaptive outcome. Thus there is widespread public awareness that excessive exposure to radiation increases the risk that the individual will develop malignant disease in later life, even though there are no clinically observable effects at the time. The protective effects of the contraceptive pill for both ovarian and endometrial cancer, as well as the slightly increased risk for myocardial infarction, also take time to develop, as do the well-established risks of lung cancer associated with smoking. Similarly, young people who suffer sports injuries may seem to recover completely only to face an increased risk of arthritic change in later life. This biological phenomenon is well established, but its operation in the domain of psychosocial risk factors is not, as yet, well demonstrated. There are, it is true, important indications that such long-term sequelae may occur. The increased risk of depression in adult life associated with a serious lack of affectionate parental care in childhood constitutes one example (Brown *et al.*, 1986). There are also suggestions that early stressful experiences may serve either to sensitize or steel individuals against the ill effects of later stress and adversity (Rutter, 1981b). It seems likely that such long-term effects may sometimes be operative but we know regrettably little about the situations in which they occur or the mechanisms involved. The questions posed by such effects point to the need for further investigation of how psychosocial influences affect the organism (Rutter, 1984b), how cognitive processes serve to mediate the persistence or otherwise both of experiential effects (Rutter, 1987c) and of the complex set of features involved in personality organization and development (Rutter, 1987b).

Conclusions

Longitudinal data provide many advantages for the study of risk and protective factors for psychopathological outcomes in childhood and adult life. Social scientists are trained to accept that causation can never be inferred from correlations. There is indeed every reason to be wary about the drawing of causal inferences from statistical associations. Nevertheless, we must all be concerned with the delineation of causal mechanisms and processes. It is unduly pessimistic to conclude that causal hypotheses can be studied only through highly controlled laboratory experiments. There are many longitudinal research strategies that can go a long way towards the testing of causal hypotheses. While it would be rarely, if ever, permissible to draw strong conclusions about causation from a single study, combinations of findings from investigations using contrasting but complementary research strategies can do much to increase our understanding of mechanisms. However, almost never will this amount to the identification of the one basic underlying cause of some maladaptive outcome. Multiple aetiologies are the rule and most causal processes operate through a series of indirectly connected sequences involving different, relatively short-term effects or operations. It is in the analysis of these chain effects over time that longitudinal data really come into their own.

References

Almqvist, F. (1983) *Psychiatric treatment and registration of social deviance in adolescence.* Helsinki: Painatusjaos.

Biddle, B. J. and Marlin, M. M. (1987) Causality, confirmation, credulity and structural equation modeling. *Child Development*, 58, 4–17.

Birch, H. G. and Gussow, J. D. (1970) *Disadvantaged children: health, nutrition and school failure.* London: Grune and Stratton.

Bradford Hill, A. (1977) *A short textbook of medical statistics.* London: Hodder and Stoughton.

Brown, G. W., Harris, T. O. and Bifulco, A. (1986) The long-term effects of early loss of parent. In Rutter, M., Izard, C. E. and Read, P. B. (eds.) *Depression in young people: clinical and developmental perspectives.* New York: Guilford Press, pp. 251–96.

Brunk, M. A. and Hengeller, S. W. (1984) Child influences on adult controls. An experimental investigation. *Developmental Psychology*, 20, 1074–81.

Chess, S., Thomas, A. and Birch, H. G. (1966) Distortions in developmental reporting made by parents of behaviorally disturbed children. *Journal of the American Academy of Child Psychiatry*, 5, 226–34.

Chrousos, G. P. and Nottlemann, E. (in press) Hormones and behavior in puberty. In Bancroft, J. and Reinisch, J. (eds.) *Adolescence and puberty.* New York: Oxford University Press.

Cloninger, C. R. (in press) A unified biosocial theory of personality and its role in the development of anxiety states. *Psychiatry Research.*

Crittenden, P. M. (1985) Maltreated infants: vulnerability and resilience. *Journal of Child Psychology and Psychiatry*, 26, 85–96.

Crowe, R. R. (1983) Antisocial personality disorders. In Tarter, R. E. (ed.) *The child at psychiatric risk.* New York: Oxford University Press, pp. 214–27.

Dumaret, A. (1985) IQ, scholastic performance and behaviour of sibs raised in contrasting environments. *Journal of Child Psychology and Psychiatry*, 26, 553–80.

Earls, F., Reich, W., Jung, K. and Cloninger, C. R. (in press) Psychopathology in children of alcoholic and antisocial parents. In *Alcoholism: clinical and experimental research.*

Eisenberg, L. (1986) When is a case a case? In Rutter, M., Izard, C. E. and Read, P. B. (eds.) *Depression in young people: clinical and developmental perspectives.* New York: Guilford Press, pp. 469–78.

Elliott, D. S. and Voss, H. L. (1974) *Delinquency and dropout.* Toronto: Lexington.

Eysenck, M. W. and Eysenck, H. J. (1980) Mischel and the concept of personality. *British Journal of Psychiatry*, 71, 191–204.

Farrington, D. P., Gallagher, B., Morley, L., Raymond, J. St. L. and West, D. J. (1986) Unemployment, school leaving and crime. *British Journal of Criminology*, 26, 335–56.

Feather, N. T. and O'Brien, G. E. (1986) A longitudinal analysis of the effects of different patterns of employment and unemployment on school leavers. *British Journal of Psychology*, 77, 459–79.

Goodman, R. (1987) The developmental neurobiology of language. In Yule, W. and Rutter, M. (eds.) *Language development and disorders*, Clinics in developmental medicine no. 101–2. London: MacKeith/Blackwell, pp. 129–45.

Gottesman, I. I. and Shields, J. (1976) A critical review of recent adoption, twin and family studies of schizophrenia: behavioral genetics perspective. *Schizophrenia Bulletin*, 2, 360–400.

Gualtieri, T. and Hicks, R. E. (1985) An immunoreactive theory of selective male affliction. *Behavioral and Brain Sciences*, 5, 427–41.

Haggerty, R. J. C. (1980) Life stress, illness and social supports. *Developmental Medicine and Child Neurology*, 22, 391–400.

Heywood, C. A. and Canavan, A. G. M. (1987) Developmental neuropsychological correlates of language. In Yule, W. and Rutter, M. (eds.) *Language development and disorders*, Clinics in development medicine no. 101–2. London: MacKeith/Blackwell, pp. 146–58.

Hinde, R. A. and Dennis, A. (1986) Categorizing individuals: an alternative to linear analysis. *International Journal of Behavioural Development*, 9, 105–19.

Hodges, J. and Tizard, B. (in press a) IQ and behavioural adjustment of ex-institutional adolescents. *Journal of Child Psychology and Psychiatry*.
(in press b) Social and family relationships of ex-institutional adolescents. *Journal of Child Psychology and Psychiatry*.

Kagan, J. J., Reznick, S. and Snidman, N. (1987) The physiology and psychology of behavioral inhibition in children. *Child Development*, 58, 1459–73.

Kendler, K. S. and Eaves, L. J. (1986) Models for the joint effect of genotype and environment on liability to psychiatric illness. *American Journal of Psychiatry*, 143, 279–89.

King, R. D., Raynes, N. V. and Tizard, J. (1971) *Patterns of residential care: sociological studies in institutions for handicapped children*. London: Routledge and Kegan Paul.

Knight, B. J., Osborn, S. G. and West, D. J. (1977) Early marriage and criminal tendency in males. *British Journal of Criminology*, 17, 64–7.

Labouvie, E. W. (1986) Methodological issues in the prediction of psychopathology: a life span perspective. In Erlenmeyer-Kimling, L. and Miller, N. E. (eds.) *Life span research on the prediction of psychopathology*. Hillsdale, NJ: Erlbaum, pp. 137–55.

Lewine, R. R. J., Watt, N. F., Prentky, R. A. and Fryer, J. H. (1980) Childhood social competence in functionally disordered psychiatric patients and in normals. *Journal of Abnormal Psychology*, 39, 132–8.

Loeber, R. (1986) Behavioral precursors and accelerators of delinquency. Paper given at the conference 'Explaining Crime', University of Leiden, Holland, June.

Maccoby, E. E. (1986) Social groupings in childhood: their relationship to prosocial and antisocial behavior in boys and girls. In Olweus, D., Block, J. and Radke-Yarrow, M. (eds.) *Development of antisocial and prosocial behavior: research, theories and issues*. New York: Academic Press, pp. 263–84.

Maccoby, E. E. and Jacklin, C. N. (1983) The 'person' characteristics of children and the family as environment. In Magnusson, D. and Allen, V. L. (eds.) *Human development: an interactional perspective*. New York: Academic Press, pp. 75–91.

McGuffin, P. (1984) Genetic influences on personality, neurosis and psychosis. In McGuffin, P., Shanks, M. E. and Hodgson, R. J. (eds.) *The scientific principles of psychopathology*. London: Grune and Stratton, pp. 190–226.

Magnusson, D. (1987) *Individual development in an interactional perspective, paths through life*, ed. D. Magnusson, vol. 1. Hillsdale NJ: Erlbaum.

Magnusson, D., Stattin, H. and Allen, V. L. (1986) Differential maturation amongst girls and its relation to social adjustment: a longitudinal perspective. In Featherman, D. and Lerner, R. M. (eds.) *Life span development*, vol. 7. New York: Academic Press.

Main, M., Kaplan, N. and Cassidy, J. (1985) Security in infancy, childhood and adulthood. In Bretherton, I. and Waters, E. (eds.) *Growing points of attachment theory and research*. Monographs for the Society for Research in Child Development 209, vol. 50, nos. 1–2.

Martin, J. A. (1987) Structural equation modeling: a guide for the perplexed. *Child Development*, **58**, 33–7.

Maughan, B. and Rutter, M. (1986) Black pupils' progress in secondary schools: II examination attainments. *British Journal of Developmental Psychology*, **4**, 19–20.

(1987) Pupils' progress in selective and non-selective schools. *School Organization*, **7**, 50–68.

Maziade, M., Boudreault, M., Thivierge, J., Capéraà, P. and Côté, R. (1984) Infant temperament: SES and gender differences and reliability of measurement in a large Quebec sample. *Merril Palmer Quarterly*, **30**, 213–26.

Mischel, W. (1979) On the interface of cognition and personality: beyond the person–situation debate. *American Psychologist*, **34**, 740–54.

Nylander, I. (1979) A 20-year prospective follow-up study of 2164 cases at the child guidance clinics in Stockholm. *Acta Paediatrica Scandinavica*, supplement no. 276.

Olweus, D. (1986) Aggression and hormones: behavioral relationship with testosterone and adrenaline. In Olweus, D., Block, J. and Radke-Yarrow, M. (eds.) *Development of antisocial and prosocial behavior: research, theories and issues*. New York: Academic Press, pp. 51–72.

Paradise, J. L. (1981) Otitis media during early life: how hazardous to development? A critical review of the evidence. *Pediatrics*, **68**, 869–73.

Parnas, J. (1985) Mates of schizophrenic mothers: a study of assortative mating from the American–Danish high risk project. *British Journal of Psychiatry*, **146**, 490–7.

Puig-Antich, J. (1986) Psychobiological markers: effects of age and puberty. In, Rutter, M., Izard, C. E. and Read, P. B. (eds.) *Depression in young people: clinical and developmental perspectives*. New York: Guilford Press, pp. 341–81.

Quinton, D. and Rutter, M. (1988) *Parenting breakdown: the making and breaking of intergenerational links*. Aldershot: Gower.

Radke-Yarrow, M., Cummings, E. M., Kuczynski, L. and Chapman, M. (1985) Patterns of attachment in two- and three-year-olds in normal families and families with parental depression. *Child Development*, **56**, 884–93.

Ramey, C. T., Yeates, K. O. and Short, E. J. (1984) The plasticity of intellectual development: insights from preventive intervention. *Child Development*, **55**, 1913–25.

Reinisch, J. M. and Sanders, S. A. (1984) Prenatal gonadal steroidal influences on gender-related behavior. In De Vries, G. D., De Bruin, J. P. C., Uylings, H. B. M. and Corher, M. A. (eds.) *Sex differences in the brain: the relation between structure and function*, Progress in brain research, vol. 61. Amsterdam: Elsevier.

Richman, N., Stevenson, J. and Graham, P. (1982) *Preschool to school: a behavioural study*. London: Academic Press.

Robins, L. N. (1966) *Deviant children grown up*. Baltimore: Williams and Wilkins.

(1979) Longitudinal methods in the study of normal and pathological development. In Kisker, K. P., Meyer, J. L. E., Müller, C. and Strömgren, E. (eds.) *Psychiatrie der Gegenwart*, vol. 1, *Grundlagen and Methoden der Psychiatrie*. Heidelberg: Springer.

(1986) The consequences of conduct disorder in girls. In Olweus, D., Block, J. and Radke-Yarrow, M. (eds.) *Development of antisocial and prosocial behavior: research, theories and issues*. New York: Academic Press, pp. 385–414.

Robins, L. N., Davis, D. H. and Wish, E. (1977) Detecting predictors of rare events: demographic, family and personal deviance as predictors of stages in the progression towards narcotic addiction. In Strauss, J. S., Babigian, H. N. and Roff, M. (eds.) *The origins and course of psychopathology: methods of longitudinal research*. New York: Plenum Press, pp. 379–406.

Robins, L. N., Schoenberg, S., Holmes, S. J., Ratcliffe, K. S., Behnam, A. and Works, J. (1985) Early home environment and retrospective recall: a test of concordance between siblings with and without psychiatric disorders. *American Journal of Orthopsychiatry*, 55, 27–41.

Roy, P. (1983) Is continuity enough? Substitute care and socialization. Paper presented at the Spring Scientific Meeting, Child and Adolescent Psychiatry Specialist Section, Royal College of Psychiatrists, London, March.

Rutter, M. (1971) Parent–child separation: psychological effects on the children. *Journal of Child Psychology and Psychiatry*, 12, 233–60.

(1974) Epidemiological strategies and psychiatric concepts in research on the vulnerable child. In Anthony, E. and Koupernik, E. (eds.) *The child in his family: children at psychiatric risk*, vol. 3. New York: Wiley, pp. 167–79.

(1977) Prospective studies to investigate behavioral change. In Strauss, J. S., Babigian, H. M. and Roff, M. (eds.) *The origins and course of psychopathology*. New York: Plenum Press, pp. 223–47.

(1979) *Changing youth in a changing society: patterns of adolescent development and disorder*. London: Nuffield Provincial Hospitals Trust (Cambridge, MA: Harvard University Press, 1980).

(1981a) Epidemiological/longitudinal strategies and causal research in child psychiatry. *Journal of the American Academy of Child Psychiatry*, 20, 513–44.

(1981b) Stress, coping and development: some issues and some perspectives. *Journal of Child Psychology and Psychiatry*, 22, 323–56.

(1982) Developmental neuropsychiatry: concepts, issues and problems. *Journal of Clinical Neuropsychology*, 4, 91–115.

(1983) Statistical and personal interactions: facets and perspectives. In Magnusson, D. and Allen, V. (eds.) *Human development; an interactional perspective*. New York: Academic Press, pp. 295–319.

(1984a) Psychopathology and development, I. Childhood antecedents of adult psychiatric disorder. *Australian and New Zealand Journal of Psychiatry*, 18, 225–34.

(1984b) Psychopathology and development, II. Childhood experiences and personality development. *Australian and New Zealand Journal of Psychiatry*, 18, 314–27.

(1985a) Resilience in the face of adversity: protective factors and resistance to psychiatric disorder. *British Journal of Psychiatry*, 147, 598–611.

(1985b) Family and school influences on cognitive development. *Journal of Child Psychology and Psychiatry*, 26, 683–704.

(1987a) Continuities and discontinuities from infancy. In Osofsky, J. (ed.) *Handbook of infant development*, 2nd edn. New York: Wiley, pp. 1256–96.

(1987b) The role of cognition in child development and disorder. *British Journal of Medical Psychology*, 60, 1–16.

(1987c) Temperament, personality and personality disorder. *British Journal of Psychiatry*, 150, 443–58.

(in press a) Psychosocial resilience and protective mechanisms. In Rolf, J., Masten, A., Cicchetti, D., Nuechterlein, K. and Weintraub, S. (eds.) *Risk and protective factors in the development of psychopathology*. New York: Cambridge University Press.

(in press b) Intergenerational continuities and discontinuities in serious parenting difficulties. In Cicchetti, D. and Carlson, V. (eds.) *Research on the consequences of child maltreatment*. New York: Cambridge University Press.

Rutter, M. and Garmezy, N. (1983) Developmental psychopathology. In Hetherington, E. M. (ed.) *Socialization, personality and social development, Handbook of child psychology*, ed. P. Mussen, vol. 4, 4th edn. New York: Wiley, pp. 775–911.

Rutter, M. and Giller, H. (1983) *Juvenile delinquency: trends and perspectives.* Harmondsworth: Penguin.

Rutter, M. and Madge, N. (1976) *Cycles of disadvantage: a review of research.* London: Heinemann.

Rutter, M. and Quinton, D. (1984) Parental psychiatric disorders: effects on children. *Psychological Medicine*, 14, 853–80.

Rutter, M., Cox, A., Tupling, C., Berger, M. and Yule, W. (1975a) Attainment and adjustment in two geographical areas I. The prevalence of psychiatric disorder. *British Journal of Psychiatry*, 126, 493–509.

Rutter, M., Yule, B., Quinton, D., Rowlands, O., Yule, W. and Berger, M. (1975b) Attainment and adjustment in two geographical areas III. Some factors accounting for area differences. *British Journal of Psychiatry*, 126, 520–33.

Rutter, M., Graham, P., Chadwick, O. and Yule, W. (1976) Adolescent turmoil: fact or fiction? *Journal of Child Psychology and Psychiatry*, 17, 35–56.

Rutter, M., Maughan, B., Mortimore, P. and Ouston, J. (with Smith, A.) (1979) *Fifteen thousand hours: secondary schools and their effects on children.* London: Open Books.

Rutter, M., Chadwick, O. and Shaffer, D. (1983a) Head injury. In Rutter, M. (ed.) *Developmental neuropsychiatry*. New York: Guilford Press, pp. 83–111.

Rutter, M., Quinton, D. and Liddle, C. (1983b) Parenting in two generations: looking backwards and looking forwards. In Madge, N. (ed.) *Families at risk.* London: Heinemann, pp. 60–98.

Rutter, M., Maughan, B. and Ouston, J. (1986) The study of school effectiveness. In van der Wolf, J. C. and Hox, J. J. (eds.) *Kwaliteit van onderwijs in het feding*. Lisse: Swets and Zeitlinger, pp. 32–43.

Rydelius, P. A. (1981) Children of alcoholic fathers. Their social adjustment and their health status over 20 years. *Acta Paediatrica Scandinavica*, supplement no. 286.

Sameroff, A. J. and Chandler, M. J. (1975) Reproductive risk and the continuum of caretaking causality. In Horowitz, F. D. (ed.) *Review of child development research*, vol. 4. Chicago: University of Chicago Press, pp. 187–244.

Schiff, M. and Lewontin, R. (1986) *Education and class: the irrelevance of IQ genetic studies*. Oxford: Clarendon Press.

Shafer, S. Q., Shaffer, D., O'Connor, P. A. and Stokman, C. J. (1983) Neurological 'soft signs': their origins and significance for behaviour. In Rutter, M. (ed.) *Developmental neuropsychiatry*. New York: Guilford Press, pp. 144–63.

Silva, P. A., Kirkland, C., Simpson, A., Steward, I. A. and Williams, S. M. (1982) Some developmental and behavioral problems associated with bilateral otitis media with effusion. *Journal of Learning Disabilities*, 15, 417–21.

Silva, P. A., Hughes, P. and Faed, J. (1985) Blood levels in 579 Dunedin eleven year old children: a report from the Dunedin Multidisciplinary Health and Development Research Unit. *New Zealand Medical Journal*, 99, 179–83.

Silva, P. A., Chalmers, D. and Stewart, I. (1986) Some audiological, psychological, educational and behavioral characteristics of children with bilateral otitis media with effusion: a longitudinal study. *Journal of Learning Disabilities*, 19, 165–69.

Simpson, A. E. and Stevenson-Hinde, J. (1985) Temperamental characteristics of three- to four-year-old boys and girls and child–family interactions. *Journal of Child Psychology and Psychiatry*, 26, 43–53.

Stevenson-Hinde, H. and Hinde, R. A. (1986) Changes in associations between characteristics and interactions. In Plomin, R. and Dunn, J. (eds.) *The study of temperament: changes, continuities and challenges*. Hillsdale NJ: Erlbaum, pp. 115–29.

Stewart, A. (1983) Severe perinatal hazards. In Rutter, M. (ed.) *Developmental neuropsychiatry*. New York: Guilford Press, pp. 15–31.

Stewart, A., Reynolds, E. O. R., Hope, P. L., Hamilton, P. A., Baudin, J., Costello, A. M. de L., Bradford, B. C. and Wyatt, J. S. (1987) Probability of neurodevelopmental disorders estimated from ultrasound appearance of brains of very preterm infants. *Developmental Medicine and Child Neurology*, 29, 3–11.

Tizard, B. and Hodges, J. (1978) The effect of early institutional rearing on the development of eight-year-old children. *Journal of Child Psychology and Psychiatry*, 19, 99–118.

Tizard, B. and Joseph, A. (1970) Cognitive development of young children in residential care: a study of children aged 24 months. *Journal of Child Psychology and Psychiatry*, 11, 177–86.

Tizard, B. and Rees, J. (1974) A comparison of the effects of adoption, restoration to the natural mother, and continued institutionalization on the cognitive development of four-year-old children. *Child Development*, 45, 92–9.

Tizard, J. (1975) Race and IQ: the limits of probability. *New Behaviour*, 1, 6–9.

Udry, J. P. (in press) Hormones and social determinants of adolescent sexual initiation. In Bancroft, J. and Reinisch, J. (eds.) *Adolescence and puberty*. New York: Oxford University Press.

Von Knorring, A.-L. (1983) *Adoption studies on psychiatric illness: epidemiological, environmental and genetic aspects*. Umea University medical dissertations no. 101.

Warr, P. B. and Jackson, P. R. (1985) Factors influencing the psychological impact of prolonged unemployment and of re-employment. *Psychological Medicine*, 15, 795–807.

Watt, N. F. (1974) Childhood roots of schizophrenia. In Ricks, D., Thomas, A.

and Roff, M. (eds.) *Life history research in psychopathology*, vol. 3. Minneapolis: University of Minnesota Press.

Watt, N. F., Anthony, E. J., Wynne, L. C. and Rolf, J. E. (eds.) (1984) *Children at risk for schizophrenia: a longitudinal perspective*. New York: Cambridge University Press.

Weissman, M. M., Gammon, G. D., John, K., Merikangas, K. R., Warner, V., Prusoff, B. A. and Sholomskas, D. (1987) Psychopathology in the children of depressed and normal parents: direct interview study. *Archives of General Psychiatry*, **44**, 847–53.

West, D. J. (1982) *Delinquency: its roots, careers and prospects*. London: Heinemann (Cambridge, MA: Harvard University Press).

Wing, J. K. and Brown, G. W. (1970) *Institutionalism and schizophrenia: a comparative study of three mental hospitals, 1960–1968*. Cambridge: Cambridge Univesity Press.

Yarrow, M. R., Campbell, J. D. and Burton, R. V. (1970) *Recollections of childhood*. Monographs of the Society for Research in Child Development, vol. 35, no. 5.

Yule, W. and Rutter, M. (1985a) Effects of lead on children's behaviour and cognitive performance: a critical review. In Mahaffey, K. R. (ed.) *Diet and environmental lead: human health effects*. Amsterdam: Elsevier.

(1985b) Reading and other learning difficulties. In Rutter, M. and Hersov, L. (eds.) *Child and adolescent psychiatry: modern approaches*, 2nd edn. Oxford: Blackwell, pp. 444–64.

Zaslow, M. J. and Hayes, C. D. (1986) Sex differences in children's response to psychosocial stress: toward a cross-context analysis. In Lamb, M. E., Brown, A. and Rogoff, B. (eds.) *Advances in developmental psychology*, vol. 4. Hillsdale, NJ: Erlbaum, pp. 285–337.

Zeitlin, H. (1986) *The natural history of disorder in childhood*. Institute of Psychiatry/Maudsley monograph no. 29. Oxford: Oxford University Press.

2 Longitudinal strategies, causal reasoning and risk research: a commentary

Norman Garmezy

Introduction

In the search for causal relationships in healthy development and mal-development, the longitudinal research strategy can play a prominent role. But the method provides a generous compound of virtue and vice. As Rutter points out (see chapter 1), the assets of the method are evident: the greater precision in the timing of significant events; the measurement of adaptational changes that accompany such events; the opportunity to examine the diversity of outcomes that are a consequence of such events (one of the most intriguing being 'the escape from the risk process'); the study of intra-individual changes over time as opposed to the analysis of inter-group or inter-individual differences; the analysis of the role of potential mediators and moderators of outcome that may be present at different temporal points in the longitudinal skein; the inferring of causal processes implicated in observed changes over time; and the avoidance of respondent error, often evident in follow-up studies, in which known outcomes shape a past that is seemingly (if not actually) coherent, consistent and continuous (Yarrow *et al.*, 1970).

However, accompanying these positives are certain inescapable negatives: the problem of selecting relevant and stable variables for longitudinal study; the extensiveness and diversity of the variables needed to ensure adequate coverage of the phenomena to be studied over time; the ubiquitous mensurational problems that plague some variables that are investigated; problems of homotypic and heterotypic continuity (Brim and Kagan, 1980) made difficult by age changes, transitional biological states, socio-cultural, psychosocial and situational factors; intervening, disruptive secular events and unanticipated environmental perturbations; subject and staff attrition; and the shifting tides of the later rejection of measures previously considered acceptable in an earlier period of life span developmental investigations.

These worrisome aspects of longitudinal study led Baldwin (1960, p. 27) to issue a cautionary note:

It should be apparent that a longitudinal study ... is a big investment for relatively small return – quantitatively speaking. It behooves us, therefore, to precede such an undertaking with careful pretesting, study of cross-sectional differences, and cruder retrospective studies to establish the likelihood of major effects. A longitudinal study is the last, not the first, step in a research program. It is an absolutely essential research method if we are to get firm knowledge of psychological change, but paradoxically it is to be avoided whenever possible.

Two key words, beyond the general admonition, are to be found in the notion of 'psychological change' as the object of study, for longitudinal research gained its initial credibility from the prediction pay-offs that resulted from long-term prospective studies of *physical* change. Again Baldwin (1960, pp. 25–6):

> Longitudinal studies, as they were originally conceived, seemed to have gambled on the existence of clear developmental trends that would shine through the welter of uncontrolled events. In physical growth the gamble paid off quite well. Many measures of physical growth are relatively uninfluenced by the disturbances found in the normal life of the child ... The general shape of the growth curve is quite apparent; and the extrinsic disturbances do not affect the individual's growth pattern enough to destroy the predictability of early or late maturation, adolescent growth rate, adult height, etc. The organism's own growth pattern can be identified despite lack of control over many environmental factors.

However, in the area of personality development, continuities are often modified by powerful environmental factors marked by biological (nutritional neglect), sociological (poverty and disadvantaged status), familial (discord, separation and loss), educational (inadequate schools), and psychological (stressful life events) disruption. Additional problems of method and measurement are posed by the search for behavioural modifiers that often interact with and influence biological, social, affective and cognitive growth patterns.

Some early history

It is interesting to examine part of the history regarding longitudinal research in the United States (MacFarlane, 1971). In the late 1920s a number of 'growth studies' of children were conducted at several major research centres: Harvard, the Fels and Merrill Palmer Institutes and, perhaps the best known of all, the Institute of Human Development of the University of California, Berkeley (Jones *et al.*, 1971). At Berkeley, two studies were initiated in 1928. The Guidance Study was designed to reveal the frequency of occurrence of behaviour and personality problems exhibited by children in preschool therapeutic clinics. Its purpose was to search for 'bioenvironmental' and family factors associated with the presence or absence of the specific presenting problems. Intended as a five-year study, the programme was converted into a longitudinal study of personality development that was then extended to age 18, accompanied by continued evaluations of child, family and environment. Eventually follow-up studies of the original cohort were conducted at ages 30 and 40 with evaluations of spouses and offspring, the latter being subject to the same age-appropriate schedules that had been administered to the parents in childhood.

The Berkeley Growth Study, begun the same year, was designed to investigate 'physical, mental, physiological, and motor development in the first fifteen months of life'. Here, too, the longitudinal skein was gradually expanded to incorporate ages from 3 to 18 years followed by a 'wide range of measurements and observation' at 21, 26 and 36 years of age. In this study, however, the cohort was a homogeneous sample of healthy infants born to white, English-speaking parents. Begun as a study of 'mental and physical growth in infancy', this programme in extension moved into adult personality evaluation, appraisal of marriages and of spouses, maternal care-taking of the offspring of the second generation, accompanied in later years by varied measures of these offspring born to members of the original cohort (Jones *et al.*, 1971, pp. 3–4).

In 1932 the Oakland Growth Study was mounted to investigate adolescent growth beginning at approximately 11 years of age. This too expanded into a life span study that finally extended up to age 45.

These pioneering investigations and their unanticipated longitudinal expansion reflect a common phenomenon. There are probably very few instances in psychology's and psychiatry's history in which a large-scale study begun in infancy, childhood or adolescence has failed to have a principal investigator who, at least once, uttered those fateful words: 'We really ought to follow up this group, given all the data we have collected from them.'

Warnings about the inevitable hold that longitudinal study has on investigators prompts an interesting story. When the Berkeley studies began, the investigators sought foundation support; foundations, in turn, sought advice-givers. In one instance an advisory committee of one foundation added an unnecessarily gratuitous comment regarding those who sally forth to do battle with developmental change via longitudinal study: 'For longitudinal research a peculiar kind of selflessness is required ... It is not obvious that such personality characteristics make a creative and productive scholar' (MacFarlane, 1971, p. 5). Needless to say the disproof lies in the achievements of the many life span investigators, both past and present.

For researchers in children-at-risk areas there is an interesting precedent to be found in several of the earliest American studies of longitudinal outcomes. Even prior to the emergence of the famed early developmental studies of child growth, a series of precedent-setting longitudinal studies of deviant children was initiated. Stone and Onque (1959), in cataloguing the early studies, provided a listing of studies conducted in 1924–5, each focused on different types of atypical children. These represent early efforts, via follow-up studies, to track the developmental outcomes of early atypicality. Conduct disorder occupied a prominent place in four of the studies centred on 'problem children', 'non-conformed boys', and 'delinquent trends' in children cited for stealing and abnormal sexual behaviour. A fifth study was entitled 'How foster children turn out' and described outcomes at age 18 of 910 children reared in foster home settings. The sixth investigation provided information at the other extreme of the atypicality spectrum in its focus on outcomes of 70 children with IQs over 120 when first seen.

It is interesting to note that the potential significance of longitudinal research was appreciated in those early years both by developmental psychologists and by mental-health practitioners. The focus of the early clinical investigators framed the same question asked of contemporary longitudinal studies of high-risk children: 'How did *they* turn out?'

Currently, there is a new interdisciplinary emphasis on issues of continuity and discontinuity from past to present adaptation that is a focal point for the emergent field of developmental psychopathology (see Cicchetti, 1984; Rutter, 1987; in press a; Sroufe and Rutter, 1984). With its emphasis on an integration of the clinical and developmental sciences, developmental psychopathology seeks to identify 'the origins and course of individual patterns of behavioral adaptation' irrespective of causation, age of onset, and the developmental transformations that ensue (Sroufe and Rutter, 1984, p. 18). Developmental psychopathology and risk research have now become inextricably linked (Masten and Garmezy, 1985) in their common focus on those ontogenetic and environmental processes that influence the longitudinal evolution of adaptive and maladaptive behaviour patterns extending from infancy to adulthood.

Types of longitudinal studies

Looking back to those initial studies of children at risk, one can see that the data-gathering was longitudinal in form (Time 1 → Time 2), but not longitudinal in analysis, and essentially unconcerned with the processes and mechanisms underlying behaviour change over time. The format of these studies was the 'follow-up' strategy, one of a quartet of methods all seemingly longitudinal in outline but not in orientation (Garmezy and Streitman, 1974). The four research approaches in the study of risk for psychopathology were described in this manner. Type I studies are those that employ clinical retrospective methods often focused on case studies, clinical interviews, or even contemporary interactional studies in which an inference of continuity extending backwards to an earlier period is assumed, the assumption itself being fraught with potential invalidity. Type II studies involve the method of 'follow-back', in which the starting point is the disordered adult, and premorbid status is evaluated from retrospective reports often based upon official records. In this method, the selection of a disordered-adult cohort as the starting point can often lead to biased overgeneralizations of continuity accompanied by an inability to track mediating processes in development unconfounded by the retrospective accounting of early development. Type III studies utilize the 'follow-up' procedures for evaluating the adult adjustment of atypical children, such as the studies of the 1920s. Initially these children, too, are likely to reflect biased cohorts for the determination of outcome data, although the prospective accounting does allow for a diversity of positive as well as negative outcome measures – an advantage that is manifestly absent in Type II studies. Type IV studies come closer to the developmental psychopathology paradigm, for these employ the 'follow-through' or longitudinal–developmental method to study children at risk and attendant comparison groups.

Type IV studies at this point in the scientific enterprise are in comparatively short supply, but they contain an essential element missing from Type III studies. As a variant of the latter, the investigator also collects data on index and control children extending from childhood to some determinate later outcome. But in addition, children are seen at different points in their development to garner evaluations of intermediate outcomes, as they may be influenced by biological, psychosocial and psychological mediators and moderators of ongoing changes in adaptation. It is the effort to study process that requires multiple evaluations over time. This is the basic characteristic of Type IV studies, and examples are to be found in the longitudinal research of a sample of non-deviant children by the Blocks (Block and Block, 1980), and the ongoing investigations of children at risk for neglect and abuse by Egeland and Sroufe (Egeland *et al.*, 1984) and by Cicchetti and his colleagues (Cicchetti and Rizley, 1981). Rutter (in press b) has written most saliently on the distinction to be made between this search for process and mechanism, as opposed to the identification of specific risk and protective factors.

Instead of searching for broadly based protective factors we need to focus on protective *mechanisms* and *processes*. That is, we need to ask *why* and *how* some individuals manage to maintain high self-esteem and self-efficacy in spite of facing the same adversities that lead other people to give up and lose hope? How is it that some people have confidantes to whom they can turn; what has happened to enable them to have social supports that they can use effectively at moments of crisis? Is it chance, the spin of the roulette wheel of life, or did prior circumstances, happenings or actions serve to bring about this desirable state of affairs?

The answer to such questions lies in the study of development over time, accompanied by the systematic exploration of typical and atypical developmental changes – an exploration that should embrace environmental circumstances, biological and psychological developmental attributes of the child, the relevant environs of the child's world, the ecological niche of the family, the educational opportunities, and the successive advantaging and disadvantaging milieus to which the child may be exposed over time. This calls for a continuity in multiple aspects of the research effort, not the evaluation of the child at Time 1 versus the same child at Time 2. It also requires a conceptual framework for development and its vicissitudes that will displace the somewhat arbitrary selection of variables for longitudinal study with a more rational selection based upon developmental and social-change variables that influence transitions that occur in childhood, adolescence and adulthood.

Developmental transitions are well known; social-change transition less so to longitudinal researchers. The work of Glen Elder points to the significance of social-change factors. Great secular events can disrupt the developmental sequence for good or for bad as the classic study *Children of the Great Depression*, attests (Elder, 1974). The Great Depression, of which Elder has written so eloquently, presented opportunities for both risk factors (family disruption, paternal explosiveness and volatility, denial of education) and protective factors to operate. For the latter, Elder (1974, p. 291) pointed to the positive consequences that followed the need for children to work in order to bring much-needed additional income into the family: 'These children had productive roles to perform. But in a more general sense they were needed and, in being needed, they had the chance and responsibility to make a real contribution to the welfare of others.'

The process implicated in the positive development of children who are called upon to help others is one that has been pointed out by Bleuler (1984) in the context of children at risk for schizophrenia, and elaborated conceptually by Rachman (1979) as the construct of 'required help-fulness.'

In citing the work of Elder, Bleuler and Rachman, three of the research strategies cited earlier appear to have been used. Bleuler used a case study of a daughter of a schizophrenic mother to reveal the protective nature of a child with talents much needed by her disabled family. Elder used a follow-back strategy to elucidate a similar viewpoint; and Rachman made use of a follow-up strategy to gain his initial insights into the importance of learned helpfulness. Do these examples derived from different modes of inquiry negate the view that Type IV studies are the primary instrument for studies of developmental processes in risk situations? Not at all.

Each of the studies cited above have in common the intensive collection of information needed to elucidate the operation of a transitional process. Bleuler knew intimately the lives and circumstances surrounding his cohort of 109 schizophrenic parents and their 184 offspring. This knowledge based on his 20-year-long contact with his families provided him with the information needed to infer process. Elder had a treasury of archival data from the Oakland Growth Study and the Berkeley Guidance Study with which to map the correlates and consequences for differential adaptation in children of the Great Depression. This permitted him to carry out in-depth studies of the likely processes that were implicated in differential patterns of adaptational outcomes in the offspring. Rachman had available to him a wealth of experimental and clinical data on fear and courage displayed by individuals under varying circumstances, none of it truly longitudinal in the long-term sense, but rather evident over a short-term period in which the repeated relationship between activity and helpfulness under stress was affirmed as a correlate of positive outcomes. This last observation suggests that the search for processes implicated in adaptive development may well be served best by short-term intensive longitudinal investigations to change over time following the subjects' exposure to stressful events.

Reflections on issues posed by Rutter

The single causal agent

In his chapter on the uses and pitfalls of studying causal processes in longitudinal data, Rutter has rightfully pointed to the inappropriate tendency of many researchers to seek the one 'breakthrough' causal agent that can explain the aetiology of a given mental disorder. A considerable portion of contemporary psychopathological research is devoted to such an effort, particularly given the impact of the current biological revolution that now energizes a large portion of psychiatric research. Thus there is the effort to discover *the* relevant neurotransmitter implicated in a disease, or *the* specific gene locus of a given mental disorder. That we are in the midst of a genuine revolution in molecular biology and genetics there can be no doubt. Clearly, that revolution will bring in its wake great advances in identifying the underlying biological processes implicated in the major mental disorders, but it is equally true that complex gene–environment interactions often tend to prevail in highly complex diseases which fail to follow a more typical Mendelian inheritance pattern. The fact that there has not been an equivalent revolution in the behavioural sciences, with the search for relevant psychological and psychosocial variables as yet unsuccessful, does not reduce the significance of Rutter's view that the search for multiple causation in mental disorder remains an important scientific future goal of psychopathologists. The assumption is a reasonable one that progress in the behavioural, cognitive and developmental sciences, accompanied by the great anticipated strides in molecular biology, biochemistry and molecular genetics, will in time resolve issues of the aetiology and the maintenance of mental disorder.

Too often, similarity of outcome, such as an identical diagnosis, fails to account for the diversity of factors that may contribute to that common end point. Robins (1978, p. 180), in commenting on environmental variation, has stated: 'There has been little research that has satisfactorily estimated the effect of the setting as distinct from the effect of the predisposition of the actors.'

Life events research that uses inventories rather than the Brown *et al.*. (1986) approach, by its very absence of context, heightens the single-causal explanation of disordered behaviour. As an example, one can select an item such as 'moved during the past year', a frequent 'stressor' in life events schedules, but in the absence of context one cannot ascertain whether such a move is reflective of upward or downward mobility, or of the absence of mobility. One cannot identify the significant antecedents to such a move, the family members involved, the interactive stressors to the event, and the types of risk or protective factors that can moderate the effects of the move.

What we do know is that settings alone do not determinately reflect positive or negative outcomes. Recent research by Long and Vaillant (1984), who followed up the Gluecks' (1950; 1968) control sample for the delinquency cohort that had been studied 40 years previously, clearly reveals a dissimilar pattern of adaptation in the offspring of these controls, who had also been reared in poverty and subjected to many of the same deprivations that marked the early years of the index children. Their findings require us to pause before unequivocally asserting the presence of a transgenerational 'permanent underclass' in America. Years previously, Pavenstedt (1965) also established the same manifest degree of variation in outcome as reflected in escape versus continued residence in the slums of Boston.

Research studies such as these point to the confound between settings and the dispositional qualities of individuals, affirming Robins' point, who also used the apparent stressor of 'moved during the past year' to demonstrate interaction of the impact of personality disposition on events and event consequences.

Laboratory research to demonstrate such a complex interaction is not an optimal strategy. Rather, naturalistic and quasi-naturalistic experiments seem the more appropriate methods for investigating such person–setting interactions.

Maladaptive outcomes as a joint function of risk, potentiating and maintenance factors

In elaborating on the interaction of risk, potentiating and maintenance factors, Rutter has alluded to studies he and his colleagues have conducted with institution-reared children, who, as adults, have become maladaptive parents. Here, contemporary disadvantaged circumstances and a non-supportive spouse appear to be contributory variables to a later negative outcome.

This example serves as an excellent illustration of the need to construct and to differentiate between aetiological and maintenance models in the study of psychopathology. There is a tendency for psychopathologists to fix on the former, but in a life span developmental view of mental disorder the neglect of maintenance models, which also requires a longitudinal strategy, can create an illusory view of an aetiological referent.

The longitudinal study of schizophrenia provides an example of such an error. In this disorder the skein must be seen as wide-ranging over time from (a) the premorbid period, (b) the introduction of possible biological and/or psychosocial potentiators of onset, (c) the morbid period of symptomatic expression of the disease, (d) treatment interventions culminating either in (e) recovery and release from hospital, or (f) chronicity and relapse.

In this disorder, over a 40-year span, the study of relationships within the family of the schizophrenic patient have traversed a spectrum that began with the false aetiologic view that the 'schizophrenogenic mother' (Fromm-Reichman, 1948) was the causative agent of the disorder to the current and more appropriate placement of the role of parental 'expressed emotion' (EE) as reflected in hostile or overemotional involvement of family members with the patient as a factor for either maintaining (low EE) or reducing (high EE) the post-hospital adaptation of the patient (Rodnick *et al.*, 1982; Leff and Vaughan, 1985). Recent research on the original conception of the aetiologic power of 'expressed emotion' has been supplanted by its more likely role as an element in family interaction that can act to modify expression of the basic disorder. First suggested as a specific to schizophrenia, recent unpublished research by Goldstein and Weissman suggests that EE may also be operative within families marked by severe depression as well. Presumably as EE comes to be regarded as a correlate of multiple disorders, its presumption as a potential specific element in causation will disappear to be replaced by its risk potential for maintaining severely disturbed behaviour.

The need to study variables that correlate with outcome
Rutter's view that one focus of inquiry in longitudinal risk studies should be the evaluation of variables that tend to accompany *differential* outcomes is an important one. There is strong supporting evidence that one category of measures – premorbid competence in terms of work efficiency, social (peer) engagement, and the ability to form intimate meaningful relationships – serves as a predictive core of outcomes in the severe mental disorders (Garmezy, 1970; Phillips, 1968; Zigler and Glick, 1986).

This relationship would suggest that laboratory and evaluation studies should be included in longitudinal research designed to elicit the degree of the presence or absence of factors that would appear to underlie competence functioning, such as attentional focusing, resistance to distraction, persistence, problem-solving activity, social cognition, school achievement, sociometric measures of peer acceptance, classroom studies of engagement and disruptiveness, and teacher judgements.

Rutter and Quinton (1984) and Quinton *et al.* (1984) have provided evidence of the power of a supportive husband in fostering the adaptation of women reared during childhood in institutional settings. This finding, too, would appear to affirm the power of competence as a protective factor in stressful circumstances. The assumption underlying this statement is that the selection of a supportive spouse-to-be is not an adventitious event. Were it to be, one would have to discard the powerful evidence of assortative mating. Competence breeds to competence; incompetence to incompetence. A supportive spouse suggests a process of evaluation and a non-random set of selection criteria indicative of a high level of competence in the co-partner.

If early competence is a basic predictor of later competence, then it should be important to include the positioning of variables to reflect this attribute at various points in the life cycle in longitudinal studies. Further, a focus on variables that can act to maintain or disrupt the continuity of competence should become an equally important aspect of life span developmental research. It is in the arena of competence that the analyses of the transactional quality of person and situation assumes great significance in longitudinal study.

This emphasis on competence, to which I ascribe, is designed to substitute for the ubiquitous popularity of the 'coping' construct. Currently favoured by numerous investigators, coping as a construct is marked by *post hoc* determination, inadequate measurement, and a lack of evidence of the transsituational generality of the category sets proposed by its adherents (Lazarus and Folkman, 1984; Moos and Schaefer, 1986).

The power of competence is illustrated by Rutter's reflections (see chapter 1) on research of Brown *et al.* (1986) indicating the ways used by single women who have to cope with an unwanted pregnancy – an event that can radically modify the women's subsequent life span trajectory. The observations of Brown *et al.* suggest that competence factors were again instrumental in solving the crisis posed by a premarital pregnancy. Successful 'coping' included seeking termination of the pregnancy, marrying someone already intended as the future spouse, or choosing as a husband a man who had not fathered the child. By contrast, unsuccessful patterns included marrying the father solely because of the illegitimate conception, becoming a long-term single parent, or bearing the child only to have it adopted later. The former, more adaptive pattern was twice as common among women of middle-class status in comparison with a group of working-class women; by contrast, a long-term cognitive set of helplessness dominated the patterns of adaptation of the unsuccessful group.

Buffering or neutralizing factors that abet stress reduction, such as supportive social networks, positive life events, intelligence, degree of engagement, good peer relations, and family cohesion and stability, all play a role in facilitating satisfactory adaptation to stress. Of equal importance is their intercorrelation with competence indices.

Similarly, Rutter's commentary (see chapter 1) on Maughan's finding in chapter 11 that a 'greater persistence' in black adolescents being educated in inner-London borough schools enabled them to counter their earlier educational disadvantage to a considerable extent is another indicator of the operation of a powerful personality disposition that serves to retain competence in difficult settings and trying circumstances.

'Escape' from the risk process

Rutter observes that continuities based on prospective study can differ markedly from those based on retrospection, citing in support the relationship between later parenting breakdown and adversities encountered in children. Although the relationship holds for the parenting breakdown on the basis of retrospective evidence, prospectively only a minority of children who had known adversity in childhood exhibited this pattern of later inadequate parenting.

This example provides another restatement of Freud's (1955, pp. 167–8) observation, made all the more masterful by Freud's weddedness to retrospective inquiry:

> So long as we trace development from its final outcome backwards, the chain of events appears continuous and we feel we have gained an insight which is completely satisfactory and even exhaustive. But if we proceed the reverse way, if we start from the premises inferred from the analysis and try to follow these up to the final result, then we no longer get the impression of an inevitable sequence of events which could not have been otherwise determined. We notice at once that there might have been another result, and that we might have been just as well able to understand and explain the latter ... Hence the chain of causation can always be recognized with certainty if we follow the line of analysis, whereas to predict ... is impossible.

Longitudinal data and the investigation of directional changes within the individual

In the context of risk research intra-individual changes can provide intriguing hypotheses for more elaborate study. Rutter (see chapter 1) refers to different outcomes in subcohorts that can result from events that occur to some persons and not to others, such as a move from the inner city that may accompany a diminution in delinquent behaviour. Such analyses of shifts in status, which may even originate in observations drawn from single cases, may reveal more basic processes at work that do affect behaviour outcome.

Robins (1966), in her classic volume *Deviant Children Grown Up*, used a control group of children whose *potential* vulnerability could have been reflected in the similarity of their disadvantaged status with that of the clinic sample. However, these control children met three minimal criteria for selection: (a) they had never been seen in a psychiatric clinic; (b) they had never repeated a full grade in elementary school; and (c) they had never been expelled from school, nor had they spent time in a correctional institution. In this subcohort it was the *absence* of negative changes that suggested a stability of function in these children.

Thirty years later when seen on follow-up as adults, these controls, despite early adversities, were remarkably resistant to psychopathology. Some 60% were living in the suburbs, they had good jobs, their divorce rate did not exceed the average, they demonstrated a high rate of stability and home ownership, they had never been incarcerated, nor had they ever been mental-hospital residents, and they were not on welfare. Thus a continuity of competence was evident in the comparison sample. The basis for selection, reflective of that competence, served as an early indicator of later stability. In assembling such a cohort, the investigator had to assay individually the early patterns of adaptive functioning. Longitudinal follow-up study revealed the long-term consequences of such stability. Thus this longitudinal study, initially derived from idiographic appraisal of childhood status, served as the nomothetic base for identifying subcohorts of deprived children whose early signs of competence, as against others marked by incompetence, helped investigators to understand differential patterns of life span trajectories.

Rutter's differentiation of risk indicators and risk mechanisms (see chapter 1) seems both timely and helpful, since it moves investigators a step closer to the integration and categorization of measures that reflect more basic processes. The suggestion is one of a need for a cluster analysis of appropriate variables that share elements in common and of an underlying mechanism or process to account for the interrelationships.

A research example may be supportive. In the Minnesota studies of children at risk for schizophrenia and in studies conducted in other laboratories, attentional dysfunction has frequently been observed in a subset of children born to schizophrenic mothers. Using the Continuous Performance Test (a measure of attentional vigilance) under a degraded stimulus condition, Nuechterlein (1983) applied signal detection analysis to the data and isolated a subset of children who showed a d' deficit, that is a more fundamental inability to discriminate relevant from irrelevant stimuli. Nuechterlein's collaborative research with Buchsbaum is now aimed at correlating PET scan data obtained from d' deficit schizophrenic persons in an effort to establish a pattern of brain–behaviour relationships that may suggest the operation of a more basic risk mechanism under which other risk factors reflective of attentional dysfunction in schizophrenic patients and in some children presumed to be at risk for the disorder can be subsumed.

Longitudinal research in the study of risk for mental disorders

Risk research in psychopathology has varied from disorder to disorder. The correlates of antisocial disorder and the antecedent behaviours implicated in the development of such disordered adults are well known and show marked cross-national stability. Studies of children at risk for schizophrenia have been given marked attention over the past two decades and the results of many of these investigations have been reported in a definitive volume (Watt *et al.*, 1984). Risk studies for affective disorder are now getting under way in which, for the most part, the range of variables studied in children born to affectively disordered parents tends to be comparatively narrow, in part because of the need to justify the diagnostic entity of childhood depression. Acceptance of that reality is warranted and the time for preoccupation with cross-sectional studies of limited variables, many focused on diagnoses, has passed. Fortunately, investigations are now beginning to be directed to developmental studies aimed at discovering measures that may reflect a continuity between childhood and adult depression.

There are many areas of investigation needed in a second wave set of research programmes of children at risk for psychopathology. Among these the following seem appropriate for consideration in future investigation:

1 Study of the components of competence reflected in the at-risk child's patterns of work, play, social attachment and educational attainment.
2 The elaboration of those components of intelligence that are instrumental for the child in meeting and overcoming stress.
3 The study of the genetics and biology of temperament and its phenotypic transformations over time. The issue here is one of heterotypic as opposed to homotypic continuity in infancy, and early and later childhood.
4 The need to track the psychophysiological and neurophysiological processes involved in attentional functioning upon which the development of a diverse set of competencies depend.
5 Social class is the great cutting variable of sociology, but the processes implicated in living under conditions of disadvantaged social status have not been adequately mapped. Block (1971) has called for a 'psychologizing' of the social-class variable into its constituent components so that those risk and escape-from-risk components that operate to express or to inhibit disorder can be better studied.
6 The nature of family constellations, the role of attachment, of discord, separation and loss, are all requisite to an understanding of the intrafamilial processes that contribute to risk in childhood. The many studies of 'expressed emotion' are steps in this direction. However, the original specificity of the construct, which was directed by studies of relapse and recovery in schizophrenia, now appears to have been a function of the failure to apply the construct in other disorders. Pilot research suggests that EE may be a significant factor in parental response in the affective disorders and other disturbing conditions as well. Mapping the correlates of low EE in high-risk families may prove to be contributory to the study of resilience under stress.
7 Needed in risk research is a careful mapping of significant events in lives through time that are found to correlate with 'turnarounds', that is changes in the life span development of individuals that are marked by shifts from adaptation to maladaptation and the reverse.

8 Finally, the case should be made for intensive short-term longitudinal studies in which the process of adaptation following specific stressful major life events can be studied for their impact on the loss of adaptive functioning in some and the retention of such functioning in others. However, the loss of adaptive functioning may not be the best indicator of risk status. Equally important is the rapidity of the recovering-of-competence function. Such studies have not been performed, but that neglect should be ended. Speed of recovery may be able to provide insights into risk or protective mechanisms that mark the passage of vulnerable and resilient children.

The longitudinal study of individuals is a vital method for studying trajectories of adaptation. Their absence condemns us to a failure to understand the present and the future in the context of the past. Samuel Coleridge (see *Oxford Dictionary of Quotations*, 1953, p. 152) used a metaphor that helps to frame the limitations under which we operate in the absence of longitudinal study:

If men could learn from history, what lessons it might teach us. But passion and party blind our eyes, and the light which experience gives is a lantern on the stern, which shines only on the waves behind us!

References

Baldwin, A. L. (1960) The study of child behavior and development. In Mussen, P. H. (ed.) *Handbook of research methods in child development*. New York: Wiley, pp. 3–35.

Bleuler, M. (1984) Different forms of childhood stress and patterns of adult psychiatric outcome. In Watt, N. F., Anthony, E. J., Wynne, L. C. and Rolf, J. E. (eds.) *Children at risk for schizophrenia: a longitudinal perspective*. Cambridge: Cambridge University Press, pp. 537–42.

Block, J. (1971) *Lives through time*. Berkeley, CA: Bancroft.

Block, J. H. and Block, J. (1980) The role of ego-control and ego-resiliency in the organization of behavior. In Collins, W. A. (ed.) *Development of cognition, affect, and social relations*. The Minnesota Symposia on Child Psychology, vol. 13. Hillsdale, NJ: Erlbaum, pp. 39–101.

Brim, O. G. Jr and Kagan, J. (eds.) (1980) *Constancy and change in human development*. Cambridge, MA: Harvard University Press.

Brown, G. W., Harris, T. O. and Bifulco, A. (1986) The long-term effects of early loss of parent. In Rutter, M., Izard, C. E. and Read, P. B. (eds.) *Depression in young people: developmental and clinical perspectives*. New York: Guilford Press, pp. 251–96.

Cicchetti, D. (1984) The emergence of developmental psychopathology. *Child Development*, 55, 1–7.

Cicchetti, D. and Rizley, K. L. (1981) Developmental perspective on the aetiology, intergenerational transmission and sequelae of child maltreatment. In Cicchetti, D. and Rizley, K. L. (eds.) *Developmental perspectives on child maltreatment*. New directions for child development, vol. 11. San Francisco: Jossey-Bass, pp. 31–55.

Egeland, B., Sroufe, L. A. and Erickson, M. A. (1984) The developmental consequence of different patterns of maltreatment. *International Journal of Child Abuse and Neglect*, 7, 459–69.

Elder, G. H., Jr (1974) *Children of the Great Depression.* Chicago: University of Chicago Press.

Freud, S. (1955) The psychogenesis of a case of homosexuality in a woman. In Strachey, J. (ed.) *The standard edition of the complete psychological works of Sigmund Freud,* vol. 18. London: The Hogarth Press and the Institute of Psychoanalysis, pp. 146–72.

Fromm-Reichman, F. (1948) Notes on the development of treatment of schizophrenics by psychoanalytic psychotherapy. *Psychiatry,* 11, 263–73.

Garmezy, N. (1970) Process and reactive schizophrenia: some conceptions and issues. In Katz, M., Cole, J. and Barton, W. E. (eds.) *The role and methodology of classification in psychiatry and psychopathology.* US Department of Health, Education and Welfare, Washington, DC: Government Printing Office, pp. 419–66. Revised and reprinted in *Schizophrenia Bulletin* (1970), 1, 30–74.

Garmezy, N. and Streitman, S. (1974) Children at risk for schizophrenia. Part I: Conceptual models and research methods. *Schizophrenia Bulletin,* 8, 14–90.

Glueck, S. and Glueck, E. (1950) *Unraveling juvenile delinquency.* New York: Commonwealth Fund.

(1968) *Delinquents and nondelinquents in perspective.* Cambridge, MA: Harvard University Press.

Jones, M. C., Bayley, N., MacFarlane, J. W. and Honzik, M. P. (1971) *The course of human development.* Waltham, MA: Xerox College Publishing.

Lazarus, R. S. and Folkman, S. (1984) *Stress, appraisal, and coping.* New York: Springer.

Leff, J. and Vaughan, C. (1985) *Expressed emotion in families.* New York: Guilford Press.

Long, C. V. F. and Vaillant, G. E. (1984) Natural history of male psychological health, XI: escape from the underclass. *American Journal of Psychiatry,* 141, 341–6.

MacFarlane, J. W. (1971) The Berkeley studies: problems and merits of the longitudinal approach. In Jones, M. C., Bayley, N., MacFarlane, J. W. and Honzik, M. P. (eds.) *The course of human development.* Waltham, MA: Xerox College Publishing, pp. 3–9.

Masten, A. S. and Garmezy, N. (1985) Risk, vulnerability, and protective factors in developmental psychopathology. In Lahey, B. B. and Kazdin, A. E. (eds.) *Advances in clinical child psychology,* vol. 8. New York: Plenum Press, pp. 1–52.

Moos, R. H. and Schaefer, J. A. (1986) Life transitions and crises. In Moos, R. H. (ed.) *Coping with life crises.* New York: Plenum Press, pp. 3–28.

Nuechterlein, K. H. (1983) Signal detection in vigilance tasks and behavioral attributes among offspring of schizophrenic mothers and among hyperactive children. *Journal of Abnormal Psychology,* 92, 4–28.

Pavenstedt, E. (1965) A comparison of the child-rearing environment of upper-lower and very low-lower class families. *American Journal of Orthopsychiatry,* 35, 89–98.

Phillips, L. (1968) *Human adaptation and its failures.* New York: Academic Press.

Quinton, D., Rutter, M. and Liddle, C. (1984) Institutional rearing, parenting difficulties, and marital support. *Psychological Medicine,* 14, 107–24.

Rachman, S. J. (1979) The concept of required helpfulness. *Behavior Research and Therapy,* 17, 1–6.

Robins, L. N. (1966) *Deviant children grown up.* Baltimore: Williams and Wilkins.

(1978) The interaction of setting and predisposition in explaining novel behavior: drug initiations before, in, and after Vietnam. In Kandel, D. B. (ed.) *Longitudinal research in drug abuse*. Washington: Hemisphere, pp. 179–96.

Rodnick, E. H., Goldstein, M. J., Doane, J. A. and Lewis, J. M. (1982) Association between parent–child transactions and risk for schizophrenia: implications for early intervention. In Goldstein, M. J. (ed.) *Preventive interventions in schizophrenia*. Washington, DC: Department of Health and Human Services, pp. 156–72.

Rutter, M. (1987) Continuities and discontinuities from infancy. In Osofsky, J. (ed.) *Handbook of infant development*, 2nd edn. New York: Wiley, pp. 1256–96.

(in press a) Psychosocial resilience and protective mechanisms. In Rolf, J., Masten, A., Cicchetti, D., Nuechterlein, K. and Weintraub, S. (eds.) *Risk and protective factors in the development of psychopathology*. New York: Cambridge University Press

(in press b) Intergenerational continuities and discontinuities in serious parenting difficulties. In Cicchetti, D. and Carlson, V. (eds.) *Research on the consequences of child maltreatment*. New York: Cambridge University Press.

Rutter, M. and Quinton, D. (1984) Long-term follow-up of women institutionalized in childhood: factors promoting good functioning in adult life. *British Journal of Developmental Psychology*, **18**, 225–34.

Sroufe, L. A. and Rutter, M. (1984) The domain of developmental psychopathology. *Child Development*, **55**, 17–29.

Stone, A. A. and Onque, G. C. (1959) *Longitudinal studies of child personality*. Cambridge, MA: Harvard University Press.

Watt, N. F., Anthony, E. J., Wynne, L. C. and Rolf, J. E. (eds.) (1984) *Children at risk for schizophrenia: a longitudinal perspective*. Cambridge: Cambridge University Press.

Yarrow, M. R., Campbell, J. D. and Burton, R. V. (1970) *Recollections of childhood: a study of the retrospective method*. Monographs of the Society for Research in Child Development 138, vol. 35, no. 5.

Zigler, E. and Glick, M. (1986) *A developmental approach to adult psychopathology*. New York: Wiley.

3 Individual and variable-based approaches to longitudinal research on early risk factors*

David Magnusson and Lars R. Bergman

Introduction

The main theme of this chapter is a discussion of a variable-based versus a person-based approach in longitudinal research on early risk factors. First the limitations of a variable approach are described and discussed, and the conclusion is drawn that this approach should be complemented with a person-oriented pattern approach. The second part of the chapter is devoted to the presentation of an empirical example of one possible pattern approach. The chapter concludes with a discussion of the implications of (a) the theoretical considerations and (b) the empirical illustration in terms of further research on early risk factors.

The variable orientation

With longitudinal risk research, the variable orientation has been a standard approach, dominating research on two main issues: (a) the stability of individual characteristics across age levels and (b) the relationship between ecological and/or person factors during childhood ('predictors'), on the one hand, and adult status on various respects, on the other ('criteria').

The first issue mentioned above, namely the stability of individual characteristics, is basic to risk research in that it includes, for example, studies of the growth and stability of various indicators of maladjustment. A sound knowledge of such fundamental phenomena is sometimes a necessary prerequisite for carrying out studies of the kind described under (b) above. Much of the research on stability has been confined to investigations of one or only a few aspects of individual functioning across time, for example aggressiveness, hyperactivity or attachment. Most of the interest has been on the same aspect of behaviour across ages, that is what Kagan (1971) referred to as homotypic continuity. Fewer studies have been made of heterotypic continuity, that is when a particular underlying disposition is manifested in different types of behaviour at

* This study was supported by grants from the Bank of Sweden Tercentenary Fund, the Swedish Council for Social Research, and the Swedish Council for Planning and Coordination of Research. We are grateful to Dr Sigrid Gustafson for many useful suggestions.

45

different developmental stages. Often in studies of homotypic continuity, stability for a certain person characteristic is expressed as the correlation among measures at different age levels. This approach implies that what is studied is mainly the stability of individual rank orders with respect to the variable under consideration.

A second, but related, variable-oriented area of early risk research is concerned with prediction studies of adulthood status. For example, various aspects of adult maladjustment are predicted from measures of individual characteristics and/or from what is assumed to be significant properties of the environment during childhood. In this tradition, factors in the childhood environment (e.g. parents' income and/or education, parents' divorce, parental behaviour) and characteristic features of individual functioning at an early age (e.g. intelligence, conduct, achievement, peer relations) are treated as predictors, and measures of criminal behaviour, mental illness, alcohol abuse, etc. at adult age are treated as criteria. Almost independent of the choice of predictors and criteria, systematic and sometimes strong correlations have been found between negative aspects of the early environment, such as low intelligence, antisocial behaviour, poor peer relations and poor achievement, and criminal activity, mental problems and alcohol abuse in adulthood.

The relations between early antecedents of adult functioning and actual measures of such variables are commonly studied within a correlational framework, for instance using regression analytic models and methods for data treatment, multiple correlation, discriminant analysis, path analysis, LISREL, etc. The common feature of these methods is that they are directed towards the analysis of variables and express the results of the analyses in terms of weights indicating the relative role in the process outcome of each of the involved variables.

An interactional view of individual development

Before discussing the limitations of a variable orientation, it is necessary to provide a brief presentation of the basic view on individual development underlying this chapter's discussion of an appropriate research strategy and methodology. The perspective has been designated an interactional view.

The following three propositions form the cornerstones of an interactional view on psychological phenomena (Magnusson, 1987; Magnusson and Allen, 1983):

1 The individual develops and functions as a total, integrated organism. Development does not take place in single aspects *per se*, in isolation from the totality.
2 The individual develops and functions in a dynamic, continuous and reciprocal interaction with his/her environment.
3 The characteristic way in which individuals develop, in interaction with the environment, depends upon and influences the continuous reciprocal

process of interaction among the subsystems of psychological and biological factors in the individual.

According to this view, development is regarded as a *process* in which cognitive–affective and biological factors in the individual, and distal and proximal factors in the environment, are involved in a constant, reciprocal interaction. The process of interaction among single operating factors in the individual takes place within this framework, and is influenced by, and influences the total organism to which they belong. The patterning of various aspects of individual functioning in an individual represents a partly specific mosaic of psychological, biological and environmental (situational) factors. To some extent the patterns themselves undergo transformations across time. These transformations are, in part, common to individuals, and age-related, and are partially specific for each individual. Thus what is characteristic of a certain individual at a certain stage of development is the patterning of relevant factors, a patterning that is the result of a life history of interaction processes (Magnusson and Bergman, 1984).

Methodological problems in a variable approach
It is important to take into consideration the theoretical view presented above when planning longitudinal risk research. A characteristic feature of research in the two areas of risk research delineated above is the reliance on linear correlations for the study of relationships among variables. From the theoretical discussion in the preceding section, it should be clear that this approach, though appropriate and effective under certain conditions, may not be as generally applicable as is often assumed. Two particular cautions are worthy of mention: (a) the existence of inter-individual differences in growth curves and (b) the existence of non-linearity and interactions among operating factors.

In a discussion regarding the methodological implications of the existence of individual differences in growth rate for single variables, Magnusson (1985) based his conclusions on two examples drawn from biological variables. These examples served as a background for the following conclusions:

1. Though all individuals pass through the transitional period in adolescence in the same lawful and predictable way, correlation coefficients among rank orders of individuals obtained for the same function at various age levels may vary substantially, exhibiting both positive and negative signs. If such results were obtained in the study of the stability of cognitive, emotional or conduct factors, they would most probably be interpreted as reflecting a lack of stability and consistency in the processes being studied.

2. The size of a correlation coefficient among rank orders taken at various age levels depends on the interval between data collections and/or

the age or the stage within a transitional period when the data are collected. For example, coefficients covering the time before and after a transitional period may be higher than coefficients covering a shorter period if data collections occur during the transitional period.

3. The size of the correlation between two variables, if at least one is strongly influenced by biological maturation, can vary considerably across different chronological ages. It is noteworthy that these observations contradict and invalidate what has been long regarded as a law of development, summarized by Clarke and Clarke (1984, p. 197) as follows: 'The second law (as noted) is that, regardless of age, the longer the period over which assessments take place, the lower the correlation is likely to be, that is the greater the change in ordinal position of individuals within a group.'

Individual differences in growth rate exist for many biological factors, with some of them exerting strong effects on mental functioning and conduct, for example those involved in the biological changes during puberty. The important consequences of inter-individual differences in biological maturation among girls, manifested in the age at menarche, have been demonstrated by Magnusson *et al.* (1986). As previously emphasized, for instance by Loevinger (1966), there are many examples of interesting psychological functions that display the same general growth curves as those shown for biological factors. The need for modelling individual differences in growth rate has been emphasized by Rogosa and Willett (1985), who also stressed the failure of the traditional regression approach to take such differences into account.

The discussion above was concerned with the implications of the existence of individual differences in growth rate. The limitations of using a linear regression analytic approach to the study of relationships among relevant factors operating in a developmental process become even more apparent when what is being considered is several factors operating together, often in a complicated, non-linear fashion. The methodological implications of the existence, in developmental processes, of non-linearity and interactions in the relationships among operating factors appear both in cross-sectional and longitudinal analyses (Bergman and Magnusson, 1987; Hinde and Dennis, 1986; Magnusson, 1985; 1987).

The limitations of a linear regression approach to the study of complex relationships among variables extend beyond the use of pair-wise correlation coefficients. They apply to other linear, regression-based methods used for the analysis of multivariate sets of data, such as multiple correlation analyses, discriminant analyses and path analyses. To some extent and for some purposes, regression analytic methods can be used to take care of non-linearity and interactions among the variables under consideration. However, as Hinde and Dennis (1986) demonstrate empirically, the applicability of such methods is restricted.

A pattern approach

The discussion and illustrations given above demonstrate the limitations of a variable-oriented, regression analytic approach to the study of certain essential topics within longitudinal risk research. The foregoing discussion does not, of course, mean that variable-directed analyses, using regression analytic methods are meaningless or unnecessary. However, the conclusions that can be drawn from the examples presented above are (a) that regression analytic methods must be used with great caution and with due consideration for the nature of the phenomena under study in each specific case, and (b) that for some purposes we must complement the variable-oriented regression analytic methods with person-oriented *pattern* approaches.

In line with the general view formulated above, Cairns (1986) drew a similar conclusion:

certain developmental outcomes are sufficiently unique as to require analysis at the individual, configural level rather than at the sample, population level. Generalizations may then be reached on the basis of the lawfulness of associations within groups of subjects (see Allport, 1937). That is, the unit of study becomes the individual, not the sample of individuals. General laws may then be identified by commonalities across persons or across relationships.

Such an approach has not only certain attractive methodological features but also the merit of yielding results that reflect more directly the functioning of individuals rather than the functioning of a statistically defined 'average' child (see Lewin, 1931).

The methodological problems connected with a pattern approach to the study of developmental problems are multifaceted. Since there is no single solution to these problems, the methodological solutions must also be multifaceted. In earlier studies within the same project as the data presented here are taken from, latent profile analysis was used to study the patterning of conduct and norm breaks (Magnusson, 1981). In this chapter another pattern approach is followed and, as an illustration, an empirical investigation of the relationship between early adjustment problems and adult maladjustment will be presented. The study illuminates a central problem that arises in variable-oriented research on early risk factors.

As was stated above, there is no single solution to the methodological problems that arise when applying the theoretical perspective presented here. Thus the methodology presented here, using a pattern approach, is only one possible way of dealing with some of the problems. Other problems, for example the ones arising from the existence of individual differences in growth rate, require other solutions.

As summarized earlier, much variable-oriented research has demonstrated significant, sometimes strong, relationships between single possible risk factors at an early age, for example aggressiveness, and adult maladjustment, for example criminality. One question that then arises is the following: To what extent does the total picture of pair-wise correlations between conduct variables at an early age and maladjustment factors at adulthood depend upon a rather limited number of persons characterized by broad syndromes of adjustment problems? Moreover, if these multi-problem syndromes account for the bulk of the pair-wise relationships, to what extent is it meaningful to interpret correlations between single conduct problems at an early age and indicators of adult maladjustment as demonstrating the significance of these early behaviours in the development process? The empirical study presented here may serve as a basis for a discussion of these and connected problems (see also Robins (1984) for a discussion of the importance of considering the correlations between problems).

Cross-sectional analyses

The data on which the present analyses are based come from the longitudinal research programme Individual Development and Adjustment (IDA), initiated and led by the first author of this chapter (Magnusson, 1987; Magnusson et al., 1975). The programme started with the first data collection in 1965. It comprised initially all boys and girls of ages 10 and 13 who attended school in a typical town in the middle of Sweden. The main group (those who were ten at the start) comprised about 1,100 children. The boys and girls represent the entire range of intelligence and social background, and empirical comparisons show that the group is fairly representative of the corresponding cohorts from other towns in Sweden. The boys and girls have been followed through the school system up to adulthood, and data for psychological and biological aspects of individual functioning, as well as data covering relevant social and physical characteristics of the environment of the youngsters, have been collected. The present study concerns the main group. Data for adjustment problems at the age of 13 and register data from adulthood for alcohol abuse, criminal offences and psychiatric care have been used. Only boys were studied.

Adjustment problems at the age of 13 were measured for four aspects of conduct (aggressiveness, motor restlessness, lack of concentration and low school motivation), for poor peer relations, and for underachievement. Official record data for alcohol abuse, criminal offences and psychiatric care cover the age span from age 18 up to and including age 23.

The total sample of boys, on which the analyses presented here are based, consisted of all boys who at any time after the second grade entered the grade cohort ($N = 707$). The total sample of boys in the grade cohort at age 13 comprised 545 boys. For adjustment data at the age of 13, data were missing for five boys. Official records of any kind were missing for three boys. Thus the analyses are based on data for a representative sample of boys with a negligible attrition.

Adjustment data from the age of 13. At the age of 13 the boys were grouped into clusters of similar patterns on the basis of the following six indicators of extrinsic adjustment problems: aggressiveness, motor restlessness, lack of concentration, low school motivation, underachievement and poor peer relations.

The first four aspects of adjustment were covered by teachers' ratings made on seven-point scales for each variable (see Magnusson *et al.*, 1975). Underachievement was measured for each individual as the residual between his obtained achievement score and the predicted score from his intelligence level. Poor peer relations were based on sociometric ratings and primarily measured unpopularity.

As emphasized by Bergman and Magnusson (1983), an optimal investigation of the development of adjustment problems in terms of individual patterns implies the use of some sort of absolute measure of the variables under investigation. This prerequisite is difficult for many relevant variables in psychological research. In order to meet the requirement in so far as is possible, the analyses reported here were based on data for what Bergman and Magnusson (1987) designated as '*semi-absolute*' scales. Using that approach, each of the above indicators was scored on a four-point semi-absolute scale, with the following tentative definitions of the adjustment scores:

Adjustment score description
0 No adjustment problem
1 The adjustment is not good but no clear problem
2 An adjustment problem
3 A pronounced adjustment problem

The scoring was based on considerations of the significance of each indicator of an adjustment problem, independent of the relative frequency of its occurence. One implication of this approach is that distinctions in the 'positive' side of the distribution of adjustment scores are neglected in this specific analysis, where the interest is devoted to maladjustment. For instance, with regard to the teachers' ratings, which were made on seven-point scales, the values 1–4 were coded 0, 5 was coded 1, 6 was coded 2, and 7 was coded 3. The reasons for the semi-absolute scaling are discussed by Bergman and Magnusson (1983; 1984a; 1987). In the first of these references, a more detailed presentation of the underlying theoretical background and taxonomy was given. The indicators are described in more detail in Bergman and Magnusson (1984b).

Pattern analysis on data from the age of 13. For the grouping of the children, a cluster analytic procedure – RESCLUS – developed in the project was applied (Bergman, 1985; Bergman and Magnusson, 1984a). The method, as it was used here, was based on existing algorithms within the statistical package CLUSTAN (Wishart, 1982). The individuals were first grouped according to a hierarchical method. This classification was then taken as input for a relocation cluster analysis. One special feature of the relocation procedure employed was that a residue of *unclassified* individuals were formed. This is important for two reasons: first, it is important from a theoretical viewpoint to recognize the fact that not all individuals fit well into one of a small number of classes or types; second, for technical reasons it may be important to remove individuals who are 'misfits' to a residue of unclassified since they otherwise might affect the clustering solution appreciably. (This argument holds whether a deviating profile is generated by deficient reliability or is a valid representation of an individual's 'true' profile). The final clustering based on data from the age of 13 is given in Table 1.

The first observation that can be made is that four out of the six indicators of maladjustment at the age of 13 do not appear as single-problem clusters. For example, aggressiveness and motor restlessness, which have been studied extensively in the variable-oriented tradition as separate indicators of maladjustment in both a cross-sectional and a longitudinal perspective, appear only in combination with other indicators. The only single-problem clusters that appear are those for poor peer relations and underachievement, respectively. These two clusters were also identified at the age of 10 and showed a significant stability from 10 to 13 (Bergman and Magnusson, 1987).

According to the solution presented in Table 1, most boys (296 out of 540) belong to a cluster characterized by no adjustment problems. Some maladjustment clusters are of particular interest, however. Three severe multi-problem clusters, indicating severe adjustment problems are identified (6, 7 and 8). The most severe is cluster 8, which is characterized by strong maladjustment symptoms at the age of 13 for all the factors investigated except underachievement. Cluster 7 is characterized primarily by high aggressiveness, motor restlessness and lack of concentration. This cluster seems to be of special interest in discussions regarding the conceptualization of the hyperactivity syndrome. The strongest indicators of maladjustment in cluster 6 are underachievement, lack of concentration and low school motivation, a syndrome which might be interpreted as indicating mainly learning problems. For a more detailed description the reader is referred to Bergman and Magnusson (1984b).

Essential for the interpretation of these results is their generalizability, the extent to which the obtained patterns are dependent on sample characteristics. An estimation of the possibility of generalizing from the results was made in an earlier study in which a pattern analysis was performed on data from the age of ten, for the same variables as presented

Table 1 *Final clustering solution for extrinsic adjustment problems (boys at age 13)*

					Cluster means			
Cluster no.	Size	Average coefficient	Aggresive-ness	Motor restless-ness	Lack of concen-tration	Low school moti-vation	Under-achieve-ment	Poor peer relations
1	296	.12	–	–	–	–	–	–
2	23	.30	–	–	–	–	–	2.4
3	40	.28	–	–	–	–	2.6	–
4	61	.39	1.3	1.4	–	–	–	–
5	41	.39	–	1.5	2.3	1.9	–	–
6	12	.56	1.7	1.8	2.3	1.9	2.6	–
7	37	.37	2.3	2.3	1.9	1.3	–	–
8	22	.48	2.2	2.7	2.6	2.4	–	1.9
Residue	8		1.5	1.4	1.3	1.3	1.3	2.3

Note: A dash means that the cluster mean of a variable is less than one in the four-point scale coded 0, 1, 2, 3. Average coefficient means average error sum of squares within the cluster.

here (Bergman and Magnusson, 1984a). The total sample was split into two random halves and the same procedure was used for clustering the individuals in the two subsamples. The solutions were similar, and there is no reason to assume that the same generalizability does not hold for the sample studied here.

Official records data. As reported above, the presence of registered alcohol abuse, criminal offences and psychiatric care was identified for the age period 18–23. These variables were operationalized as follows:

1 Alcohol abuse was measured by counting the number of registrations of alcohol offences, such as being arrested by the police for drunkenness, etc.
2 Criminal offences were measured as the number of court decisions. In this analysis, pure alcohol offences and minor traffic offences were not counted in order to avoid contamination with records for alcohol abuse. (For further details, see Stattin *et al.*, 1986.)
3 Psychiatric care was defined as having had an interview with a psychiatrist that led to a DSM-III diagnosis (von Knorring *et al.*, 1987). A pure alcohol diagnosis was counted as severe alcohol abuse, not as psychiatric care. A pure drug diagnosis, other than alcohol, was not counted at all. (Only two persons were thus categorized.)

Pattern analysis of data from official records. The pattern analysis of data from official records was performed with configural frequency analysis (CFA). This type of analysis tests whether an observed value pattern occurs significantly more often (a type) or significantly less often (an antype) than expected by an independence model (Krauth and Lienert, 1982; Lienert, 1969). In the testing of the significance of the findings, the exact binomial probability model was used to avoid the problems with small expected values (Bergman, 1985). The significances were corrected according to the so-called Bonferroni method (see Krauth and Lienert, 1982), a necessary correction to take into account the fact that several simultaneous and dependent tests were performed. In Table 2 the results are given of a configural frequency analysis (CFA) of official records data.

The results presented in Table 2 show three significant types: (a) not in the official records at all, (b) in the official records for both criminality and alcohol abuse, and (c) in all three kinds of record. It should also be noted that being only in *one* of the three types of official record is a significant antitype, that is it occurs significantly less frequently than expected, if the occurrences were randomly distributed in the sample.

The result of this analysis in terms of patterns has relevance for further discussions about variable- versus pattern-oriented research on maladjustment.

Longitudinal analyses

In Table 3, the results are reported of the analyses of the longitudinal relationship between school adjustment clusters at age 13 and adjustment problems at age 18–23, as they are reflected in criminal, psychiatric, and alcohol records. For each of the clusters of males, in terms of their pattern of adjustment scores from the school, Table 3 presents the percentage appearing in records for criminal acts, in records for psychiatric care and in records for alcohol abuse, respectively. The significance testing of types and antitypes for each percentage was performed using exact hypergeometric tests (see Bergman and El-Khouri, in press).

Of particular interest for the elucidation of the developmental process underlying adult maladjustment are the significant types and antitypes that appear in Table 3. Four significant types emerge: those who were characterized by the patterns for the severe, multi-problem clusters 7 and 8 at the age of 13 (see Table 1) were registered significantly more often for criminality and for alcohol abuse at adulthood than expected by chance.

It is worth noting that neither of the single-problem clusters characterized by underachievement or poor peer relations nor the multi-problem cluster characterized solely by weak aggressiveness and weak motor restlessness at age 13 was significantly related to being registered at adulthood. There is not even a conspicuous tendency in that direction. At first glance, this result may appear contradictory to the sizeable relationships often reported between these variables and adult maladjustment of various kinds. However, viewed from the pattern approach perspective, there is no contradiction. Subjects with several conduct problems as the core symptoms appear to be responsible for these often observed relation-

Table 2. *Cross-sectional configurations of data from records for criminal acts, psychiatric care and alcohol abuse*

Configuration				
Criminality	Psychiatric care	Alcohol abuse	Observed frequency	Expected frequency
No	No	No	504[t]	443.10
No	No	Yes	22[at]	66.50
No	Yes	No	25[at]	41.22
No	Yes	Yes	6	6.19
Yes	No	No	71[at]	117.73
Yes	No	Yes	48[t]	17.67
Yes	Yes	No	13	10.95
Yes	Yes	Yes	16[t]	1.64

[t] Type, significant at the 5% level after Bonferroni correction.
[at] Antitype, significant at the 5% level after Bonferroni correction.

Table 3 *Relation between adjustment clusters at age 13 according to school data, and criminality, psychiatric care, and alcohol abuse at age 18–23 (males, N = 538)*

Cluster at age 13	N	Percentages that appear in records for		
		Criminality	Psychiatric care	Alcohol abuse
1 No problems	295	13.6[at]	6.4	7.5[at]
2 Poor peer relations	23	13.0	13.0	4.3
3 Underachievement	40	10.0	5.0	12.5
4 Weak aggression, weak motor restlessness	61	18.0	0.0	13.1
5 Lack of concentration, low motivation	40	30.0	15.0	27.5
6 Multi-problems – severe underachievement and lack of concentration	12	33.3	0.0	8.3
7 Hyperactivity with aggressiveness	37	48.6[t]	16.2	37.8[t]
8 Severe multi-problem	22	50.0[t]	13.6	36.4[t]

[t] Problem type, significant at the 5% level after Bonferroni correction.
[at] Problem antitype, significant at the 5% level after Bonferroni correction.

ships. Boys with poor peer relations or underachievement, but not characterized by the general syndrome(s), do not exhibit later maladjustment. In concordance with the results summarized above, antitypes appeared for those who belonged to the group with no problems at age 13 and who were registered for criminality or alcohol abuse at adulthood.

If we turn to each kind of registered problem, a strong relation to adjustment clusters at age 13 arises for criminal records. It is interesting to note that for clusters 2, 3 and 4 the percentage of those who have criminal records does not deviate to any marked extent from what is the case for males from the 'no problem' cluster. However, in examining the multi-problem clusters, clusters 5, 6, 7 and 8, strong relationships appear, with the strongest ones emerging for clusters 7 and 8, in which about half of those who belong to these clusters appear in criminal records at age 18–23.

For alcohol abuse at age 18–23 there is a strong relation to three clusters at school age: clusters 5, 7 and 8. As for criminal records, the strongest relationship appears for cluster 7, in which the boys were characterized primarily by high aggressiveness, high motor restlessness, and a strong lack of concentration, and for cluster 8, in which the boys were characterized by all problems included in the analyses, except underachievement.

The relation to adjustment clusters at school age is much weaker for psychiatric care at age 18–23 than for criminality and alcohol abuse. For the clusters 3, 4 and 6, the percentage of males having a psychiatric record is actually smaller than the percentage for those who belonged to the 'no problem' cluster. In two of these three, rather large clusters (clusters 4 and 6), no male has a psychiatric record. The strongest relationship appears for clusters 2, 5, 7 and 8. However, the percentages for those having a psychiatric record in these four clusters are not very high.

Thus the total picture is that there is a strong relationship between syndromes of maladjustment in terms of teachers' ratings at age 13 and adult criminal offences and alcohol abuse as reflected in official records. The relation is markedly weaker for the relation between maladjustment syndromes at the age of 13 and adult psychiatric care. Chi-square tests for each type of official record showed that the overall relationship between categorization in terms of ratings at age 13 and categorization on the basis of official records at age 18–23 was significant at the 0.1% level for criminal and alcohol records, and at the 5% level for records for psychiatric care.

In a preceding section a crucial question was raised regarding the importance, in generating the observed pair-wise relationships between an early risk factor and adult maladjustment, of a small group of children with severe multi-problems. To illustrate this question, the following analysis was performed. First, the relationship between aggression at age 13 and each of criminality and alcohol abuse at age 18–23 was studied for the whole sample by computing chi-squares for the corresponding 2×2 tables (all variables were dichotomized). The results, which are displayed in Table 4, indicate strong positive relationships, as could be expected. Second, the children belonging to the severe multi-problem clusters, clusters 6, 7 and 8, were removed and the same relationships were then computed for the reduced data set. As can be seen, the longitudinal

Table 4 *Longitudinal relationship between aggression at age 13 and criminality or alcohol abuse at age 18–23: (a) for all men (N = 538); (b) for men after removal of those belonging to a severe multi-problem cluster at age 13 (N = 467). Frequencies (percentages within parenthesis)*

			Age 18–23			
			Criminality		Alcohol abuse	
			No	Yes	No	Yes
Age 13			$p < .001$		$p < .001$	
(a)	Aggression	No	383 (84.7)	69 (15.3)	405 (89.6)	47 (10.4)
		Yes	50 (58.1)	36 (41.9)	62 (72.1)	24 (27.9)
			ns		ns	
(b)	Aggression	No	373 (84.8)	67 (15.2)	395 (89.8)	45 (10.2)
		Yes	22 (81.5)	5 (18.5)	24 (88.9)	3 (11.1)

Note: The significance of a relationship was tested using a chi-square with one *df*, corrected for continuity.

relationships between aggression and criminality or alcohol abuse completely disappeared.

Discussion

The results presented above demonstrate that the strong coefficients obtained in IDA and elsewhere for the relationship between single aspects of early adjustment problems and alcohol abuse, criminal offences and mental problems at a later stage of development can sometimes be explained by the existence of a small number of groups of boys who are characterized by patterns or syndromes of adjustment problem indicators. Even in the cases when single adjustment problems formed significant clusters of boys at ages 10 and 13 (for poor peer relations and underachievement, respectively) their relationship to registered alcohol problems, criminal offences and psychiatric care was non-significant and negligible.

The results obtained for the two adjustment problem indicators at age 13 – poor peer relations and underachievement – illustrate one essential aspect of the problem under consideration. With regard to poor peer relations, for example, the results indicate the existence of at least two distinct groups: one group with only this problem and the other group with a general syndrome of adjustment problems, including severe conduct problems. This result gives a less rigid interpretation to the relationship between poor peer relations and later maladjustment than that given by, for instance, a correlation coefficient between an indicator of poor peer relations and an indicator of later maladjustment.

One conclusion for research on peer relations and their psychological significance is that the issue cannot be dealt with as a characteristic of an individual, one that has the same meaning independent of the context formed by the whole individual and his environment (see Lewin, 1931). This conclusion can be generalized to hold for other aspects of individual functioning. To take one further example from the study, it is not certain that aggressiveness has the same role in the dynamic functioning of an individual when it appears in a syndrome together with restlessness and low school motivation as it has when it appears in another individual together with lack of concentration and underachievement. This conclusion is in line with the general interactional formulations that form the theoretical framework for IDA and which were discussed earlier in this chapter. For the planning and interpretation of empirical research, such findings have far-reaching implications.

The above illustrates that the higher-order interaction structure found in pattern analysis cannot always be reduced to pair-wise relationships as is often done in variable-oriented analysis. It appears doubtful that even a more sophisticated variable-oriented analysis, where, for instance, some indicators of conduct problems were controlled for before studying the correlation, would reveal the structure found in the pattern analysis.

Consequently, the results indicate that observed relationships in a set of adjustment variables (in a cross-sectional as well as in a longitudinal perspective) may only be an expression of the fact that a small group of subjects are characterized by a general syndrome of problems. When the subjects that were characterized by several severe adjustment problems (clusters 6, 7 and 8) at age 13 were removed before analyses of the relationships between single early behaviours and adult adjustment were made, the systematic relationship of aggressiveness to adult criminality and to adult alcohol abuse disappeared completely. Thus aggressiveness, when not combined with other adjustment problems, does not seem to be the important antecedent it is assumed to be by theorists, and which empirical research in the variable-directed tradition supposes. This result, however, did not occur to the same extent for other conduct variables analysed in the same way. An essential task for further risk research is to investigate to what extent stability and prediction coefficients in this field can be explained by the presence of a small group of multi-problem boys who are stable in their behaviour across time, and to what extent single factors have an impact *per se*, independent of whether or not they occur together with other factors.

A central issue in developmental research is concerned with stability and change of single aspects of individual functioning. This issue is of central importance in the two main areas of developmental risk research that were identified in the introduction to this chapter. The first one is concerned with the stability of single aspects, either because this consistency is of interest *per se* or in order to elucidate the issue of personality consistency. Results from such studies have been used as arguments by both sides in the battle regarding the consistency of personality (see Mischel, 1968; and Olweus, 1979). The second area has been concerned with the prediction of adult criminality, mental illness and/or alcohol problems, etc. from single early symptoms of maladjustment, for example aggressiveness and hyperactivity. One implication of the results presented here is that, to some extent, the stability coefficients and the coefficients for prediction of adult functioning from single maladjustment symptoms at an early age can be accounted for by the fact that the males who are characterized by several problem indicators at an early age are stable in their patterns of maladjustment through the life course up to adulthood.

The present longitudinal analysis was concerned only with the relationship between belonging to one of the behaviour patterns at age 13 and each of the aspects of registered maladjustment covered by official records for alcohol abuse, criminality and psychiatric problems. Thus the relationship between the patterning at age 13 in terms of maladjustment problems and patterning in terms of registered maladjustment was not elucidated since the criterion variables were considered individually rather than as a pattern. Such analyses will yield more information about the developmental processes underlying adult maladjustment and will be carried out in the project. For example, the developmental background of the appearance of only alcohol abuse or only criminality may be different from the developmental background of alcohol abuse and criminality combined with other aspects of maladjustment at adult age. From this point of view, the separation of research on alcoholism, criminality and mental illness into separate fields, each looking at one of these aspects in the variable tradition, has its drawbacks. The study of possibly significant patterns of individual functioning may progress further towards understanding the developmental background of adult maladjustment. One of the major advantages of IDA is that we have access to information about various aspects of individual functioning from the age of ten to adulthood, and this will be used for further analyses of this issue.

It was pointed out above that, in risk research, a configural approach cannot generally substitute for common variable-oriented methods like regression analysis; the approaches are complementary. Besides in some situations being the natural way to analyse the data, a pattern approach may in other situations be a useful *complement* to more conventional procedures in that a configural analysis can be used exploratively in the first analyses to help the researcher obtain information with respect to the relevant variables and interactions. Such information could then be used in making the conventional variable-oriented analysis more refined. It is a task for future research to investigate more carefully the merits and limitations of the two approaches as scientific tools in risk research.

References

Allport, G. W. (1937) *Personality: a psychological interpretation.* New York: Holt, Rinehart and Winston.

Bergman, L. R. (1985) En personansats för att studera utveckling i ett interaktionistiskt perspektiv (A person approach to the study of development in an interactional perspective). In Törestad, B. and Nystedt, L. (eds.) *Människa–omvärld i samspel* (Man-environment in interaction). Stockholm: Natur och Kultur, pp. 195–211.

Bergman, L. R. and El-Khouri, B. (in press) EXACON – a Fortran 77 program for the exact analysis of single cells in a contingency table. *Educational and Psychological Measurement.*

Bergman, L. R. and Magnusson, D. (1983) *The development of patterns of maladjustment.* Reports from the project Individual Development and Environment, Department of Psychology, University of Stockholm, no. 50.

(1984a) *Patterns of adjustment problems at age 10. An empirical and methodological study.* Reports from the Department of Psychology, University of Stockholm, no. 615.

(1984b) *Patterns of adjustment problems at age 13. An empirical and methodological study.* Reports from the Department of Psychology, University of Stockholm, no. 620.

(1987) A person approach to the study of the development of adjustment problems: an empirical example and some research strategy considerations. In Magnusson, D and Öhman, A. (eds.) *Psychopathology: an interactional perspective.* New York: Academic Press, pp. 383–401.

Cairns, R. B. (1986) Phenomena lost: issues in the study of development. In Valsiner, J. (ed.) *The individual subject and scientific psychology.* New York: Plenum Press, pp. 97–111.

Clarke, A. D. B. and Clarke, A. M. (1984) Constancy and change in the growth of human characteristics. *Journal of Child Psychology and Psychiatry,* **25**, 191–210.

Hinde, R. A. and Dennis, A. (1986) Categorizing individuals: an alternative to linear analysis. *International Journal of Behavioral Development,* **9**, 105–19.

Kagan, J. (1971) *Change in continuity in infancy.* New York: Wiley.

Krauth, J. and Lienert, G. A. (1982) Fundamentals and modifications of configural frequency analysis (CFA). *Interdisciplinaria,* **3**, 1–14.

Lewin, K. (1931) Environmental forces. In Murchison, C. (ed.) *A handbook of child psychology.* Worcester, MA: Clark University Press, pp. 590–625.

Lienert, G. A. (1969) Die 'Konfigurationsfrequenzanalyse' als Klassifikationsmittel in der klinischen Psychologie. In Irle, M. (ed.) *Bericht über den 26. Kongress der Deutschen Gesellschaft für Psychologie.* Tübingen, Göttingen: Hogrete, pp. 244–53.

Loevinger, J. (1966) Models and measures of developmental variation. *Annals of the New York Academy of Sciences*, **134**, 585–90.

Magnusson, D. (1981) Some methodology and strategy problems in longitudinal research. In Schulsinger, F., Mednick, S. A. and Knop, J. (eds.) *Longitudinal research: methods and uses in behavioral science*. Boston: Nijhoff.

(1985) Implications of an interactional paradigm for research on human development. *International Journal of Behavioral Development*, **8**, 115–37.

(1987) Individual development in an interactional perspective. *Paths through life*, vol. 1. Hillsdale, NJ: Erlbaum.

Magnusson, D. and Allen V. L. (1983) *Human development: an interactional perspective*. New York: Academic Press.

Magnusson, D. and Bergman, L. R. (1984) On the study of the development of adjustment problems. In Pulkkinen, L. and Lyytinen, P. (eds.) *Human action and personality*. Jyväskylä: University of Jyväskylä, Finland, pp. 163–71.

Magnusson, D., Duner, A. and Zetterblom, G. (1975) *Adjustment: a longitudinal study*. Stockholm: Almqvist and Wiksell.

Magnusson, D., Stattin, H. and Allen, V. (1986) Differential maturation among girls and its relation to social adjustment: a longitudinal perspective. In Featherman, D. L. and Lerner, R. M. (eds.) *Life-span development*, vol. 7. New York: Academic Press, pp. 135–72.

Mischel, W. (1968) *Personality and assessment*. New York: Wiley.

Olweus, D. (1979) Stability of aggressive reaction patterns in males: a review. *Psychological Bulletin*, **86**, 852–75.

Robins, L. N. (1984) Longitudinal methods in the study of development. In Mednick, S. A., Harway, M. and Finello, K. M. (eds.) *Handbook of longitudinal research*. New York: Praeger, 31–54.

Rogosa, D. R. and Willett, J. B. (1985) Understanding correlates of change by modeling individual differences in growth. *Psychometrika*, **50**, 203–28.

Stattin, H., Magnusson, D. and Reichel, H. (1986) *Criminality from childhood to adulthood*. Reports from the project Individual Development and Adjustment, Department of Psychology, University of Stockholm, no. 63.

Von Knorring, A.-L., Andersson, O. and Magnusson, D. (1987) Psychiatric care and course of psychiatric disorders from childhood to early adulthood in a representative sample. *Journal of Child Psychology and Psychiatry*, **28**, 329–41.

Wishart, D. (1982) *CLUSTAN: User manual*. Edinburgh: Program Library Unit, Edinburgh University.

4 Statistical modelling of longitudinal data

Andrew Pickles

1 Introduction

In chapter 3 Magnusson and Bergman argued convincingly for the use of pattern-based as well as variable-based methods for the analysis of longitudinal data. They quote approvingly Cairns (1986) that 'certain developmental outcomes are sufficiently unique as to require analysis at the individual, configural level rather than at the sample, population level'. Pattern-based methods, they suggest, are better suited to this task than variable-based methods because they make the unit of study the individual, not the sample of individuals.

Such a description has immediate intuitive appeal, especially to the clinician familiar with a case-by-case synthetic view of the many and particular characteristics and circumstances that describe each individual. Nor can one deny that the use of the technical tools suggested for this task of pattern analysis – configurational frequency analysis and cluster analysis – has proved illuminating in the Magnusson and Bergman study. However, I believe some further discussion of pattern- and variable-based methods to be desirable, in order to clarify several issues.

To the statistician, the focus of the debate revolves around the question of the independence or form of dependence between observations from the same individual. Typically our data consist of observations on several response variables thought to describe the same, related or unrelated, characteristics of each individual, together with some explanatory covariates. How do we summarize those variables and how do we identify and describe the processes that generated their values? Where independence between the response processes can be assumed the analyses can be undertaken variable by variable, with each response variable being taken in turn and its relationship to the explanatory variables examined. However, where the response variables are related to each other, such a 'variable-based' analysis is clearly not ideal. We do not need to postulate any direct causal relationship amongst the response variables to suggest this. Evidence for the effects of the explanatory covariates on each response variable separately may be weak, whereas taken together the evidence may be more persuasive. In other words, unless the response variables are independent of one another the analysis may be inefficient.

Achieving greater efficiency involves using several of the response variables together, but how do we do this? The most obvious approach, particularly where the several response variables are essentially repeated measures of the same variable, is to include each observation as if it were a new case. For most of the simple statistical techniques potential efficiency is increased by so doing, but an assumption of independence remains, though now of a weaker form requiring the observations to be independent, conditional upon the explanatory variables included in the analysis. Exactly what this means will be elucidated later, but the very fact that the analysis would now be treating a longitudinal study of N individuals with R repeated measures as if it were a larger $(N \times R)$ cross-sectional study must seem worrying. It is the implausibility of this assumption of conditional independence that provides one of the major justifications for doing longitudinal studies in the first place. Ignoring it at the analysis stage is well known to be potentially highly misleading.

So how, then, should analyses be undertaken where dependence among the observations must be suspected? Must we abandon those techniques commonly used in variable-by-variable analyses and which seem to rely upon the assumption of independence? Section 2 of this chapter examines these issues, attempting to place the debate within the larger context of statistical modelling and regression, and illustrating the ideas using a growth curve example from Magnusson and Bergman (see chapter 3). Section 3 itemizes the major alternative statistical methods for dealing with dependencies among observations for continuous variables. Section 4 shows how essentially similar approaches can be used with non-continuous response variables, using as an example mother–child interaction data. Section 5 offers some conclusions.

2 Statistical modelling

The research literature is full of arguments concerning the superiority of statistical procedure A over procedure B. Rarely do such arguments advance the cause of science to any significant degree. Of greater importance are the rules by which the various techniques are being assessed. At the risk of overgeneralizing, statistical techniques used within psychology and psychiatry are divided between those appropriate to exploration and data reduction and those appropriate to hypothesis-testing. Factor analysis and analysis of variance are classic examples of each type. Judged by the rules pertinent to the context of their application, both techniques remain important and valuable tools; rarely is one suggested as a replacement of the other. Techniques such as regression analysis, which can be used as both exploratory and hypothesis-testing tools, are frequently discredited when used for the one purpose and then judged by the rules of the other. Such criticism is not only unfair but fails to appreciate the central importance of the transition from exploration to hypothesis-testing. This transition, involving the sequential development of our knowledge of the data, and of the relevant theory of the process under study, encapsulates much of the 'science' of survey research. In statistics this process of building up a probabilistic representation of the process of interest is now generally referred to as statistical 'modelling'. The modelling approach is becoming of increasing importance within statistics in response to the increasingly complex questions being asked by researchers and the ability of statisticians to be able to answer them within a framework of 'regression' – like procedures.

Magnusson and Bergman discuss regression analysis as one of those variable-based techniques ill-suited for longitudinal research. In the manner in which it often seems to be used one could only agree, if it was not for the fact that so many other techniques poorly used are equally ill-suited. The validity of any statistical test relies on its appropriateness for the data at hand. This requires us either to select a test that is undemanding in its assumptions about the data – the tradition of non-parametric statistics – or to check that the assumptions that the test requires are not falsifiable from the data at hand. Thus the use of regression to perform hypothesis tests should involve not only the calculation of the test statistic but a considerable effort in checking the assumptions of the regression and in the modification of that regression where appropriate.

It is the checking and modification that distinguishes the modelling approach from the use of regression that Magnusson and Bergman have in mind. Let me illustrate this by a consideration of their example concerning growth curves with typical data, as shown in Figure 1a for four girls A, B, C and D. Such curves look an unpromising area for the application of linear regression.

We might begin with the obvious approach, as described in the Introduction, of fitting to the 12 sample data points (4 individuals by 3 time points) the simple model in which the height y_{it} of individual i at time t increases linearly with t:

$$y_{it} = \alpha + \beta t + \varepsilon_{it} \quad \text{and} \quad \begin{aligned} \varepsilon_{it} &\sim G(0,\sigma^2) \\ E[\varepsilon_{it}\varepsilon_{is}] &= 0 \\ E[\varepsilon_{it}\varepsilon_{jt}] &= 0 \end{aligned} \tag{1}$$

This gives an R^2, proportion of explained deviance, of .72 and estimated slope coefficient β of 2.0 with a 't-test' of significance of 5.03 ($p < .001$).

However, before we can place any faith in the meaningfulness of these 'results' we must check that the model is appropriate. The model specification includes not only the linear relationship between height and time posited by Equation (1), but a set of assumptions about the errors $\{\varepsilon_{it}\}$ listed next to it. The first of these indicate that the errors should have

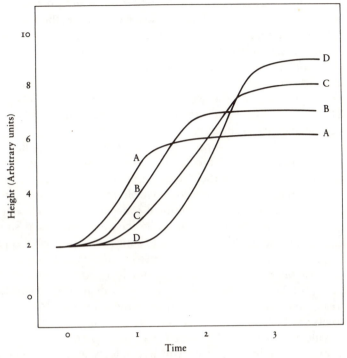

Figure 1a   Hypothetical growth curves

mean 0 and a constant variance σ^2. The second and third of these indicate that the error for individual i at time t should be uncorrelated with that at any other time s, and similarly for the errors from any two individuals i and j at the same time t. These last are the requirements for conditional independence described earlier, and which must be examined critically.

Procedures for model-checking can be usefully divided into two groups. The first of these is mis-specification tests, which examine aspects of the model looking for something wrong. These are usually rather general in nature, the cause of the possible faults suspected rarely being made explicit beforehand. Specification tests, by contrast, examine aspects of the model looking for improvements. These are usually motivated by clearer hypotheses about the nature of the process under study. We shall consider examples of each in turn.

Within simple regression models the familiar measure of goodness of fit is R^2, the proportion of explained deviance. We have become accustomed to expecting rather poor levels of R^2, so we tend to give this relatively little attention, though we continue to wish it was larger! Of practical interest, however, is to discover where the model is fitting well and where it is fitting poorly. Examining global measures will be of no value here, whereas examining the degree of ill-fit for particular subgroups of the data may prove more insightful. In the illustrative example, the values of the unexplained variance have been calculated for each of the four individuals to be 4.66, 2.33, 0.66 and 5.00 respectively, and for each of the three time periods to be 5.11, 2.44 and 5.11 respectively. The first set suggests that the model fits better for some individuals than for others, but to some degree that would not be unexpected. The second set suggests that the model fits better in the middle than at the extremes. This should make us suspect the linearity of the data.

Another check for mis-specification is to plot the residuals – the difference between the observed and predicted response values – against the predicted value to test their constant variance (or homoscedasticity) and to plot them against time (distinguishing residuals from different individuals) to assess their conditional independence. In this instance these two plots turn out to be essentially the same, and one is shown in Figure 1b. It suggests a clear pattern of change from positive residuals at time 1 to negative at time 3 or vice versa. Such a pattern is inconsistent with the notion of uncorrelated errors and also suggests that the rates of change in height vary from individual to individual. This would explain the greater unexplained variance at times 1 and 3 found earlier as these are the points at which the misapplication of average rates of change would be most evident. Cook and Weisberg (1982) provide details of numerous other procedures by means of which residuals and the influence of individual data points may be examined.

Specification tests in searching for deficiencies in the model often cure them at the same time. A typical specification test involves adding terms to a model or otherwise modifying its specification. The form of the term

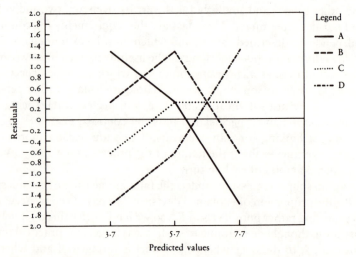

Figure 1b   Checking residuals: plot of residuals against predicted values

added may have already been suggested by the previous diagnostic checks, or by one's own suspicions, or by the theoretical discussions and empirical findings of other researchers. If these additional terms substantially improve the performance of the model, or if a modified model, which may represent some alternative theory of the process, performs almost as well as the current model, then further consideration should be given to them. More importantly, however, is the question of whether the additional/ modified terms remove any of the statistical pathologies previously identified, or substantially alter the inference that would be made on those aspects of the model which are of major interest. In this instance the diagnostic checks suggested exploring a curvilinear relationship of height with age and a model in which the rates of growth varied from individual to individual. The addition of a quadratic in time to the model of Equation (1) provided no significant improvement, but allowing for person-specific slopes resulted in a notable improvement. The estimated parameters and predicted values from that model suggested the relationships shown in Figure 1c. Although the underlying process as sketched in Figure 1a was curvilinear, the time points of observation are such that the linear relationships of Figure 1c clearly give a fair approximation, showing, in particular, that those tallest at the first time period are the shortest by the end. Thus regression-type methods can be used with longitudinal data without 'averaging' away important aspects of individual variability and, moreover, unless proper account is taken of that heterogeneity, model-checking procedures should indicate a violation of the assumption of conditional independence.

However, in no sense could this be regarded as a final model or the end point of an analysis. Theoretically, it does not seem reasonable to use a

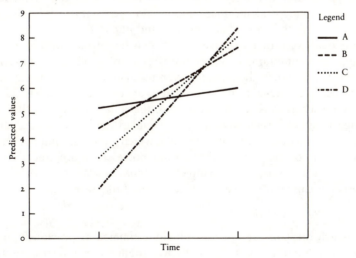

Figure 1c   Modified model: predicted values against time

simple linear relationship when we know that the rate of growth of height first increases with age and then declines to zero as adult height is reached. Furthermore, in order to allow initial heights and rates of increase to vary from individual to individual we have had to specify a model of the form

$$y_{it} = \alpha_i + \beta_i t + \eta_{it} \tag{2}$$

in which there are as many α and β parameters as individuals. This is neither efficient parsimony nor good statistical practice, for it exposes us to the risk of bias arising from the 'incidental parameter' problem described by Neyman and Scott (1948). Finally, we have not subjected this new model, in its turn, to specification- and mis-specification-testing, and so should not accept its appropriateness without question. Thus although the regression model has been able to give us some very useful insights into the structure of the data, we should pursue an alternative model structure in which the curvilinear relationship which theory requires is an integral element and in which the variability between individuals is more efficiently accounted for. The clear relationship between initial growth and smaller eventual stature immediately presents the basis for a more parsimonious account for this individual variability. However, rather than proceed to examine such a model in detail using the very limited data of the example, I refer the interested reader to more complete sources, such as Goldstein (1979; 1986).

3 Linking observations with continuous response variables

As the preceding section suggests, the key issue in longitudinal data analysis is how the observations from an individual can be made conditionally independent, that is how do we characterize the overall structure of the individual process and those persistent qualities of individuals such that whatever variation is left unexplained is consistent with the assumptions of randomness that are implied by our assumed error distribution? The previous example achieved this by using person-specific, but time-constant, parameters or 'dummy variables'. Had the person-specific effect been restricted to the constant α_i rather than to the slope β_i as well, then a set of quite standard and rather more efficient procedures would have been available, which would decompose the error term ε_{it} into components that would possess a more tractable interdependence. Thus, for example, analysis of variance for repeated measures can be used to estimate a model of the form

$$y_{it} = \alpha_i + \beta t + v_{it} \tag{3}$$

in which the $\{\alpha_i\}$ are not individually estimated as previously, but are treated as 'random constants', with the variance of their distribution being estimated on the assumption that it is independent of the new error term

v_{it}. Where such independence cannot be assumed or where we have observed several response variables that we wish to examine together, then an appropriate MANOVA analysis (sometimes referred to as profile analysis) would be more appropriate. Bock (1975) provided a simple example and comparison of the use of AOV and MANOVA for repeated measures. If the impact of individual variability extends beyond the constant to the β slope coefficients, then 'random coefficient' models may be necessary. These are now frequently referred to as multi-level, hierarchical or variance components models. Although some programs are available for their estimation there is a trade-off between their ease of use and the generality of the model specification possible. Aitkin and Longford (1986) provide a comparison of the dummy-variable and random-coefficient models in the context of the assessment of school performance, and Goldstein (1986) discusses random-coefficient models for growth curves.

Both AOV and MANOVA are referred to as 'marginal' procedures in that they attempt to account for individual effects by considering the distribution of the various possible values for the individual component. An alternative approach using a 'conditional' procedure essentially removes from the data that part associated with the individual effect, and examines the remaining variation for the influence of the systematic effect of the explanatory variables. For a model of the form of Equation (3) we can see that the individual effect α_i contributes only to the mean response and not to the temporal variation. Thus subtracting the mean value of the x and y variables of each individual from their corresponding values at each time point leaves data from which temporal variation in the y variable is then to be explained by the temporal variation in the x variable, both measured about their respective individual means, and which therefore excludes the individual component.

The form of individual effects appropriate to different contexts can vary since they may arise from quite different sources, and each form may then require a different model specification to achieve conditional independence. In the above examples the error terms at each time point are broken down into an individual effect, reflecting a fixed propensity or sensitivity, and a simple error, to reflect period-specific chance. If we expect that there might be 'drift' over time in this underlying individual propensity, then an alternative breakdown is to allow for auto-correlated errors, in which the error term ε_{it} from the original Equation (1) is correlated with its previous value such that

$$\varepsilon_{it} = \delta_{it} + \varrho\varepsilon_{it-1} \tag{4}$$

In developmental studies, in which, although there are repeated measures, the instrument used to obtain the measure or the interpretation that can be placed upon it often varies from occasion to occasion, a somewhat different approach may be required. The analysis of covariance structure assumes that the interdependency is generated by an 'auto-regressive' process

$$y_{it} = \alpha + \beta_t + \gamma_t y_{it-1} + \tau_{it} \qquad (5)$$

in which the previous value of the response variable directly influences the current value. Where the causal ordering among a set of interdependent response variables is unknown, then path or simultaneous equation regression methods are more appropriate (see, for example, Johnston, 1984, chapter 11).

Lastly, latent-variable models provide a very general framework within which information from several response variables can be combined and within which various models of measurement error can be examined. A useful introduction to such models, and some examples estimated using the computer package LISREL (Jöreskog and Sörbum, 1981), can be found in the chapters by Brown and by Fergusson and Horwood (see chapters 17 and 19). Some varied examples of its use can be found in *Child Development*, vol. 58, no. 1 (1987). Such models provide a means of distinguishing circumstances in which response variables really do interact with each other from those situations where they are simply different observed variables contributing to the measurement of the same underlying latent variable. This distinction would seem to be important in attempting to interpret the results of the Magnusson and Bergman study. To what extent is a syndrome more than the 'sum' of the indicator variables used to define it?

It should be clear that there are a variety of ways in which 'individual effects' can be represented and that to empirically establish the best representation can be arduous. This emphasizes the importance of clarifying the available theory in order to select from the outset that approach most likely to achieve the conditional independence that is sought.

4 Non-continuous response variables

Of course, many data, in particular many longitudinal data, do not come in the form of continuous measurements but in the form of possession of, or the switching between, nominal or ordinal states, or in the form of occurrence of a sequence of events. All of these would seem unpromising areas for the use of regression models. However, since the mid-1970s there has been substantial development in regression methods for just this type of data. This now very general regression framework is referred to as the generalized linear model (GLM) even though it includes many models that were previously described as non-linear. The appeal to the researcher of the GLM is not only that the basic specification of the model can be selected to match the fundamental theoretical characteristics of the data at hand, but that the procedures for model development, the sequential addition (or removal) of terms, and other aspects of model checking, are largely similar to ordinary linear regression. Moreover, the results can be presented in a relatively uniform fashion, thus simplifying interpretation.

As our second example, we shall consider a very different form of longitudinal data, those from the observation of dyadic interaction. The data come from 44 mothers observed with their children over two two-hour periods and is more fully described elsewhere (Dowdney *et al.*, 1984). The immediate concern here will be to analyse the frequency of occurrence of certain behaviours and their relationship to some explanatory covariates, notably fixed measures/characteristics of the individuals concerned. We postulate that we can achieve a reasonable approximation to the 'systematic' relationship by combining these covariates into a linear predictor, on the surface identical to the linear combination of coefficients and variables of a normal linear regression model. This linear predictor provides predicted 'scores' for any setting of the explanatory variables, which when transformed (in this case by exponentiation) yields a predicted rate of occurrence of the behaviour in question. Considerations from simple probability theory would suggest how this rate of occurrence can be related to the pattern of counts expected from the dyads. Thus, with a rate Z, we would typically expect $Z \times T$ occurrences during the observation period of length T, and that this count would be Poisson distributed, for that is the natural distribution for counts for independent events and is the one, for example, assumed within contingency table analysis.

The above description is that for a standard Poisson regression model. In our case the y or response variable is the observed count for each dyad of the times the mother approached the child, and the x or explanatory variables are the age, sex and ordinal position of the child, the age of the mother at time of birth, and whether she had been raised in an ordinary family setting or in an institution ('in care'). We regress a suitable combination of the x variables against the y variable but with a model that now assumes that the residuals or errors will be Poisson, rather than Normally, distributed. This is readily done within the package GLIM (Baker and Nelder, 1978). Examining various models suggested a complex relationship between the rate of mother approaches and all the explanatory variables available. Such a complex of significant relationships seemed implausible. What else should we be keeping in mind?

As with the ordinary regression model, assumptions about the conditional independence of observations must be examined critically when dealing with longitudinal data. There are two main sources of likely non-independence in these data. First, there is the dependence arising through the rhythms, cycles and other internal dynamics of behaviour, in which some behaviours can be expected to occur clustered in time or, more rarely, to be more regularly and evenly spaced than expected. The second source is that the expected rate of occurrence for each dyad is derived from a relationship estimated from all dyads in the sample. Whilst we can hope that the estimated relationship captures some of the impact of the observed explanatory variables on the rate of occurrence, we should expect each dyad to exhibit some idiosyncrasy arising from unobserved explanatory variables and the approximate nature of the model. Thus each dyad may have a rate consistently higher or consistently lower than that which their observed characteristics and our estimated relationship would have predicted. This is more fully explained in Pickles and Dowdney (1987). In the growth curve example each individual contributed three observations and heterogeneity showed its presence through the correlation between the residuals corresponding to these points. In this example each dyad contributes just a single count, and heterogeneity will now show its presence through our mis-specifying the error variance or size of the residuals to be expected.

As before, we can use goodness-of-fit measures and plots of residuals to check our suspicions. The Normal distribution has separate parameters for the mean and variance. This means that in a regression model assuming Normally distributed errors the variance of the residuals, or in other words the unexplained variance, is something that is estimated from the data. The Poisson distribution has just a single parameter, the variance being determined by the mean and equal to it. Thus, in the usual Poisson regression model (as in a contingency table) the amount of unexplained variance is not a free parameter. Simply put, the model is assumed to fit and if it does not, then our inference about significant effects may be quite spurious. In our case the model with the complex of apparently significant effects fits with a Pearson χ^2; of 237 with 36 *df*, much larger than the value of around 36 that we should have obtained for a properly fitting model. Confirmation and further illumination of this problem is obtained from the Q–Q plot of the residuals, shown in Figure 2, in which the cumulative distribution function of the (appropriately transformed) residuals is compared with that expected from a Poisson error distribution. The substantial departure from the 45-degree line shows that there is much greater variability in the observed occurrence rates than the model allows, with both more large negative and more large positive residuals than expected.

Various authors have proposed solutions to this problem of overdispersion, as it is called (e.g. Williams, 1982). The solution adopted here is probably the simplest and follows that of McCullagh and Nelder (1983, p. 138). It is clear that the Poisson distribution does not allow sufficient variability, and so a 'scale parameter' is estimated which allows the unexplained variance in the data to match that allowed for in the model in an almost equivalent way to that in the Normal linear regression case. The scale parameter is estimated by the ratio of the Pearson χ^2 to the (residual)

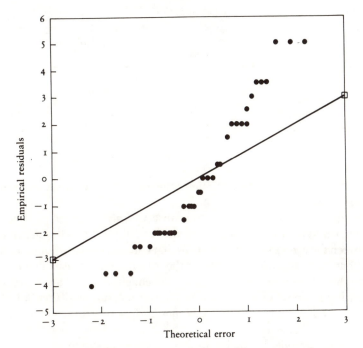

Figure 2   Q–Q plot from Poisson regression model

degrees of freedom. The model that estimates the effects of the explanatory variables is then re-estimated with this new scale parameter value. For the standard Poisson regression model a likelihood equation may be written down and the parameter estimates and test statistics justified using likelihood theory. For the more general model in which the scale parameter is estimated, only sometimes can a corresponding likelihood equation be found. However, a justification for the estimation and inference can be found in the concept of 'quasi-likelihood' (Wedderburn, 1974; Nelder, 1985) which promises a very fruitful generalization of both likelihood and least-squares statistical theory.

As with a difference-of-means *t*-test in which one has underestimated the within-group variance, allowing for the larger correct variance results in some previously significant findings no longer being so. In our case concerning mother approaches, the complex of previously 'significant' effects is quickly reduced to a few simple effects all related to the experience of the mother; these are summarized in the estimated model of Table 1. This model shows that first-born children receive more mother approaches than second-borns but that this declines as the child gets older, until at the age of 35 months they receive the same as second-borns, for whom there is no variation with age. There is also more marginal

Table 1 *Final model for mother approaches data*

Variable	Parameter estimate	Standard error	p value
Constant	4.865		
First-born	1.404	0.4868	0.004
First-born age (months)	− 0.0405	0.0155	0.009
Mother's age (years)	− 0.0647	0.0379	0.090

Scale parameter = 6.409

evidence for lower rates of mother approaches as the age at birth of the mother increases.

In the above analysis the multiple observations of each dyad have been summarized by a single count, and the lack of conditional independence between the events that contribute to that count has been accounted for by estimating an appropriate value for the scale parameter, usually one larger than the value of unity expected for independent events. This approach of reducing multiple observations to a single measure and then analysing these within a model that includes an appropriate error distribution is of very general application. The approach is an example of one in which, by specifying a model at the level of the individual, summary measures or 'parameter estimates' for each individual can be obtained that focus upon particular behavioural features of interest and which are then examined for evidence of any systematic relationship to explanatory variables.

It does not deal with circumstances in which the explanatory variables are time-varying, for then the analysis of multiple observations from each individual, one for each setting of the explanatory variables, seems inevitable. Section 3 suggested several statistical techniques for multiple continuous observations which linked together such non-independent data points. Although the particular computer programs for these techniques are no longer applicable, the underlying concepts remain so. Thus the use of dummy variables, random coefficients, variance components, conditional methods and structural equation models are all possible with non-continuous data, but for the most part the computation is difficult and time-consuming.

5 Conclusions

In the previous sections, the statistical methods outlined are, for the most part, familiar from 'variable-based' analysis. It has, however, been emphasized that greater attention must be paid to the specification of the individual effects to make them more appropriate to longitudinal data analysis. In most analyses within medical statistics, sociology or econometrics, these individual effects are of no particular interest, indeed they are often referred to as 'nuisance parameters', their role within the model being to allow the sound estimation of some structural or systematic relationship of the process to an explanatory variable. In psychopathology, in which one of the major foci of interest is individual heterogeneity, these individual effects may themselves be of rather greater interest. The dummy-variable approach provides a direct estimate of each individual's 'baseline', and similar indicators can be obtained using residual-like quantities from variance components models (see Aitkin and Longford, 1986) and from the other techniques described. These may be usefully interpreted as measures which, having accounted for those known systematic adverse and constructive factors present in the individual's life history and included in the model, describe the individual's 'frailty' or 'latent score'. Particular attention might then be paid to those within the extremes of such distributions.

The debate concerning individual- versus variable-based approaches should be about the theoretical issues concerning the specification of the process and of the individual effects within that process, rather than about statistical techniques. The great majority of those statistical techniques with which researchers are already familiar are capable of yielding both sound and interesting results, but each requires that the theory concerning the individual effects be characterized within the technique in an appropriate fashion. Increasing the facility with which this can be done is important, but current difficulties should not be used as an argument to restrict the analyst to a narrow set of 'approved' longitudinal techniques. Magnusson and Bergman's use of pattern-based methods, such as cluster analysis and configural frequency analysis, may be seen in the terms of this chapter as an effective example of model-checking. However, those methods do not, themselves, provide much of an inferential framework for the analysis of longitudinal data. Rather, they point to the risks of spurious inference were cross-sectional-type procedures to be used and suggest specifications for the 'individual effects' appropriate within a more process-oriented longitudinal analysis.

References

Aitkin, M. and Longford, N. (1986) Statistical modelling issues in school effectiveness studies. *Journal of the Royal Statistical Society A*, **149**, 1–44.

Baker, R. J. and Nelder, J. A. (1978) *The GLIM systems, release 3: Generalized Linear Interactive Modelling*. Oxford: Numerical Algorithms Group.

Bock, R. D. (1975) *Multivariate statistical methods in behavioral research*. New York: McGraw-Hill.

Cairns, R. B. (1986) Phenomena lost: issues in the study of development. In Valsiner, J. (ed.) *The individual subject and scientific psychology*. New York: Plenum Press, pp. 97–111.

Cook, R. D. and Weisberg, S. (1982) *Residuals and influence in regression*. London: Chapman and Hall.

Dowdney, L., Mrazek, D., Quinton, D. and Rutter, M. (1984) Observation of parent–child interaction with two- to three-year-olds. *Journal of Child Psychology and Psychiatry*, **25**, 379–407.

Goldstein, H. (1979) *The design and analysis of longitudinal studies*. New York: Academic Press.

—— (1986) Efficient statistical modelling of longitudinal data. *Annals of Human Biology*, **13**, 129–41.

Johnston, J. (1984) *Econometric methods*, 3rd edn. Singapore: McGraw-Hill.

Jöreskog, K. G. and Sörbum, D. (1981) LISREL V: analysis of linear structural relationships by maximum likelihood and least squares methods. Research Report 81–8, Department of Statistics, Uppsala, Sweden.

McCullagh, P. and Nelder, J. A. (1983) *Generalized linear models*. London: Chapman and Hall.

Nelder, J. A. (1985) Quasilikelihood and GLIM. In Gilchrist, R., Francis, B. and Whittaker, J. (eds.) *Generalized linear models*. New York: Springer, pp. 120–7.

Neyman J. and Scott E. J. (1948) Consistent estimates based on partially consistent observations. *Econometrica*, **16**, 1–32.

Pickles, A. R. and Dowdney, L. R. (1987) Observed interaction between mother-child dyads: analysis, models and diagnostics. Mimeo. London: Institute of Psychiatry.

Wedderburn, R. W. M. (1974), Quasi-likelihood functions, generalised linear models and the Gauss–Newton method. *Biometrika*, **61**, 439–47.

Williams, D. A. (1982) Extra-binomial variation in logistic linear models. *Applied Statistics*, **31**, 144–8.

5 Risk/protective factors for offending with particular reference to deprivation*

I. Kolvin, F. J. W. Miller, M. Fleeting and P. A. Kolvin

Introduction

In this chapter we describe the use of longitudinal data to explore early risk and protective factors for later offending. This theme had its origins in observations arising from other research that many youths from 'high-risk' backgrounds do not become delinquent and a small proportion of youths from 'low-risk' backgrounds do. We sought to highlight factors that allowed us to discriminate between such youths.

A number of approaches were considered. First, there is the biographical anecdotal approach whereby a small number of families are studied at considerable depth so as to provide information about possible protective and risk factors. Unfortunately our data lacked the quality of clinical case records and therefore could not be used as a source of information and insights (as used, for example, by Coffield *et al.*, 1981).

Second, we were tempted to move directly into multiple regression analyses, using a diversity of explanatory variables in order to seek significant predictors, but for good reasons we decided there was no virtue in rushing into this. Multiple regression gives information about significant predictors, irrespective of risk or protection, and this is likely to give rise to the banal conclusion that protection is merely the flip side of risk. The results of prediction analysis (based on prediction coefficients) may be dependent on a relatively small subgroup of individuals lying at the extreme of multi-problem behaviour, but the prediction model itself does not give much idea about the details of such subgroups. However, it does allow a view of the relative importance of predictors within a specified prediction set.

Finally, some of the factors appeared to operate at different stages of development and hence path analysis appeared a more appropriate model, but at this early stage it was not clear which variables should have been included.

* This research was supported by a grant from the DHSS/SSRC and by supplementary support from the Home Office, the City of Newcastle Priority Area Projects, the Rowntree Trust, the W. T. Grant Foundation and the J. Joffe Trust. We are grateful to Mrs N. Nelson for her help in sorting the criminal data. And to Dr D. P. Farrington for advice on method and theory. We would like to thank Mrs M. Blackburn for administrative assistance and Mrs K. McAneney, Mrs A. Alexander and Mrs J. Lee for secretarial support.

We therefore decided on a four-stage approach. The first established operational definitions of deprivation and of offending. The second did the same for other stress factors. These included social, family, personal and biological factors. Thirdly, we had to consider how to reorganize and analyse our data in order to obtain a better understanding of the extent to which these factors influenced risk and of the possible mechanisms involved. This was a flexible approach that allowed an exploration of variations in outcome, escape from risk and also heterogeneity of outcome in relation to similar orders of risk. In this sense the method is quasi-experimental. Fourth, we complemented the above with appropriate multivariate analyses.

Background

The Newcastle Thousand Family Study began in 1947 and continued until 1962 when the children were 15 years of age. The data on these families had been preserved and, using a 'catch-up' longitudinal design, it proved possible to examine whether boys who grew up in deprived families were more at risk for offences in later childhood and adulthood than those from families who did not experience deprivation.

In 1978–80, we were granted access to the relevant criminal records for the 847 families in the study in 1952; the results provide the material for this report. There are good reasons for the focus on the 847 families. When the children of these families were in their fifth year, extensive social data were collected which proved crucial to the definition of deprivation. For this reason the fifth-year cohort of 847 families constitutes our baseline for the research into deprivation and criminality. Further, only attrition from this baseline is of consequence to the findings reported here.

Concept of deprivation

Our method demanded that we identify cardinal criteria of deprivation. Briefly the criteria were determined by the range of social and family information available in the archives and by theoretical views about their relevance. In other words we had to rely on concepts and measures adopted by research workers thirty years earlier. We first explored the data (Miller et al., 1960) for features representing deprivation. We then grouped those features that reflected similar concepts of deprivation; this gave rise to six clusters. We went on to examine the frequency of features and also their intercorrelation within clusters, and on this basis we selected six features representative of each broad area of deprivation that consituted our cardinal criteria. We assumed that each of the criteria had the same value and confirmed that it was reasonable to sum the scores of deprivation by subjecting the data to principal components analysis. Naturally, adverse family factors are not confined to these cardinal criteria.

In 1952 the main areas of deprivation in the families were:

1 Family/marital instability	14.5%
2 Parental illness	12.2%
3 Poor care of children and homes	12.7%
4 Social dependence (families dependent upon state or community subsistence)	17.5%
5 Housing (overcrowding, as defined by the Housing Act 1936)	18.7%
6 Poor mothering	15.1%

All families were given a score of zero or one on each of the above six criteria and their scores were added to give a total deprivation rating. The percentage of families affected ranged from 12% to 19%

Choice of samples

The next step was to identify all the families with evidence of 'deprivation' in any of these six areas at five years of age. From the records, it was found that of the 847 families then present in the survey, 482 (57%) were not deprived in any respect, 365 (43%) were deprived on at least one criterion, and 116 (14%) were deprived on at least three criteria.

Subsamples were then isolated for special study with three main objectives. First, the basic aim of the research was to compare a sample that was representative of *all* the deprived families with a sample in which there was no evidence of deprivation. Second, we examined the effect of each type of deprivation separately. The subsamples consisted of the following:

1 Not deprived: families in which there was no evidence of deprivation (57%).

2 Deprived group: families deprived in at least one respect (43%). This sample includes the multiply deprived.

3 Multiply deprived: families deprived in at least three respects (14%).

The above selection is based on the use of the cardinal defining criteria of deprivation outlined above. A distinction needs to be made between the defining criteria and associated criteria. For instance, overcrowding and unemployment contributed to the defining criteria, whereas father in an unskilled job did not. However, being categorized as deprived does not prevent within-group variation on other measures of social dysfunction.

Rates of offending

In this chapter, we combine evidence about offending from two sources – the archives of the Thousand Family Study and information about

Table 1 *Deprivation and offending: per cent of men from deprived families who offend*

	Marital disturb- ance		Parental illness		Poor physical care		Social depend- ency		Over- crowding		Poor mothering	
	N	% offend ing	N	% offend ing	N	% offend ing	N	% offend ing	N	% offend ing	N	% offend ing
Specified deprivation alone	21	38	12	17	4	50	12	33	30	27	11	18
Specified deprivation plus one other deprivation	14	36	16	25	11	73	22	36	16	75	19	58
Specified deprivation plus two or more other deprivations	25	60	25	68	39	59	39	68	36	64	40	65
Total	60		53		54		73		82		70	

Note: Not corrected for attrition.

criminality available from official criminal records (Home Office data) until the individuals were 33 years of age (Kolvin *et al.*, 1988a, b). Prior to the minimum school-leaving age of that period 83 persons offended, and of these, three-quarters went on to commit further offences after that age. In addition, a further 66 individuals acquired a criminal record for the first time after the age of 15. This gives a total of 149 persons who had offended at some time up to the age of 33. At all ages, offences were overwhelmingly committed by males. By the age of 33, more than one in every four males had offended, but only about one in twenty females. The rate of 31% of the general population for male criminality is suprisingly robust. It is similar to the rate reported for an inner London area (West, 1982) and in a national survey (Home Office, 1985).

Relationship between deprivation and offending

Two basic questions were asked. First, does coming from a deprived back-ground give rise to a higher rate of offending? The proportion of males who offended varied according to the degree of deprivation, ranging from one in six males from non-deprived families, to over six in ten males from multiply deprived families. The answer is 'yes' and, furthermore, offending appears to be closely related to the degree of deprivation.

The second question is whether a single criterion of deprivation, when it occurs truly in isolation, carries a greater risk of offending than when there is no deprivation? Such circumstances are rare but it will be noted (see Table 1) that when a specified deprivation was present on its own, the

Table 2 *Combinations of major deprivations and offending* (men only)

	1 Poor physical care or mothering		2 Social, i.e. overcrowding or social dependency		3 Marital disruption	
	N	%	N	%	N	%
Alone	27	41	61	34	23	35
Plus 1	–	–	36	64	9	66
Plus 2	36	64	–	–	15	33
Plus 3	9	66	15	33	–	–

Note: Not corrected for attrition.

rates of subsequent offending varied little from the rate (17.7%) in those families with no deprivation (with the exception of marital disturbance and possibly social dependence).

When a specified deprivation coexisted with one other criterion in the same family, the rate of offending varied from 25% to 75%. When it coexisted with two or more other deprivations, the rate varied from 59% to 68%. Pooling data gives rates of 29% for one criterion alone, 69% for two and 66% for three.

Parental illness, when on its own or combined with any one other deprivation, appeared to carry the lowest risk. Our other analyses also suggested that parental illness has the lowest effect on many different types of outcome (Kolvin *et al.*, 1988b). The rest of the table merely reveals what has already been demonstrated, namely that the more deprivations there are coexisting in the family, the higher the rate of subsequent offending.

We examined this hypothesis further by ascertaining the effects of combinations of the cardinal deprivations. For these purposes, we devised three major deprivation indices to reflect:

1 Poor mothering (to reflect both poor physical care and poor mothering).
2 Adverse social influences (as reflected by dependence on social welfare and overcrowding).
3 Marital disruption.

The rates of offending in males brought up in families where each of these deprivations existed on their own was roughly similar (see Table 2). However, poor mothering, when combined with the other deprivations, appears to exert the most powerful effect.

Continuities and discontinuities of risk factors

So far, deprivation has been examined as if it were a static phenomenon, but family deprivation fluctuates over time. This gives rise to the question

Table 3 *The offence rates of men whose families moved in and out of deprivation*

	Family never deprived	Family moving into deprivation (1952–7)	Family moving out of deprivation (1952–7)	Family always deprived
N	207	19	92	84
Offending %	16	26	32	54

Note: Not corrected for attrition.

of whether an increase in family deprivation over time (e.g. 1952 to 1957) increases the risk of offending and, conversely, whether a reduction of family deprivation acts as a protective factor in relation to offending. To examine this question, the families were divided into those who were never deprived, those who moved into deprivation over that period, those who moved out of deprivation, and those who were deprived in both 1952 and 1957. The data in Table 3 suggest that if the family moves into deprivation, there is a 50% increase in the rate of offending. If the family moves out of deprivation, there is a 40% decrease in the rate of offending.

Exploring the importance of risk and protective factors

For the purpose of exploring these notions we divided our cohort into subgroups (see Figure 1). First, in the non-deprived group we tried to identify features that discriminate between individuals who do and those who do not become delinquent; these are the stress factors. Secondly, in the deprived group, we sought factors to explain the resilience of certain of its members; these are the protective factors. An important question was whether protective factors operated across the spectrum of depri-vation. We also tried to determine whether these two kinds of factor operated in a similar way in both boys and girls. Unfortunately the low incidence of female delinquency confined us to a study of protective factors and we have not been able to study sex differences in vulnerability to stress. Finally, we tried to discover if these factors remained potent over time (Werner, 1985) or changed in significance as the child developed. For these purposes data were drawn from the children's records at 5, 11 and 15 years.

The first five years
Stress factors. By the age of five a small number of factors that tolled the bell of later delinquency had already emerged in the non-deprived group. The main ones were a relative reduction in personal territory (40% of eventual delinquents in this group had experienced less personal 'space' as against 18% of non-delinquents), mother's young age at her first

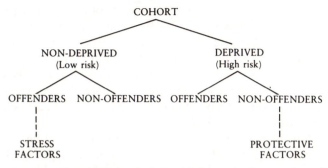

Figure 1   Flow chart of method. For girls, protective factors only studied; for boys, stress and protective factors studied

marriage (29% as against 11%), and the breadwinner being in semi-skilled/unskilled work or unemployed (33% as against 18%). An ancillary factor was relatively poor physical growth at the age of three.

Protective factors. The absence of specific deprivations against a background of general deprivations (as reflected by less overcrowding and smaller family size perhaps giving rise to greater living and elbow space) proved to be an important protector. In addition, only 46% of delinquents in the deprived group as against 68% of non-delinquents had had the benefit of good mothering, of good maternal health (68% as to 82%), of being well mothered in a good home (76% as to 93%), or of employment of the breadwinner (60% as to 77%). Being elder-born appeared to mitigate the ill-effects of underprivilege: 49% of the deprived group who became delinquent had at least two elder siblings as opposed to 26% of those who remained crime-free. There was also an undeniable statistical link with good early physical development, the absence of a medical history, including the relative absence of neonatal complications, fewer hospital outpatient attendances and fewer accidents. Accidents and hospital outpatient visits seemed to operate only at the extremes of deprivation. All of these probably reflect a more favourable standard of child-rearing.

The protective factors identified by the age of five for females were fewer than for their male counterparts. A secure socio-economic status of the breadwinner appeared to act as a bulwark against criminal activity as did a healthy mother and an accident-free early childhood. All of these factors may in turn reflect better care of the child.

The tenth/eleventh year
Stress factors. By the age of 11 many more factors concerning a child's interaction with his social and school environment were measurable and the emergent stress factors seem to cover the whole range of the child's non-family activities.

The stress factors were of four main types: physical, temperamental, cognitive and attitudinal. It is not that factors that were striking at the age of five ceased to be significant; rather, other factors became predominant. School proved a veritable almanac of stress factors, with the scholastic underachiever who had a negative attitude to education most likely to fall foul of the law. Good concentration was more than three times as frequent among potential law abiders than among nascent delinquents. A similar pattern occurred with reliable behaviour in class. There was also a marked difference in abilities: 35% of the delinquent group had poor handwriting as against 20% of the non-delinquent group. Further, intelligence and educational achievements in the 'core' educational sub-jects diverged considerably between the groups. Even at this age, negative attitudes to education and authority were developing amongst the even-tual delinquents: for instance, 62% of the eventual delinquent group were anti-police as against 35% of the non-delinquent group. Whether a symptom or cause of antisocial behaviour, this was startling as a statistic.

Protective factors. For those from high-risk backgrounds a respectable school career blunted the propensity to crime. The proportion of the non-delinquent deprived group who either performed well scholastically or concentrated in class, or showed persistence and reliability, or whose IQ was 100+, varied from between twice and five times that of the delinquent deprived group exhibiting these qualities. Only 10% of the deprived delinquent group had an IQ of 100+ as against 43% of the non-delinquents. Good parental supervision had an ameliorating effect: 28% of the delinquent group, but only 10% of the non-delinquent group, had been poorly supervised at this age. Finally, whereas 76% of deprived children who later stayed out of trouble belonged to youth clubs, only 55% of those who later offended were members. This suggests that identification with positive peer group activities gives some protection.

The effect of protective factors stood out even more starkly in the multiply deprived group, spectacularly so in the case of educational achievements during the 11+ examination, particularly with arithmetic, reading and spelling. Good behaviour and reliability ratings in the classroom were also moderately protective. The majority of those who stayed out of trouble were members of youth clubs (72%) compared with a minority (41%) of those who did not.

No less plain were the protective factors in females at this age. Of the eventual delinquents 28% experienced poor supervision as against 7% of the non-delinquents. In only 61% of the delinquent group was the natural father still present compared with 81% of non-delinquents. The future delinquent was also nearly twice as likely to be unreliable in the classroom and four times as likely as her non-delinquent contemporary to be unsociable.

The fifteenth year

As might be expected, school factors that operated *stressfully* at 11 continued to do so at 15, particularly poor intelligence, poor concentration, low persistence and a poor attitude to schoolwork. Not surprisingly, therefore, only 36% of the future delinquents expressed a desire to stay at school beyond the minimum leaving-age compared with 61% of the non-delinquents. What is more, the families' interest in maintaining contact with the school seemed to reflect their offsprings' achievements there: 83% of parents of the non-delinquents compared with 48% of the parents of delinquents. Only 32% of the delinquent group as against 61% of the non-delinquent group had fathers with an 'effective' personality (based on judgements which were reached by a team of doctors and community nurses who had known the family over 10 to 15 years). Of those from non-deprived homes who became or who were already delinquent 43% were missing at least one school day in ten, compared with only 13% of those who did not become delinquent; 59% of the delinquents as against 24% of the non-delinquents had a hostile attitude to school work. Furthermore, while only 45% of the delinquent group participated in family activities, 70% of the non-delinquent group did so.

A similar series of factors proved to be protective in the case of the deprived, and once again those factors that reflected a positive motivation and attitude in the deprived child (particularly willingness to continue at school, good school attendance and attitude to school work) were prominent discriminators. Only one-quarter of the delinquent group concentrated well in class, whereas over half of the non-delinquent group did so, a finding that suggests the protective effect of positive temperamental features. Good intelligence and educational achievements and a positive family interest were also powerful protectors. A few of these were also protective at the extremes of deprivation.

There was a smaller set of protective factors for girls; four of these overlapped with those applying to boys. They were good concentration and persistence in class, a non-hostile attitude to school, a willingness to stay on at school, and a family that maintained contact with the school. The constant presence of the natural father was a powerful protector; in the non-delinquent group 57% of fathers were always present as against 21% in the delinquent group. A new factor was good growth at thirteen years.

The effects of pairs of explanatory variables in predicting criminality in the family of formation

As risk factors do not operate in isolation, another question posed was whether there would be an independent main effect of each risk factor (a specific deprivation) after all other risk factors had been taken into

Table 4 *Risk factors, IQ and criminality: loglinear analysis*

	Explanatory variables	df	G	Significance
(N = 356)	RF1	1	12.23	p < .01
	IQ	1	18.89	p < .01
	(interaction)	1	2.86	ns
(N = 356)	RF2	1	6.01	p < .05
	IQ	1	23.80	p < .01
	(interaction)	1	2.12	ns
(N = 356)	RF3	1	5.54	p < .05
	IQ	1	30.27	p < .01
	(interaction)	1	0.63	ns
(N = 427)	RF1	1	22.06	p < .01
	RF2	1	9.09	p < .01
	RF3	1	3.36	ns
	(interactions)	4	2.27	ns
(N = 427)	RF1	1	24.48	p < .01
	RF2	1	10.33	p < .01
	(interaction)	1	0.02	ns
(N = 427)	RF1	1	33.25	p < .01
	RF3	1	4.61	p < .05
	(interaction)	1	0.02	ns
(N = 427)	RF2	1	20.28	p < .01
	RF3	1	5.78	p < .05
	(interaction)	1	2.79	ns

RF1   Defective care and/or poor mothering.
RF2   Overcrowding and/or social dependence.
RF3   Marital disruption.
IQ   0 = 100+, 1 = 99–.
ns   Not significant.
The dependent variable is the proportion offending.

account. For these purposes, the pairs of risk factors were analysed formally using the technique of loglinear analysis. This gives an estimate of the independent effects of each of the explanatory variables and of any interaction between them. We used the same main deprivational explanatory variables described in the section on the relationship between deprivation and offending, with the data organized into categories. An additional explanatory variable employed was intelligence as measured at the age of 11 (comparing youths scoring 100 or more with those scoring 99 or less). The most powerful explanatory variable was IQ. Of the family risk factors, poor mothering showed the highest level of statistical significance; and when the three were put into the same analysis, marital disruption no longer had a significant effect. We had anticipated considerable statistical interaction between our risk factors but none occurred.

It is noteworthy that this last finding on marital disturbance seems to run counter to that in Table 1, where it was noted that of all the indices of deprivation, marital disturbance had one of the *greatest* effects when it occurred in the absence of other deprivations. The contradiction arises because an independent effect after taking account of other variables is not synonymous with an effect in the absence of other variables (see Rutter, 1983). The implication is that marital disruption probably *is* a significant risk factor on its own but that (at least in the deprived sample we studied), when it is associated with several other deprivations, its effect tends to be swamped by the impact of multiple other adversities.

Mechanisms of operation of risk factors using path analysis

Finally, we wished to explore possible mechanisms using path analysis. One problem was how to select the variables of importance for this exercise. We decided to look at key early-life, social and family experiences to ascertain (a) if their effects were mediated through individual differences of intelligence and temperament (i.e. indirect influences); or (b) whether they operated directly; and (c) to see if an overall deprivation index masks the pattern of contribution of specific deprivation criteria (see Figures 2 and 3).

One of the major limitations of path analysis is that the causal path may account for a small proportion of the variance of subsequent dysfunction. There are many possible reasons for this, but we highlight those that strike us as important:

1 The insensitivity of the measures included as causal influences.
2 The use of measures which broadly reflect the same underlying construct, that is duplication of explanatory measures.

Heath (1981) wrote that many variables, such as marital disruption, overcrowding, poor health and unemployment, may add very little to the prediction if they are strongly correlated. Each new variable may produce only a small increment in explanatory power. To discover more about the unknown sources of variation we must add variables not correlated with those already included and preferably not correlated with each other. Further, it is often assumed that such independent variables are unrelated, but frequently there is much collinearity. Thus there are strong reasons for adding psychological and biological variables to the sociological ones.

We studied mechanisms using path models with a hypothesized network of specific causal associations. Intelligence was measured at the 11+ examination, and temperament was represented by an index of poor concentration and persistence in the early years of secondary school. (Figure 2A represents the proposed simplest model.) The unbroken lines represent causal links where the association between the two factors in question was significantly different from zero. The relevant coefficient is termed a path coefficient. The broken lines represent proposed paths that have been omitted as no significant causal associations emerged, and the proposed linkage therefore is implicitly set equal to zero. The curved lines

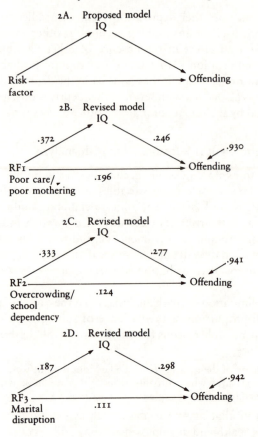

Figure 2   Risk factors, individual differences and criminality

represent simple non-causal correlations. More complex models may be erected but for the purposes of this paper simpler models have been proposed. Figures 2B, 2C and 2D suggest that all three of the main specified family risk factors have both direct and indirect influences on offending. In such a simple model, the explained variance never amounts to more than 16%.

Figure 3A represents a slightly more complex model. Figure 3B also suggests that the deprivation indeed has both direct and indirect influences on offending, but such an overall index may mask the pattern of contribution of the specific deprivational criteria. Figure 3C also suggests that poor mothering in the preschool years has a prior causal influence on measured intelligence and on temperament, and therefore a direct or indirect influence on criminality. The explained variance is 16%. The other two risk factors (see Figures 3D and 3E) have only indirect influences mediated by intelligence and temperament, and each of the causal models accounts for only 13% of the explained variance.

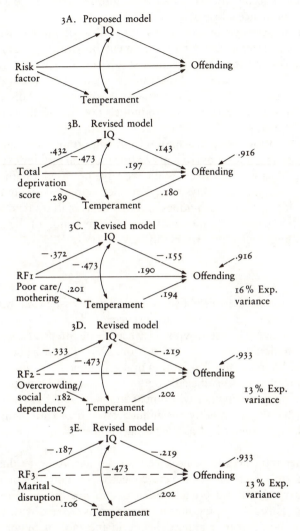

Figure 3   Risk factors and criminality

The path analysis employed in this study is based on linear multiple regression models, which assume that any interval data are normally distributed and that other data are measured on nominal or ordinal scales. In some respects our data fall short of such requirements. First, criminological data usually have a skewed distribution. While some authors claim that the path analysis technique is relatively robust in relation to violation of the normality assumption, and the inefficiencies incurred may be slight (Macdonald, 1976), caution is needed in interpreting the percentage of variance explained. Further, we converted our data on offending into a categorical form despite the fact that the dichotomy gives rise to a loss of information and hence a loss of sensitivity.

Second, there were also questions of scaling. Most of our data were not recorded at an interval level of measurement but rather as binary or ordinal variables. What therefore is their status? Binary variables used as predictor variables in path analysis can be regarded as interval level variables (Macdonald, 1977). Furthermore, 'though technically improper, the use of ordinal variables in path models does not lead to disaster' (Macdonald, 1977, p. 95).

These qualifications about assumptions are important as the adoption of a purist view may mean loss of a powerful statistical tool for exploring the sequence of cause and effect. While we have not used a path model that is based on loglinear analysis, we have noted in other analyses that linear multiple regression techniques and loglinear analyses tend to give similar results. These similarities are probably a reflection of the general linear model underlying the two methods.

Discussion

In this study we tried to establish 'stress' factors associated with the occurrence of offences despite the absence of deprivation and also 'protective' factors associated with the absence of offences despite the presence of moderate or severe deprivation. Deprivation in our population was widespread. But deprivation in itself, while correlating highly with offending, was not a sufficient condition for its development. Other factors within the care-giving environment and in the children themselves appeared to be able to modify the influences of deprivation; in some situations these factors acted as mediating influences and in others as moderating ones.

These other influences have been categorized according to the three main periods in which the data were collected: roughly the preschool years, primary school and pre-adolescence and, finally, the adolescent school years. This allows pinpointing of factors associated with vulnerability in the non-deprived and resiliency in the face of major deprivational experiences.

In the first five years, the resilient, despite a background of some deprivation, were characterized by having good parental care, more positive social circumstances, and less adverse physical experiences in the perinatal period and early childhood. The vulnerable, despite a background without deprivation as we had defined it, were characterized by having some adverse social circumstances not sufficient to constitute deprivation but enough to act as stress, poor growth, which probably also reflects their poorer social circumstances and a greater number of accidents by the age of five.

In the pre-adolescent period, the resilient were characterized by five different kinds of protective factors: first, a care-giving environment that provides good supervision of children; second, the absence of developmental delays; third, relatively good cognitive development and educational achievements; fourth, positive temperamental qualities; and, finally, positive responses from peers and also social activities, such as membership of a youth club. The features that characterized the vulnerable (again despite a background without deprivation) relate to the children themselves, their poorer intelligence and achievements, their adverse temperamental qualities and behaviour in class, and their attitudes, rather than to aspects of their care-giving environment.

In adolescence, the factors associated with resilience proved to be similar to those in pre-adolescence, namely good cognitive development, scholastic progress and positive school factors. At this stage, we have to question the viability of the concepts of stress and protection, as the majority of the delinquents have actually already become delinquent. Nevertheless, the pattern of the factors identified in adolescence is similar to that in pre-adolescence and it is not unreasonable to think that many of the identified factors are merely continuations of the stress and protective influences of pre-adolescence. In addition, there were two important parent and family factors: family contact with the school and in girls the continuous presence of the natural father. The 'stress' factors associated with vulnerability were again similar to those in pre-adolescence. However, there were at this stage important family and parental factors: the family showed little interest in maintaining contact with the school; the youth did not participate in family activities; and, finally, the mother and father lacked effective personalities.

Are the above factors responsible for, or merely associated with, resilience in the face of deprivation, and vulnerability against a background of 'non-deprivation'? And how reliable are they as predictors?

Peer influences

It is often argued that delinquent activities may reflect the example set by friends with whom the potential delinquent associates. We examined the converse proposition that positive peer influences are associated with a decreased risk of delinquency in high-risk children. Taking the deprived group at 11 years of age, we found that whereas only 33% of youth club members were to become offenders, 54% of non-members would do so. While it is difficult to disentangle cause and effect, the above differences may be explicable not on the grounds of the positive effects of youth club membership, but on the basis that potentially delinquent youths choose delinquent friends, whereas non-delinquent youths seek more approved forms of recreation as provided in the youth club setting. Nevertheless, our findings do support the suggestion that beneficial social influences were associated with protection from delinquency even in high-risk children.

Family factors

Long before children reach the age of criminal responsibility, data obtained from the home environment can be used to forecast later delinquency, at least as effectively as other predictors. For example, we found that of those deprived children receiving poor mothering before five years of age, 71% became delinquent, with only 39% of those receiving good care becoming delinquent. In other words, good parenting protects against the acquisition of a criminal record; the likely explanation is that good affectionate mothering is complementary to good physical care and supervision and it is not surprising that a similar pattern emerges. Research data often imply that the mechanism by which good care is translated into relatively good behaviour is simply that the caring parent had jurisdiction over the child's choice of friends and recreation, but given the early age at which the correlation emerges, the argument must be that good parental care and supervision is itself capable of giving rise to beneficial personal qualities (such as internal controls) that influence behaviour at a later stage.

'Good parenting' is by no means the only measure of a family's beneficial involvement in a child's development. Even for high-risk children, the probability of later delinquency was substantially reduced from 57% to 28% if the family wished to maintain contact with the school when the youths were aged 15.

Positive qualities of the father's behaviour appear to go some way towards nullifying the detrimental effects of a deprived background. In high-risk 15-year-olds, the presence of an 'effective' father decreased the probability of delinquency from around one-half to one-third, whereas among low-risk youths 'ineffective' fathers raised the probability from 11% to 28%. The same increased vulnerability was found in those youths who did not share or participate in family activities.

Social factors

Social stresses appear to have been operative in high-risk families even before the children were five. These included greater density of the home territory, the family breadwinner having low occupational status, and the mother being young when first married. The effects of these stresses taken individually is significant rather than startling, but their combined effects may be more substantial. However, households that were smaller and had 'older mothers and employed breadwinners' had a positive influence.

Childhood accidents

The word 'accident' carries many shades of meaning: at one extreme, it describes in neutral terms an occurrence that was not intentional. But the term also encompasses 'negligence', as when the occurrence was occasioned by the child's carelessness, or by the parent's lack of foresight (possibly reflecting generally ineffective care and control).

In the absence of deprivation, accidents in the preschool years did not appear to be a stress factor. However, in the deprived group, a relative absence of accidents proved to be associated with resilience; it is reasonable to speculate that in the multiply deprived group accidents probably represented a combination of carelessness and ineffective care, or even abuse.

School factors

Much research has shown an association between dull intelligence and delinquency (Rutter and Giller, 1983). Our own data tend to bear out this proposition. In the high-risk group, 43% of those who did not become delinquent had IQs above 100, compared with 10% of those who did become delinquent. Only 18% of the high-risk group with arithmetical ability above the mean became delinquent, whereas 58% of those whose ability was below the mean did so. Results for ability in English were similar, but not so impressive. It seems sensible that positive attitudes to school, educational attainment and conduct in class should go hand in hand, but it is nevertheless noteworthy that positive temperamental and behavioural qualities in the classroom were strongly associated with reduced risk of delinquency, even among deprived, and therefore vulnerable, children. Only 17% of those vulnerable children who were described as having a good ability to concentrate in class at ten years of age went on to acquire a criminal record, but of those whose concentration was poor, over 45% became offenders. Conversely, low cognitive ability and scholastic achievements and poor temperamental and classroom attitudes in youths from non-deprived backgrounds appeared to render them more vulnerable. The great majority of these data were collected prior to the emergence of delinquency and this supports the notion that the sense of stability and esteem derived from meritorious school performance persists as a protective factor into later life (Rutter and Giller, 1983). Alternatively, of course, factors encouraging positive academic performance might in themselves be protective. The mechanisms are still far from clear. For example, is a distressing home atmosphere balanced by a fulfilling school career (Rutter, 1979), or does the teacher react favourably to the high-risk, yet intellectually able child, and elicit from him a positive identification with the teacher's own values? Because of the complexity of interactions, these theoretical speculations may be as near to the mark as any.

Male–female difference

We found only a few factors that protected females from delinquency and they differed from those in boys. In addition, at 15 years, protective factors were associated with a smaller decrease in risk of delinquency in

males than in females. In other words, not only are females less pre-
disposed to delinquent acts, but they also have stronger shields to guard
against the risks. At age five, the major protective factors in the deprived
female groups were a father in skilled employment, a family not dependent on social welfare, an accident-free life, and a mother in good health. A
girl with any one of these factors was between three and four times less
likely to acquire a criminal record than a girl without them.

By the tenth year, the importance of parental care was evident in both
males and females; only one in ten of the deprived youths who did not
become delinquent were experiencing poor parental supervision, in
contrast to one in four of those who did become delinquent. Among girls,
the continuous presence of a natural father was also important. Good
reliability in the classroom was protective for both boys and girls, and a
good ability to socialize was protective for females but not for males.

At age 15 a greater number of protective factors emerged in females;
not only did more of them overlap with male factors, but where they did,
the protective element was as great or greater than in males. The
overlapping factors mostly concerned scholastic ability and interest, and
included level of concentration, attitude to schoolwork, willingness to
continue at school, and interest of the family in maintaining contact with
the school. Of course, by this stage, the majority of delinquents already
have a criminal record, so that the presence of adverse attitudes may
merely reflect an already acquired delinquent predisposition.

The same cannot, however, always be said of certain other factors,
peculiar to girls, that are reflections not of attitude but of development.
For example, good physical growth at age 13 was associated with an 8%
delinquency rate, whereas poor growth portended a 63% rate; a wet bed
at age five or later entailed a threefold increase in risk for later delinquency. Finally, more than half of the females who did not offend had
fathers who were continually present over their preschool and school
years, compared with only one in five of offenders. The mere presence of
the natural father seems protective in females but presumably the quality
of the fathering is also important (McCord, 1982).

Relationship of cardinal defining criteria and offending

There was an independent main effect of both poor mothering and
adverse social circumstances, but whereas marital disturbance was a stress
factor in its own right, it was not so in the presence of severe multiple
deprivation. It seems that the effects of marital disturbance are mediated
through a consequent poor quality of care and mothering, and through
relatively impoverished social circumstances.

Discontinuities in family deprivation appear to give rise to a degree of
protection; conversely, movement into deprivation in previously non-
deprived families increases the vulnerability of their offspring to

offending. The risk of offending for males was three and a half times greater in males whose families showed a consistent pattern of deprivation than in those who were never deprived.

The association between deprivation and offending was almost always entirely mediated indirectly through a prior effect on IQ and temperament. This was not true for poor care and mothering, which had an additional significant direct effect.

There remains the question of the mechanisms of action of the intervening variables – are the effects of offending facilitated or 'mediated' by these variables? Or are the effects 'moderated' by these variables? Unfortunately path analysis cannot tease out which intervening variables act as mediators or moderators. In attempting to answer this question, less complex statistical analyses may prove more helpful.

References

Coffield, F., Robinson, P. and Sarsby, J. (1981) *A cycle of deprivation? A case study of four familes.* London: Heinemann.

Heath, A. (1981) *Social mobility.* London: Fontana.

Home Office (1985) *Home Office statistical bulletin*, April. ISSNO 143, 6384.

Kolvin, I., Miller, F. J. W., Scott, D. McI., Gatznis, S. R. M. and Fleeting, M. (1988a) *Adversity and destiny: explorations in the transmission of deprivation – Newcastle '1000' Families Study.* Aldershot: Gower.

Kolvin, I., Miller, F. J. W., Fleeting, M. and Kolvin, P. A. (1988b) Social and parenting factors affecting criminal offence rates (findings from the Newcastle Thousand Family Study, 1947–1980). *British Journal of Psychiatry*, 152, 80–90.

McCord, J. (1982) The relation between paternal absence and crime. In Gunn, J. and Farrington, D. P. (eds.) *Abnormal offenders, delinquency, and the criminal justice system.* Chichester: Wiley.

Macdonald, K. I. (1976) Causal modelling in politics and sociology. *Quality and Quantity*, 10, 189–208.

Macdonald, K. I. (1977) Path analysis. In O'Muircheartaigh, C. A. and Payne, C. (eds.) *The analysis of survey data*, vol. 2. Chichester: Wiley, pp. 87–104.

Miller, F. J. W., Court, S. D. M., Walton, W. S. and Knox, E. G. (1960) *Growing up in Newcastle upon Tyne.* London: Oxford University Press.

Rutter, M. (1979) *Changing youth in a changing society.* London: Nuffield Provincial Hospitals Trust (1980: Cambridge, MA: Harvard University Press).

Rutter, M. (1983) Statistical and personal interactions: facets and perspectives. In Magnusson, D. and Allen, V. (eds.) *Human development: an interactional perspective.* New York: Academic Press, pp. 295–319.

Rutter, M. and Giller, H. (1983) *Juvenile delinquency: trends and perspectives.* Harmondsworth: Penguin.

Werner, E. E. (1985) Stress and protective factors in children's lives. In Nicol, A. R. (ed.) *Longitudinal studies in child psychology and psychiatry: practical lessons from research experience.* Chichester: Wiley, pp. 335–55.

West, D. J. (1982) *Delinquency careers and prospects.* London: Heinemann.

6 A person–process–context approach

Rainer K. Silbereisen and Sabine Walper

The work of Glen Elder *Children of the Great Depression* (1974) represents a cornerstone of modern research into the effects of family deprivation on offsprings' long-term personality development. Its major contribution lies in the study's attempt to provide insight into the mechanisms that gradually transform the experience of deprivation into quite stable attributes of the family members, as well as the circumstances that determine destructive or constructive outcomes. In a series of analyses, Elder and his colleagues (Elder, 1974; Elder *et al.*, 1984a; Elder *et al.*, 1984b; Elder *et al.*, 1985; Elder *et al.*, 1986) revealed some major mediating mechanisms and moderating factors operating in family adaptation and the children's development throughout the lifespan.

One of the most instructive findings indicates that the effect of deprivation on juvenile problem behaviour is moderated by the vulnerability of the family system produced by impaired relationships prior to economic loss. As Rockwell and Elder (1982) demonstrated for boys, but not girls, financial loss led to increased problem behaviour only in those families who entered the Depression period with an incompatible marriage. For families with compatible marriages, however, the effect was even slightly reversed. At the same time, the impact of parents' earlier marital relations on boys' later problem behaviour was more pronounced under conditions of economic loss than among the non-deprived. Since economic deprivation is likely to exacerbate previous tensions in family relations (Liker and Elder, 1983), this accentuation of given tendencies of the family system may have led to more consistent differences in the children's development. Indeed, it has been shown that strains in the marital subsystem of the family contributed to punitive parenting, one of the mediating processes that influenced children's problem behaviour (Elder *et al.*, 1984a).

The work by Elder on longitudinal archives dating back to the end of the 1920s (Berkeley Guidance Study, Oakland Growth Study) shares some important features with the equally impressive Newcastle Thousand Family Study initiated in 1947 (Spence *et al.*, 1954; Miller *et al.*, 1960; Miller *et al.*, 1974). In both cases the original investigations were based on local samples that were followed up in the community. Furthermore, by using catch-up strategies the ultimate time range observed in the studies is very long: for the Newcastle Study more than 30 years, and almost 40 years in the case of the Berkeley Guidance Study. The attrition rate is moderate because of the care and advice given to the families by the research team.

There is, however, a remarkable difference concerning the general political and economic climate during the early years of the studies. Whereas Elder's study took the Great Depression as a point of departure, comparing families who moved into deprivation and those who did not, the Newcastle Study was undertaken in a period of economic expansion in post-war Britain. A comparison of the families' adaptational mechanisms and the respective outcomes for children's development could shed light on the possibility of generalizing across such differing historical contexts, but so far analyses of the Newcastle data have taken a more descriptive approach, and chaining effects between deprivation and psychosocial development have not yet been addressed (Miller *et al.*, 1985). Thus the ultimate contribution of the study to our knowledge of the mechanisms and outcomes of deprivation is still to be seen.

Starting from this background, Kolvin *et al.* (see chapter 5) report further attempts towards a better understanding of the transmission of deprivation. Based on more than 800 Newcastle families, they present a rich body of data on factors associated with vulnerability to delinquency in adolescents and young adults coming from privileged homes, and factors associated with resilience despite a history of deprivation in the family background.

In this chapter three topics related to this approach will be discussed: (a) Starting with a description of the analyses carried out in order to identify factors and mechanisms that promote delinquency or protect from it, some shortcomings and problems will be characterized; (b) the basic structure of a more comprehensive and, at the same time, more dynamic approach towards this aim will be presented; and (c) these methodological issues will be complemented, and their advantage exemplified, by substantive results from our own research on the processes mediating between economic hardship and psychosocial functioning in adolescence.

The Newcastle approach

Apart from a great number of communalities, longitudinal research has well-known features that cannot be met by cross-sectional data (see Schaie and Hertzog, 1982). A prominent advantage is related to one's knowledge about the temporal relationships between and among variables as provided by this strategy. It allows for the disregarding of at least some of the potential effects of one variable on another because of their sequence across time.

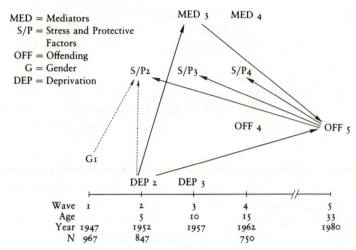

Figure 1 Strategies used in analysing the Newcastle Thousand Family Study. Strategies depicted are (a) retrospective evaluation (arrows from right to left, dotted arrows) and (b) prospective assessment (arrows from left to right)

In the following the conceptual framework and the statistical analyses accomplished thus far by Kolvin and his colleagues will be discussed with regard to the advantages of the longitudinal nature of the study. In Figure 1 the kinds of data gathered and the strategies used are schematically depicted. In all, five waves of data covering an age range of 33 years have been gathered: after birth (1947), at ages 5 (1952), 10 (1957), 15 (1962) and 33 (1980).

Several classes of concept were operationalized and measured at some or all of the waves, the numbers attached to the variable designations indicating the respective wave. These classes were:

1 Family deprivation (DEP), the major antecedent variable. Several categories were used to distinguish the quality of deprivation (family/marital instability, parental illness, poor care of children and homes, dependence on public subsistence, overcrowding in the home, poor mothering) and its severity (not deprived, deprived in at least one aspect, deprived in at least three aspects). Both were gathered at waves 2 and 3.

2 Gender (G). This is taken into account as another antecedent variable which, of course, had to be recorded only once.

3 The frequency of offending (OFF) as documented in official sources and project files of the Newcastle Study. This represents the major consequent variable. This was assessed at waves 4 and 5, but until now only life time prevalence (offences ever committed) at age 33 has been used in the analyses.

4 So-called stress or protective factors (S/P). A considerable number of these were measured at waves 2, 3 and 5. Although the investigators' term 'stress factor' is used in Figure 1, 'risk factor' will be preferred in the following because of its descriptive status. These factors are considered

to moderate or shape the relationship between family deprivation and the prevalence of criminal offences. If the likelihood of offences under relatively privileged conditions is seen to increase depending on a certain variable, this variable is addressed as a risk factor. For example, low participation in family activities at age 15 has been shown to increase the risk of offending. Likewise, protective factors are defined as reducing the likelihood of offences under deprived family environments. A case in point is adolescents' membership of youth clubs at age 10 which turned out to reduce the risk of offending.

5 A class of variables that may be called *mediators* (MED), so called because they are conceived as transmitting or linking effects between antecedent and outcome variables. Deprivation, instead of influencing delinquency directly, is thought to exert its effect by changing such mediators, for example temperamental characteristics such as poor concentration in school, which in turn lead to a variation in the prevalence of delinquency.

Turning to the data analyses conducted so far, the following two strategies may be deemed representative of Kolvin and his colleagues' approach. For ease of communication they will be called (a) retrospective evaluation of risk and protective indicators and (b) prospective assessment of processes of vulnerability and resilience. As underscored by these catchphrases, the two strategies not only emphasize different time perspectives but also provide different concepts of the linkage between deprivation and offending. Whereas the first strategy is characterized by a static, descriptive vein, the latter requires modelling of the dynamic nature of risk and protective mechanisms.

Retrospective evaluation

We questioned whether the longitudinal nature of the data is adequately represented in the analyses accomplished thus far. A closer look at the approach of retrospective evaluation will help to develop the argument a step further.

In Figure 1 the strategy of retrospective evaluation is characterized by the solid arrows from offending (OFF5) to the risk and protective factors (S/P2). As symbolized by the dotted arrows connecting gender (G1) and deprivation (DEP2) with the risk and protective factors, statistical tests were run separately for the sexes and the categories of deprivation. In order to identify protective factors (a) those participants whose records did not show a history of offending, although they lived in deprived conditions through childhood and adolescence were compared with (b) those who offended given the same circumstances. Risk factors, on the other hand, were analysed by comparing (c) those participants whose records showed a history of offending, although they lived in privileged conditions, with (d) those who did not offend given the same circumstances.

One may question the adequacy of this strategy with statistical arguments. Instead of using multivariate analysis of variance and planned contrasts in comparing the four groups, only the above-mentioned comparisons were made, using univariate tests on differences in central tendency. Thus the large number of tests will inevitably result in a considerable inflation of alpha levels. More importantly, however, the equivalence of offenders (groups (b) and (c)) and non-offenders (groups (a) and (d)), irrespective of differences in the state of deprivation, has not been tested.

Investigating age-related change in vulnerability and resilience represents the actual challenge of a developmental point of view on problem behaviour. Further insight concerning these issues was gained by replicating the retrospective evaluation for other waves. In Figure 1 this is indicated by the arrows from OFF5 to S/P3 and S/P4. Again, the analyses were accomplished separately for the sexes and categories of deprivation. Following this developmental approach, Kolvin and his colleagues report differences in the pattern of risk and protective factors at different stages of the life span. For instance, cognitive and scholastic progress proved to be associated with resilience at ages 10 and 15, whereas a lack of participation in family interaction was related to vulnerability only at age 15.

This approach to the longitudinal data has formed a most useful first step but it is restricted to features shared by cross-sectional analyses. No use is made either of information concerning the stabilities of the variables or of the time-lagged and reciprocal influences between them. With regard to the latter, one should bear in mind that risk and protective factors at a given time may influence the future trajectory of other variables, and vice versa. For example, while a lack of family cohesion and low participation in family activities may put the children at risk of developing delinquent affiliations and behaviours at one point, the child's delinquency itself may contribute to strained family relations and an isolation of the child from common family activities (Bahr, 1979).

The distinction between risk and protective factors in offending helps to widen the view on the multitude of developmental avenues that may ultimately lead to delinquency. Indeed, the analyses are quite complex, as the influences of both inter-individual differences (gender, essentially a stable person variable) and contextual variations (status of deprivation) are distinguished. However, no evaluation of their joint effect on delinquency has yet been provided, and the mediating developmental processes which link deprivation and delinquency are not addressed in these analyses.

In sum, the reported retrospective evaluations come close to an approach that Bronfenbrenner (Bronfenbrenner and Crouter, 1983; Bronfenbrenner, 1986) called the 'social address' model: no explicit consideration is given to intervening structures or processes through which the course of development might be affected.

Prospective assessment

In contrast, the second strategy used in the Newcastle Study is explicitly aimed at analysing processes intervening between deprivation and offending. This is exemplified in Figure 1 by the triangle comprising solid arrows connecting deprivation (DEP2), mediating variables (MED 3), and offending (OFF5). Although there is no restriction as to the psychological quality of mediation, fairly stable personal attributes were used, for example general intelligence and temperamental characteristics.

Formally, the concept of mediation is used in order to describe indirect influences in path analyses and structural modelling. Whereas Judd and Kenny (1981) maintain that the first and last variables in a chain (for instance, DEP2 and OFF5) must be significantly related before any intermediate variable can be said to be a mediator, other authors (Elder *et al.*, 1985; Galambos and Silbereisen, 1987b) have used the concept in a broader sense to explain the lack of uniform direct effects between variables.

As the psychological salience of a mediating variable is evaluated in contrast to the magnitude of the corresponding direct effect, it is worthwhile to consider the adequacy of the model itself. With just-identified models the only indicator is the proportion of explained variance. If intelligence and temperament should function as mediators – for a thorough proof the correlation matrix would have to be checked – their effect on offending seems to be small (10–15%), as Kolvin and his colleagues report (see chapter 5). Given the usually much more complex models of the relationship between deprivation and non-normative behaviour (see Elliot *et al.*, 1985), this result may have been expected. In order to increase the proportion of explained variance, variables such as parental monitoring or peer group affiliation have to be taken into account (Patterson and Stouthamer-Loeber, 1984). At least some information on these variables could be drawn from the long list of potential risk and protective factors provided by the Newcastle Study.

Another issue to be mentioned relates to the distinctions made as to qualitative aspects or severity of deprivation. While separate analyses for more severely deprived subgroups as conducted so far provide some descriptive information, adequate dummy-coding techniques (Cohen and Cohen, 1975) would allow differences in the effects of, for example, multiply deprived environments in comparison to less severely influenced, or even privileged, homes to be tested.

Although a prospective view is taken of the data, the analyses carried out are still not longitudinal in the strict sense, because time-lagged relationships are taken into consideration only between different variables, not among the same variables across time. Concerning deprivation, only data gathered at wave 2 was used. Thus it remains open whether deprivation (DEP2) has to be conceived as a reasonably stable or a transitional experience in a given family.

When analysing processes that result in vulnerability and resilience, a prospective assessment of mediating mechanisms is generally more promising than a retrospective evaluation of moderator effects. In the following, an attempt will be made to optimize the prospective strategy, and to suggest more elaborated conceptualizations and statistical models for further analyses of the Newcastle Study.

A person–process–context approach

Bronfenbrenner (see Bronfenbrenner and Crouter, 1983) strongly advocated the use of 'person–process–context' models as a frame of reference for developmental studies. Essential to this paradigmatic approach is the assumption that – contrary to the common presupposition in research practice – developmental processes are *not* invariant across both person and context. There is now growing evidence (for an overview, see Bronfenbrenner, 1986) that processes of age-related change do not only vary in magnitude but also in direction as a function of the interplay between both the nature of the context and the characteristics of the person. Potential variations in the process of developing a history of offending should thus be analysed as a function of characteristics of the person, the context, and any (statistical) interaction between them.

Drawing from this general background, an alternative approach is suggested for the analysis of the Newcastle Study. It is schematically depicted in Figure 2.

Features of design

As compared to the strategies used thus far by Kolvin and his colleagues (see chapter 5), some new features are realized in this design.

Moderating factors. First of all, the sample of families is assumed to be broken down into several subgroups that are characterized by the systematic combination of person and context variables. This allows us to disentangle possible interactions between these variables, as suggested by Bronfenbrenner (1986). We may assume that gender and deprivation represent the two basic concepts, but, of course, the argument is not confined to these variables. For ease of communication, the time-graded structural relationships are shown for the first subgroup only.

Secondly, instead of using the concurrent state of deprivation as a context variable, *change* in deprivation across time is analysed as an antecedent factor. In order to accomplish this, categories may be formed

Modelling separately per
Gender (<u>M</u>ale, <u>F</u>emale) × Change
in Deprivation (<u>N</u>ever, <u>I</u>nto, <u>O</u>ut of,
<u>A</u>lways) Group

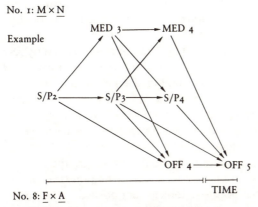

No. 1: <u>M</u> × <u>N</u>

Example

MED 3 ——→ MED 4

S/P2 ——→ S/P3 ——→ S/P4

OFF 4 ——→ OFF 5

TIME

No. 8: <u>F</u> × <u>A</u>

Figure 2   Person–process–context approach suggested for future analyses.
Sample assumed to be broken down into eight subgroups according to gender
and change in state of deprivation

as depicted in Figure 2: never in deprivation, moved into deprivation, moved out of deprivation, and always in deprivation.

As there are two (gender) and four (change in deprivation) categories in the present example, the sample is assumed to be broken down into eight subgroups. Depending on the marginal distributions of gender and – more importantly – change in deprivation, the cell sizes in this two-way classification scheme may vary remarkably. According to the data reported in the Newcastle Study, only a minority of families moved into deprivation as compared to those who moved out of, or remained in, deprivation throughout. As this is often the case in normal population samples, the prevalence of the phenomenon in which one is actually interested is rather small. Thus the sample size, and the reduction in statistical power related to it, already set limits to analyses applying the person–process–context approach.

As already mentioned, the main goal of the proposed approach is to reveal variations in processes as a function of both person characteristics and change in the nature of the context. That different mechanisms may be operative in the various subgroups is already suggested by the small proportion of families which moved into deprivation at this time of relative prosperity in Britain. Deprivation hit families selectively (Miller *et al.*, 1985), and such conditions, confounded with deprivation, may well contribute to different trajectories in the children's development. Of course, it will be necessary to disentangle the effects of change in deprivation and selectivity factors by controlling for the latter if the former is to be estimated properly.

Some further remarks on investigating changes in deprivation may be helpful at this point. Whereas effects of the current state of deprivation are worth studying, a systematic comparison of the effects of deprivation, measured concurrently, with those relating to its trajectory across time would be even more valuable. A case in point is provided by research on economic deprivation that took both approaches (see Horwitz, 1984; and Siegal, 1984) but hardly ever combined them in one single study, and hence leaves many questions unanswered. For example, it is conceivable that a lack of strong significant findings concerning the effects of economic disadvantage, assessed concurrently, on deviance (see Bahr, 1979) are due to the low stability of deprivation. As far as studies on economic change are concerned, important subgroups may have been neglected by the adoption of a restricted definition of deprivation. For example, it has often been overlooked that normal variations in income across the family cycle may be even greater than the financial effects of unemployment, which more often than not is a transitional experience (Moen *et al.*, 1983). Again, the latter point supports the notion that differences in the fabric of risk and protective factors – for example as related to family development (Hill and Mattesich, 1979) – may influence, and may be influenced themselves by, moving in and moving out of deprivation.

Stability. There is another specificity in the suggested design. In contrast to the earlier approaches, the prediction of a variable accounts for separate effects of stability and cross-lagged influences from other variables. For instance, the variance of mediating variables at age 15 (MED4) is explained by the combined effect of this variable measured at an earlier wave (MED3), and the effect of risk and protective factors at age 10. In the same vein, the effect of offending at age 33 (OFF5) is explained by the combination of earlier offending (OFF4), risk and protective factors at ages 10 and 15 (S/P3, S/P4), and the influence of mediating variables (MED4).

The importance of stability effects is quite obvious in the case of irritability and other temperamental characteristics, which may represent mediating variables. These variables are conceived as revealing a strong hereditary component and this should result in reasonably high stabilities across time. The same effect seems to be true for other personality variables as well. Self-esteem, for instance, has been shown to play an important role in vulnerability to negative outcomes of social and economic strains (see Werner and Smith, 1982). Except for short periods in the life of some adolescents, however, the stability of self-esteem is remarkably high (Silbereisen *et al.*, 1986). As the prevalence and incidence figures of delinquency show pronounced peaks in early adulthood (see Elliot *et al.*, 1985), the stability of offending may be much lower than that of the mediating variables throughout the time span covered in the study. Even in this case, it is essential to take into account stabilities of the variables in order to avoid failures in interpretation.

Mediation. The predominant goal in the study of mediational processes is to analyse explanatory links between antecedent and consequent variables. It complements the study of moderating factors in that it may reveal differences and communalities in causal processes as a function of the specific constellation of person and context.

In fact, there are two distinct processes of mediation depicted in Figure 2. Mediation – as characterized when we introduced Kolvin and his colleagues' prospective assessment strategy – is represented by the triangle composed of directed effects between S/P2, and MED3 and OFF4. Self-esteem may be taken as an example. If low participation in family activities exerts its effect on offending predominantly by reducing one's self-esteem first, which consequently leads to an increase in future offending, this chain of effects would indicate mediation. Indeed there is evidence in the literature confirming this assumption concerning self-esteem (Kaplan *et al.*, 1984). A comparison of the mediational effect on offending at wave 4 with its potential replication at the next wave (S/P3–MED4–OFF5) may shed light on what one could call a 'critical periods' concept of the vulnerability to delinquency.

The other process of mediation depicted in Figure 2 is exemplified by the triangle composed of S/P2, S/P3 and OFF4, and its counterpart at the next wave. Intuitively one would assume that the effect of earlier risk and protective factors (S/P2) on future offending (OFF4) would be relatively small as compared to the more recent history of risk and protective factors (S/P3). If not, findings would probably have to be conceptualized in terms of a 'sleeper' effect. This is exemplified by Bronfenbrenner's (1979) interpretation of findings from the Elder studies demonstrating that effects of family deprivation do not manifest themselves before adolescence.

Cross-lagged effects. The original data do not allow the analysis of many hypothetical cross-lagged effects that would be of interest. For example, influences of offending (OFF4) on future risk and protective factors or mediating variables cannot be assessed due to lack of measurement. Needless to say, however, a developmental orientation in research on delinquency would strongly recommend the analysis of mutual influences between the two sets of variables. It should then be clear that offending –

depending on its severity or quality – will show differential feedback into the system of variables depicted in the model.

The only possibility of testing for mutual cross-lagged effects is to be found in the relationship between risk and protective factors, and mediating variables. Complementary to the path S/P3–MED4, influences are also assumed to take place in the opposite direction – MED3–S/P4. Irritability (MED4), for example, may be less influenced by earlier risk and protective factors in family interaction (S/P3), as irritability itself (MED3) could have an impact on these factors, for example it could lead to reduced participation in family activities (S/P4). Indeed, recent research on temperament (Lerner and Lerner, 1983) suggests that this possibility needs to be taken into account.

In order to avoid a possible misunderstanding, it should be emphasized that the model shown in Figure 2 is not meant to represent a specific theory of the development of offending or the transmission of deprivation. Rather, it is aimed at demonstrating the kind of concepts (moderating factors, stability, mediating mechanisms, cross-lagged effects) one should bear in mind. On the other hand, its general outline comes close to models suggested by others (see especially Elder *et al.*, 1984b). Some of its features also guided our own research on economic hardship and psychosocial development in adolescence. Before we proceed to the results of this research, some remarks on technical aspects of the approach may be helpful.

Modelling and statistical analysis

Although the person–process–context approach suggested is principally open for different statistical and modelling devices, the assessment of time-graded structural differences among and between subgroups requires complex statistical procedures.

In many cases the use of LISREL (Jöreskog and Sörbom, 1984; Biddle and Marlin, 1987; Fergusson and Horwood, chapter 19) may be a very good solution because of its special feature for multi-group comparisons. When compared to ordinary regression and path analysis, a major advantage is the capacity to differentiate between latent variables and their multiple indicators, and the availability of a maximum-likelihood goodness-of-fit test. It is possible, for instance, to compare alternative models that assume different constraints in the structural relationships of a given subgroup or to test the equality of structural relationships between all the subgroups. This is especially valuable in testing the relative importance of direct, as compared to indirect, effects (mediation).

Recently researchers have stressed the methodological difference between variable-based and person-oriented strategies (see Magnusson and Bergman, chapter 3), and have recommended qualitative statistical approaches for the latter. One of these approaches is configural frequency analysis (Krauth and Lienert, 1982). It allows for the identification of patterns that occur significantly more or less often than predicted by an independence model. As there are also procedures to compare patterns of various subgroups, configural frequency analysis seems to be especially appropriate for person–process–context models. Furthermore, instead of assuming linear relationships, as in the case of LISREL, the possibility of higher-order interactions among categorical variables is taken into account.

Throughout this chapter the effects of variables on each other were assumed to take considerable time. This is indicated in Figure 1 by the lagged effects which parallel the time span between data gatherings. Alternatively, contemporaneous effects may be assumed. In principle a decision between these conceptualizations has to be based on theoretical considerations that reflect the state-like versus trait-like quality of the variables and/or longitudinal evidence concerning the relative strength of cross-lagged and contemporaneous effects. As the general argument would not be changed when assuming contemporaneous effects, we will not go further into detail on these (see Hertzog and Nesselroade, 1987).

In the following, results from our own research will be reported. The presentation will demonstrate differences in the transmission of economic deprivation depending on context variables such as the level of education.

Moderating and mediating effects in the transmission of economic hardship

In 1982, the Berlin Youth Longitudinal Study was started utilizing a cohort-sequential design. Representative samples drawn from three cohorts of adolescents have been interviewed at yearly intervals. In nearly 70% of the cases, the parents are being followed up. The study is still active. So far, the analyses on economic hardship make use of only one or two of the waves, although the data collection has been accomplished for five waves.

Taking findings from the Great Depression (Elder, 1974) as a reference point, Walper and Silbereisen (1987a) investigated whether losses in family income were related to the adolescent children's transgression proneness at present, and whether family integration and self-esteem played a mediating role in this respect. Furthermore, differences in the patterns of structural relationships were tested as a function of the level of parental education. The latter was thought to indicate socio-economic and problem-solving resources.

In order to investigate economic hardship in this sample of about 800 families, the selectivity of deprivation in the normal population had to be controlled for. A target group of deprived families was identified who had lost at least 5%, the majority more than 25%, of their income during the previous year. These families were matched with families of stable income (i.e. who had experienced changes of less than 5%) on criteria such as parental education, occupation, and age and sex of the child. As only two-parent families with complete data sets were included in the analyses, the sample consisted of 92 cases (38 deprived, 54 non-deprived) with children in the age span from 9 to 16 years. Data were gathered independently from children and both parents.

The reader may doubt whether the income loss reported by the Berlin families is comparable to the deterioration of living conditions in the 1930s. Although in the Depression study of Oakland and Berkeley families economic deprivation was defined as a loss in family income of at least 35%, in practice this financial loss was compensated for by a parallel 25% decrease in living expenses (Elder *et al.*, 1985). The communalities of deprivation now and then are underscored by the fact that many of the reported adaptive changes in the household economy could be replicated in the Berlin sample (Walper, 1988). Furthermore, different effects of income loss according to the degree of deprivation were taken into account by adequate dummy-coding.

Family integration, an indicator of cohesion and positive emotional relations in the overall family system, was measured using reports from both parents. The items were drawn from subscales evaluating the dimension of relationships in family climate (Moos, 1974). The scale on adolescents' self-esteem used items provided by Kaplan *et al.* (1984). Transgression proneness was assessed by items such as 'Sometimes I really feel like doing something forbidden', which had already been used by Silbereisen and Zank (1984).

Following Elder *et al.* and taking into account results of our own previous research (Galambos and Silbereisen, 1987a), higher transgression proneness was expected for deprived adolescents than for those from families with stable income. In line with our moderation hypotheses assuming a greater vulnerability of families with lower resources, this effect of income loss was restricted to adolescents in the low-education group. The degree of deprivation had no influence on this finding.

As far as the transmission of economic hardship is concerned, our hypotheses focused on two interrelated mediators. Ordinary path analysis techniques were used for the assessment of mediation effects in the two groups. With reference to Kaplan (Kaplan, 1980; Kaplan *et al.*, 1984), self-esteem was hypothesized as playing a mediating role in linking economic hardship to adolescents' transgression proneness. Again, self-esteem was not affected by deprivation in the high-education group, while findings for the adolescents of low educational background confirmed our expectations. In this case, only severe hardship led to a reduction in adolescents' self-esteem, which, in turn, contributed to increased transgression proneness.

In addition, and causally prior to self-esteem, family integration was assumed to function as a mediator that links economic hardship with transgression proneness through its effects on self-esteem. This hypothesis was based on the report by Elder *et al.* (1984a) on the detrimental effects of economic hardship on the marital relationship and on parent–child interaction as mediators to children's problem behaviour, as well as on earlier qualitative research on the negative impact of income loss and unemployment on family integration and the provider's authority within the family (Angell, 1965; Komarovsky, 1940). The results obtained required some revision of this view. Although family integration was reduced by financial hardship and, in turn, influenced the adolescents' self-esteem, economic loss still exerted an additional direct effect on the latter. Thus self-esteem seems to represent the more potent mediator between income loss and transgression proneness.

Despite the reported differences in effects of income loss among families of high and low parental education, LISREL multi-group comparisons demonstrated that the similarities in structural relationships prevailed. As group-specific features, only differences in self-esteem as a function of gender emerged. Interestingly enough, the widespread belief that female adolescents score lower on self-esteem was true only for the high-education group. This result draws attention to a restriction of the study. Due to a limited sample size, the moderating effect of educational context and gender could not be tested in the same model.

Even though the overall pattern of structural relationships seems to hold for both educational groups, the more pronounced effects of income loss for families with low parental education may be interpreted in terms of differences in the resources available for adaptation to economic change. This view corresponds with results of research on life events, which also claimed a higher vulnerability of groups low in social and educational resources (Liem and Liem, 1978).

Using the same sample and measurement of economic hardship, Walper and Silbereisen (1987b) broadened the view on other moderating and outcome variables. In these analyses, family integration and adolescents' peer relationships were taken into account as moderating factors. Regarding the latter, membership in a friendship clique, an indicator of the density of the peer network, was of prime interest. Besides transgression proneness, social criticism (critical, rejecting attitudes towards social norms, regulations and institutions), and deviant contacts (contact with peers and adults showing rule-breaking, deviant behaviour) were included as other aspects of contranormative orientations.

An important common feature of friendship cliques is that they provide a feeling of belonging and solidarity beyond that of single friendships (Hallinan, 1980). Such an advantage of clique membership is also suggested by research on the effects of dense social networks, which are considered to be especially successful in providing emotional support (Wood, 1984). In line with these assumptions, findings reported by Kolvin and his colleagues (see chapter 5) show that deprived children who were members of a youth club at age ten were less at risk for offending in adolescence and early adulthood than those who did not participate in such groups.

The main questions raised were whether adolescents who lack the supportive background of an integrated family system and/or who are not integrated in a peer group show stronger effects of economic deprivation than members of a clique. Instead of using path analysis, as in the earlier study, analysis of variance techniques was employed to test for interaction effects.

Peer integration (categories: socially isolated, single friendships, member of a friendship clique) showed no main effect on the dependent variables, nor did it interact with family integration. However, in the case of adolescents' contact with deviance, there was an interaction effect – though only a marginally significant one – between income loss and peer integration. The expected advantage of those who belonged to a friendship clique could be confirmed. They did not manifest any effect of economic loss at all, while deprived youth with single friendships indicated significantly more deviant affiliations than their non-deprived counterparts. At the same time, a comparison among adolescents from families with financial loss revealed that this latter finding was not due to particularly high deviant contacts of deprived adolescents who could only rely on single friendships. Rather, it seems that among non-deprived youth, those who are neither socially isolated nor members of a clique have lower contacts with deviance than the other non-deprived adolescents, but this advantage is lost in a situation of economic deprivation. This suggests that under stable economic conditions adolescents with only single friendships tend to be protected from deviant affiliations. Yet at the same time, this lack of a firm and dense network in peer relationships puts them more at risk of changes towards more deviant affiliation if stressful conditions are encountered. Somewhat similarly, only adolescents from poorly integrated families reported more deviant contacts due to economic deprivation, while those from well-integrated families did not show any effect of income loss.

In these analyses, no effect of economic deprivation on transgression proneness was obtained. At first glance one may assume this to be contradictory to the earlier findings reported by Walper and Silbereisen (1987a). However, the main effect of family integration on transgression proneness shown in the analyses of variance is in accord with previous results. In fact, since family integration is included as a factor, the lack of an independent effect of income loss meets our assumptions concerning the mediating role of family integration in the causal process. The analysis-of-variance approach does not address (nor do findings exclude) indirect effects of income loss mediated through its negative impact on family integration as demonstrated in the path analysis.

In conclusion, it should be clear that the analysis of mediating and moderating effects deserves more attention in research on the transmission of deprivation. The person–process–context paradigm seems to be especially helpful in the conceptualization of adequate strategies for research on risk and protective factors in psychosocial development.

References

Angell, R. C. (1965) *The family encounters the Depression.* Gloucester, MA: Peter Smith (1st edn 1936).

Bahr, S. J. (1979) Family determinants and effects of deviance. In Burr, W. R., Hill, R., Nye, F. I. and Reiss, I. L. (eds.) *Contemporary theories about the family,* vol. 1. New York: Free Press, pp. 615–43.

Biddle, B. J. and Marlin, M. M. (1987) Causality, confirmation, credulity, and structural equation modeling. *Child Development,* 58, 4–17.

Bronfenbrenner, U. (1979) *The ecology of human development.* London: Harvard University Press.

(1986) Recent advances in research on the ecology of human development. In Silbereisen, R. K., Eyferth, K. and Rudinger, G. (eds.) *Development as action in context.* Berlin, New York: Springer, pp. 287–309.

Bronfenbrenner, U. and Crouter, A. C. (1983) The evolution of environmental models in developmental research. In Kessen, W. (ed.) *Handbook of child psychology,* vol. 1, *History, theories, and methods,* 4th edn. New York: Wiley, pp. 357–414.

Cohen, J. and Cohen, P. (1975) *Applied multiple regression/correlation analysis for the behavioral sciences.* New York: Wiley.

Elder, G. H., Jr (1974) *Children of the Great Depression: social change in life experience.* Chicago: University of Chicago Press.

Elder, G. H., Jr, Caspi, A. and Downey, G. (1984a) Problem behavior and family relationships: life course and intergenerational themes. In Sorensen, A., Weinert, F. and Sherrod, L. (eds.) *Human development and the life-course: multidisciplinary perspectives.* Hillsdale, NJ: Erlbaum, pp. 293–340.

Elder, G. H., Jr, Liker, J. K. and Cross C. E. (1984b) Parent–child behavior in the Great Depression: life course and intergenerational influences. In Baltes, P. B. and Brim, G. O., Jr (eds.) *Life-span development and behavior,* vol. 6. New York: Academic Press, pp. 109–58.

Elder, G. H., Jr, van Nguyen, T. and Caspi, A. (1985) Linking family hardship to children's life. *Child Development,* 56, 361–75.

Elder, G. H., Jr, Caspi, A. and van Nguyen, T. (1986) Resourceful and vulnerable children: family influences in hard times. In Silbereisen, R. K., Eyferth, K. and Rudinger, G. (eds.) *Development as action in context.* Berlin, New York: Springer, pp. 167–86.

Elliot, D. S., Huizinga, D. and Ageton, S. (1985) *Explaining delinquency and drug use.* Beverly Hills: Sage.

Galambos, N. L. and Silbereisen, R. K. (1987a) Influences of income change and parental acceptance on adolescent transgression proneness and peer relations. *European Journal of Psychology of Education,* 1, 17–28.

(1987b) Income change, parental life outlook, and adolescent expectations for job success. *Journal of Marriage and the Family*, 49, 141–9.

Hallinan, M. T. (1980) Patterns of cliquing among youth. In Foot, H. C., Chapman, A. J. and Smith, J. R. (eds.) *Friendship and social relations in children*. New York: Wiley, pp. 321–42.

Hertzog, C. and Nesselroade, J. R. (1987) Beyond autoregressive models: some implications of the trait-state distinction for the structural modeling of developmental change. *Child Development*, 58, 93–109.

Hill, R. and Mattesich, P. (1979) Family development theory and life-span development. In Baltes, P. B. and Brim, O. G., Jr (eds.) *Life-span development and behavior*, vol. 2. New York: Academic Press, pp. 162–204.

Horwitz, A. V. (1984) The economy and social pathology. *Annual Review of Sociology*, 10, 95–119.

Jöreskog, K. G. and Sörbom, D. (1984) *Lisrel VI: analysis of linear structural relationships by the method of maximum likelihood*. Mooresville, IN: Scientific Software.

Judd, C. M. and Kenny, D. A. (1981) Process analysis: estimating mediation in treatment evaluations. *Evaluation Review*, 5, 602–19.

Kaplan, H. B. (1980) *Deviant behavior in defense of self*. New York: Academic Press.

Kaplan, H. B., Martin, S. S. and Robbins, C. (1984) Pathways to adolescent drug use: self-derogation, peer influence, weakening of social controls, and early substance use. *Journal of Health and Social Behavior*, 25, 270–89.

Komarovsky, M. (1940) *The unemployed man and his family: the effect of unemployment upon the status of the man in fifty-nine families*. New York: Dryden.

Krauth, J. and Lienert, G. A. (1982) Fundamentals and modifications of configural frequency analysis (CFA). *Interdisciplinaria*, 3, 1–14.

Lerner, J. V. and Lerner, R. M. (1983) Temperament and adaptation across the life: theoretical and empirical issues. In Baltes, P. B. and Brim, O. G., Jr (eds.) *Life-span development and behavior*, vol. 5. New York: Academic Press, pp. 198–231.

Liem, R. and Liem, J. (1978) Social class and mental illness reconsidered: the role of economic stress and social support. *Journal of Health and Social Behavior*, 19, 139–56.

Liker, J. K. and Elder, G. H., Jr (1983) Economic hardship and marital relations in the 1930s. *American Sociological Review*, 48, 343–59.

Miller, F. J. W., Court, S. D. M., Walton, W. S. and Knox, E. G. (1960) *Growing up in Newcastle upon Tyne*. London: Oxford University Press.

Miller, F. J. W., Court, S. D. M., Knox, E. G. and Brandon, S. (1974) *The school years in Newcastle upon Tyne*. London: Oxford University Press.

Miller, F. J. W., Kolvin, I. and Fells, H. (1985) Becoming deprived: a cross-generation study based on the Newcastle upon Tyne 1000-family survey. In Nichol, A. R. (ed.) *Longitudinal studies in child psychology and psychiatry*. Chichester: Wiley, pp. 223–40.

Moen, P., Kain, E. L. and Elder, G. H., Jr (1983) Economic conditions and family life: contemporary and historical perspectives. In Nelson, R. and Skidmore, F. (eds.) *American families and the economy: the high costs of living*. Washington, DC: National Academy Press, pp. 213–59.

Moos, R. H. (1974) *Family environment scale (FES): preliminary manual*. Palo Alto: Social Ecology Laboratory, Department of Psychiatry, Stanford University.

Patterson, G. R. and Stouthamer-Loeber, M. (1984) The correlation of family management practices and delinquency. *Child Development*, 55, 1299–1307.

Rockwell, R. C. and Elder, G. H., Jr (1982) Economic deprivation and problem behavior: childhood and adolescence in the Great Depression. *Human Development*, 25, 57–64.

Schaie, K. W. and Hertzog, C. (1982) Longitudinal methods. In Wolman, B. B., Stricker, G., Ellman, S. J., Keith-Spiegel, P. and Palermo, D. S. (eds.) *Handbook of developmental psychology*. Englewood Cliffs, NJ: Prentice-Hall, pp. 91–115.

Siegal, M. (1984) Economic deprivation and the quality of parent–child relations: a trickle-down framework. *Journal of Applied Developmental Psychology*, 5, 127–44.

Silbereisen, R. K. and Zank, S. (1984) Development of self-related cognitions in adolescents. In Schwarzer, R. (ed.) *The self in anxiety, stress and depression*. Amsterdam: North-Holland, pp. 49–60.

Silbereisen, R. K., Reitzle, M. and Zank, S. (1986) Stability and change of self-concept in adolescence: self-knowledge and self-strategies. In Klix, F. and Hagendorf, H. (eds.) *Human memory and cognitive capabilities: mechanisms and performances. Symposium in memoriam Hermann Ebbinghaus.* Amsterdam: North-Holland, pp. 449–57.

Spence, J. C., Walton, W. S., Miller, F. J. W. and Court, S. D. M. (1954) *A thousand families in Newcastle upon Tyne*. London: Oxford University Press.

Walper, S. (1988) *Familiäre Konsequenzen ökonomischer Deprivation*. Munich: Psychologie Verlags Union.

Walper, S. and Silbereisen, R. K. (1987a) Familiäre Konsequenzen ökonomischer Einbußen und ihre Auswirkungen auf die Bereitschaft zu normverletzendem Verhalten bei Jugendlichen. *Zeitschrift für Entwicklungspsychologie und Pädagogische Psychologie*, 19: 3, 228–48.

 (1987b) Economic loss, strained family relationships, and adolescents' contranormative attitudes. Paper held at the biennial meeting of the Society for Research in Child Development, 23–6 April, Baltimore, MD.

Werner, E. E. and Smith, R. S. (1982) *Vulnerable but invincible: a study of resilient children*. New York: McGraw-Hill.

Wood, Y. R. (1984) Social support and social networks: nature and measurement. In McReynolds, P. and Chelune, G. J. (eds.) *Advances in psychological assessment*, vol. 6. San Francisco: Jossey-Bass, pp. 312–53.

7 Follow-up of biological high-risk groups

Alex F. Kalverboer

Introduction

The early condition of the central nervous system (CNS) is of great importance for the organism's cognitive and behavioural development. The CNS is especially vulnerable in these most rapid, early phases of the developmental process (Dobbing, 1976). Early damage to the central nervous system can have strong effects on the organism's mental and behavioural development; however, this is not necessarily so, due to the great potential for functional recovery of the CNS: there does not exist a one-to-one relationship between early neurological condition and behavioural outcome.

During the last 20 to 30 years, there has been a shift from main effect models, with an overestimation of both constitutional and environmental direct contributions to developmental outcome, to more subtle concepts of complex interactions and transactions between the developing organism and its social and physical environment. We are learning more and more about these early phases of CNS development and also about early mechanisms in social and cognitive development. However, there is still a serious lack of knowledge on *how* early biological risk might have its effects on the individual's social and cognitive functioning.

The study of the effects of early biological risk factors for development is complicated by the great differences in various parts of the world with respect to mortality and morbidity. Infantile mortality remains a major concern in developing countries of the Third World. As the death rate in early life has fallen in industrialized nations, so increasingly attention has turned to the possibility that categories of children who would have died in days gone by remain represented in the morbidity statistics through behavioural and learning problems deriving from (often subtle) malfunctioning of the CNS (Werner, 1986). This implies that the study of the impact of early CNS damage and of the recovery or 'escape' from early biological risks has become a field of crucial importance in research.

There has been a growing interest in preventive health care since about 1950. In many countries nationwide screening programmes have been introduced for the detection of early risk factors (such as inborn errors of metabolism). In this connection, 'early' generally refers to pre-, peri- and neonatal periods. However, no sharp demarcation exists. Some genetic-

114

ally based risk factors, present since conception, may not manifest themselves until long after birth (Shields, 1980). In all instances the aim is to detect factors that may lead to a disorder (primary prevention) or to detect disorders at such an early state that the likelihood of a serious developmental course can be reduced (secondary and tertiary prevention).

There are very few well-defined specific biological risk factors that can be detected early and for which there is an adequate treatment. Congenital hypothyroidism (CH) and phenylketonuria (PKU) constitute exceptions but even with these conditions treatment is not always completely efficient and screening programmes may give false positives if they are done in such a way as to avoid false negatives. It is much more common for both biological risk factors and their possible effects to be vaguely defined, with the mediating mechanisms uncertain or unknown.

Biological risk and cause–effect relationships

Both the terms 'biological' and 'risk' present their specific difficulties. The term 'biological' is used in the literature with at least three different connotations (Kalverboer and Hopkins, 1983), signifying genetic (versus environmental), structural (versus functional) or adapted on the basis of an evolutionary process (versus adapted on the basis of extraneous cultural influences). In clinical psychiatry the term generally refers to brain structure or function, whereas in ethology, the term refers to an intrinsic relation between functionally adapted patterns of behaviour on the one hand and natural conditions on the other. Much confusion is due to these different connotations of the term 'biological'. Rose (1976) has presented a helpful model of a hierarchy of biological explanations (see Figure 1).

Rose, however, warns against attempts to postulate causal relationships between phenomena at various levels; causality is in the first instance a within-level category not a between-level category. Each level has its own set of concepts and we lack an adequate theory for postulating connections between phenomena at different levels of explanation.

There are also at least three implicit assumptions in the application of the term 'risk': knowledge of the adverse effects for development (often such knowledge is not available), knowledge of the place where a cutting point could be put between risk and non-risk values of a certain factor, and knowledge of the conditions under which a potential risk factor becomes a real danger for the development of the organism.

'Optimality' concept

Many so-called risk factors have no implications in isolation but become important in interaction with other factors. In recognition of this, Prechtl coined the term 'optimality' to describe the condition of the CNS as a risk factor. The term was later also applied to the domain of pre- and perinatal

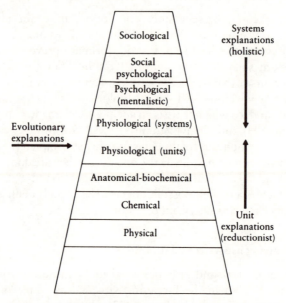

Figure 1   Hierarchies in biological explanation (Rose, 1976)

(obstetrical) complications that may affect the development of the CNS (Prechtl, 1977; 1980). Prechtl claimed that the term 'optimality' allows for a more precise definition of the quality of the CNS and the seriousness of factors that might adversely affect CNS development than the term 'risk'. Optimality refers to the 'best' (most adaptive) manifestation of a function, given a certain level of maturation (development) of the CNS. More generally, such an optimality concept allows for the ordering of values of functions/conditions within a certain domain (the domain of obstetrical complications, of neurological functions discernible in the neonate, etc.), along the dimension running from 'optimal' through 'less optimal' to 'non-optimal.'

The implicit assumption behind the optimality scores is that the more non-optimal signs there are, the more serious the condition is. Applied to the CNS this means that its quality is indicated by the number of optimal neurological signs. Therefore such an optimality score is considered as an index for the integrity of the central nervous system.

There are two problems in the application of this concept:

1 A thorough knowledge of the development of the CNS is necessary to decide whether a neurological function is optimal for that particular age.
2 It requires the availability of normative data.

The problem is exemplified in Figure 2 on the development of aquatic behaviour in the human infant.

Figure 2, derived from McGraw (1939), indicates that in the develop-

Figure 2 Three phases in the development of aquatic behaviour in the human infant. (A) Reflex swimming movements. (B) Disorganized behaviour. (C) Voluntary or deliberate movements. The drawings were made by tracing successive frames of 16 mm ciné film illustrating the quality of consecutive movements at different chronological ages and developmental stages (from McGraw, 1939)

ment of aquatic behaviour 'reflex swimming' is the rule for the one-month-old child, 'disorganized movements' are the rule for the five-month-old child and 'deliberate voluntary movements' are the rule for the one-year-old child. It is not easy to answer the question as to what would be optimal for the one-, five- or twelve-month-old child. Is a particular series of movements the full-blown function, as shown at one year of age, or is it the disorganized or reflex swimming pattern? And if it is not in all instances the fully developed pattern, what is the moment at which one description of optimal aquatic behaviour 'switches' to another?

Molfese and Thompson (1985) assessed the predictive power of two types of perinatal scale, namely the 'complications' scale and the 'optimality' scale, both of which are concerned with the neonatal status of the CNS as well as obstetrical history. Both types of scale predicted medical outcomes much better than they did behavioural measures. There was some association with neurobehavioural development in the neonatal period but neither scale provided substantial predictions of functioning in infancy or beyond. In general the predictive power of complications scales was somewhat stronger than that of optimality scales.

In conclusion, the optimality concept may be helpful when precise criteria for neuropathology are lacking. Where it is clear which features should be included in the index, although not how they hang together, it may serve roughly to categorize groups on the basis of the overall quality of CNS functioning. However, it has only a temporary value. Different types of dysfunction, such as hypertonia and hypotonia, with quite different implications for adaptive behaviour, are components of such an optimality score. It is not very useful merely to correlate such an optimality score, obtained in early development, with behavioural outcomes at a later age. Rather, it is necessary to complement such analyses with evaluations of specific subsystems, such as postural control or sensory motor functions (Touwen *et al.*, 1980). Consequently, the concept seems to be more applicable in the domain of developmental neurology, where such knowledge is to some extent available, than in other areas, where most diverse elements make up optimality scores.

Agreement on the definition of risk factors in the various domains (condition of nervous system, perinatal complications) is an important prerequisite for comparability of research findings. However, we lack adequate theories on which to base quantification of biological risk.

Brain-imaging techniques

Two factors have strongly complicated the detection of early brain pathology, namely the loose structure–function relationships in the developing nervous system and the lack of direct measures of brain function and dysfunction. Severe early brain damage may have benign effects on later functioning (see, for example, Windle's (1968) experimental studies using Rhesus monkeys). In humans, too, there is good clinical evidence that children who have suffered early brain damage may appear neurologically normal at a later age. Neurological examinations do not provide a direct assessment of CNS integrity.

The situation has changed, however, with the development of non-invasive brain-imaging techniques (Mazière, 1986; Roland, 1985; Ross, 1984; Hope and Reynolds, 1985). The first advance came in the 1970s with the advent of procedures that allowed examination of the structure of the brain and the ventricular system without the need for injection of air or radio-opaque dyes. Real-time ultrasound has become the method of choice for the imaging of the brains of newborns and infants (see, e.g., Pape *et al.*, 1979; and Thorburn *et al.*, 1982). It is able to detect peri-ventricular haemorrhage and parenchymal echo densities, and follow-up studies have shown that these are highly predictive of neuro-developmental abnormalities (such as cerebral palsy, developmental delay, and disorders of tone and reflexes) as assessed at one year of age (Stewart *et al.*, 1987). It allows for the assessment of congenital abnor-malities as well as ventricular size (Slovis, 1982; Slovis and Shankaran, 1984), and it is in widespread use now to evaluate hypoxic, ischemic insults and intracranial haemorrhage in preterm and term infants (Hill *et al.*, 1982). Important new insights into normal and abnormal develop-ment are provided by the ultrasound study of foetal motility (de Vries *et al.*, 1985).

In older age groups, computerized axial tomography (CT or CAT scans) perform a similar function. Early reports argued that findings suggestive of cortical atrophy or asymmetry might be useful in detecting 'minimal brain dysfunction' as indicated by signs of motor inco-ordination (Bergstrom and Bille, 1978). However, similar abnormalities have been found in a range of psychiatric disorders and it is evident that there are a variety of methodological problems in interpretations (Jaskiw *et al.*, 1987). Precise computerized quantification of ventricular size has helped in that connection. It is also possible now to measure tissue densities and, although this is prone to artefact (Jacobson *et al.*, 1985), it carries the promise of being able to detect subtle abnormalities in brain structure.

Nuclear magnetic resonance imaging (NMR or MRI) became available in the 1980s and ultimately it may take over from CT scans (see Jaskiw *et al.*, 1987; Levine, 1985; and Rea *et al.*, 1985, for reviews). It relies on the detection of radiofrequency signals from the spin and wobble of photons when placed in a strong magnetic field. The major advantage of NMR over CT scans is in the excellent grey–white matter resolution that it provides. NMR uses hydrogen nuclei to generate structural information but because it can also use other elements it carries the potential of studying amino-acid metabolism, and hence brain function as well as brain structure (Hope and Reynolds, 1985).

Finally, there are the brain-imaging techniques explicitly designed to assess brain function (Morihisa, 1987). Xenon inhalation was the first of these methods through its use in the measurement of regional cerebral blood flow; however, it has little ability to investigate subcortical structures. Nevertheless, cerebral blood flow can be used as an indicator of neuronal activity (Roland and Friberg, 1985) and it has been employed to study regional activation in relation to particular mental or perceptual motor functions. Positron emission tomography (PET) uses positron emitting radio-isotopes to create three-dimensional maps of brain metabolism. Glucose has been most used for this purpose but potentially the method can allow study of the activity of a range of neurotransmitters, as well as regional metabolic activity associated with different types of mental task demand. Single photon emission computed tomography (SPECT) provides an alternative approach based on the detection of gamma radiation from single-photon-emitting radionuclides.

At about the same time as the new imaging techniques arrived on the scene, advances in the computerized analysis of electrophysiological data began to provide the means of studying the brain in action through measurement of responses to stimuli or task performance. The study of event-related potentials (ERP) is one approach that has promise (see Courchesne and Yeung-Courchesne, 1988) and neurometrics (the computerized combination of a variety of electrophysiological measures) is another (Prichep *et al.*, 1983). Neither is yet at the stage for clinical application to individual patients, but interesting group comparisons have been made.

So far, all these techniques are in their infancy, but they have greatly extended our capacity to study brain function and malfunction. Exploration of the links between brain activity and behavioural functioning or psychological development has scarcely begun, but the potential is there.

The definition of 'effects' of brain damage
In research and clinical practice explicit criteria are required for the diagnosis of the possible sequelae of early risk factors. Such diagnostic criteria should be clearly, unambiguously defined and should be operationalized in terms of well-validated measuring instruments and procedures. Unfortunately this is not the case for many frequently used clinical categories, such as 'minimal brain dysfunction', hyperactivity and dyslexia, despite all the international efforts to improve diagnostic systems. The problem is that there is a lack of agreement on the concepts, and hence on the disorders that they are intended to encompass. The 'minimal brain dysfunction' (MBD) concept is a case in point. The initial assumption was that particular patterns of behaviour could be used to

infer CNS malfunction. However, precise observational studies have shown the looseness of the connection between neurological and behavioural variables (Kalverboer, 1975; 1979).

At the behavioural level MBD can be considered as a waste-basket. At least four groups of phenomena can be subordinated under the term MBD, namely:

1 Disorders of attention and concentration, with or without hyperactivity.
2 Disorders in the organization of body postures and movements, often termed 'clumsiness'.
3 Specific learning disorders, such as dyslexia and dyscalculia.
4 Disorders in social interactive and emotional functions (anxiety, impulsivity, aggressiveness, poor verbal communication, etc.).

These groups can be represented by various individual behavioural profiles. Intercorrelations between them are often mildly positive (as between hyperactivity and disturbed social behaviour), but they can be negative (as between hyperactivity and clumsiness – Kalverboer, in press). The internal consistency within groups can be rather low (inattention may be present without hyperactivity, or the reverse).

Recent diagnostic refinements have slightly improved the situation. Conceptually ambiguous terms like MBD have been replaced by behavioural diagnoses, such as attentional deficit disorder with hyperactivity (ADD(H)). However, to some extent the improvement is illusory. Confusion over the nature of inattention is nearly as great as it was over MBD.

Research by Sergeant and van der Meere (Sergeant, 1981; van der Meere and Sergeant, 1987) has shown that children with so-called ADD(H) do *not* show the impairment in sustained attention that is thought to characterize the attention deficit (see Schneider and Shiffrin, 1977; and Shiffrin and Schneider, 1977). When these children are brought into the right experimental conditions, they do not demonstrate any attentional deficit in terms of the model; neither their focused attention nor their sustained attention is disturbed. The only consistent finding in this series of experiments was that the children were slightly slower in handling information, irrespective of variations in task load.

A similar story can be told for other clinical entities such as dyslexia. There are widely differing subclassifications (Decker and deFries, 1981; Vernon, 1979) and contrasting views on the processes involved in relationships between dyslexia and antisocial behaviour (see Sturge, 1982). It is completely fruitless to look for specific risks for such ambiguous entities. The prerequisite for progress in research and the improvement of clinical practice is agreement on concepts and diagnostic criteria. Both DSM-III (American Psychiatric Association, 1980) and ICD 9 (World Health Organization, 1978), the two most widely used classification systems, lack adequate operationalization of many categories.

Empirical research is needed to test diagnostic concepts, but also better theories are required in order to bridge the gap between field and laboratory.

Mediating factors between 'risk' and 'effects'

Problems in the definitions of 'risk' and 'effects' only partly explain the lack of clarity of association between early biological risk factors and later disorders. Most crucially we lack knowledge about the mediating factors and how they work. This is illustrated by the fact that in retrospective studies more pre- and perinatal complications are reported for individuals with most types of psychiatric disorder than for controls, whereas in prospective studies, almost no substantial relationships have been found between early biological risk factors and later psychopathology (see Bellak, 1978, for a review of retrospective studies; and Sameroff and Chandler, 1975, for a review of the impact of early biological risk factors). Evidently, knowledge about conditions under which certain risk factors may have adverse effects for development is still very limited. Of course, in view of the continuous reorganization of behaviour during development one may seriously doubt whether substantial relationships can ever be found between 'risk' factors early in life and behavioural deviance in later childhood. However, ignorance regarding the mechanisms means that the limits of our predictive powers remain unknown.

Evidently, many pieces of the puzzle have already been suggested as important biological and contextual variables which may affect the impact of specific risk factors. Touwen *et al.* (1980) pointed to the very limited prognostic value of separate risk factors. Obstetrical risk factors lead to adverse sequelae only when combined with low neurological optimality scores. Similarly, the contribution of asphyxia at birth to neonatal dysfunction is strongly dependent on additional factors, such as low birth weight, foetal growth retardation or complications during pregnancy (Dijxhoorn, 1986). Interaction and transaction models have come 'into vogue' during the last two decades, with increasing attention being paid to the influence of social context on the developmental impact of early biological risk factors. Factors at the *macro-level* include maternal psychiatric disorder, familial discord, paternal criminality, and hospitalization of the child (see Rutter and Madge, 1976). Traditionally, socioeconomic status was considered the key social variable, but it is evident now that this overall concept includes a variety of family risk variables that need separate specification. Factors at the *micro-level* that may modify the impact of early biological risk include parental sensitivity to the child's signals, patterns of acceptance, and goodness of fit between the child's temperament and the parents' behavioural patterns. That both biological and psychosocial risk factors are important is clear; moreover, it seems probable that one may potentiate the other. However, the mechanisms involved in such interactions remain largely unknown. There are large individual differences in vulnerability for the development of deviant behaviour. In this respect, Waddington's (1975) notion of a 'self-righting tendency of the organism' may be a fruitful concept (see also Dunn, 1976; and Bateson, 1978). Evidently, there are genetically based differences in vulnerability to stress but how they operate remains obscure.

Pre-, peri- and postnatal risk factors

Traditionally there has been a strong emphasis on biological risk factors that operate in the *early* developmental process. The assumption has been that the earlier a risk factor occurs, the stronger the impact for development. A growing system is thought to be particularly vulnerable to biological hazards (Dobbing and Smart, 1974). Potentially, it might be thought that the possiblities for minimizing negative sequelae were greatest when there was early identification of risk. Mortality, for instance, is some four times as high during the first two months as in the subsequent ten months, dropping still further after the first year. Many handicaps, such as congenital malformations, some types of deafness and blindness, and cerebral palsy, stem from pre- and perinatal disorders. Niswander and Gordon (1972) estimated that approximately 10% of the American population suffer from disorders that manifest themselves shortly after birth.

Predictive power can be improved by going to earlier phases of development. An abnormal electrocardiogram, which is indicative of asphyxia, can be obtained even before birth (Dijxhoorn, 1986). It has a higher predictive power for neonatal neurological morbidity than is the case with perinatal measures, such as blood-gas values and Apgar scores (this is especially the case in growth-retarded foetuses). In a study on relationships between foetal growth retardation and neurological condition at four and six years of age, neurological deviance was found only in those cases where chronic asphyxia was already present before birth. Moreover, in early screening programmes for metabolic disorders (such as for congenital hypothyroidism and phenylketonuria) it became evident that some children were already brain-damaged before birth.

Risk and protection in early CNS development
There is not a simple linear relationship between (gestational) age and vulnerability. Ebels (1980) referred to 'changing patterns of *selective vulnerability*'. Effects of noxious factors generally depend on the maturational state of the system. Proliferating cells are especially vulnerable to agents such as X-rays and toxins. Some noxious factors are particularly damaging to immature organisms; however, some others have a prefer-

ence for mature cells (such as the virus of poliomyelitis – Jilek *et al.*, 1964). On the other hand sensitivity to anoxia increases with increased maturation of cells. Clearly the rule 'the quicker the growth of a certain system, the more vulnerable it is' is not generally true. A further point is that animal species differ in their timing of growth (e.g. the rat is very immature at birth compared with the pig). In man, brain weight increases exponentially after birth; a newborn's brain weight is approximately 350 grams, whereas adult brains have a weight of 1,300 grams (in women) to 1,350 grams (in males). In man, the time scale is much longer than in lower animals; consequently, vulnerable periods are both more extensive and less well defined in humans.

Roughly there are three phases in early brain development (Parmelee and Sigman, 1983). In the first phase (in man until about one month before birth), cortical neurones are largely protected against stimulation. Brain maturation seems to go its own way. This is due to the fact that brain and central sensory pathways develop functionally somewhat ahead of the peripheral receptors. In the second phase, external sensory stimulation becomes very important. Defects will occur in its absence. Here, ethology has provided us with a wealth of data from non-human as well as from human primates. This period is thought to be the period of fine tuning, where the effects of first experiences depend on the maturity of the brain. In humans this is thought to last from approximately the last month before, to several months after, birth. The third phase is characterized, in humans, by rapid cognitive growth, some aspects of which may not be dependent on major identifiable structural changes in terms of synaptic or axonic/dendritic growth. In this stage there is an integration of previous sensory perceptions with as yet no recognized structural correlations.

Risk and protective factors play a major role in the early structural and functional development of the brain and of the auditory and visual systems. Although in recent years there have been rapid developments in neurosciences, we are still far away from a theoretical basis for linking complex cognitive and social developments to structural changes in the brain.

Early biological risk factors

In our series of follow-up studies over the last twenty years we have found only minor differences in neurological and psychological outcome at five and ten years that were attributable to obstetric or neonatal biological risk factors of mild to moderate degree (see Kalverboer, 1975; 1979). Two types of finding are most prominent in the literature as a whole. First, early biological risk factors have the most serious impact on children's further development if they grow up in social disadvantage. Thus Werner *et al.* (1971), in the Kauai longitudinal study, found strong interaction effects between perinatal risk variables and social circumstances with respect to physical and mental development. At two years of age perinatal complications were associated with a 5–7 Developmental Quotient points deficit in the higher social economic subgroup, but a 19–37 point difference in the lower social strata. The possible mechanisms involved have been an important topic of study from about 1975 onwards (Werner, 1986; Werner and Smith, 1982).

The second main finding concerns the very limited prognostic value of *specific* risk factors of all kinds when considered in isolation. Even in combination predictive power is still limited. Scarcely any meaningful relationships have been found between specific perinatal risk factors and psychological measures after the first year of extra-uterine life (apart, of course, from sequelae in children with overt neurodevelopmental disorders). However, it goes too far to claim that the importance of perinatal factors 'pales in comparison to the massive influences of socioeconomic factors on both prenatal and postnatal development' (as stated by Sameroff and Chandler, 1975, p. 192). This statement is an overgeneralization because, not surprisingly, the relative importance of the two domains of risk factors varies with their seriousness.

Prematurity and early growth retardation (low birth weight)
The problems in searching for causal connections between biological risk and later cognitive and social emotional development are evident from the variety of developmental outcomes in groups at risk (Kopp, 1983). From the early 1960s onwards, when simple linear models were abandoned, the focus has been on the possible explanations for the well-demonstrated marked individual differences in outcome. System-analytic approaches have been applied and complex catalogues of protective and risk factors have been produced (see Werner, 1986). Rather than review those individually, I shall discuss the conceptual and methodological issues involved, using prematurity and low birth weight as exemplars of a recognized risk factor.

Prematurity is usually defined in terms of gestational age (e.g. before 37 weeks), and dysmaturity, or early growth retardation, in terms of birth weight (e.g. less than 2,500 grams). Even within ethnically homogeneous populations these cutting points are very arbitrary because there may be uncertainty about the precise date of conception and, more particularly, because of the large normal biological variation in the defining parameters. Such cutting-point problems are even larger in multi-ethnic, mixed societies as found in most countries. Concomitants of both maturity and dysmaturity also vary. Sometimes there is a direct connection with some associated factor (e.g. prematurity and thyroid dysfunction), sometimes they are unconnected, and often we simply do not know (for example, we lack data on the differences in intra-uterine experiences between pre-term and full-term infants). The definition of risk groups is

126   *Alex F. Kalverboer*

problematic if concomitant risk factors are not taken into account. However, the mere listing of risk factors is no answer; knowledge about their interdependencies is also required and often this is lacking. In summary, biological risk research is hampered by a lack of clarity on the validity of pre- and perinatal risk indices by the limited reliability of some measures, and by the uncertainties involved in extrapolations across socio-cultural groups.

The loose connections between risk indices and risk mechanisms
Particular attention has been paid to two main groups of factors thought likely to influence developmental outcomes, namely (a) the 'integrative' capacities of the CNS and (b) the quality of the care-giving environment. Thus trauma may prevent the proper functioning of the organism's self-righting capacities, and adverse forces may prevent normal integration (see Sameroff and Chandler, 1975; and Werner, 1986).

There are only weak relationships between prematurity and low birth weight as risk *indices*, on the one hand, and the risk *mechanisms*, such as impaired integrative capacity of the CNS, by which adverse sequelae are thought to be brought about, on the other. As the brain-imaging studies have shown, there is gross brain damage in only a minority of cases. Nevertheless, there are modest statistical relationships between perinatal risk indices and indicators of CNS dysfunction, such as irregularity of the sleep–wake pattern, problems in postural control, and inconsistencies in motor and sensory function. These indicators may reflect CNS damage, but equally they may reflect a temporary interference with function in the absence of damage. Similarly, the effects of development may be either direct or indirect (with sequelae a consequence of interference between the infant and its social environment). Thus there may be impairment in the development of secure attachment relationships or in feelings of competence. Two core aspects of the integrity of the CNS, early behavioural organization and the temporal regulation of behaviour, seem to be involved in risk mechanisms.

The CNS can be considered as an 'apparatus' for information-processing. As Prechtl (1982, p. 29) put it:

The nervous system is now seen as an information processing apparatus in that it *generates* activity, receives, transmits, conducts, transforms, stores and compares messages. With the aid of these processes it *initiates* and keeps neural activity going, it *regulates* non-neural functions such as respiration, circulation, thermal balance, food intake and many others, it *adapts* the organism's posture and orientation in space, adapts social behaviour states to the demands of the environment. Furthermore, it may *anticipate* events and may change responses according to previously *stored* experiences (habituation and learning). By no means is the nervous system an instrument which becomes only active by the grace of stimuli; on the contrary, it may seek for particular stimuli.

Care-taking has to respond to these characteristics of the organism. Even the very young child has a highly organized behavioural repertoire that allows for a flexible adaptation to the environment. Examples can be found in orienting behaviour, sucking and rooting movements (Prechtl, 1958; Papousek, 1977). Already in the first weeks of life, children show highly developed skills in the perception of depth, acoustical discrimination and imitation (Bower, 1974; Meltzoff and Moore, 1977). The newborn is already able to relate information from various sensory and motor areas to each other. Meltzoff and Moore hypothesized 'supra sensorial representation of functions' as a mechanism. This is still a strongly debated concept.

Behavioural reactions depend on the behavioural state of the child. A healthy newborn has a characteristic organization of sleep and wake states; other vital functions (such as sucking and crying) also have a periodic character. This temporal organization of behaviour seems to be an important determinant of social reactions from the environment. The care-taker makes use of it in the interaction processes and adapts behaviour to fluctuations of the child's state and orientation. Alberts *et al.* (1983) found that both child and mother have their own periodicities in behaviour. The child exhibits alternations between periods of sucking and pausing and the mother shows temporal patterning in her tactile stimulation of the child. Moreover, the mother adapts her pattern of tactile stimulation so that it mainly occurs during the pauses in the child's sucking. Some researchers consider this pattern of alternation as a precursor of the later process of role-taking (Kaye, 1977).

If this organization of behavioural states is upset, that could have repercussions for the ability of the care-taker to respond appropriately to the child. One may postulate that the less stable the behavioural organization of the child, the more difficult it is for the mother to vary her behaviour in correspondence with that of the child. This, in turn, may have effects on the child's cognitive processes. Thus Seligman (1974) introduced the concept of 'learned helplessness' to describe feelings of 'lack of perceived control over the environment'. This state of learned helplessness would be more likely to arise if the child lived in situations in which no consistent relationships could be perceived between vital behaviours and their effects.

Some individuals have a higher chance to develop signs of 'learned helplessness' than others. Children with a rather unstable behavioural pattern, as is often found in relation to early neurological disorders, may be at higher risk. Behavioural inconsistencies and stereotypes are well-known manifestations of early neurological disorder; in both instances there is a lack of flexible adaptation to variations in the environment, which in turn makes it more difficult for the social partner to react sensitively to the child. A promising line in early risk research is the close follow-up of children with a 'non-optimal' early behavioural organization, which may negatively affect the development of attachment relationships and competence.

However, such refined analyses are only focusing on a limited fragment of the social structure. Studies at macro-level have to be added. Seligman and his co-workers (1979) have reformulated their helplessness theory; they postulate that the chronicity and generality of signs of helplessness and depression partly depend on the attribution style of the individual. Individuals who tend to ascribe the uncontrollability of events to internal, stable, global factors are thought to be most at risk.

Main-effect, interactional and transactional models

Main-effect models, following a nature–nurture dichotomy, postulate independent effects of constitutional and environmental factors on the development of behavioural deviance. Many follow-up studies based on early biological risk factors have shown that such factors account for only a small proportion of the behavioural variance at ages later than two years. The correlations are too low to allow for any prediction in individual cases. Main-effect models are applicable only in very extreme conditions, as with serious brain damage that leads to severe mental retardation, cerebral palsy and the like.

Follow-up studies based on models that postulate an interaction between constitution and environmental conditions show statistically significant relationships between early biological complications and deviance at a later age. However, such models are too static to detect the developmental mechanisms involved. Characteristics of child and environment change over time, partly in dependence on each other. More dynamic concepts than social economic status (SES) or constitution were needed; Sameroff and Chandler's (1975) 'transactional model' aimed to meet this need. They argued, in the tradition of Piaget's notions of assimilation and accommodation in individual development, that children actively organize and structure their environment and that development involves a continuing mutual influence between the organism and its surroundings. The implication is that potentially all elements in a system may affect the development of all others and that there are no inherently stable characteristics of either individuals or their circumstances (see also Sameroff *et al.*, 1982).

Sameroff and Chandler's ideas had a far-ranging influence on the study of early biological risk. From about 1975 onwards longitudinal studies sought to chart transactions between child and environment through repeated measurements over time of child characteristics and features of the environment. In a few instances, statistical techniques like path analysis and LISREL (analysis of linear structural relationships) were used to examine mutual dependencies (see Hagekull and Berit, 1982, for an example using children's temperament in groups at risk).

The transaction model presupposes *continuous* behavioural changes in each of the interacting partners during development, in part through mutual dependence. In practice, however, most research has taken some risk factor (such as prematurity or neonatal hyperexcitability) as a starting condition and followed this by repeated measurements of selected characteristics of children and their environments. Intercorrelations between successive measurements are then used to make inferences about continuities and discontinuities in development and about the mutual dependence of dyadic partners. The notion that young children and their care-takers mutually shape each other's behaviour has been taken up in longitudinal studies of 'temperament'. The basic concept is that there are inter-individual differences in biologically rooted styles of behaviour. Such differences are thought to affect children's interactions with their social environment.

Early temperament and developmental risk

Modern research into temperament originated from Thomas, Chess and Birch's New York Longitudinal Study (Thomas *et al.*, 1963; Thomas and Chess, 1977). Temperament was considered to refer to 'the behavioural style of the individual', 'the *how* of behaviour'. Differences in behavioural style of children and social partners would imply differences in transactions during the developmental process. Thomas *et al.* distinguished nine dimensions of temperament (e.g. 'activity level', 'rhythmicity of biological function' and 'approach–withdrawal').

During the last three decades investigators have varied in whether they have viewed temperament as confined to genetically determined characteristics or rather have used the term in a purely descriptive sense to refer to behavioural characteristics that tend to be pervasive over situations and persistent over time. The choice of the term 'temperament', with its historical connotation of a basis in body type and hereditary factors, was perhaps unfortunate as Thomas *et al.* considered that temperamental traits are likely to be influenced by environmental circumstances. Since 1970 numerous symposia and review articles have been concerned with temperament and over 20 scales (most of dubious validity and reliability) have been introduced for its measurement.

Thomas and Chess did not assume that any particular type of temperament would lead directly to problems in psychosocial development. Rather, it was hypothesized that the developmental impact of temperamental features would depend on the congruence ('goodness of fit') between the child's behaviour and environmental demands and expectations (see also Lerner and Lerner, 1983).

In recent times there has been increasing interest in a temperamental constellation termed 'difficult temperament' (Carey, 1985). The concept is in keeping with transactional models in its emphasis on the likelihood that care-givers will find some behaviours more difficult than others and that that will shape parent–child interactions. However, it seems contradictory that it has been defined in a way that presupposes that the same behaviours will prove 'difficult' in all circumstances. It is true that characteristics such as high emotional intensity, negative mood and low adaptability form a rather coherent group of phenomena that tend to be predictive of later behavioural problems (see Maziade and Capéraà, 1985). Nevertheless, the implications of temperamental differences for later development seem to be strongly dependent on socio-cultural and material circumstances. For example, 'arhythmicity' in sleep–wake cycles poses problems for white middle-class families in the United States, who expect their children to follow predictable routines, but not for Puerto Rican families, whose expectations are different (Korn and Gammon, 1983). Similarly, de Vries (1984) found that Masai infants with a 'difficult' temperament were *more* likely than other infants to survive severe drought conditions in the lower Sahara area. It seems that 'difficult' infants were better able than those with an 'easy' temperament to elicit maternal care-giving behaviour. Both sets of data are compatible with the goodness-of-fit model. However, such suppositions can be crucially tested only if multivariate measurements of aspects of temperament and contextual variables are obtained repeatedly over time and related to each other. As yet, such analyses are lacking.

Carey (1985) summarized the clinical conditions that may affect temperamental development:

1 Prenatal conditions (genetic deviations, chromosome disorders, etc.).
2 Stress during pregnancy and birth.
3 Postnatal damage to the central nervous system.
4 Nutritional deficiences.
5 Conditions like mental retardation and 'cerebral palsy'.
6 Allergies, endocrine disorders (such as congenital hypothyroidism).

As yet, this enumeration of factors is only suggestive, because we lack good data on the connections between such risk factors and the development of temperament. Unfortunately, much research on temperament lacks the theoretical clarity and methodological rigour necessary for the longitudinal study of neurobehavioural relationships in children.

There is a lack of reliable and well-validated instruments, with, as a good exception, Bates' Infant Characteristics Questionnaire (Bates *et al.*, 1979). A Dutch adaptation of this questionnaire has been applied in a large study on the social development of so-called hyperexcitable children (Swets-Gronert, 1986).

The characteristics of 'high activity level', 'low attention span' and 'impulsivity' are key features in both temperamental research and the study of the clinical syndrome of attention deficit disorder with hyperactivity. Unfortunately, there has been a lack of theoretical and methodological coherence between these two lines of study. The longitudinal study of biological risk would profit considerably from a fundamental reflection on concepts and research diagnostic tools, applied in various stages of development.

Ethology and information-processing in risk research

Approaches to early risk

Ethology and information-processing both constitute approaches that have much to offer in the study of early biological risk for psychopathology.

Two key notions characterize the ethological approach: (a) the concept of an intrinsic relationship between the organism and its (natural) environment (in Papousek's opinion an inborn co-ordination meets a suitable stimulation (Papousek, 1977)) and (b) the view that the developing organism actively explores the environment. Intrinsic relationships between behavioural systems and the environment are studied, guided by the following types of question: How is the behaviour of partners functionally organized? What is the spatial and temporal structure of the behaviour? and Which rules govern interaction processes? (Kalverboer and Hopkins, 1983). The organism is equipped with highly organized, functionally adaptive behavioural patterns, which develop in a complex interplay with the social environment. Consequently, there is much interest in periodic/rhythmic basic processes (sleep–wake–alternation, regulation of wake states) that directly affect the reactivity of the organism (Kalverboer, 1983). Disorders in the early behavioural organization and regulation of behavioural states may have repercussions for the social and cognitive development of the organism, and an ethological approach can make an important contribution to our insight into the repercussions of such problems for individual development.

A good example of how an ethological and a system-analytic approach can fertilize each other in developing useful models for core phenomena in human development is given by Bischof (1975). Bischof drafted a 'causal' network of interacting observable and hypothetical factors that can account for basic processes in attachment development. This model simulates the transaction from a stage of attachment to familiar conspecifics and fear of strangers to a stage of detachment from the familiar and exploration of the stranger. It is a control model from which testable hypotheses can be derived. It seems that students of human attachment development have not yet made sufficient use of such formulations.

In learning psychology, strong emphasis is laid on contingencies between behaviours and effects and their effect on the perception of control. Initially, attention was mainly paid to inconsistencies with respect to the external stimulation of the organism. In later stages organismic factors that might affect processes of operant learning came into focus. The approach has much to offer in the study of normal and deviant interactions.

Experimental–psychological models allow for the systematic study of structural and functional disorders of information-processing. Although experimental approaches have rarely been applied below the age of five, in principle they can be adapted for lower ages. In this information-processing approach, the organism is considered as a system with a limited capacity for processing information. Therefore it is bound to react selectively. In the course of development the system can 'save' capacity by handling certain information automatically. By doing so, capacity can be reserved for problems that demand a controlled handling of information. Consequently, after sufficient development and training, skills like locomotion or adjustment of body postures can occur without attention. When these skills become automatic, they can be combined with other behaviours that do demand specific processing. Thus a child can write and, at the same time, concentrate on the content of what is being written. Similarly, an experienced driver can negotiate traffic while holding a conversation with a passenger. Structural limitations in information-processing capacity concern stimulus selection and response selection as well as response execution. In groups at risk, such processes may be slower than normal. This was found to be the case in many ADD(H) children (Sergeant and Scholten, 1985; and van der Meere and Sergeant, 1987).

It is also possible that reactions that are automatic in the normally developed individual demand controlled processing in children with handicaps. Thus automatization of responses may be impaired in children with minor neurological signs. It seems that many of these children have a less stable processing of information. One can postulate that this lability may be associated with less stable physiological processes and with a less stable behavioural regulation. Porges (1976) used the term 'autonomic imbalance' to refer to a lack of balance between the activity of the parasympathetic and the sympathetic nervous system. In this theory sympathetic and parasympathetic reactions are under the control of a central neurotransmission system that may be affected by stimulants; this is one rationale for their use to treat hyperactivity. Some workers consider that such stimulants restore the balance between autonomic subsystems, a process that suggests autonomic imbalance in the untreated individual. Higher and more variable heart rhythms may play a role in attentional deficits in children. Such an 'autonomic imbalance' may manifest itself in very early stages of development, indicated by disorders in sleep–wake regulation and the child's inability to maintain a state of alertness during a longer time.

Analysis of clinical entities, such as ADD(H) in terms of an information-processing model can make an important contribution to the study of sequelae of early biological risk factors. Important questions remain on how the organism copes with a high information load and how it makes use of compensatory mechanisms in case of (sensory or motor based) information-processing deficits.

Problems and perspectives

Basic research is essential in order to enable biological risk factors to be identified early and to develop appropriate strategies for dealing with risk groups in preventive health care. Such research is methodologically difficult, if only because of the complexity of transactions between individuals and their social and physical environment during the developmental process. There are problems in the definition of 'determinants', 'effects' and 'mediators'. In this respect the development of well-described diagnostic categories and theoretically based measurement instruments is of the utmost importance.

Research focusing on the sequelae of early biological risk factors has four key intrinsic problems:

1 The long time lapse between the first manifestations of risk and their possible effects requiring longitudinal studies over a large time period.
2 The difficulty in defining behavioural disorders in various stages of development in a theoretically consistent way.
3 Difficulties in the early assessment of the central nervous system.
4 The continuous reorganization of behaviour during development.

The optimism of the 1950s that it would be possible to predict developmental outcomes in later childhood on the basis of pre- and perinatal history has disappeared. However, we now have improved techniques and methods for a precise study of brain-behaviour relationships from the earliest phase of development onwards. There are growing insights into the reciprocal relationships between characteristics of the child and of the social environment. At the same time, more suitable statistical techniques are available for the analysis of complex transactions. Important technical and theoretical advances have come from neurophysiology, ethology and information-processing theory. The best practical tool is a good theory. This is particularly important in the study of biological high-risk groups, which until recently was mainly 'atheoretical' and 'descriptive' in character.

References

Alberts, E., Kalverboer, A. F. and Hopkins, B. (1983) Mother–infant dialogue in the first days of life: an observational study during breast-feeding. *Journal of Child Psychology and Psychiatry*, **24**, 145–61.

American Psychiatric Association (1980) *Diagnostic and statistical manual of mental disorders (DSM-III)*. Washington, DC: APA.

Bates, J. E., Freeland, C. A. and Loundsbury, M. L. (1979) Measurement of infant difficultness. *Child Development*, **50**, 794–803.

Bateson, P. P. G. (1978) How does behavior develop? In Bateson, P. P. G. and Klopfer, P. H. (eds.) *Perspectives in ethology*, vol. 3. New York: Plenum Press, pp. 55–66.

Bellak, L. (1978) *Psychiatric aspects of minimal brain dysfunction in adults*. New York: Grune and Stratton.

Bergstrom, K. and Bille, B. (1978) Computed tomography of the brain in children with minimal brain damage: a preliminary study of 46 children. *Neuropädiatrie*, 9:4, 378–84.

Bischof, N. (1975) A systems approach toward the functional connections of attachment and fear. *Child Development*, 46, 801–17.

Bower, T. G. R. (1974) Development of infant behaviour. *British Medical Bulletin*, 30, 175–8.

Carey, M. D. (1985) Interactions of temperament and clinical conditions. In Wolraich, M. and Raith, D. K. (eds.) *Advances in development and behavioural pediatrics*, vol. 6. Greenwich, CT: JAI Press.

Courchesne, E. and Yeung-Courchesne, R. (1988) Event-related brain potentials: a critical assessment of the use of this method in research on developmental psychopathologies. In Rutter, M., Tuma, H. and Lann, I. (eds.) *Assessment, diagnosis and classification of child and adolescent psychopathology*. New York: Guilford Press.

Decker, S. N. and deFries, J. C. (1981) Cognitive ability profiles in families of reading-disabled children. *Developmental Medicine and Child Neurology*, 23, 217–27.

De Vries, J. I. P., Visser, G. H. A. and Prechtl, H. F. R. (1985) The emergency of fetal behavior, II. Quantitative aspects. *Early Human Development*, 12, 99–120.

De Vries, M. W. (1984) Temperament and infant mortality among the Masai of East Africa. *American Journal of Psychiatry*, 141, 1189–94.

Dijxhoorn, M. J. (1986) Asphyxia at birth and neonatal neurological morbidity. Ph.D. thesis, University of Groningen.

Dobbing, J. (1976) Vulnerable periods in brain growth and somatic growth. In Roberts, D. F. and Thomson, A. M. (eds.) *The biology of human fetal growth*. London: Taylor and Francis, pp. 137–47.

Dubbing, J. and Smart, J. L. (1974) Vulnerability of developing brain and behaviour. *British Medical Bulletin*, 30, 164–71.

Dunn, J. (1976) How far do early differences in mother-child relations affect later development? In Bateson, P. P. G. and Hinde, R. A. (eds.) *Growing points in ethology*. Cambridge: Cambridge University Press, pp. 481–96.

Ebels, E. J. (1980) Maturation of the central nervous system. In Rutter, M. (ed.) *Scientific foundations of development psychiatry*. London: Heinemann, pp. 25–39.

Hagekull, K. and Berit, K. (1982) *Measurement of behavioural differences in infancy*. Uppsala, Sweden: Acta Univ. Uppsala.

Hill, A., Melson, L., Clark, B. and Volpe, J. J. (1982) Hemorrhagic periventricular leukomalacia: diagnosis by real time ultrasound and correlation with autopsy findings. *Pediatrics*, 69, 282–91.

Hope, P. L. and Reynolds, E. O. R. (1985) Metabolism in newborn infants. *Clinics in Perinatology*, 12, 261–75.

Jacobson, R. R., Turner, S. W., Baldy, R. E. and Lishman, W. A. (1985) Densitometric analysis of scans: important sources of artefact. *Psychological Medicine*, 15, 879–89.

Jaskiw, G. E., Andreasen, N. C. and Weinberger, D. R. (1987) X-ray computed tomography in magnetic resonance imaging in psychiatry. In Hales, R. E. and Frances, A. J. (eds.) *American Psychiatric Association annual review*, vol. 6. Washington, DC: American Psychiatric Press, pp. 260–99.

Jilek, L., Fischer, J., Krulich, L. and Trojan, S. (1964) The reaction of the brain to stagnant hypoxia and anoxia during ontogeny. In Himwich, W. E. and Himwich H. E. (eds.) *Progress in brain research*, vol. 9, *The developing brain*. Amsterdam: Elsevier, pp. 113–31.

Kalverboer, A. F. (1975) *A neurobehavioural study in preschool children.* Clinics in developmental medicine, vol. 54. London: Heinemann.
(1979) Neurobehavioural findings in preschool and school-aged children in relation to pre- and perinatal complications. In Shaffer, D. and Dunn, J. (eds.) *The first year of life.* New York: Wiley, pp. 55–67.
(1983) Neurobehavioural organization at early age and risk for psychopathology. In Mendlewicz, J. and van Praag, H. M. (eds.) *Biological rhythms and behaviour, Advances in biological psychiatry,* vol. 11. Basel: Karger.
(in press) Hyperactivity and observational studies. In Sergeant, J. A. and Bloomingdale, L. F. M. *Attention deficit disorder,* vol. 6. New York: Spectrum.
Kalverboer, A. F. and Hopkins, B. (1983) General introduction: a biopsychological approach to the study of human behaviour. *Journal of Child Psychology and Psychiatry,* 24, 9–10.
Kaye, K. (1977) Towards the origin of dialogue. In Schaffer, H. R. (ed.) *Studies of mother–infant interaction.* London: Academic Press.
Kopp, C. B. (1983) Risk factors in development. In Haith, M. M. and Campos, J. J. (eds.) *Infancy and developmental psychobiology, Handbook of child psychology,* ed. P. Mussen, vol. 2. New York: Wiley, pp. 1081–1188.
Korn, S. and Gammon, S. (1983) Temperament, culture variation and behavior disorders in preschool children. *Child Psychiatry and Human Development,* 13, 203–12.
Lerner, J. V. and Lerner, R. M. (1983) *Temperament and adaptation across life: theoretical and empirical issues. Life-span development and behavior,* vol. 5. New York: Academic Press.
Levine, M. I. (1985) The role of NMR and other techniques in neonatal imaging. *Journal of Perinatal Medicine,* 13, 259–64.
McGraw, M. (1939) Swimming behaviour of the human infant. *Journal of Pediatrics,* 15, 485–90.
Maziade, M. and Capéraà, P. (1985) Value of difficult temperament among 7-year-olds in the general population for predicting psychiatric diagnosis at age 12. *American Journal of Psychiatry,* 142, 943–6.
Mazière, B. (1986) In vivo studies of brain receptors using positron emission tomography. In *ESF European Training Programme in Brain and Behaviour Research 'Brain Imaging',* no. 37. Strasbourg: European Science Foundation.
Meltzoff, A. and Moore, M. K. (1977) Imitation of facial and manual gestures by human neonates. *Science,* 198, 75–8.
Molfese, V. J. and Thompson, B. (1985) Optimality vs complication: assessing predictive values of perinatal scales. *Child Development,* 56, 810–23.
Morihisa, J. M. (1987) Functional brain imaging techniques. In Hales, R. E. and Frances, A. J. (eds.) *American Psychiatric Association annual review,* vol. 6. Washington, DC: American Psychiatric Press, pp. 300–35.
Niswander, K. R. and Gordon, M. (eds.) (1972) *The collaborative perinatal study of the National Institute of Neurological Disease and Stroke: the women and their pregnancies.* Philadelphia: Saunders.
Pape, K. E., Blackwell, R. J., Cusick, G., Sherwood, A., Houang, M. T. W., Thorburn, R. J. and Reynolds, E. O. R. (1979) Ultrasound detection of brain damage in preterm infants. *The Lancet,* 1, 1261–4.
Papousek, H. (1977) Entwicklung der Lernfähigkeit im Säuglingsalter. In Nissen, G. (ed.) *Intelligenz, Lernen und Lernstörungen.* Berlin: Springer.
Parmelee, A. H. and Sigman, M. (1983) Perinatal brain development and behavior. In Haith, M. M. and Campos, J. J. (eds.) *Infancy and developmental psychobiology, Handbook of child psychology,* ed. P. Mussen, vol. 2. New York: Wiley, pp. 95–155.

Porges, S. W. (1976) Peripheral and neurochemical parallels of psychopathology: a psychopathological model relating autonomic imbalance to hyperactivity, psychopathy and autism. *Advances in Child Development and Behaviour*, 11, 35–65.

Prechtl, H. F. R. (1958) The directed head turning response and allied movements of the human baby. *Behaviour*, 13, 212–42.

(1977) *The neurological examination of the full-term newborn infant*. Clinics in developmental medicine, vol. 63. London: Heinemann.

(1980) The optimality concept. *Early Human Development*, 4, 201.

(1982) Assessment methods for the newborn infant, a critical evaluation. In Stratton, P. (ed.) *Psychobiology of the human newborn*. New York: Wiley, pp. 21–52.

Prichep, L., John, E. R., Ahn, H. and Kaye, H. (1983) Neurometrics: quantitative evaluation of brain dysfunction in children. In Rutter, M. (ed.) *Developmental neuropsychiatry*. New York: Guilford Press, pp. 213–38.

Rea, P. A., Crowe, J., Wickramasinghe, Y. and Rolfe, P. (1985) Non-invasive optical methods for the study of cerebral metabolism in the human newborn: a technique for the future? *Journal of Medical Engineering and Technology*, 9, 160–6.

Roland, P. E. (1985) Cortical organization of voluntary behaviour in man. *Human Neurobiology*, 4, 155–67.

Roland, P. E. and Friberg, L. (1985) Localization of cortical areas activated by thinking. *Journal of Neurophysiology*, 53–5, 1219–43.

Rose, S. (1976) *The conscious brain*, London: Penguin.

Ross, B. D. (1984) Diagnostic potential of NMR. In Price, C. P. and Alberti, K. G. G. (eds.) *Recent advances in clinical biochemistry*, vol. 3. Edinburgh: Livingston.

Rutter, M. and Madge, N. (1976) *Cycles of disadvantage: a review of research*. London: Heinemann.

Sameroff, A. J. and Chandler, M. J. (1975) Reproductive risk and the continuum of caretaking casualty. In Horowitz, F. D. (ed.) *Review of child development research*, vol. 4. Chicago: University of Chicago Press, pp. 187–244.

Sameroff, A. J., Seifer, R. and Zax, M. (1982) *Early development of children at risk for emotional disorders*. Monographs of the Society for Research in Child Development 199, vol. 47, no. 7. Chicago: University of Chicago Press.

Schneider, W. and Shiffrin, R. M. (1977) Controlled and automatic human information processing, I. Detection, search and attention. *Psychological Review*, 84, 1–66.

Seligman, M. E. P. (1974) Depression and learned helplessness. In Friedman, R. J. and Katz, M. M. (eds.) *The psychology of depression*. Washington, DC: Winston, pp. 83–125.

Seligman, M. E. P., Abramson, L. Y., Semmel, A. and van Bayer, C. (1979) Depressive attributional style. *Journal of Abnormal Psychology*, 88, 242–7.

Sergeant, J. A. (1981) Attentional studies in hyperactivity. Ph.D. thesis, University of Groningen.

Sergeant, J. A. and Scholten, C. A. (1985) On data limitations in hyperactivity. *Journal of Child Psychology and Psychiatry*, 26, 111–24.

Shields, J. (1980) Genetics and mental development. In Rutter, M. (ed.) *Scientific foundations of developmental psychiatry*. London: Heinemann, pp. 8–24.

Shiffrin, R. M. and Schneider, W. (1977) Controlled and automatic human information processing: II Perceptual learning, automatic attending and a general theory. *Psychological Review*, 84–2, 127–90.

Slovis, T. L. (1982) Neonatal intracranial ultrasound. In Sanders, R. C. (ed.) *Ultrasound annual*. New York: Raven Press.

Slovis, T. L. and Shankaran, S. (1984) Ultrasound in the evaluation of hypoxic-ischemic injury and intracranial hemorrhage in neonates: the state of the art. *Pediatric Radiology*, 14, 67–75.

Stewart, A. L., Reynolds, E. O. R., Hope, P. L., Hamilton, P. A., Baudin, J., Costello, A. M. de L., Bradford, B. C. and Wyatt, J. S. (1987) Probability of neurodevelopmental disorders estimated from ultrasound appearance of brains of very preterm infants. *Developmental Medicine and Child Neurology*, 29, 3–11.

Sturge, C. (1982) Reading retardation and antisocial behaviour. *Journal of Child Psychology and Psychiatry*, 23, 21–31.

Swets-Gronert, F. (1986) *Temperament, taalcompetentie en gedragsproblemen van jonge kinderen*. Lisse: Swets and Zeitlinger.

Thomas, A. and Chess, S. (1977) *Temperament and development*. New York: Brunner-Mazel.

Thomas, A., Birch, H. G., Chess, S., Hertzig, M. E. and Korn, S. (1963) *Behavioral individuality in early childhood*. New York: University Press.

Thorburn, R. J., Reynolds, E. O. R., Blackwell, R. J., Cusick, G., Shaw, D. G. and Smith, J. E. (1982) Accuracy of imaging of the brain of newborn infants by linear-array real time ultrasound. *Early Human Development*, 9, 31–46.

Touwen, B. C. L., Huisjes, H. J., Jurgens van der Zee, A. D., Bierman, M. E. C., Smrkovsky, M. and Olinga, A. A. (1980) Obstetrical conditions and neonatal neurological morbidity. An analysis with the help of the optimality concept. *Early Human Development*, 4, 207–28.

Van der Meere, J. J. and Sergeant, J. A. (1987) A divided attention experiment with pervasively hyperactive children. *Journal of Abnormal Child Psychology*, 15, 379–91.

Vernon, M. D. (1979) Variability in reading retardation. *British Journal of Psychology*, 70, 7–16.

Waddington, C. H. (1975) *The evolution of an evolutionist*. Edinburgh: Edinburgh University Press.

Werner, E. E. (1986) The concept of risk from a developmental perspective. In *Advances in special education*, vol. 5, pp. 1–23. Greenwich, CT: JAI Press.

Werner, E. E. and Smith, R. S. (1982) *Vulnerable but invincible*. New York: McGraw-Hill.

Werner, E. E., Bierman, J. M. and French, F. E. (1971) *The children of Kauai*. Honolulu: University of Hawaii Press.

Windle, W. F. (1968) Brain damage at birth: functional and structural modifications with the time. *Journal of the American Medical Association*, 209: 9, 1967–72.

8 Longitudinal and systemic approaches in the study of biological high- and low-risk groups[1]

Klaus E. Grossmann

Thoughts about assessment of individuals' adaptive functioning

The many difficulties involved in biological risk research are aptly summarized by Kalverboer (see chapter 7). In this chapter, I compare the issues with those raised in our longitudinal research with low-risk samples. Nomothetic or group-based research is contrasted with idiographic or individual-focused research. Whereas nomothetic research is essential for drawing general inferences about determinants of development, the idiographic approach brings an understanding that is helpful in planning preventive, remedial and therapeutic interventions.

There is much uncertainty in the elucidation of cause–effect relationships. This is not only a reflection of hierarchies in biological explanations, as depicted in Rose's model (see figure 1 in chapter 7); it is also a matter of deciding on the most relevant level of assessment and of integration.

This decision on the choice of level of behavioural integration for the study of risk factors in the negotiation of environmental challenges or developmental risks is of foremost importance in the conceptualization of research. It may even be the key to the solution for some of the major problems outlined by Kalverboer.

The task is the assessment of the individual's capacity to adapt and to develop under more or less adverse living conditions. In that connection, rather than dichotomize high and low risk it may be preferable to deal with risk as a continuous dimension. Prechtl's concept of 'optimality' appears to come close to that notion. The optimality score, based on pregnancy and perinatal measures, is conceptualized as an index for the integrity of the central nervous system, although it provides only an indirect reflection of such integrity.

The uncertainty about effects seems to be a consequence, in part, of a lack of adequate diagnostic criteria. Again, a behavioural focus on the

[1] This chapter was prepared while the author was on leave on a grant from the Volkswagen Foundation. Thanks are due for critical comments to Elisabeth Fremmer-Bombik, Karin Grossmann, Gerhard Suess and Gottfried Spangler. Research was supported by grants Gr299/11/12/13 from the Deutsche Forschungsgemeinschaft.

individual's coping abilities may, perhaps, ease some of the problems associated with concepts of minimal brain dysfunction (MBD) or its partial replacement by attention deficit disorder, with or without hyperactivity (ADD(H)).

The ignorance concerning mediating factors between 'risk' and 'effect' is a real problem at any level of behavioural assessment. It will be aggravated, however, by a concentration on single variables, such as neonatal asphyxia, which usually creates a biological risk only in the context of other circumstances. As Kalverboer notes, there may be genetically based differences in the organisms' capacities to maintain functional integrity in the presence of external stress.

Pre- and perinatal traumata or abnormalities may, of course, be associated with severe brain damage, as associated with intraventricular haemorrhage or periventricular anoxia. In these cases, the biological risk is strong and direct. However, this risk operates only in the uncommon situation of severe damage. In the more usual circumstance of milder perinatal risk factors with just an inference of possible organic brain dysfunction, the sequelae are mainly seen in children from a socially disadvantaged background. Kalverboer argues for a concentration on composite factors that have been shown to be associated with adverse outcomes. Such factors include both the 'integrative' capacities of the organism, and the quality of the care-giving environment. We need to study how an individual who is at risk functions under circumstances threatening to his integrity.

An ethological approach, using careful descriptions of how the individual handles environmental challenges, may serve to delineate possible qualitative differences in both normal and biological high-risk samples. Intergenerational continuities in the quality of attachment relationships as shown by Main in California (Main *et al.*, 1985), as well as by us in our Bielefeld and Regensburg longitudinal projects, may serve to elaborate some of the issues raised by Kalverboer. At the same time, it may become clear that the transactional model proposed by Sameroff and Chandler (1975) does not provide much help in this complex context. The transactional model is, however, useful for guarding against any simple-minded main-effect conceptualizations of organismic damage or environmental deficiencies. It warns also against solutions on the level of statistical interactions, rather than on an empirical assessment of 'real' transactions between individuals with different levels of emotional, motivational and cognitive integrity in the face of adaptive tasks. Such tasks result in assimilation of, and accommodation to, environmental events that matter, that is that are meaningful to the individual (Grossmann, K. E. *et al.*, 1986).

The transactional model, in other words, is necessary, but methodologically insufficient to deal with the issues raised by Kalverboer. An assess-

ment of individual integrative capacities is needed to capture the resources
and deficiencies available. However, it is also necessary to move induc-
tively upwards in the hierarchy of behavioural integration. As Hinde
(1979) has pointed out, there is no rational way of constructing the
qualitative properties of any system from the knowledge of operations on
the level of the elements of which the system is composed. Als has
proposed a transformational model which adds to and includes the
'changing nature and composition of the infant's capacities with age'.
Impairment may not show until later ages (Als, 1985, p. 68).

Since environmental factors (experiences) operate on behavioural
systems of different degrees and kinds of behavioural integration, the
behavioural systems have to be assessed first. Traditionally, psychology
has dealt with three overriding adaptive systems: emotional, motivational
and cognitive ones. The emotional system is well handled by attachment
theory. The motivational system has a long tradition, especially regarding
the need for achievement and the development of intentions on the basis
of more or less flexible goals. The cognitive system has been dealt with as
one of handling knowledge in a goal-oriented manner, that is using
thinking for solving problems. Cognitive functioning requires recognition
of the relationship between existing or forthcoming events and the most
likely changes to be expected, with or without personal intervention. Of
course, these different systems are not separable. Only together do they
make up the characteristics of any individual. For the purpose of assessing
the individual's functioning, however, they may be profitably considered
separately. The questions are: How does the emotion system respond
(coherent–disruptive)? What action goals are available? What knowledge
and creative thinking patterns are available?

Modern approaches to the study of early risk for pathology have been
presented towards the end of Kalverboer's chapter. I agree that the best
practical tool is a good theory. However, such a theory, according to the
experiences we have had so far with our own approach – going from an
individual approach to a variable approach, and then back to the
individual – must be formulated somewhat along the following lines:

1 There should be a focus on contiguities between behaviours and consequences, instead of separate assessments of behavioural organization
  and environmental factors.
2 Integrative resources of adaptive coherence need to be assessed at the
  individual level in order to develop systemic hypotheses about their role
  in the person's meeting of developmentally relevant challenges.
3 These data then need to be reorganized in order to group individuals on
  the basis of their behavioural patterning so that nomothetic statistical
  comparisons can be made using either single variables or behavioural
  composites.
4 Finally, these statistical abstractions need to be retranslated back to
  provide a qualitative description of individuals' functioning.

The idea behind these four postulates is as follows: the individuals are assessed in representative 'ecologically valid' situations that are relevant for his or her development (McClelland, 1973). Working within the context of attachment theory means that the attachment system has to be activated, as in the Strange Situation designed by Ainsworth (Ainsworth *et al.*, 1978). If the attachment system is not activated, then we may not be able to state that we are actually observing behaviour relevant for attachment. The activation of the attachment system (a metaphor as heuristically useful as the internal working model – see below) means that some kind of emotional insecurity or conflict must occur in the individual, which is to be solved within the attachment relationship (the attachment system), or on the basis of the (perhaps) resulting differences between individuals (the internal working model).

The familiarity with different qualities of adaptive functioning will guard the researcher against premature definitions and against isolated, non-systemic variables. Admittedly, the idiographic assessment is closely tied to qualitative and descriptive data, and does not *per se* provide the kind of data needed for nomothetic treatment. However, it provides the knowledge base necessary for evaluating the meaning of any set of single variables. In other words, both approaches are necessary, but each in itself is insufficient to solve the problems raised by Kalverboer. My proposal is that only data sets using both individual and variable approaches together will facilitate progress (Grossmann, K. E., 1986).

The grouping of individuals according to similarities and differences involves a degree of arbitrariness, but, if handled flexibly and knowledge-ably, it may provide a much better basis for longitudinal research than traditional statistical strategies, such as factor analyses or multiple discrimination procedures, or even path analyses and LISREL (see chapter 17; and Cairns, 1986). Although, in the end, statistical (sometimes called 'objective') procedures eventually have to be applied, it seems to be a matter of integration in the scientist's mind in the first place whether he successfully accomplishes the task of *discovering* the most appropriate level of behavioural integration. Statistics, then, is applicable to any level of analysis.

The retranslation of data to the individual level has a two-fold purpose. First, it provides a check on the validity of the prior translation of individual idiographic features into nomothetic variables. Second, as longitudinal data accumulate, the findings may be used to derive new groupings that provide a better picture, as part of a hypothesis-generating rather than as part of a hypothesis-testing procedure. This qualitative judgement needs to take account of the possibility that different observed behaviours may reflect similar underlying behavioural strategies. In this respect, there is a parallel with clinical approaches. If one is lucky, this may eventually approximate to the phenomena observed at the individual level. The validation of such hypotheses is a matter of quantitatively tying appropriate longitudinal data sets together.

The synactive approach to development

Brazelton's neonatal assessment scale (BNAS) has been used in one of our two longitudinal studies (Bielefeld). It follows a conceptualization that resembles the optimality notion of Prechtl. While the infants are being tested, the tester observes their states and state changes very closely. The aim is to tap each baby's optimal performance. In our own Bielefeld longitudinal project the quality of orientation (closely tied to state 4 – attentive alertness) was as strongly predictive of quality of attachment relationship to mothers at 12 months of age, and to fathers at 18 months of age, as was maternal sensitivity assessed in the families' homes during the infants' first year of life (Grossmann, K. *et al.*, 1985).

For infants at risk, Als (1985, p. 67) noted that later organizational deficits (e.g. in dyslexia) 'do not just arise when the child is exposed to formal education, but have been part of the child's neuro-integrative makeup potentially from birth'. Children who are born very prematurely have a raised incidence of school and behaviour problems that cannot be explained by social class alone. Half of them, however, do not show such deficiencies. Als set out to identify 'early organizational analogues of later functioning' that would provide a basis for early intervention and therapy, and would thereby alleviate or ameliorate the later difficulties.

Idiographic data, in Als' research, form the necessary complement to variable research. Both together form a kind of *via regia* to better definitions of behavioural problems. Als' synactive model of development 'outlines the degree of differentiation and of modulation of behavioural functioning as main parameters of the human's individuality and uniqueness recognizable over time ... [it] focuses on the way the individual infant appears to handle his experience of the world around him rather than on the assessment of skills per se' (Als, 1985, p. 68; 1986). The questions she asks are, among others: 'How well differentiated and modulated are the various subsystems in their functioning and mutual balance, given varying demands placed on the infant and varying developmental tasks attempted by him as a result of his intrinsic biological developmental motivation?' and 'When does smoothness and balance become strained or stressed and coping behaviours become costly, bare subsistence protections or even counterproductive maladaptations?' (Als, 1985, p. 69).

In line with our own data, Als states: 'the differentiation of the attentional–interactive system is the most rapidly changing, apparently newly emerging, salient agendum of the human organism' (p. 69). For some of the newborns this differentiation is a very difficult task, especially for thin-for-height newborns (p. 71). Als developed an assessment of pre-term infants' behaviour procedure (APIB). One important insight from working with many maturely and immaturely born newborns has been termed 'dual antagonist integration of avoidance': 'stimulation, if inappropriately timed or inappropriate in its quality and intensity, will cause the infant to defend himself against it: if properly timed and appropriate in its quality and intensity, stimulation will cause the infant to seek out and to move toward it, while maintaining himself at a balanced level' (p. 75).

There were impressive differences between pre-terms and full-terms on indices of the following subsystems: physiological, motor, states, attentional–interactive, regulatory, and overall system organization. So-called packages of manipulation, such as sleep/distal stimulation, uncovering, supine position, low, medium and high tactile, and vestibular stimulation were consistently more taxing to the pre-terms in terms of system organization. The amount of examiner facilitation necessary to maintain and support the pre-term during those package manipulations was consistently higher for the prematures than for the full-term infants. This corresponds to the first point in my own theoretical notions outlined on p. 140: the joint assessment of contiguities between organismic behaviours and environmental consequences.

The second point had to do with the idiographic knowledge of the researcher. This, in Als' work, was the basis for developing the APIB.

The third point was that similar individuals had to be grouped together, and had to be compared to other groups of individuals that were similar among themselves in other ways. There is great reluctance among scientists to consider this procedure as suitable. In the case of the Brazelton test (BNAS), however, qualitative 'a priori' groupings had consistently yielded better results than traditional statistical procedures like factor analysis, which, of course, is unable to take fine-tuned systemic aspects into consideration. In the case of the APIB a clustering analysis system called the Taxonomic Intracellular Analytic System (TICAS), developed by Bartels and Wied for the detection of groups of cancerous lymphocytes within a group of normal lymphocytes (Als, 1985, p. 81), was used. The grouping was based mainly on the infants' system organization, the most comprehensive scores available. Four clusters of infants resulted. They were rank-ordered from good to poor. The most important finding was that there were only full-terms in cluster I, there were four pre-terms and one full-term in cluster II, one pre-term and one full-term in cluster III, and one full-term and five pre-terms in cluster IV. Als (1985, p. 82) found it encouraging that cluster membership 'cuts across the medical classification of pre-term and full-term status and appears to yield conceptually meaningful, behaviourally distinct subgroups of infants', because not all of the prematures suffered from adverse consequences.

Grouping of variables according to qualitative criteria seems to be of major concern. Farrington (see chapter 9) also combined many variables into one global rating called parental child-rearing behaviour. He comments: 'This data reduction technique was more subjective than the factor analysis described in West (1969) but, taking account of the different kinds of variable involved, it was felt to be more appropriate' (Farrington, p. 176).

The retranslation to the level of the behavioural phenomena is maintained in Als' procedure, and the fourth aspect of my own theoretical considerations stated above has been satisfied, that is the necessity of retranslating abstractions back to the phenomena shown by the individuals of the research project.

Longitudinal validations are possible with this approach. Als invented a Kangaroo-box to assess the behavioural organization of the older infants. The K-box is made of transparent plexiglass with a latch door and has a hopping, wind-up kangaroo inside. The box was presented to the infants at 9 and 18 months. A more complex, larger version has also been developed for five- to seven-year-old children.

The infants' capacities are taxed in terms of autonomic organization, gross- and fine-motor organization, symmetry of tonus, movement and posture, apparent cognitive functioning, language and vocal organization, affective organization, competence in play with object, competence in combining object play and social interaction, degree of self-regulation, degree of facilitation and structure necessary, and degree of pleasure and pride displayed by infants. Attention is paid to the infants' autonomic reactions, movements, tone, vocalizations and facial expressions during their interplay. Scores for the parents, as well as interactive scores, were also available. As Als (1985, p. 85) put it: 'The K-box scales were developed to be directly related to the assessment scales of organizational capacities on the APIB.'

The strongest feature in developing clusters was the degree of flexibility in integrating social and object play. Other important contributions were self-regulation, pleasure and pride, fine-motor co-ordination and flexibility.

Cluster classification stability from newborn age to nine months yielded only 2 infants who had changed, whereas 18 infants showed the continuity of behavioural organization postulated by the synactive model. The fact that such indices of competence cut across traditional medical variables may be an indication of the fact that the phenomena have not been caught at the optimal level of integration, and have not been captured by the most suitable or *niveauadäquate* terminology (see below). I fully agree with Als (1985, p. 86), who stated: 'We anticipate that the identification of such patterns will make the diagnosis of an individual infant's developmental functioning more succinct and will help in structuring appropriate early support and intervention and in measuring the effect of such support and intervention.' New data, as yet unpublished, for the same children at three years of age show an impressive stability. The approach taken by Als is highly encouraging, and promises to solve many of the problems raised by Kalverboer in a most elegant, insightful, albeit enormously laborious, manner.

Children's disposition and maternal responsivity

We attempted to look at the different styles of communication directly. Having observed that the infants/children themselves behaved differently on different occasions, Spangler (1986) looked at the quality of different everyday experiences of two-year-olds again. He used a small independent sample in order to take differences in individual dispositions of the children (to avoid the term temperament) into consideration.

When the infants were 12 months old, their Mental Development Index (MDI), their emotional disposition and their social index were assessed. One group of seven children with high emotional excitability was compared with a group of seven children with low excitability. Ten children were in between the two groups, and were used for comparison purposes (total $N = 24$). The two groups of high and low excitable children were observed six times at home, every two weeks, between 14 and 17 months of age in order to evaluate the content and qualities of their experiences. The infants' competence was observed at 24 months in an open-play situation with the mother, and in a structured-play session with a stranger.

The individual differences during the second year of life were not very stable; in fact, there were definite changes in the individual children's MDIs between 12 and 24 months. In contrast, the emotional disposition of the high and low excitable groups remained highly stable. There were, however, definite changes over the year within each of the two groups. Despite large individual differences between the children, the level of their everyday experiences correlated with their MDI. The quality of mother–child interactions correlated with the emotional disposition of the child. In general, level of play and the children's play motivation correlated significantly with the social competence of the children, and with the interaction quality of the mothers. A most interesting difference was seen in connection with differences in the mothers' interaction styles in play situations in which the children showed negative emotions. The data suggested that the children's emotional disposition did not have a direct influence on their competence development. Rather, the quality of the experiences made by them within a certain interaction style with their mothers appeared to be the most effective process variable.

We had too few subjects for a meaningful variable approach. Therefore only patterns of correlations that provided coherent pictures of the differently disposed children with mothers who responded positively or negatively to their children's mood in the context of everyday experiences were interpreted. Single correlations outside that context were not considered.

The correlations between quality of play at 24 months and preceding experiences when the children were in a good mood were positive for the mothers' interest in the children's activities, the quality of their participation in the children's activities, and for their sensitivity towards the children's needs. Negative correlations occurred for the frequency of the children's passive participation in their mother's activities (watching). When children were in a poor mood, negative correlations for frequency of interaction with the mothers and their children's constructive play $(-.67^{**})$, as well as level of play $(-.51^{*})$ were found, together with a positive correlation for inactivity $(-.69^{**})$. However, there was a positive correlation with the frequency of harmonic interactions ($.69^{**}$), and a corresponding negative correlation with the frequency of conflicting interactions $(-.48^{*})$. The mothers seem to be responsible for the quality of interaction, indicated by the positive correlation of $-.61^{*}$ between the mothers' sensitivity to their children's signals and the children's constructive play (although, of course, it is possible that there were also child effects on parents).

Emotionally unco-operative mothers often ignored the needs of the children, as indicated by their uninvolved expressions and by their delayed responses and assistance. Often they responded only verbally and also rejected the children's bids for assistance. Often they did not seem to understand their children's intentions and did not try to find out either. When the children cried or appeared to be sad, these mothers did not show much sympathy for their children's feelings. There was less warmth and consideration for the child as a person than there was with the emotionally co-operative mothers.

The emotionally co-operative mothers, in contrast, reacted promptly and without delay to the children's expressed needs, even when the signals were rather subtle. They seldom ignored their approaches and they did not postpone their assistance. Usually, they provided the kind of assistance desired by the child, and questions were answered appropriately. When the child cried or was sad, the emotionally co-operative mothers consoled them with words and/or with bodily contact. They showed an understanding for their children, by for example, paraphrasing their children's feelings.

Five of the seven difficult children, compared with only two of the seven easy children had emotionally unco-operative mothers. The two difficult children with emotionally co-operative mothers had high concentration, were high in social competence, and had a high MDI. The five difficult children with emotionally unco-operative mothers had low concentration, low social competence and a low MDI. The two difficult children with co-operative mothers resembled the five easy children with co-operative mothers.

In the case of Spangler's research, only hypotheses could be formulated. However, they are supported by the correlational data presented above. It may be suggested that the children's difficulties influence the mothers' response qualities, which in turn have an effect on the children's competence development. However, the mothers' responses could also be a reaction to the competence and emotional disposition of the children. Our two difficult children with co-operative mothers suggest the following hypothesis: if a mother, despite her child's dispositional difficulties, is or *remains* responsive and co-operative, then the child's competence will develop favourably. Otherwise, it will develop less favourably.

We have also analysed audiotapes and whispered observational comments of the everyday experiences of the children in the Bielefeld longitudinal project at two years of age (Grossmann K., 1984; Loher, 1984; Weigert, 1986). These suggest very similar conclusions. Most of the Bielefeld children's 'intellectually valuable experiences' (Carew, 1980) were made in conjunction with mothers who were intellectually demanding and emotionally responsive at the same time. Again (correlational) variable research had provided the nomothetic data, but retranslation to the level of the individuals provided the necessary insights about the actual psychologically important processes.

The development of emotional coherence and integrity

Quality of attachment in two longitudinal studies
A third example of the benefits of concentrating on individuals within a longitudinal frame comes from our own two longitudinal studies. In close co-operation with Mary Main, and inspired by her own notion of emotional coherence and integrity, we assessed the mothers' memories of their own childhood relationships with their own mothers. The attachment relationship of these mothers with their own infants had been assessed four years earlier by using the now (in)famous Strange Situation developed by Ainsworth and her co-workers (Ainsworth *et al.*, 1978; Grossmann, K. E. *et al.*, 1981).

The Strange Situation provided observational data. In Bielefeld they had been preceded by direct observations during birth and during the first week in the hospital, as well as through direct home observations at two, six and ten months of age. This study was a kind of ethologically oriented discovery study, plus a partial replication of the main findings of Ainsworth: the close connection between maternal sensitivity and classifications of the infant–parent dyads into securely (B = four subgroups) and insecurely attached (A = insecurely avoidant – two subgroups; and C = insecurely ambivalent – two subgroups). About 10% of the dyads did not fit into the classifications at the time of our analyses (Grossmann, K. *et al.*, 1985).[2]

Our Strange Situation data were based on the Ainsworth classification scheme (Ainsworth *et al.*, 1978). In addition, however, we applied a detailed communication model for a sequence-by-sequence reanalysis (Grossmann, K. E. *et al.*, 1986). This method revealed definitely different communication patterns in the infants' non-verbal expressions for the securely as against the insecurely attached dyads. The securely attached infants communicated directly, particularly when they showed mixed feelings and signs of misery. The insecurely avoidant infants ceased to communicate directly, in similar circumstances. In addition, the social consequences were quite different for the two groups (we did not have enough cases for the insecurely ambivalent C categories). Whereas the securely attached dyads achieved some kind of trustful togetherness, the consequences for the insecure dyads were increased separation, and independence. This was evident at both the microanalytic (Grossmann, K. E. and Grossmann, K. 1986) and the macroanalytic level (Grossmann, K. E., 1987).

In our further longitudinal analyses we considered the differences in emotional expressiveness in the presence of a particular attachment figure. This is a 'synactive' (Als, 1986) characteristic of emotional organization of the child in the presence of that attachment figure. From here we had to pursue two longitudinal perspectives: one on the possible dynamic stability of the special communicative quality of the *relationship* between the infant/child and its mother (father), and the other on *individuals* using Bowlby's concept of an 'internal working model'. Empirically, this meant looking for behavioural patterns in the *absence* of attachment figures. The hypothesis was that an insecure relationship eventually gave rise to a working model characterized by mistrust, brittleness and difficulties in sympathy, sensitivity and the emotional gratifications of loving relationships. Main (in prep.) made a most efficient use of that notion in her analyses of the mothers' attachment as regards their own childhood memories. We proceeded along the same heuristic lines in our analyses.

---

[2] Mary Main has reanalysed her videotapes for signs of disturbed behaviours in the infants. A major part of the infants' behaviours that did not fit into the Ainsworth classification scheme in fact showed signs of disturbance, labelled 'D' by Main. Wartner (1987), who conducted the six-year follow-up study in Regensburg, was able to identify the 'disturbed' infants on the basis of disturbance scores given to them in a different videotaped situation, the so-called clown situation (Main and Weston, 1981). A blind reanalysis of the Strange Situation videotapes confirmed the Main and Wartner notion: the same infants were also identified in the SS when the criteria developed by Main were applied by us. Future longitudinal analyses will have to take these additions into consideration. At the present time, however, we have to confine ourselves to the original SS classification data, because a

Observations in preschool: consequences for the individuals in non-risk groups

When the Regensburg children were five years old they were observed in preschool (all but two children being in different groups). The observers described each child's social behaviour in the context of other children and the preschool teacher (without knowledge of earlier data). Three different contexts were considered: quality of play, interpersonal encounters without a play theme, and behaviour problems.[3]

Play behaviour did not differ very much between the children who had been classified as securely and insecurely attached with their mothers four years earlier. The group means for the securely attached children showed a tendency towards longer play periods as compared to the insecures ($p = .07$): they spent as much time in group play as the insecures, but somewhat more time in solitary play ($p = .11$). The narrative reports of the preschool observations allowed for a reconstruction of the actual behaviour patterns. They revealed that the secures played in a more concentrated manner. They were less easily disturbed than the insecures, acting purposefully and in an organized way for about twice as long as the insecures ($p < .01$); they appeared more relaxed, as judged from their facial and gestural expressions, whereas the insecures were somewhat more erratic, more tense, and more fidgety ($p < .10$). The insecures went from one thing to the next, their motor movements appearing somewhat more unco-ordinated and aimless. During play the insecures showed a tendency towards more frequent conflicts ($p < .10$).

The probabilities on the variable level are certainly not very impressive. But these are data in the making. Quite often we first find a picture as outlined above. We usually try then to move back to the individual approach. From our variable approach we know what to look for in the original protocols. Our goal is to find a level of integration and coherence of behaviour patterns that can be reliably recognized by well-trained observers, and in which the children differ noticeably. Of course, we do not always succeed with our attempts to supplement the variable approach by the individual approach. In many cases, however, we find very large statistical differences if we succeed in finding typical behaviour *strategies* in which subgroups of children definitely differ. Sometimes these differences are significantly related to our heuristic model of a

reanalysis of all the data sets for which this new discovery may be relevant is very time-consuming and had not been anticipated.

[3] The detailed work on the level of individuals had been preceded by judgements made by the children's kindergarten teachers on Block's California Child Q-Sort. Some of the relevant items showed in fact a highly significant difference between the mean values of those children who, as 12- or 18-month-olds, had been classified securely attached to their mothers and/or fathers and those classified insecurely attached to both parents. (The child–father data are not considered here because they would complicate the picture without furthering the argument in favour of a synactive approach on the level of the functioning individual.) (Suess *et al.*, 1985).

developing 'internal working model' (IWM) suggested by attachment theory. For the preschoolers' play behaviour this has not been done yet. The quality of integration of each single child is, indeed, a concept that is difficult to define.

The preschoolers' interpersonal encounters were analysed next. The secure children showed a tendency towards more friendliness in their social contacts, with open facial expressions ($p < .08$). The insecures were more sober and tense, although on the variable level this did not reach statistical significance ($p < .11$). As in the play situations, they appeared to be more tense and fidgety, with sometimes somewhat twitchy facial expressions and body movements. Another tendency was seen in their more frequent dissatisfaction and poor mood during social encounters. Again, the complex picture, statistically not very impressive on the variable level, may still come out as a much more impressive difference when the individual children are compared on a 'synactive' level of behavioural organization.

Social conflicts were analysed in the same way. Mostly, partners wanted to have the same toy or to play the same part in a role play. The styles of handling such conflict situations were quite different between the children. Some of them tried to solve the conflicts themselves and asked for help only after they had failed. They did not draw others into their quarrels, and they did not retreat and leave the conflict unsolved. This group of children was compared with a group of children who retreated before the conflict was solved, who transferred the quarrel to other previously uninvolved children, and who generally showed little self-confidence in their handling of social conflicts. The first group, labelled 'competent', contained 14 of 21 secure children, but only 3 of 11 insecure children. The second group, called 'incompetent', contained 8 of 11 insecure children, but only 7 of 21 secure children ($p = .041$). Three children, all secures, did not get involved in social conflicts at all.

Finally, we looked at possible behaviour problems in our children from quite normal families, that is those families without any of the traditional indications for risk factors. There were, for a primary analysis, two groups. One group contained children with no or only marginal problems. The other group contained children who were somewhat hostile, that is aggressive, or scapegoating, or isolated, or with multiple problems such as stereotyped or definitely inappropriate behaviours. Of the 24 secure children 18 belonged to the 'competent' group, but only 2 of the 11 insecures did. The 'incompetent' group contained 9 of the 11 insecure children, but only 6 of the 24 secure children ($x_2 = 15.36$; $df = 1$; $p < .002$).

Part of the analysis of the data consists of a time-consuming search for behaviour patterns, strategies, coherency, and level of integration, as well as a corresponding search for a terminology appropriate to the level of integration found (*niveauadäquate Terminologie* – von Holst and Saint Paul, 1969, pp. 228ff). We aim to be able to retranslate our data base from single variables to the actual phenomena shown by individuals, and, if we are successful in our discovery of relevant behaviour patterns, we are sometimes able to enhance our statistical confidence level in order to reject the null hypothesis. At the variable level we could only achieve mere tendencies towards statistical significance. At the individual level, in comparing synactive strategies, however, we were able to show highly significant differences between the five-year-old children who were classified as insecurely (A) or securely attached (B) to their mothers four years earlier in Ainsworth's Strange Situation.

The results show a different style of functioning of the individual children in a social context in the *absence* of the attachment figure. We consider this to be an indication of the emerging internal working model (IWM). Of course, as Hinde points out (see chapter 21), the data base only tells us that there are certain conspicuous differences in the behaviour of a majority of insecurely avoidant attached children in comparison to the children who at 12 and 18 months of age had been identified as securely attached to their mothers. But for the process of finding synactive perspectives of the children's more or less integrated social–emotional functioning, neither Main nor we could have done without the heuristic value of the IWM as a 'conceptual metaphor' to integrate diverse facts. Once *all* the phenomena that occur on the level of the individuals' 'synactive' functioning have been discovered, then *all* of the phenomena will be isomorphic with the model, and the model can then be easily discarded because it will have served its purpose and will then (and only then) have become perfectly redundant.

Observations in preschool: consequences for the individuals in high-risk groups

A highly comparable approach was taken by Erickson *et al.* (1985) in their study of the relationship between quality of attachment and behaviour problems in 40 preschool children from a high-risk sample of 267. Their analysis was based on the proposal of Erickson *et al.* (1985, p. 148) that 'disturbances of the attachment relationship are the main cause of psychopathology characterized by chronic anxiety or distrust, placing children doubly at risk. First, they render the child less able to cope with later adverse experiences, and, second, they increase the likelihood that the child will behave in such a way as to bring about more adverse experiences.' There is coherence in optimal adaptational strategies as well as in maladaptive ones: 'Thus, pronounced difficulties with impulse control, aggression, and other antisocial behaviours, prolonged emotional dependency, and extreme difficulty in relating to other children may be linked to adaptational failures during earlier periods when the major developmental issues were attachment and autonomy' (Erickson *et al.*, 1985, p. 148). Children who were securely attached as infants at 12 and again at 18 months 'were found to be more ego resilient, independent, compliant, empathic and socially competent; they had greater self-esteem and expressed more positive affect and less negative affect than did children who were anxiously attached as infants' (Erickson *et al.*, 1985, p. 149).

An additional 56 children from preschool and daycare centres throughout Minneapolis were observed, with some gain in ecological validity. The children were 4½–5 years old when they were seen, on at least two days, in a variety of teacher-directed and free-play activities. It is important to note that their mothers were not present while the assessments were made, giving support to the idea of the operation of an 'inner working model' in the individual children.

Problem children were identified by observers and teachers and compared with children without recognizable problems. Only 2 of the children who had been insecurely attached with their mothers as infants were in the well-functioning group in preschool; 14 were in the behaviour problem group. In contrast, 16 of 22 secure children functioned well.

There were some exceptions from these continuities. Secure children with problems had less support and encouragement from their mothers earlier in life. Insecure children without problems, at 42 months of age, had mothers who were more respectful of the children's autonomy, were more supportive, were firmer, gave clearer instructions, and were less hostile than mothers of insecure children with problems (Erickson *et al.*, 1985, p. 151).

There was a distinct difference in the overall social and emotional functioning in the children. The characteristic elements of children with an insecurely avoidant history were dependency, non-compliance, poor skills in social interaction, hostility, impulsiveness, giving-up easily, and withdrawal. They had extensive and varied behaviour problems.

In a high-risk sample such as that used by Erickson *et al.* (1985) the differentiation between well-adapted and poorly adapted children was obviously very clear. In contrast, those children whose attachment classification as infants had been *different* at 12 and 18 months of age (38% of the high-risk sample) were not clearly predictable.

In our two non-risk samples, where adaptational strategies showed only more subtle differences, it was necessary to follow the group variable-based comparisons with a detailed analysis of *individual* behavioural strategies. We needed to examine 'how the child monitors impulses and modulates his or her responses to stimuli' (Erickson *et al.*, 1985, p. 152) in order to derive the 'working model' behind the observable behaviour. At first sight this may seem less necessary when there are strong behavioural differences between high-risk children and normals.

However, even with high-risk samples, it is often the case that the differences lie in the overall patterns of low-frequency behaviours rather than in any marked excess in any single high-frequency variables.

The Minnesota high-risk children, in contrast to the Regensburg 'normal' children, had only minimal possibilities to compensate for an insecure attachment relationship with the mother by a secure one with the father. Therefore the continuities obtained with the 'normal' sample can be considered to be more ecologically representative (Schmidhuber, 1987). They lend convincing support to the notion that the behaviour of the high-risk children is not special, but only an exaggeration of qualitatively different behaviour strategies as a consequence of different attachment histories.

Replication of the dyadic patterns at six years of age

At six years of age another reunion with the mother in a nicely furnished playroom was studied. The mothers were interviewed in one room, while in another room the children performed a number of tasks and were interviewed by an 'owl' who wanted to know 'everything' about him or her. After about one hour the mothers returned and the child's socio-emotional response was analysed, using videotapes. Again, following a variable-based analysis, we sought to assess individual behaviour patterns in order to create groups, using criteria relevant for attachment theory.

In terms of their attachment classification at 12 and 18 months, 80% of the children were correctly identified on the basis of their behavioural patterns at the age of six (Wartner, 1987). That meant that, in line with the concept of trustful sharing and open social–emotional communication, the individual patterns of the children in the *presence* of the mother remained stable over a period of five years. For us this is a good example of dyadic stability. The preschool data, in the light of these relationship stabilities, provide some indication that at least some transfer to the individual child's functioning outside the actual child–mother attachment relationship had occurred (Suess, 1987).

Interviews with the mothers about childhood attachment memories

The latest set of data in our attempt to make explicit the IWM metaphor consists of interviews with the mothers about their own childhood memories about attachment-related issues. The 'adult attachment interview' has been designed by George *et al.* (in prep.). A method was developed that made the components of the interview transcripts somewhat more explicit and transparent than the rather complex and difficult to handle adult attachment classification system devised by Main and Goldwyn (in prep.). The 'adult attachment interviews' were conducted at the time when the children were observed in preschool at five years of age, four years after the SS assessments. We were able to pinpoint variables in line with the IWM, in which mothers with a secure relationship four years earlier in the SS differed greatly from mothers with an insecure relationship four years earlier.

One group of mothers was open to attachment-related topics. They gave detailed reports on their attachment figures. Some of them reported supportive relationships, but there were also a few mothers who were open and sympathetic to attachment issues despite memories of problematic and unsupportive parents. One other group of mothers had memories of unsupportive attachment figures, and little thinking about, and strong avoidance of, attachment-related issues. In line with our preferred metaphor, the IWM, we called the first pattern 'securely organized representation of attachment' and the second pattern 'insecurely organized representation of attachment'. Again, we were able to undertake variable-based, as well as individual, approaches. The variable approach helped us to find those variables and combinations of variables that best differentiated between mothers with secure and insecure attachments. A few variables were sufficient for a correct identification of the secure and insecure mothers. However, an understanding of the function of the IWM was not to be expected from this approach. Only the individual approach provides enough information for a glimpse into the actual functional differences in the mothers' handling of attachment-related issues. In this manner 78.6% of the mothers who at 12 or 18 months had shown a secure or insecure relationship with their infants in Ainsworth's Strange Situation could be correctly identified (Fremmer-Bombik, 1987). With a different method of transcript analysis, in a different culture (California), and in a different language, Main and her co-workers had achieved a corresponding hit-rate of about 80%.[4]

Follow-up of high-risk groups in comparison with normal groups

Our data and conceptions stem from longitudinal research with normal children and their families. Risk factors had been explicitly excluded by eliminating all factors related to developmental complications in our research. All of the children were full-term, healthy and had normal families with working, reliable fathers and available mothers in nicely furnished apartments or houses, mostly not in affluence, but without signs of poverty. Our original intention was to get some ideas about the lives of such families, usually unknown to researchers interested in remedial and/or prophylactic interventions. Can anything be learned from this research for high-risk individuals?

[4] Our hit-rate from Strange Situation data to the assessment at the age of six was between 83.3% and 88.9% (31 hits, 4 misses) (Wartner, 1987). Our hit-rate from Strange Situation to adult attachment interview was 78% (32 hits, 9 misses) (Fremmer-Bombik, 1987). The hit-rate from the age of six to the mothers' adult attachment interviews was only 67.5% (25 hits, 12 misses).

The approach presented here is, of course, related to Kalverboer's ethological one: the adaptation of functionally adapted patterns to natural conditions. Most of the problems outlined by Kalverboer cannot be solved by a simple switch from a variable-based to an individual-based approach. However, I believe that some of the problems of longitudinal high-risk research have a better chance of being solved if both approaches are being used in conjunction with each other, more or less simultaneously. The variables and the statistical tools behind them have the predictive power of well-defined variables. The synactive functioning of the individual, on the other hand, provides the basis for judging the proper place of the identified variable within the context of the individuals' adaptive functioning. Enhancing the predictive power of combinations of variables should eventually match the predictive power of the synactive approach for individuals with comparable synactive functioning. Many of the phenomena involved are known to experienced clinicians; they also know the particular situations – mostly challenging ones – in which the synactive capacities of such persons are actually impaired. And they have interpretative models, that is they assume different functional models behind these different styles of functioning of the individuals involved (e.g. Dührssen, 1984). The interpretative model may still be wrong. A better model, however, may come about only when 'properties are added to the working model as new phenomena require explanation', so that in the end the new 'properties [of the model] are isomorphic with the phenomena they purport to explain' (Hinde, p. 379). This, and the plea for a complementary strategy of variable and individual orientation, is most meaningful and promising in longitudinal developmental studies. Non-longitudinal studies, in contrast, do not provide the data base for testing the more or less grave implications of biological high risk in individuals under different social and cultural challenges.

References

Ainsworth, M. D. S., Blehar, M. C., Waters, E. and Wall, S. (1978) *Patterns of attachment: a psychological study of the Strange Situation*. Hillsdale, NJ: Erlbaum.

Als, H. (1985) Patterns of infant behavior: analogs of later organizational difficulties? In Duffy, F. H. and Geschwind, N. (eds.) *Dyslexia: current status and future directions*. Boston: Little, Brown, pp. 67–92.

(1986) A synactive model of neonatal behavioral organization: framework for the assessment of neuro-behavioral development in the premature infant and for support of infants and parents in the neo-natal intensive care enviroment. In Sweeney, J. K. (ed.) The high risk neonate. Developmental therapy perspectives. *Physical and Occupational therapy in pediatrics*, 6: 3–4, 3–55.

Bowlby, J. (1973) *Attachment*, vol. 2. London: Hogarth Press.

(1980) *Attachment*, vol. 3. London: Hogarth Press.

(1982a) *Attachment*, vol. 1, 2nd edn. London: Hogarth Press.

(1982b) Attachment and loss: retrospect and prospect. *American Journal of Orthopsychiatry*, 52, 664–78.

Cairns, R. B. (1986) Phenomena lost: issues in the study of development. In Valsiner, J. (ed.) *The individual subject and scientific psychology*. New York: Plenum Press, pp. 97–111.

Carew, J. V. (1980) *Experience and the development of intelligence in young children at home and in daycare*. Monographs of the Society for Research in Child Development 187, vol. 45, nos. 6–7.

Dührssen, A. (1984) Risikofaktoren für die neurotische Krankheitsentwicklung. *Zeitschrift für Psychosomatische Medizin*, 30, 18–42.

Erickson, M. F., Stroufe, L. A. and Egeland, B. (1985) The relationship between quality of attachment and behavior problems in preschool in a high risk sample. In Bretherton, I. and Waters, E. (eds.) *Growing points of attachment theory and research*. Monographs of the Society for Research in Child Development 209, vol. 50, nos. 1–2, pp. 147–66.

Fremmer-Bombik, E. (1987) Beobachtungen zur Beziehungsqualität im zweiten Lebensjahr und ihre Bedeutung im Lichte mütterlicher Kindheitserinnerungen. Ph.D. dissertation, University of Regensburg.

George, C., Kaplan, N. and Main, M. (in prep.) Adult attachment interview. In Main, M. (ed.) *Behavior and development of representational models of attachment: five methods of assessment*. Cambridge: Cambridge University Press.

Grossmann, K. (1984) Zweijährige Kinder im Zusammenspiel mit ihren Müttern, Vätern, einer fremden Erwachsenen und in einer Überraschungssituation: Beobachtungen aus bindungs-und kompetenztheoretischer Sicht. Ph.D. dissertation, University of Regensburg.

Grossmann, K., Grossmann, K. E., Spangler, G., Suess, G. and Unzner, L. (1985) Maternal sensitivity and newborns' orientation responses as related to quality of attachment in northern Germany. In Bretherton, I. and Waters, E. (eds.) *Growing points of attachment theory and research*. Monographs of the Society for Research in Child Development 209, vol. 50, nos. 1–2, pp., 233–56.

Grossmann, K. E. (1986) From idiographic approaches to nomothetic hypotheses. In Valsiner, J. (ed.) *The individual subject and scientific psychology*. New York: Plenum Press, pp. 37–69.

(1987) Die natürlichen Grundlagen zwischenmenschlicher Bindungen. In Niemitz, C. (ed.) *Erbe und Umwelt: Zur Natur von Anlage und Selbstbestimmung des Menschen*. Frankfurt: Suhrkamp, pp. 200–35.

Grossmann, K. E. and Grossmann, K. (1986) Phylogenetische und ontogenetische Aspekte der Entwicklung der Eltern-Kind Bindung und der kindlichen Sachkompetenz. *Zeitschrift für Entwicklungspsychologie und Pädagogische Psychologie*, 18, 287–315.

Grossmann, K. E., Grossmann, K., Huber, F. and Wartner, U. (1981) German children's behavior toward their mothers at 12 month and their fathers at 18 month in Ainsworth's strange situation. *International Journal of Behavioral Development*, 4, 157–81.

Grossmann, K. E., Grossmann, K. and Schwan, A. (1986) Capturing the wider view of attachment: a reanalysis of Ainsworth's Strange Situation. In Izard, C. E. and Read, P. (eds.) *Measuring emotions in infants and children*, vol. 2. Cambridge: Cambridge University Press, pp. 124–71.

Hinde, R. A. (1979) *Towards understanding relationships*. London: Academic Press.

Loher, I. (1984) Intellektuell wertvolle Erfahrungen beim Zusammenspiel von zweijährigen Kindern mit ihren Müttern. *Diplom* thesis, University of Regensburg.

McClelland, D. C. (1973) Testing for competence rather than for 'intelligence'. *American Psychologist*, **28**, 1–14.

Main, M. (ed.) (in prep.) *Behavior and development of representational models of attachment: five methods of assessment*. Cambridge: Cambridge University Press.

Main, M. and Goldwyn, R. (in prep.) Adult attachment classification system. In Main, M. (ed.) *Behavior and development of representational models of attachment: five methods of assessment*. Cambridge: Cambridge University Press.

Main, M. and Weston, D. R. (1981) The quality of the toddler's relationship to mother and to father: related to conflict behavior and the readiness to establish new relationships. *Child Development*, **52**, 932–40.

Main, M., Kaplan, N. and Cassidy, J. (1985) Security in infancy, childhood and adulthood: a move to the level of representation. In Bretherton, I. and Waters, E. (eds.) *Growing points of attachment theory and research*. Monographs of the Society for Research in Child Development 209, vol. 50, nos. 1–2, pp. 66–104.

Sameroff, A. J. and Chandler, M. J. (1975) Reproductive risk and the continuum of caretaking casualty. In Horowitz, F. D., Hetherington, M., Scarr-Salapatek, S. and Siegel, G. (eds.) *Review of development research*, vol. 4. Chicago: University of Chicago Press, pp. 187–244.

Schmidhuber, M. (1987) Die Qualität des Spiels von Fünfjährigen im Kindergarten im Zusammenhang mit der frühen Eltern–Kind Bindung. *Diplom* thesis, University of Regensburg.

Spangler, G. (1986) Der Einfluß von alltäglichen Erfahrungen auf die kindliche Kompetenzentwicklung: eine Analyse aufgrund von natürlichen Beobachtungen im zweiten Lebensjahr. Ph.D. dissertation, University of Regensburg.

Suess, G. (1987) Auswirkungen frühkindlicher Bindungserfahrungen auf Kompetenz im Kindergarten. Ph.D. dissertation, University of Regensburg.

Suess, G., Escher-Gräub, D. and Grossmann, K. E. (1985) Different patterns of adaptation in preschool: relations to early attachment classifications. Paper presented at the eighth biennial meeting of the International Society for Study of Behavioral Development (ISSBD), Tours, France.

Von Holst, E. and Saint Paul, U. (1969) Vom Wirkungsgefüge der Triebe. In von Holst, E. (ed.) *Zur Verhaltensphysiologie bei Tieren und Menschen. Gesammelte Abhanddlungen*, vol. 1. Munich: Piper, pp. 204–39.

Wartner, U. (1987) Attachment in infancy and at age six, and children's self-concept: a follow-up of a German longitudinal study. Ph.D. dissertation, University of Virginia.

Weigert, D. (1986) Intellektuell wertvolle Erfahrungen von zweijährigen Jungen und Mädchen in ihrer häuslichen Umgebung. *Diplom* thesis, University of Regensburg.

West, D. J. (1969) *Present conduct and future delinquency*. London: Heinemann.

9 Studying changes within individuals: the causes of offending

David P. Farrington

Introduction

The concept of cause inevitably involves the concept of change within individual units. A factor X causes a factor Y if, with some specified degree of regularity, changes in X are followed by changes in Y. For example, the death of a father may cause a decrease in the economic status of his family. As this example shows, the factors X and Y can be dichotomous (father living or dead), continuous (economic status), or of some intermediate kind. Equally, the individual unit can be the family rather than an individual person, although I will concentrate in this chapter on changes within individual persons, primarily in connection with the study of the causes of offending.

Causes are often inferred from variations between individuals rather than from changes within individuals. For example, a study might demonstrate that males were more likely to be convicted offenders than females, and that this relationship held after controlling statistically for other measured variables. It might then be concluded that gender was a cause of offending. However, drawing conclusions about causes, or in other words about the effect of changes within individuals, on the basis of variations between individuals, involves a conceptual leap that may not be justifiable. For all practical purposes, we cannot investigate whether changing males into females would lead to a decrease in their offending.

Furthermore, the control of extraneous causal factors is usually poorer in studies of variations between individuals than in studies of changes within individuals, where each person essentially acts as his or her own control. Non-experimental studies of variations between individuals inevitably have low internal validity because of the impossibility of measuring and controlling for all the possible factors that might influence the dependent variable. This is not true of randomized experiments on variations between individuals, because – with large samples – the randomization ensures that the average individual in one condition is equivalent to the average person in another, on all possible extraneous factors. However, it is difficult to study the causes of offending in randomized experiments.

My key argument is that the causes of offending can be investigated most effectively in studies of changes within individuals. Such studies inevitably require longitudinal rather than cross-sectional data, and their internal validity can be increased by combining experimental or quasi-experimental designs with longitudinal data (see Farrington *et al.*, 1986b). The remainder of this chapter essentially expands the arguments summarized in this introduction.

The focus of this paper is on causal analyses, but longitudinal data are, of course, useful for many other purposes: they can be used to document the natural history and course of development of offending and criminal careers, the onset of offending, numbers and types of offences committed at different ages, specialization or escalation in offending, lengths of criminal careers, and the termination of offending. An investigation of causes leads to an emphasis on change. However, it should not be forgotten that longitudinal data are also useful in studying the opposite of change: the degree of consistency and continuity in behaviour over time.

Towards a causal theory of offending

Characteristics of a causal theory

In studying the causes of offending, I assume that the aim should be to develop an explicit scientific theory that yields unambiguous quantitative predictions that can be tested against empirical data. The stress is not so much on falsifiability as on the ability of a theory to fit the data. The aim should be to compare theories in a way that makes it possible to conclude that one is better than another.

One important criterion by which to compare theories is the agreement between quantitative predictions and empirical data. However, this is not the only criterion. A simple theory that provides an approximate fit to the data may be preferable to a more complex one that provides a more exact fit. A general theory with wide applicability may be preferable to a specific theory with limited applicability, other things being equal (e.g. empirical fit and complexity). There should be more discussion of what are the characteristics of a 'good' theory and more attempt to reach a consensus on this among social scientists.

In developing and testing any theory, there is a fundamental distinction between theoretical constructs and empirical variables (sometimes called 'concepts' and 'indicators' respectively). I assume that statements about causal relationships between theoretical constructs lie at the heart of any theory. Theory testing requires operational definitions of theoretical constructs so that they can be measured by empirical variables. For example, the theoretical construct of 'criminal potential' might be measured by the empirical variable of the self-reported offending rate (the number of crimes committed within a certain time period). It is important for social scientists to develop agreed standard yardsticks to measure theoretical constructs, just as physicists have developed yardsticks to measure their theoretical constructs such as length.

Reduced to its simplest elements, a causal relationship between theoretical constructs is essentially of the form:

$$T_y = f(T_x) \tag{1}$$

This equation indicates that a theoretical construct T_y is some function of another theoretical construct T_x. Hence, a specified change in T_x will cause a specified change in T_y within an individual unit. Pursuing a physics analogy, Boyle's Law specifies that decreasing the volume of a gas will cause a predictable increase in its pressure, implying that T_y (pressure) is an inverse function of T_x (volume). To take a criminological example, it might be proposed that increases in the level of school failure (T_x) of an individual cause increases in his or her criminal potential (T_y).

The main questions about the concept of cause centre on whether a causal relationship is probabilistic or deterministic and on the time delay between the change in the cause and the change in the effect. I would not draw a clear distinction between causal and purposive (or teleological) theories; for example, T_x could be the perceived attractiveness of a future reward or the perceived probability of a future punishment. Early philosophers, such as Hume, assumed that there was a deterministic (100%) relationship between cause and effect, but this seems unnecessary and inappropriate for causal statements about human behaviour.

It is more plausible to assume that causal relationships are probabilistic: that a change in T_x has a certain probability of being followed by a change in T_y. Even better, the functional relationship could specify a range of changes in T_y that occurred according to a certain probability distribution. In the interests of simplicity, the key equation could specify how the average (or expected) value of T_y changed as a function of changes in T_x. The time delay between cause and effect could also have a probability distribution, and the average or expected time could perhaps be hypothesized in the light of empirical research. (I am assuming that theory development involves repeated interaction and feedback between theory and data.)

The discussion so far has concentrated on individuals as the units of interest. However, as mentioned earlier, causal theories could be based on larger units, such as groups or areas. A theory could also specify how individual criminal potential combined or interacted to produce group criminal potential. Similarly, it would be interesting to know how individual offending was linked to changes in more fundamental units, such as biochemical or physiological constructs. A lack of knowledge about constructs at one level does not necessarily preclude knowledge about constructs at another; for example, a lack of knowledge about electrons does not prevent people knowing how to switch an electric light on and off.

Key theoretical constructs

A key issue is what should be the theoretical constructs (T_ys in Equation (1)) which are causally influenced by other constructs (T_xs). I have chosen to focus on 'criminal potential' as a middle-range construct. It is plausible to suggest that, as criminal potential increases, so does the rate of committing crimes, on average.

More specific constructs could be proposed, such as stealing potential, vandalism potential, violence potential, and so on. However, all types of crime tend to be associated, so that persons who commit one type also tend to commit others. Since people tend to be versatile rather than specialized in their offending patterns (Klein, 1984), it is reasonable to propose a general construct of criminal potential. Even more general constructs could be proposed, such as antisociality or antisocial personality. Criminal acts such as stealing, violence and drug use tend to be associated with other antisocial acts such as heavy drinking, reckless driving and sexual promiscuity (West and Farrington, 1977). The concentration on a wide-ranging syndrome of antisociality would have the advantage of emphasizing the continuity between criminal and non-criminal behaviour, but for illustrative purposes here I will limit the key construct to criminal potential.

It could be argued, of course, that crime is a legally defined construct that varies over time and place. Hence, it might be better to define criminal potential behaviourally according to the kinds of act included in it (theft, property damage, and so on) rather than according to what is legally prohibited. The emphasis could be on explaining acts that have been classified as crimes at some time or in some place (probably limited to Western society in recent years) rather than acts currently classified as crimes in England. The consistency in definitions of crime over time and place is, however, more striking than the variability, and whether an act is legally classified as a crime may have an important effect on the likelihood that it is committed.

It is easy to see similarities between criminal potential and key constructs in existing theories. For example, a key construct in social-learning theories of crime (e.g. Trasler, 1962; and Eysenck, 1964) is conscience, and it is assumed that the commission of criminal acts varies inversely with the strength of the conscience. Hence criminal potential could be the inverse of the strength of the conscience. Similar comments apply to the social-control theory of Hirschi (1969), which assumes that the commission of criminal acts varies inversely with the strength of the bond to society. In the slightly more complex strain theories of Cohen (1955) and

Cloward and Ohlin (1960), it is postulated that the commission of criminal acts depends on the difference between a person's aspirations and his or her ability to achieve goals of status or material success. Criminal potential may also be related to a criminal self-concept or criminal attitudes, but whether these are different names for the same construct or different constructs that are causally related is not immediately obvious (and requires careful empirical investigation).

Empirical variables

After theoretical constructs have been chosen, it is important to define them operationally and measure them using empirical variables. For example, self-reports of offending during the past year could be used as an index of criminal potential. The extent to which each empirical variable is a valid measure of the underlying theoretical construct is usually called 'construct validity' (Cook and Campbell, 1979). One way of establishing whether any empirical variable E_y is a valid measure of a theoretical construct T_y is to compare it with other measures of the same theoretical construct. For example, if T_y is criminal potential, E_{y1} could be the conviction rate, E_{y2} self-reports of offending, E_{y3} parent reports, E_{y4} teacher reports, and E_{y5} peer reports. To the extent that these empirical variables are interrelated, they may all be measuring the same underlying theoretical construct.

The measured value of an empirical variable depends partly on the value of the underlying theoretical construct and partly on measurement error. For example, the conviction rate may depend partly on criminal potential and partly on selection biases by the police and courts that are caused by other features (e.g. poverty or having criminal parents).

In discussing theoretical constructs and empirical variables, it is important to consider the types of variable involved. A key distinction is that between discontinuous and (tolerably) continuous variables. For example, whether or not someone is convicted is a discontinuous (dichotomous) variable, whereas the number of self-reported acts is often a continuous variable. In addition, discontinuous variables may be nominal or ordinal, and continuous variables may be measured on ordinal or interval scales. The distribution of theoretical constructs and empirical variables over people is important. For example, the distribution of self-reported offending scores is usually J-shaped at any given age, with most people admitting very few acts and a few people admitting many acts. If criminal potential was assumed to have a J-shaped rather than a normal distribution, this would have important statistical implications for between-subjects analyses.

Perhaps the simplest assumption is that criminal potential is a dichotomous variable. It could then be hypothesized that, at some age, a proportion p of a sample are offenders, while a proportion $1-p$ are non-offenders. This immediately raises the question of how people move between offender and non-offender states with age. These kinds of issue have been discussed by Blumstein *et al.* (1985) and by Barnett *et al.* (1987). There could be a probabilistic relationship between the theoretical construct of criminal potential and the empirical variable of conviction; for example, offenders could have a probability q of being convicted during a certain period, and non-offenders a probability r. It could also be assumed that offenders and non-offenders had different probability distributions of self-reported offending scores.

Another possibility would be to assume that criminal potential was a continuous variable with a specified distribution over people at any given time. It could then be hypothesized that the probability of being convicted increased for each person with increasing criminal potential, and there could be a probabilistic mapping of criminal potential onto self-reported offending scores. Again, it would be important to investigate how criminal potential varied with age.

One complication is that it may be difficult to get comparable measures of theoretical constructs at different ages. This is because the behavioural manifestation of a theoretical construct might vary with age because of either individual or environmental changes. For example, high criminal potential might be reflected in troublesome school behaviour at age 8, in burglary at age 15, and in welfare benefit fraud at age 25. Self-reported offending items that are applicable at one age may not be applicable at others. Similarly, the behavioural manifestation of a theoretical construct may vary with other factors, such as gender. High criminal potential in males may be reflected in different behaviour than high criminal potential in females.

It is useful to draw a distinction between long-term and immediate influences on offending. The level of criminal potential at any age may depend on historical factors, such as a history of rewards and punishments following deviant acts, as suggested by social-learning theories. Whether a person with a given degree of criminal potential commits a crime in a particular situation may depend on immediate situational factors, such as the existence of an opportunity, the immediate level of boredom or anger, peer pressure, the value of property which can be stolen, and the probability of being caught (see, for example, Clarke and Cornish, 1985). The distinction between long-term and immediate influences is related to the distinction between explaining the development of criminal people and explaining the occurrence of criminal events. My focus in this chapter is on long-term influences and on explaining the development of criminal people.

Returning to criminal potential, it is not difficult to understand why its behavioural manifestation might vary with changes in life style, opportunities and immediate situational factors. The behavioural manifestation may vary even though the level of criminal potential itself stays constant. The challenge to researchers is to measure theoretical constructs using valid empirical variables.

Developing a causal theory

As already mentioned, the basic building block of a causal theory is the specification of the functional relationship between T_y and T_x, as indicated in Equation (1). For illustrative purposes, Figure 1 shows some possible functional relationships between a T_y of criminal potential and a T_x of school failure. It is assumed that the relationship will only be studied within certain boundary conditions (T_{x1}, T_{y1} and T_{x2}, T_{y2}), which may possibly correspond to floor and ceiling effects. Perhaps school failure has no effect below a certain level and no further incremental effect above a certain level. School failure may only have causal effects when a person is at school, since school failure will only vary during this time.

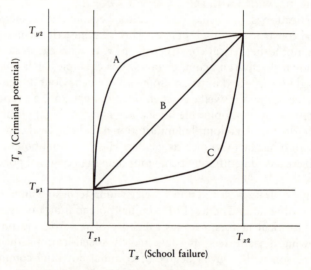

Figure 1   Some possible functional relationships

Between the boundaries, curve B shows that the relation is linear; for any given person, criminal potential increases in direct proportion to increases in the degree of school failure. Curve A shows that the first few degrees of school failure cause a big increase in criminal potential, while further increases have a lesser incremental effect. Conversely, curve C shows that it takes a great deal of school failure before there is any marked effect on criminal potential. These curves draw attention to the importance of the slope f' (T_y) and the acceleration f'' (T_y). The acceleration is zero for B, negative for A, and positive for C. An emphasis on change naturally focuses attention on differential equations. The relationship between T_y and $d(T_y)$ – the change in T_y – T_x and $d(T_x)$ – the change in T_x – could be investigated.

There are other possible uses of boundary conditions. For example, they might specify the range within which a functional relationship was reversible. Just as a spring becomes permanently distended after a certain degree of stretching, there may be a point beyond which decreases in T_x (after a series of increases) would not cause the predicted decreases in T_y. Boundary conditions might also mark turning points, where one functional relationship ends and another begins. They might also specify a range of applicability of theoretical constructs. For example, the effect on offending of getting married in England at present could not be studied under age 16, the minimum age for marriage.

Another use of boundary conditions would be to specify interactions. For example, the relationship between T_x and T_y may differ according to the value of another theoretical construct. This comes close to Rutter's (1985, p. 600) definition of protective factors: influences that 'alter a person's response to some environmental hazard that predisposes to a maladaptive outcome'. For example, if increases in school failure caused increases in criminal potential only among children from low-income families, and not among children from higher-income families, higher income would be a protective factor.

The term 'protective factor' could also be used to refer to changes in theoretical constructs that cause decreases in offending. For example, in curve B in Figure 1, a decrease in school failure from high to low causes a corresponding decrease in criminal potential. Hence just as high school failure is a risk factor, low school failure is a protective factor. However, this is not always true. In curve C, there is little change in criminal potential between medium and low levels of school failure, but there is a large change between medium and high levels. Hence a functional relationship like curve C could perhaps be interpreted as showing that high school failure was a risk factor but that low school failure was not a protective factor (in comparison with medium school failure). The reverse conclusions might follow from curve A. In discussing risk and protective factors, it is clearly desirable to specify the complete functional relationship, as in Figure 1.

More complex issues
Discussing this functional relationship draws attention to the importance of the time dimension and to the possibility of reciprocal causal relationships. If an increase in school failure causes an increase in criminal potential, then T_x is causally prior. On the other hand, an increase in criminal potential may also cause an increase in school failure, so T_y may be causally prior. Of course, both effects may happen, although this might lead to an unstable (positive feedback) system. In real life, it is more

common to have reciprocal functional relationships that maintain some kind of equilibrium, as in a homeostatic system.

The time dimension could be considered explicitly, as in the following equation:

$$T_y (t + d) = f [T_x (t)]$$ (2)

This indicates that the value of T_y at time $t + d$ is some function of the value of T_x at time t. As mentioned earlier, it would be interesting to try to investigate the time delay d between a cause and an effect, assuming that both occur at specific points in time. A more complex possibility is that the causal effect depends on the recent history of values of T_x. For example, a given level of school failure maintained over a long time period may have more effect on offending than the same level maintained over a shorter period.

There has been some concern in recent years with 'sleeper effects', which are long delayed after the causes. For example, the long-term effects of a pre-school intellectual enrichment programme on offending (Berrueta-Clement et al., 1984) have been cited as an example of this. However, it may be more plausible to hypothesize that sleeper effects really reflect a long chain of causal relationships between theoretical constructs rather than a long-delayed effect (see, for example, Woodhead, 1985). It would be useful to try to elucidate causal chains. For example, increased school failure may cause an increased self-concept of being a failure, which in turn may cause increased frustration, which in turn may cause increased criminal potential.

This discussion has assumed that T_y and T_x are continuous variables, which of course they may not be. As mentioned earlier, it is important to investigate the nature of all theoretical constructs. If T_y and T_x were hypothesized to be discontinuous variables, the functional relationship could be summarized by a transition matrix. For example, it could be proposed that, when T_x changed from state s_1 (unmarried) to state s_2 (married), T_y changed from state s_3 (high criminal potential) to state s_4 (low criminal potential) with a certain probability.

Equation (1) specifies only the most basic building block of a theory. We might wish to hypothesize that T_y is not only a function of T_x but also a function of other theoretical constructs T_a, T_b, T_c, and so on. This raises the question of how these constructs interact with, or add to, each other. In general, it will be difficult or impossible to specify all theoretical constructs that influence T_y, and the complete forms of their interacting functional relationships. It is much easier to specify the functional link between a change in T_x and a change in T_y than between a value of T_x and a value of T_y. This is another reason to concentrate on changes rather than absolute values. There might be a longitudinal sequence of changes, so that T_a is some function of T_b, T_x is some function of T_a, and finally T_y is some function of T_x. For example, Elliott *et al.* (1985) hypothesized that strain, inadequate socialization, and social disorganization jointly led to weak conventional bonding, which led to strong delinquent bonding, which in turn led to delinquent behaviour.

In testing a theory, it is necessary to measure the theoretical constructs T_y and T_x by corresponding empirical variables E_y and E_x, and to investigate how the empirical variable E_y changes as a function of the empirical variable E_x:

$$E_y = f(E_x) \tag{3}$$

In general, relationships between empirical variables are probabilistic. The form of the function relating E_y and E_x should give some clue about the form of the function relating T_y and T_x. If E_y and E_x are not functionally related, this may mean either than T_y and T_x are not functionally related or that E_y and/or E_x are not valid measures of the theoretical constructs.

As mentioned earlier, the measured value of any empirical variable is some function of the underlying theoretical construct and of the method of measurement. Hence, if self-reports of offending were significantly related to self-reports of school failure, this could mean that the theoretical constructs were functionally related or it could reflect common measurement bias (for example, if those who were willing to report their offences were also willing to report their school failure). In order to distinguish relationships between theoretical constructs from relationships caused artefactually by measurement bias, it is desirable to have multiple measures of each theoretical construct and to relate them to each other.

Unfortunately, few researchers attempt to investigate functional relationships such as those shown in Figure 1. In principle, such relationships could be studied by taking individuals with a low degree of school failure and systematically increasing this in stages, measuring the offending rate at each stage. This would be similar to a physics experiment to investigate how the length of an iron bar changed with increases in its temperature when other physical conditions were controlled for. In practice, for ethical reasons, attempts would have to be made to decrease school failure rather than to increase it. However, it is difficult to carry out such experiments with people, although they are analogous to the study of the dose–response relationship in medicine. Perhaps biological influences (e.g. the effect of drugs or diet) could be studied more adequately than social or psychological ones if the effects of biological manipulations were large in comparison with individual variation. Ultimately, however, criminological researchers should aim to develop mathematically specified theories and to plot graphs such as those shown in Figure 1 in order to establish causal relationships.

Changes within, and variations between, individuals

Experimentation and internal validity

An important implication of this discussion about causes is that causal relationships can only be established with high internal validity (Cook and Campbell, 1979) if theoretical constructs can vary within individuals. In other words, it must be possible to study the change in T_x and any related change in T_y for one individual or experimental unit. A key problem in demonstrating a causal relationship is to control extraneous theoretical constructs so that the effect of T_x can be isolated. A causal relationship can be established most securely if T_x can be experimentally manipulated, while holding constant all other theoretical constructs that influence (have causal effects on) T_y. In a Boyle's Law experiment, the volume of a gas can be experimentally manipulated while holding constant extraneous influences (e.g. temperature) in the controlled conditions of the physics laboratory.

In the social sciences, the best way of controlling for all extraneous influences is to assign people at random to different experimental conditions (values of T_x). The main advantage of a randomized experiment lies in the control of independent and extraneous variables to demonstrate causal effects. Providing that a fairly large number of people are randomly assigned to experimental conditions, those in one condition will be equivalent (within the limits of statistical fluctuation) to those in another condition in all theoretical constructs except those manipulated experimentally. Hence any variation in a dependent variable can be shown, quite conclusively, to be a function of the deliberate variation in the independent variable. The main theoretical problem would then be to elucidate the causal chain linking the independent and dependent constructs.

As an example of a randomized experiment on offending, Farrington and Knight (1980) studied stealing by leaving stamped, addressed, unsealed, apparently lost letters in the street, each containing an amount of money and a handwritten note indicating the intended recipient. Members of the public who picked up these letters had the opportunity to be dishonest and steal the money or to be honest and post the letter. Since all experimental conditions were in a random order, people were essentially assigned at random to them. Several independent variables were studied, but one result was that more letters containing £5 were stolen than letters containing £1. The researchers were testing the theory that stealing involved a rational decision. They concluded that stealing (operationally defined by non-return of the letter) increased as a function of its increased utility or benefits (operationally defined by the amount of money in the letter). Of course, in plotting the functional relationship between stealing and utility, it would have been better to study the effect of several different values of utility, but lack of resources made this impossible in practice.

An important difference between this experiment and the Boyle's Law one is that this involves a between-subjects design. The Boyle's Law experiment essentially involves a within-subjects design, since the independent variable of volume is varied over the same experimental unit (the gas). In the lost-letter experiment, each person was exposed to only one value of the independent variable of the amount of cash. This was necessary for practical and methodological reasons. If a within-subjects design had been used and people had picked up more than one letter, they might have guessed that they were participating in an experiment and hence behaved atypically. The danger of the within-subjects design in experiments with people is that a person in one condition may not be equivalent to the same person in another condition afterwards. In other words, there may be testing effects.

In investigating causes, it is convenient to distinguish *changes* (within subjects) from *variations* (between subjects). My definition of a causal relationship involves changes in T_x producing changes in T_y, not variations in T_x producing variations in T_y. However, when subjects are randomly assigned to experimental conditions, variations can be regarded as equivalent to changes. This is because, if samples are large, the randomization ensures that the experimental units (people) in one condition are equivalent to those in another. It is plausible to argue that the people in the £1 condition would have behaved like people in the £5 condition if the £1 people had been in the £5 condition. Clearly, if T_x can be manipulated, its causal effect on T_y could in principle be investigated in a randomized experiment. Furthermore, the extent to which the functional relationship between T_x and T_y is different for different classes of people could be investigated, by randomly assigning within classes.

Unfortunately, in most cases the causes of offending cannot be investigated experimentally. (For reviews of randomized experiments in criminology, see Farrington, 1983b; and Farrington *et al.*, 1986b.) However, by using the techniques of quasi-experimental analysis, it is possible to draw convincing conclusions about causal relationships from non-experimental data. My main argument is that, in the absence of random-ized experiments, longitudinal data are required to draw causal conclu-sions with high internal validity. This does not necessarily mean that a longitudinal *survey* is required, since longitudinal *data* can be collected (retrospectively) in cross-sectional surveys. However, because of methodological difficulties associated with retrospective data, such as retrospective biases and forgetting, prospective longitudinal surveys should usually be preferred.

Problems of cross-sectional data

Many researchers draw causal conclusions from cross-sectional (corre-lational) data, accepting that one variable causes another if (a) the two variables are statistically associated, (b) one variable occurs before the other, and (c) the association holds independently of other (measured) variables (see, for example, Hirschi and Selvin, 1967). However, it is impossible with cross-sectional data to control for all extraneous influences or to eliminate many of the threats to valid causal inference listed by Cook and Campbell (1979). Hence causal conclusions based on cross-sectional data inevitably have low internal validity.

Even the best cross-sectional data can only suggest that variations (between subjects) in T_x lead to variations in T_y, and it may not be justifiable to make the conceptual leap and conclude that changes (within subjects) in T_x would cause changes in T_y. This depends on the nature of the theoretical constructs. For all practical purposes, some constructs – such as gender and race – can vary *only* between subjects. In cross-sectional data, since all variation is between subjects, no distinction is typically made between constructs that can only vary between subjects and constructs that can also vary within subjects. If the concept of cause depends on changes within subjects (as I have argued), then it is not possible in practice to demonstrate conclusively the causal effect of changes in gender or race on any other theoretical construct. Hence it may be inadvisable to include constructs that can only vary between subjects – such as gender and race – in a theory as possible causes.

The empirical variables of gender and race might be included in a theory if it was assumed that they were measuring theoretical constructs that changed within subjects. For example, it might be hypothesized that gender was related to crime because of the underlying theoretical construct of the testosterone level, which is higher in males than in females, and which varies with age (see Gove, 1985). Alternatively, gender and race might be viewed as boundary conditions, so that the effect of a T_x on a T_y was different for boys and girls (for example).

Longitudinal data make it possible to study both changes within subjects and variations between subjects separately. Because of this separation, and because of the high internal validity of quasi-experimental analyses, longitudinal data are far more suitable than cross-sectional data for testing causal hypotheses. Furthermore, causal conclusions based on changes within subjects in longitudinal data could in principle have practical implications for preventive or rehabilitative treatment designed to change people, providing that the construct that varies within subjects is manipulable. No possible treatment implications could follow from the argument that a construct that varied only between subjects – such as gender or race – was a cause of offending, since we cannot change a person's gender or race. Similarly, no possible treatment implications could follow from the argument that a non-manipulable construct that varied within subjects – such as age – was a cause of offending.

Treatment implications can readily be drawn from manipulable theoretical constructs. For example, it could be predicted that a decrease in school failure would cause a decrease in offending. This prediction was indeed supported by the Head Start experiment of Berrueta-Clement *et al.* (1984). They found that a preschool intellectual enrichment programme led to decreases in school failure and decreases in offending. In another test of this hypothesis, Gold and Mann (1984) compared badly behaved juveniles assigned to alternative schools, which aimed to increase their success experiences, with similar juveniles in regular schools. Disruptive school behaviour was less in the alternative schools; however, the schools had no differential effect on offending in the community. In many respects, a good way to test a hypothesis about the causes of offending is to carry out a prevention or treatment experiment. This clearly requires a manipulable theoretical construct.

Problems of existing research

Most behavioural researchers, even if they have longitudinal data, carry out essentially between-subjects analyses (Labouvie, 1986), and this is certainly true in criminology. Most existing studies of the causes of offending have low internal validity because of the inadequate control of extraneous variables in cross-sectional (between-subjects) analyses. Even longitudinal researchers on crime and delinquency have used essentially cross-sectional methods of analysing their data. Hence, it is rare to find a convincing demonstration that any given theoretical construct is a cause of offending, and little is known about how offending can be prevented or treated successfully.

After the Second World War, the first important demonstration of the correlates of offending was completed by Glueck and Glueck (1950), in a comparison of 500 institutionalized male delinquents and 500 relatively well behaved male non-delinquents from the same areas of Massachusetts. However, the Gluecks made little attempt to establish which factors were related to offending independently of others, and it was not clear in this retrospective study whether their measured variables preceded or followed offending.

Perhaps the best-known delinquency research of the 1960s was the survey of over 4,000 California juveniles by Hirschi (1969). This was an advance on the Gluecks' work in that it was theoretically guided and focused on self-reported delinquency, thereby avoiding some of the objections which emphasized biases in official processing. However, Hirschi's research was still essentially cross-sectional in nature, and it did not demonstrate independent influences of different variables or overcome problems of causal ordering.

Research projects of the 1970s showed more sophistication in multivariate analyses. This was true, for example, in Johnson's (1979) cross-sectional self-reported delinquency survey of over 700 Seattle juveniles. He used path analysis to investigate causal relationships between such factors as attachment to parents, school success, delinquent associates and delinquent behaviour. Unfortunately, Johnson's data (as in most criminological surveys) clearly violate the statistical assumptions underlying path analysis, and he was not able to demonstrate causal order unambiguously. It is unfortunate that some of the most widely used methods of analysing cross-sectional data are, strictly speaking, inapplicable in most social-science surveys.

The major assumptions underlying path analysis (and multiple linear regression, another commonly used technique) are that the variables are measured on interval scales and are normally distributed. Most criminological variables are measured on nominal or ordinal scales or have highly skewed distributions, making it difficult to interpret the percentage of variance explained. Another assumption is that the independent variables are unrelated, but usually there is a multicollinearity, which makes it impossible to draw conclusions about the relative effects of different variables (Gordon, 1968). It is also assumed that relationships between independent and dependent variables are linear and additive, but this is rarely tested. Because of the violation of statistical assumptions, it is a mistake to assume that path coefficients (or beta weights in multiple regression) represent the direct causal effect of an independent variable on a dependent one (Palmer and Carlson, 1976).

The most influential delinquency research project of the 1980s is probably the American national longitudinal survey of over 1,700 juveniles by Elliott *et al.* (1985). Unlike much previous longitudinal research, this was theoretically guided, and was intended to test Elliott's integration of strain, control and social-learning theories. However, the only book that has yet been published from this project essentially treats the data in the same way as Johnson (1979), using path analysis. Elliott and his colleagues tried to use LISREL, but the highly skewed self-reported delinquency scales meant that 'either the iterative minimization procedure used in obtaining maximum likelihood estimates would not converge and successive estimates were becoming more and more unreasonable or the converged solutions were nonsensical, providing negative estimates of variances and inconsistent estimates of certain relationships' (Elliott *et al.*, 1985, p. 118).

Virtually all existing research on offending uses between-subjects analyses in which, for each relationship between T_x and T_y, each individual essentially contributes one observation to a scattergram. The extent to which this scattergram approximates to a straight-line relationship is rarely investigated. As already mentioned, these analyses cannot demonstrate causal relationships convincingly because of their inability to control effectively for extraneous variables. Put simply, two people who differ in any given factor (e.g. school failure) also differ in numerous other factors that may be causally related to offending, and many of these other factors are inevitably unmeasured in cross-sectional research and hence are uncontrollable statistically.

No conceivable development of appropriate statistical techniques could overcome this fundamental problem of between-subjects analysis. It is better to study relationships within subjects in longitudinal research, so that each person essentially acts as his or her own control. John Smith at one level of school failure will be equivalent to John Smith at another level on all individual difference factors, and other possible threats to valid inference (e.g. maturation and testing effects – see Cook and Campbell, 1979) can be eliminated in quasi-experimental analyses. Furthermore, the problem of causal order can be resolved more effectively in longitudinal research. Providing that measures are taken frequently, the relative timing of changes can be established.

An advantage of plotting relationships for individuals (or classes of individuals) rather than for the whole sample is that the disaggregation may reveal important individual differences or interactions. When each individual contributes only one observation to a scattergram, there seems to be an implicit underlying assumption that all individuals are homogeneous: that John Smith at one level of school failure is essentially the same as Robert Brown at another (or can be made to look the same as Robert Brown by appropriate statistical controls). When relationships are plotted within individuals, it can be explicitly acknowledged that John Smith's functional relationship between school failure and criminal potential may be quite different from Robert Brown's. Perhaps John Smith belongs to a class of people resembling curve A in Figure 1, while Robert Brown belongs to a class of people resembling curve C. A between-subjects analysis might produce the aggregated curve B, which does not apply to either class of people.

The relationship between age and crime provides a good example of differences between aggregate and individual curves. The aggregate cross-sectional curve is well known (see Farrington, 1986a). For males in England and Wales, the official crime rate (including convictions and cautions) increases from age 10 to reach a marked peak at age 15, and then declines with age, at first quickly but later more slowly. Aggregate self-report curves are similar. However, the individual longitudinal curves seem to be quite different. For those who are offenders, their rate of offending does not change consistently with age (Farrington, 1983a). Contrary to the impression conveyed by the aggregate curve, an offender at age 25 apparently commits just as many offences as an offender at age 15. The main reason for the aggregate curve is that many more persons are offenders at age 15 than at age 25. In other words, the aggregate curve reflects the prevalence of offenders rather than the frequency of offending by offenders. This shows the importance of plotting individual curves in trying to draw conclusions about individuals.

The Cambridge Study in Delinquent Development

Description of the survey

I will illustrate between-subjects and within-subjects analyses of longitudinal data by discussing the Cambridge Study in Delinquent Development, a project on which I have worked for many years. This project was originally directed by Donald West, and I am now in charge of it. It is a prospective longitudinal survey of 411 males. When they were first contacted at age 8–9 in 1961–2, the vast majority were on the registers of six state primary schools within a one-mile radius of our research office in a working-class area of London. The boys were overwhelmingly white, working class, and of British origin. More details of the survey can be found in four books (West, 1969; 1982; West and Farrington, 1973; 1977), and a concise summary is also available (Farrington and West, 1981).

The aim in this investigation of the development of juvenile delinquency and adult crime was to measure as many factors as possible that were alleged to be causes or correlates of offending. Most information was derived from interviews. The males in the study were interviewed and tested in their schools by psychologists and social scientists when they were aged about 8, 10 and 14, and they were interviewed in our research office at about ages 16, 18 and 21. They were then seen in their homes at age 24, and in 1984–6 they were interviewed again in their homes at age 32. Information has been collected about such factors as living circumstances, employment histories, relationships with females, leisure activities such as drinking and fighting, and offending behaviour. The interviews at age 18 and later ages were fully tape-recorded and transcribed, making verbatim quotations possible.

The boys' parents were also interviewed, by psychiatric social workers. These interviews took place about once a year from when the boy was aged 8–9 until when he was 14–15 and in his last year of compulsory schooling. The parents provided details about such matters as family income, family size, their employment histories, their child-rearing behaviour (including attitudes, discipline and parental agreement), their degree of supervision of the boy, and temporary or permanent separations of the boy from them.

The boys' teachers also completed questionnaires when the boys were aged about 8, 10, 12 and 14. These provided information about the boys' troublesome and aggressive school behaviour, their school attainments, and their truancy. Ratings were obtained from the boys' peers when they were in their primary schools about such matters as their daring, dishonesty, troublesomeness and popularity.

Searches were also carried out in the central Criminal Record Office in London to try to locate convictions of the boys, of their parents, of their brothers and sisters, and (in recent years) of their wives and cohabitees. Convictions were only counted if they were for offences normally recorded in the Criminal Record Office, thereby excluding minor crimes such as traffic offences and drunkenness. The most common offences included were thefts, burglaries and unauthorized takings of motor vehicles.

Up to the 25th birthday, about one-third of the males were convicted of criminal offences (Farrington, 1983a). The peak age for the number of different persons convicted was 17, which is the age at which a juvenile becomes an adult in English criminal law. There was a strong relationship between juvenile and adult convictions. For example, 77% of those with four or more convictions as juveniles went on to have four or more convictions as adults, and conversely 84% of those with no juvenile convictions also had no adult convictions.

The boys who began their conviction careers at the earliest ages (10–12) tended to become the most persistent offenders. During every age range, they averaged more convictions per person than those first convicted at later ages. The concentration of offending in a small number of boys was remarkable. Only 23 boys (less than 6% of the sample) accounted for half of all the criminal convictions of the sample up to the 25th birthday. Every one of these boys was first convicted by age 15.

To a considerable extent, the self-reports and official records identified the same youths as offenders. For example, between ages 15 and 18, 11% admitted burglary and 7% were convicted of it, including 5% both convicted and admitting it. The 80 boys who admitted the highest number of delinquent acts at ages 14 and 16 overlapped significantly with the 84 convicted juvenile delinquents, since 41 boys were in both groups. Consequently, conclusions about characteristics of offenders based on convictions were generally similar to conclusions based on self-reports of offending. For ease of exposition, the worst offenders in the sample will be termed 'the offenders' and the remainder 'the non-offenders'.

The offenders differed significantly from the non-offenders on almost every factor we measured. In terms of statistically significant relationships, we had an embarrassment of riches. In some ways this was surprising, because to a large extent the sample was homogeneous in important factors such as age, gender, ethnicity, social class, neighbourhood, and of course culture. However, the fact that most variables measured in this survey were significantly related to most other variables caused great problems of analysis.

Between-subjects analyses

One problem was to reduce the large number of measured variables in the Study (200 at age 8 alone) to a more manageable number. The guiding aim was to eliminate redundancy and to have each distinct theoretical construct measured by one empirical variable. This was achieved by identifying clusters of variables that were related empirically and theoretically, and then either choosing one variable as the best representative of the cluster or combining a number of the variables in the cluster into a single composite variable (see Farrington and West, 1981). This data reduction technique was more subjective than the factor analysis described in West (1969) but, taking account of the different kinds of variable involved, it was felt to be more appropriate.

About 20 key variables measured at age 8–10 remained after this data reduction process was completed. The final stage in the analysis described by West and Farrington (1973) was to investigate, using a matching technique, whether each key variable predicted delinquency independently of each other key variable. For example, low family income and large family size were significantly related to each other and to delinquency. It might be argued, for example, that poverty was the real cause of delinquency and that offenders only appeared to come from larger families because they came from poorer families that tended also to be larger. If this were true, offenders and non-offenders would not differ significantly in family size when matched on family income. However, they did. Furthermore, offenders and non-offenders differed significantly in family income when matched on family size. These results showed that family income and family size were independently predictive of delinquency.

These analyses showed that, at age 8–10, the boys who later became offenders tended to be rated troublesome or daring, and that they tended to come from the poorer families, the larger-sized families, those with criminal parents, those suffering poor (erratic or harsh) parental child-rearing behaviour, and those with low intelligence. These were the most important independent predictors of offending.

The matching analyses described by West and Farrington (1973) were undoubtedly rather crude. We chose to do them in the late 1960s and early 1970s because we were concerned only to use statistical techniques that were appropriate to our (usually categorical) data. Our data clearly violated the assumptions of multiple linear regression and related techniques. When loglinear and logistic techniques – which were applicable to categorical data – became available, we used them, and some of the major conclusions can be found in Farrington (1986b). We were interested in how far the occurrence of offending and other factors at any given age acted as 'stepping stones' on the progressive path towards offending at a later age. Hence we used loglinear and logistic techniques to investigate the independent predictors of offending at different ages.

In general, the best independent predictor of offending at any age was the measure of offending at the immediately preceding age. For example, the best predictor of offending at age 21–4 was offending at age 17–20, closely followed by offending at age 14–16. The best predictor of offending at the earliest age (10–13) was troublesomeness at age 8–10. Hence there did seem to be a progression from child troublesome behaviour to juvenile delinquency and adult crime.

It is important to distinguish between predictors that measure the same theoretical construct as the dependent variable, but at an earlier time, and predictors that measure different theoretical constructs. It seems more reasonable to argue that offending at one age predicts offending at the next age because of the relatively consistent ordering of persons over time on the underlying theoretical construct (e.g. 'criminal potential') rather than to argue that offending at one age in some way causes offending at the next age. Hence only different theoretical constructs can be causes. However, it might alternatively be suggested that the theoretical construct underlying child troublesomeness is different from that underlying adult crime, and that troublesomeness leads to (but does not cause) crime in a manifestation of a progressively developing syndrome. These kinds of syndrome have been investigated most thoughtfully by Robins and Wish (1977). In either case, troublesomeness does not cause crime.

Over and above the behavioural continuity or progression from troublesomeness to crime, four factors were independently important predictors: (a) economic deprivation, including low income and poor housing, (b) family criminality, including convicted parents and delinquent siblings, (c) parental mishandling, including poor supervision and poor child-rearing behaviour, and (d) school failure, including low intelligence and attainment. Farrington (1986b) proposed a theory to explain why these factors might be possible causes of offending.

Interestingly, the valid loglinear and logistic techniques gave rather similar results to invalid multiple regression, probably reflecting the general linear model underlying all of these methods. Again, these techniques were similarly efficient in predicting delinquency in validation samples (Farrington, 1985). However, the major problem is that all of these techniques use essentially between-subjects comparisons. Even the successive prediction exercises in the 'stepping stones' model does not take full advantage of the longitudinal nature of the data to investigate changes within individuals.

Within-subjects analyses

A number of within-subjects analyses have been carried out in the Cambridge Study. Perhaps the best example of an explicitly quasi-experimental analysis is the investigation of the effects of convictions on offending (Farrington, 1977). This contrasted two theories: labelling and

178 David P. Farrington

deterrence. According to labelling theory, one effect of a conviction should be to amplify delinquent behaviour, perhaps because of the effect of stigmatization on a person's self-concept. According to deterrence theory, the effect of a conviction should be to decrease delinquent behaviour, because detected offenders become more afraid of the possible consequences of offending.

In comparing these theories, the basic design was to investigate the self-reported offending of persons before and after they were convicted for the first time (between ages 14 and 18). All sample members were assigned percentile scores between 0 and 100 according to their admitted offences, and it was found that the average score of convicted youths increased significantly, from 59 before the conviction to 69 after. In this test, each youth acted as his own control, and it was clear that the convicted youths became relatively more delinquent. This was especially true when they were compared with an individually matched sample of unconvicted youths, whose scores decreased from 59 to 51 during the same period. The increased offending of the convicted youths could not be explained by reference to individual difference factors which stayed constant over time. However, it was necessary to test a number of plausible alternative explanations of the effect (or threats to internal validity).

The results could not have been caused by maturation (processes within the subjects operating as a function of the passage of time), history (events occurring between the first and the second test), testing (the effect of taking one test on the scores in a second) or instrumentation (changes in the measuring instruments or scoring methods). Each of these factors would have been expected to affect the whole sample equally. The results could not have been caused by mortality (differential loss of subjects from the comparison groups) because the analysis was based only on youths interviewed at all three ages (14, 16 and 18). Furthermore, statistical regression to the mean could not explain the results because the scores of the convicted youths became even more extreme at 18 than they had been at 14.

The major plausible alternative explanation of the results was selection: the convicted youths could possibly have differed from the unconvicted ones on some factor unrelated to conviction that caused an increase in offending. However, no other factor was found that caused such an increase. The convicted youths were individually matched with unconvicted ones at age 14 not only on self-reported offending but also on a prediction score based on the best predictors of delinquency (troublesomeness, low family income, large family size, parental criminality, poor parental child-rearing behaviour and low intelligence). This did not significantly change the results. While these factors predicted high self-reported delinquency at age 18, they did not predict an *increase* in percentile scores between 14 and 18.

One key advantage of this kind of within-subjects analysis is that all individual difference factors are controlled for. Another is that causal-order questions can be resolved more satisfactorily than in a between-subjects analysis. The main problem of causal order here was whether the conviction preceded the increased offending or whether the increased offending preceded the conviction. The percentile self-report scores at age 16 showed that there was no sign of an increase in offending by convicted youths before the conviction occurred, and so it was concluded that the conviction preceded the increased offending.

Some remaining uncertainties about the interpretation of these results centre on the theoretical constructs underlying the empirical variables. Did offending increase, or did the likelihood of admitting offending increase? A study of the dates of reported offences suggested that both effects happened, since the convicted youths at age 16 were more likely to admit offences committed before age 14 but not admitted at that age. What constructs intervened between convictions and increased offending? One construct that increased in the same way as self-reported offending was a hostile attitude to the police, and so this may have been one link in the causal chain. Finally, did the increase in offending reflect labelling or decreased deterrence? A later study by Farrington *et al*. (1978) was able to replicate the delinquency-amplifying effects of convictions between ages 18 and 21 and suggested that decreased deterrence was happening. The increase in offending was most marked for those who received the lightest possible sentences, whereas labelling theory might have predicted the opposite.

A number of other within-subjects analyses have been carried out in the Cambridge Study. Farrington (1972) investigated the effects of going to different secondary schools on offending, and concluded that whether a boy went to a school with a high or low delinquency rate had only a small effect on his later probability of offending. In this example, two different dependent measures were used since the focus was on the effect of different secondary schools on the transition from troublesomeness in the primary school to juvenile delinquency. Farrington (1978) reported that newly emerging parental disharmony when a boy was aged 14 tended to be followed by his own newly emerging aggressiveness at 16–18. This was essentially a comparison between changes in one factor and later changes in another.

In an analysis that was more similar in conception to the study of the effects of convictions, Osborn (1980) found that moving out of London was followed by a decrease in convictions and in self-reported offending. Similarly, West (1982) showed that marriage was followed by a decrease in convictions and in self-reported offending, especially if a man married an unconvicted woman. Most recently, Farrington *et al*. (1986a) discovered that youths were more likely to commit offences when they were unemployed than when they were employed, especially offences involving material gain.

In all of these analyses, each youth essentially acted as his own control. In my opinion, these within-subjects demonstrations of the causal influence of one factor on another are more compelling than between-subjects analyses involving statistical control of extraneous variables. However, I would not suggest that between-subjects analyses should not be carried out. Some of the individual-difference factors that are controlled in a within-subjects analysis may be so important that they should be studied in between-subjects analyses. A great advantage of longitudinal surveys is that they permit both kinds of analysis.

Conclusions

Clearly, there is a considerable gulf between my discussion of the functional relationship between theoretical constructs and the within-subjects analyses that have been carried out in longitudinal research projects. In some ways this is not surprising since the physics analogy is merely a heuristic model to guide theoretical thinking about causes. It is always easier to specify what should be done in an ideal world to advance knowledge about the causes of offending than to actually do it. However, the theoretical discussions in this paper do have implications for future research and analysis.

Explicit distinctions should be drawn between theoretical constructs and empirical variables, and the main aim of causal research should be to specify functional relationships between theoretical constructs. This involves the study of change within subjects in longitudinal data. A risk factor could be viewed as a value of a theoretical construct associated with high offending, whereas a protective factor could be a value associated with low offending. Alternatively, risk and protective factors could be other theoretical constructs which influence the form of a functional relationship with offending.

Changes within subjects can only be equated with variation between subjects in a randomized experiment. Such experiments on offending should be carried out where possible. In other circumstances, the next best method of establishing causal influence is through the quasi-experimental analysis of longitudinal data. In such analysis, each person acts as his or her own control, so extraneous independent influences on offending connected with individual differences are held constant. Other threats to valid causal inference (e.g. maturation and testing effects) can be eliminated by appropriate design. Between-subjects analyses are less satisfactory because of their poorer control of extraneous independent influences and because they cannot resolve problems of causal order.

It is important to distinguish between different kinds of variable. It is extremely difficult, if not impossible, to demonstrate conclusively the causal effect of variables – such as gender and race – that only vary between subjects. It is most feasible to establish causal effects of manipulable variables that vary within subjects. If a manipulable variable was shown to have a causal effect on offending, this would have implications in principle for prevention and treatment.

Future longitudinal studies should aim to have frequent, repeated measurement of theoretical constructs. These studies do not necessarily have to extend over a long time period. Where the values of constructs are changing rapidly, repeated measurements could be over days, weeks or months rather than over years. More attempts to establish the exact timing of events and changes should be made. Multiple data sources are required to establish the validity of operational definitions of theoretical constructs. Quasi-experimental or experimental research should be planned from the outset, perhaps including time series analysis based on individuals or classes of individuals.

This new generation of longitudinal studies will not be cheap. However, their pay-off in increasing our knowledge of the causes, prevention and treatment of offending could be greater than that obtainable by any other method.

References

Barnett, A., Blumstein, A. and Farrington, D. P. (1987) Probabilistic models of youthful criminal careers. *Criminology*, 25, 83–107.

Berrueta-Clement, J. R., Schweinhart, L. J., Barnett, W. S., Epstein, A. S. and Weikart, D. P. (1984) *Changed lives*. Ypsilanti, MI: High Scope.

Blumstein, A., Farrington, D. P. and Moitra, S. (1985) Delinquency careers: innocents, desisters and persisters. In Tonry, M. and Morris, N. (eds.) *Crime and justice*, vol. 6. Chicago: University of Chicago Press, pp. 187–219.

Clarke, R. V. and Cornish, D. B. (1985) Modelling offenders' decisions: a framework for research and policy. In Tonry, M. and Morris, N. (eds.) *Crime and justice*, vol. 6. Chicago: University of Chicago Press, pp. 147–85.

Cloward, R. A. and Ohlin, L. E. (1960) *Delinquency and opportunity*. New York: Free Press.

Cohen, A. K. (1955) *Delinquent boys*. Glencoe, IL: Free Press.

Cook, T. D. and Campbell, D. T. (1979) *Quasi-experimentation*. Chicago: Rand-McNally.

Elliott, D. S., Huizinga, D. and Ageton, S. S. (1985) *Explaining delinquency and drug use*. Beverly Hills, CA: Sage.

Eysenck, H. J. (1964) *Crime and personality*. London: Routledge and Kegan Paul.

Farrington, D. P. (1972) Delinquency begins at home. *New Society*, 21, 495–7.

(1977) The effects of public labelling. *British Journal of Criminology*, 17, 112–25.

(1978) The family backgrounds of aggressive youths. In Hersov, L., Berger, M. and Shaffer, D. (eds.) *Aggression and antisocial behaviour in childhood and adolescence*. Oxford: Pergamon, pp. 73–93.

(1983a) Offending from 10 to 25 years of age. In van Dusen, K. T. and

182   David P. Farrington

Mednick, S. A. (eds.) *Prospective studies of crime and delinquency*. Boston: Kluwer-Nijhoff, pp. 17–37.

(1983b) Randomized experiments on crime and justice. In Tonry, M. and Morris, N. (eds.) *Crime and justice*, vol. 4. Chicago: University of Chicago Press, pp. 257–308.

(1985) Predicting self-reported and official delinquency. In Farrington, D. P. and Tarling, R. (eds.) *Prediction in criminology*. Albany, NY: State University of New York Press, pp. 150–73.

(1986a) Age and crime. In Tonry, M. and Morris, N. (eds.) *Crime and justice*, vol. 7. Chicago: University of Chicago Press, pp. 189–250.

(1986b) Stepping stones to adult criminal careers. In Olweus, D., Block, J. and Yarrow, M. R. (eds.) *Development of antisocial and prosocial behavior*. New York: Academic Press, pp. 359–84.

Farrington, D. P. and Knight, B. J. (1980) Four studies of stealing as a risky decision. In Lipsitt, P. D. and Sales, B. D. (eds.) *New directions in psycholegal research*. New York: Van Nostrand Reinhold, pp. 26–50.

Farrington, D. P. and West, D. J. (1981) The Cambridge Study in Delinquent Development. In Mednick, S. A. and Baert, A. E. (eds.) *Prospective longitudinal research*. Oxford: Oxford University Press, pp. 137–45.

Farrington, D. P., Osborn, S. G. and West, D. J. (1978) The persistence of labelling effects. *British Journal of Criminology*, 18, 277–84.

Farrington, D. P., Gallagher, B., Morley, L., St Ledger, R. J. and West, D. J. (1986a) Unemployment, school leaving and crime. *British Journal of Criminology*, 26, 335–56.

Farrington, D. P., Ohlin, L. E. and Wilson, J. Q. (1986b) *Understanding and controlling crime: toward a new research strategy*. New York: Springer.

Glueck, S. and Glueck, E. T. (1950) *Unravelling juvenile delinquency*. New York: Commonwealth Fund.

Gold, M. and Mann, D. W. (1984) *Expelled to a friendlier place*. Ann Arbor, MI: University of Michigan Press.

Gordon, R. A. (1968) Issues in multiple regression. *American Journal of Sociology*, 73, 592–616.

Gove, W. R. (1985) The effect of age and gender on deviant behaviour: a biopsychosocial perspective. In Rossi, A. S. (ed.) *Gender and the life course*. Hawthorne, NY: Aldine, pp. 115–44.

Hirschi, T. (1969) *Causes of delinquency*. Berkeley, CA: University of California Press.

Hirschi, T. and Selvin, H. C. (1967) *Delinquency research*. New York: Free Press.

Johnson, R. E. (1979) *Juvenile delinquency and its origins*. Cambridge: Cambridge University Press.

Klein, M. W. (1984) Offence specialization and versatility among juveniles. *British Journal of Criminology*, 24, 185–94.

Labouvie, E. W. (1986) Methodological issues in the prediction of psychopathology: a life-span perspective. In Erlenmeyer-Kimling, L. and Miller, N. E. (eds.) *Life-span research on the prediction of psychopathology*. Hillsdale, NJ: Erlbaum, pp. 137–56.

Osborn, S. G. (1980) Moving home, leaving London, and delinquent trends. *British Journal of Criminology*, 20, 54–61.

Palmer, J. and Carlson, P. (1976) Problems with the use of regression analysis in prediction studies. *Journal of Research in Crime and Delinquency*, 13, 64–81.

Robins, L. N. and Wish, E. (1977) Childhood deviance as a developmental process: a study of 223 urban black men from birth to 18. *Social Forces*, 56, 448–73.

Rutter, M. (1985) Resilience in the face of adversity: protective factors and resistance to psychiatric disorder. *British Journal of Psychiatry*, **147**, 598–611.

Trasler, G. B. (1962) *The explanation of criminality*. London: Routledge and Kegan Paul.

West, D. J. (1969) *Present conduct and future delinquency*. London: Heinemann.

(1982) *Delinquency: its roots, careers, and prospects*. London: Heinemann.

West, D. J. and Farrington, D. P. (1973) *Who becomes delinquent?* London: Heinemann.

(1977) *The delinquent way of life*. London: Heinemann.

Woodhead, M. (1985) Pre-school education has long-term effects: but can they be generalised? *Oxford Review of Education*, **11**, 133–55.

10 Delinquent development: theoretical and empirical considerations

Lea Pulkkinen

Theoretical issues in delinquency causation

An approach to the study of delinquent development

Among the adolescent outcomes of social development, delinquency occurs with a certain probability. What are the risk factors that predispose an individual to juvenile delinquency and perhaps to a criminal career at a later age, and what are the protective factors that prevent him or her from this course? These are questions that puzzle researchers as well as parents and educators. There are empirical data available about group differences in criminality and on the predictability of criminal behaviour based on characteristics of an individual's earlier behaviour as well as home environment, but our theoretical understanding of the developmental processes involved is inadequate.

As Farrington (see chapter 9) argues, studies in which one theoretical construct, such as gender, varies between groups, and another construct, such as delinquency, varies within subjects, cannot yield unambiguous causal conclusions. A discovery of a difference between males and females in delinquency does not allow one to draw the conclusion that gender is a cause of delinquency. In order to understand reasons for delinquency, data on causal factors should be drawn from an individual's developmental history. The research strategy that renders this possible is a longitudinal study. In the context of developmental histories, group comparisons may yield information about risk factors in development; for instance, one may find some risk factors in male upbringing and development that increase the likelihood of norm-breaking behaviour.

The above-mentioned approach to the study of delinquency causation reflects an interest in developmental processes. To date, only a few long-term longitudinal studies have been carried out on delinquent development. Empirical data are, however, accumulating, and at the same time, the need for a theory that would integrate empirical findings has become apparent. Farrington stresses that there is a need for a theory that uses theoretical constructs that refer to, and which provide an explanation for, changes in behaviour within individuals. A critical question is what the necessary and sufficient developmental model for explaining delinquent development is (for philosophical models of development, see Reese and Overton, 1970; and Lerner, 1986). One may also ask whether criminality is at all a phenomenon which can be explained by an individual psychological model, or should it rather be understood as a societal phenomenon?

Developmental models

In natural sciences the ideal test of causal inferences is provided by randomized experiments, in which an independent variable is varied systematically, while other variables are controlled for, so that the effects on some dependent variable may be examined. An adoption of this ideal in the social sciences might mean that a potential risk factor, for instance school failure, should be systematically increased and its effects on criminal potential measured. Much criticism has been, however, presented against this kind of mechanistic or positivistic approach in the social sciences. A model of a physics experiment, such as how the length of an iron bar changed with increases in its temperature when other physical conditions were controlled, is too mechanistic for causal thinking and for experimental verification of hypotheses on delinquency. How could we, ethically and practically, systematically increase, for example, a child's failure at school to see what criminal potential it produces? School success, as a theoretical construct, depends on several organism variables, such as an individual's intelligence and aims, and therefore it cannot be randomly assigned to an individual.

From the mechanistic, behavioural perspective no strong view of development is present; the concept of development is reduced to a concept of change. What we need for the analysis of causes of delinquency are, instead of randomized experiments, natural experiments in which the effects of real-life changes, such as unemployment and employment, on criminal behaviour are studied in an individual's life span framework. The relevant empirical method is a longitudinal study. An excellent illustration of this approach has been given by Farrington *et al.* (1986) and another one by Farrington (chapter 9) on the effects of convictions on offending.

Two other philosophical models, the organismic model and the contextual model, take the nature of an organism into account. Organismic-type theories stress that as people develop they pass through a universal and unchangeable sequence of qualitatively different phases, levels, or stages of development. The contextual model, on the other hand, implies that developmental changes occur as a consequence of reciprocal relations between the active organism and the active context. By being both products and producers of their contexts, individuals affect their own development (Lerner, 1986, pp. 25–6).

Both models raise interesting questions of delinquency. From the framework of the organismic model one may ask whether there are qualitative changes in delinquency that could be understood on the basis of the stages of the development of an organism. Silbereisen and Noack (1988) maintain that some aspects of problem behaviour, for example the use of alcohol, nicotine, or even marijuana, are purposive and aimed at coping with problems of self-regulation in development and may thus play a constructive role in adolescent development. The high frequency of undetected, self-reported criminality in adolescence (Hirschi, 1969; Sipilä, 1982) might express the corresponding function of delinquency on personality development. Moreover, the analysis of the relationship between age and crime reveals a peak in teenage years, but offending is not predominantly a teenage phenomenon (Farrington, 1986). Most young-sters give up after the first convictions in middle adolescence. Some people develop a criminal career which has the peak of offences at a later age. These people's development may be qualitatively different from that of juvenile delinquents.

From the framework of the contextual model one may ask how the development of a criminal career is related to normative events such as separation from parents and getting married, and what the function of a peer group in offending is. There are also non-normative events in people's lives. How do happenings, such as dropping out of school, parental divorce, and an individual's severe illness, contribute to the development of criminal people? How does the historical time influence criminality?

West (1982) has reported that marriage decreases offending if a man is married to a non-delinquent woman, but if he is married to a delinquent woman, his offending seems to increase. The increase of offending in teenage years has been explained by the fact that teenagers gradually break away from the control of their parents and become influenced by their peers; delinquent friends encourage offending (Elliott *et al.*, 1985). According to a Swedish study by Sarnecki (1986) on delinquent networks, half of all juveniles in a municipality were affiliated with a delinquent network and they entirely dominated the juvenile problems in the municipality. Most of the juveniles abandoned their delinquent activity after a short time, but those who played a central role in the network faced a greater risk of persisting in their delinquent activity, which often gradually led to drug addiction, imprisonment, and the like.

Causal relationships and explanation

What do we mean when we maintain that we have found some of the causes of delinquency? Homans (1967) states that any science has two main jobs: discovery and explanation. Discovery means stating and testing more or less general relationships between properties in nature. When we predict and find an association between, for example, poor academic performance and delinquent behaviour we have discovered a relationship. Only when we are able to demonstrate that the finding follows a logical conclusion from more general propositions have we explained the phenomenon.

Delinquent behaviour has multiple causation. Furthermore, some variables may have a direct influence on delinquent behaviour, while some have an indirect influence. The latter was demonstrated by Johnson (1979) in a study of whether adolescents who do poorly in school are more likely to commit offences than those who do well in school. He discovered that school performance did not have a direct effect on delinquent behaviour, but poor school performance was directly related to the frequency with which adolescents had delinquent friends. Delinquent friends, in turn, increased the probability of delinquent behaviour among those adolescents. Thus poor school performance was indirectly related to delinquent behaviour.

There may be many alternative explanations for a certain discovery. Because of the complexities of real-world relationships and the difficult question of ultimate or final causes, many social scientists prefer to speak of relationships or associations, rather than of causes. Since facts are unlimited in number, some kind of theory is required to control data gathering. A theory is a set of propositions comprising defined and interrelated constructs that integrate laws concerning regular, predictable relationships among variables (Lerner, 1986, p. 42). Scientists working with, for instance, problems of delinquency do not agree about their observations, laws and theories, because they make different philosophical assumptions about the nature of the world. Theories of delinquency (the social control/disorganization perspective, the strain theory, the radical/economic conflict perspective, and the cultural transmission/ socialization perspective – see Gibbons and Krohn, 1986) differ in regard to their assumptions about what factors are more important in producing delinquency rates and/or individual delinquent behaviour. These assumptions reflect basic differences in the way the theorists view the social order and the nature of human interaction.

Regularities in delinquent behaviour and development

The replication of empirical discoveries constitutes an essential part of a scientific activity. For practical reasons, experimental results are more often replicated than developmental findings drawn from longitudinal studies. By coincidence, two longitudinal studies have been carried out in different cultures, one in England by Farrington and his collaborators and another in Finland by the present author, which share basic assumptions on delinquency to the extent that data gathering and, consequently, empirical findings are comparable.

In both studies, data collection was started at the age of eight to nine and follow-up data were available in adulthood (see Table 1). The

Table 1 *Two longitudinal studies on delinquent development*

	Cambridge study in delinquent development	Jyväskylä study in social development
Subjects	Males 411	Males 196, Females 173
Sample	Working-class area in London	Town of Jyväskylä in Central Finland
First wave	At age 8–9, in 1961–2	At age 8–9, in 1968
Last wave	At age 24, in 1977	At age 27, in 1986
Methods	Teacher ratings	Teacher ratings
	Peer ratings	Peer ratings
	Interviews	Interviews
	Criminal records	Criminal records
	Self-reports of offending	

samples represent different age cohorts and different living environments. The English sample was born in the early 1950s, the Finnish sample in the late 1950s. The English sample was drawn randomly from the working-class area of London, the Finnish sample from the town of Jyväskylä, which has about 60,000 inhabitants. Jyväskylä is the centre of the county of Central Finland and is located approximately 250 km north of the capital, Helsinki.

In both studies, teacher and peer ratings were employed for studying, for example, the subjects' aggressive behaviour in childhood. Interviews of the subjects and their parents were used for obtaining data on social background. In the Finnish study, data were collected at the ages of 8, 14, 20 and 27 (for methods used, see Pulkkinen (1982), and for data on criminality through to the age of 20, see Pulkkinen (1983)); in the English study data were collected more frequently (see chapter 9). Searches were also carried out in the Criminal Record Offices. In Finland, the central register kept by the Ministry of Justice contains all offences for which the sentence has been imprisonment. The local criminal register kept by the police also includes information on petty offences for which the person was not necessarily prosecuted. For children under 15 years no registers are kept in Finland, while in England criminal registers are available from the age of 10. Therefore data for early adolescence are not comparable in these countries.

In spite of the differences in cultural settings, the results were in many respects very similar for prevalence (the proportion of persons who are offenders) and incidence (the rate of offending by offenders). Results for females were only available in the Finnish study.

1. Prevalence. The number of individual males convicted at least once in a year reached its peak at the same age, 17, in both samples. After that age, prevalence remained high until the age of 20. For females there was no peak age (see Figure 1). Another peak age for males emerged at the age of 24 in the Finnish sample. Farrington (in chapter 9) explains the peak

age of prevalence by the fact that at the age of 17 a juvenile becomes an adult in English criminal law. This explanation does not, however, fit Finland. In Finland, there is no juvenile court, but the Law on Young Offenders terms individuals aged 15 to 20 guilty of an offence 'young offenders'. The special status means, for instance, that in the investigation of the offence an offender's personal history must be investigated, and the trial takes place behind closed doors when the case involves an offence alleged to have been committed by a person under 18 at the time (Joutsen, 1976). Age 18 is the full age of majority in Finland.

2. Cumulative prevalence. About one-third of males had been convicted for reasons more serious than drunkenness and traffic offences by the age of 24 in England; the figure was 28.1% in Finland. The rate of convicted females was much smaller (9.2%). When all convictions (including drunkenness and traffic offences) were considered, 47.4% (93/196) of the Finnish male sample and 15.6% (27/173) of the Finnish female sample had been convicted at least once by the age of 27. Few people committed several offences, and therefore the distribution of convictions is highly skewed even when drunkenness and traffic offences were included (see Figure 2).

3. Concentration of offences. Offences are highly concentrated. A small number of people accounted for half of all the criminal convictions: 5.5% of males in England, 4.1% of males (8 men out of 196) in Finland. For females, the concentration was even more obvious: 1.2% (2 women out of 173) accounted for half of all the convictions.

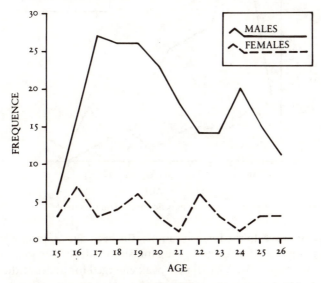

Figure 1   Prevalence: the number of different persons convicted in the Finnish sample at each age

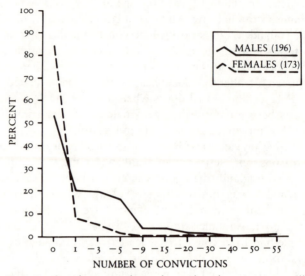

Figure 2   Cumulative prevalence: the number of convictions per offender in the Finnish sample

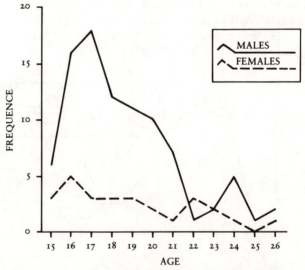

Figure 3   Age of onset of delinquency in the Finnish sample

4. Age of onset. In the English sample, the peak age of onset was at 13 to 17 (Farrington, 1986), and in the Finnish sample, correspondingly, at 16 to 17 (see Figure 3). A small new peak emerged for males at the age of 24 in the Finnish sample resulting from recruiting new cases for drunkenness and traffic offences. Adult convictions are normally preceded by

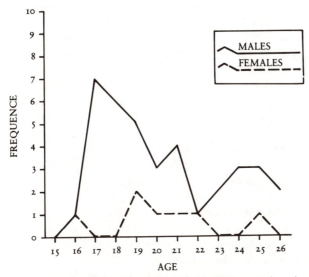

Figure 4   Peak age of incidence: the age of the highest number of convictions of each individual in the Finnish sample

juvenile convictions. In the English sample, 84% of the males with no juvenile convictions also had no adult convictions. In the Finnish sample, the corresponding percentage was 83% for males and 94% for females.

5. The peak age in incidence. Each person has his or her own pattern of convictions in relation to age. Farrington (1986) has, however, found that the highest number of convictions for a given individual is mostly found at ages 15 to 18. In the Finnish male sample, the peak in the number of convictions was correspondingly at age 17, but new peaks emerged at ages 21 and 24 to 25 (see Figure 4). The peaks in prevalence (see Figure 1) coincide with incidence, except at age 21, which means that the number of individual convictions is high at about the same age as the number of offenders. There seems to be two risk periods for offences; the first one in middle adolescence and the second one in early adulthood.

6. Age and convictions. Farrington (1986) remarks that the age–crime curve may reflect the peak in the number of different offenders (prevalence) or the number of offences by each offender (incidence). The total number of convictions (excluding drunkenness) for the whole Finnish male sample reached its peak at age 18, and by age 22 this total number had decreased to about a third of the peak value (see Figure 5). The shape of the curve is quite similar to that found by Farrington (1986) and, according to him, to those based on official criminal statistics for any given year; the curve reaches a peak in adolescence and then declines, at first quickly, but gradually more slowly. However, a new peak emerged at age 24 in the Finnish sample. There was an increase in violence, drunken

driving, and various types of traffic offence. When drunkenness was included (see Figure 6) the curve for the total number of convictions maintained the same shape; however, the peaks in every third year, at the ages of 18, 21 and 24, emerged more clearly.

To study the age–crime curve in different subgroups the male 'chronic offenders', that is those eight men who accounted for half of all convictions and whose individual convictions by the age of 27 numbered from 17 to 55 (see Figure 2), were excluded. The second and third peak almost disappeared; 'petty offenders' (85 men whose individual convictions numbered from 1 to 15) had committed the most offences at age 17; thereafter a clear decline was observable (see Figure 7). The total number of convictions for 'chronic offenders' (see Figure 8) had a peak later, at age 18, and the number of convictions remained high at a later age. Thus the total number of convictions in the whole sample (see Figure 6) was constituted by two different patterns of age–convictions curves. One was obtained for 'chronic offenders', which confirmed Farrington's (chapter 9) argument that for those who are chronic offenders, their rate of offending does not change consistently with age. The other curve was obtained for 'petty offenders', who commit a few offences mostly by the age of 20.

7. Predictability of convictions. Farrington (chapter 9) has found that the best independent predictor of offending at any age was the measure of offending at the immediately preceding age. The same result was obtained for the Finnish male sample (to be published in another context). Among

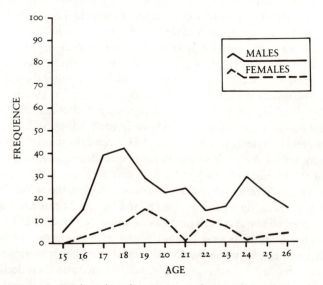

Figure 5   Total number of convictions in the Finnish sample at each age, drunkenness excluded

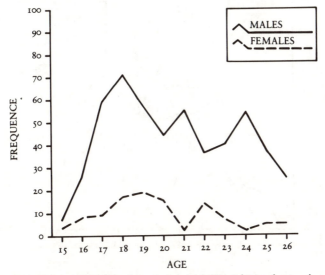

Figure 6   Total number of convictions in the Finnish sample at each age, including drunkenness

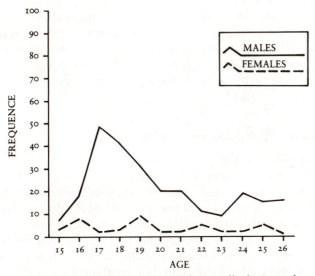

Figure 7   Total number of convictions of 'petty offenders' at each age in the Finnish sample, 'chronic offenders' excluded

the early behavioural characteristics that predict later criminality trouble-some behaviour, including aggression, is often mentioned by Farrington and other researchers. Correspondingly, logistic regression analyses revealed that peer-nominated aggression predicted convictions in the male

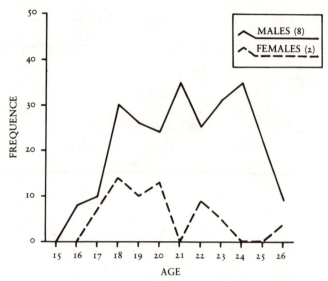

Figure 8   Number of convictions of 'chronic offenders' at each age in the Finnish sample

Finnish sample. Furthermore, a teacher rating made on a three-point scale at age eight based on the teacher's worries about the child's future because of ensuing antisocial symptoms, predicted convictions, especially those at a later age (at age 24 or later). The 12 class teachers whose classes were randomly included in the sample were worried, even at age eight, about the behaviour of those boys who developed a criminal career in the years to come.

Towards a theory of delinquent development

A universal phenomenon
The regularities obtained in the two longitudinal studies imply that the phenomenon of male delinquency is structurally similar in different communities: in a working-class area of a metropolis (London) and in a town in a country the total population of which scarcely numbers half of that of the metropolis. In both communities (a) the same proportions (about a third) of males are convicted for reasons more serious than drunkenness and traffic offences; (b) the convictions are concentrated in a small proportion (about 5%) of males; and (c) the peak age of onset, prevalence and incidence in males is about the same – around the age of 17. As mentioned above, it is not the age when a juvenile becomes an adult in Finnish criminal law, although it is in England.

The results for females were available only for Finland. The proportion of females convicted was a third that of males and half of the convictions were concentrated in only 1% of females. Official statistics also show that far fewer girls than boys commit offences. Campbell (1981) mentions that the official figures for 1976 concerning the ratio of males to females with respect to convictions give a figure of 8.95 to 1. For self-reported delinquency the sex ratio is less, although males still predominate; the ratio 2.5 to 1 is is often found. She gives several reasons for lower official statistics of females, for instance the nature of female delinquent acts, which makes them less threatening to the police. According to her conclusion (Campbell, 1981, p. 25), 'it is clear that both institutionalization and official statistics must be rejected as a working guide to the nature of female delinquency. Self-report studies can give us a more accurate picture.' In the Jyväskylä longitudinal study, the age–conviction curves for females had no regular shape, nor was there any consistency in predictive correlations, possibly because of the small number of convictions and convicted females in registers. Therefore females have been omitted in the discussion which follows.

Breaking norms is only possible if norms exist. It seems to be a universal phenomenon that there are always some people in a community who test the tolerance of others and demonstrate their existence by abandoning conventional norms. The prevalence of norm-breaking behaviour shows that these people are mainly juveniles. Most of them adjust to norms in late adolescence. Few people become chronic offenders.

Chronic offenders and juvenile delinquents

A small group of people accounts for half of all convictions. Magnusson and Bergman (see chapter 3) have correspondingly found that criminal development at a later stage can largely be explained by the existence of a small number of multi-problem boys. They consider it essential to investigate if, and to what extent, stability and prediction coefficients can be explained by the occurrence of the multi-problem group. Their own results show that if children belonging to the severe multi-problem cluster were removed, relationships between aggression and criminality or alcohol abuse would completely disappear. In the Jyväskylä longitudinal study, the multi-problem characteristics of becoming chronic offenders were obviously recognized by the class teachers, whose worries about the eight-year-old boys' future because of ensuing antisocial symptoms strongly predicted criminality at a later stage. The highest concurrent correlations between this future-oriented teacher rating and the ratings of children's actual behaviour were found for aggressive behaviour towards other children, disobedience towards the teacher, and a lack of constructive activity.

Half of convictions belong to a much higher number of people who do not develop a criminal career, but commit offences possibly only once or a few times in their life, mostly in adolescence. Problem behaviour in adolescence may facilitate establishing contacts with peers as Silbereisen and Noack (1988) have suggested for drinking alcohol and smoking cigarettes. The results from Sarnecki's (1986) study on delinquent networks were in accordance with this hypothesis. The assumption is that, to a large extent, juvenile delinquency constitutes a context and opportunity for associating with peers. His data showed that the juveniles appeared to be recruited into the network by coming into contact with some individuals in it of only slightly greater age and delinquent experience. He assumes that these were responsible for the transmission of the norms and values involved in delinquent behaviour. The playful and social aspects of delinquent behaviour are thought to be of great significance.

Another side of this juvenile behaviour may involve testing the limits of norms. Undetected criminality is frequent as self-reports show (Campbell, 1981). It has been estimated that everybody at some time breaks a law, and that the likelihood of being caught increases with the frequency of delinquent acts. Sipilä (1982) has noted that, of those adolescents who had broken a law only once according to their self-reports, 9% were caught, but when the number of self-reported offences increased, convictions became more likely.

Most juveniles abandon their delinquent activity after some time, while some continue it up to the age of 20 and beyond. Abandoning delinquent behaviour may be related to contextual changes, such as separation from peer group influences and improvement of livelihood, and/or to developmental processes, such as identity formation and increased consciousness of one's social responsibilities after finishing school, leaving home, and entering the work market. Farrington *et al.* (1986) have shown that employment decreases crime rates, particularly offences involving material gain. Osborn (1980) also found that moving out of London was followed by a decrease in convictions. Correspondingly, Sarnecki's (1986) results showed that the longer the juvenile had been associated with a delinquent network and the more central the role he played in the network, the greater the risk he faced of continuing this delinquent career.

Presumably the values in the juvenile's home may facilitate accepting the values of a delinquent network; at least the parents' and siblings' criminality predicts a boy's criminality (Farrington, chapter 9; McCord, 1983). Delinquent peers and values that make criminal activity approved in a certain subculture are also learnt in reformatory schools and prisons. Becoming a member of a network of chronic offenders may play a crucial role in continuing a criminal career. Labelling may make criminal activity acceptable to oneself, while membership of the criminal network may make it socially approved. As West (1982) remarked, the relationships with other deviants are of great significance in the delinquent way of life.

Some boys are more liable to associate with a delinquent network and to employ delinquent activity as a means of establishing social contacts than other boys. My previous results (Pulkkinen, 1982; 1983) showed that delinquent and other problem behaviour in adolescence was consistently related to the line of development characterized by weak self-control. In late adolescence (at age 19 to 20) it manifested itself in the style of life of the 'reveller' (Pulkkinen, 1982; 1983). The revellers' behaviour was typified by gathering with friends, drinking, smoking, heterosexual interaction, and weak tolerance. This pattern of behaviour was preceded by orientation towards peers at age 14, including free time in streets and discos, friends whom the parents disliked, and troubles at school, as well as aggressive behaviour at age 8. An opposite pool from the 'reveller' style of life was termed 'loner', which involved refraining from problem behaviour and peer companionship. It was preceded by dependence on the parents at age 14 and submissive behaviour in childhood.

Another developmental line that also included social activity with many friends, but which was characterized by strong control of behaviour, was not related to delinquent behaviour. It consisted of socially skilled, constructive behaviour at age 8, orientation towards responsibility at age 14, and the style of life of the 'striver' in late adolescence. The latter implied, for example, an integration into society and the assumption of responsibility for oneself and others. An opposite pool from this style of life was that of the 'loser', which represented negative and alienated attitudes, a lack of plans for the future, failure in studies, low self-confidence, and problems in adjustment. It was preceded by negativism at age 14, including, for example, truancy and poor school reports, and socially helpless, anxious behaviour in childhood. The number of convictions in late adolescence was related to the 'loser' style of life and negativism preceding it six years earlier.

In the impulse control model (Pulkkinen, 1986) both the 'reveller' and the 'loser' style of life manifest weak self-control, while the 'striver' and the 'loner' express strong self-control. Convictions in adolescence were related to both types of weak self-control, but not to either type of strong self-control (Pulkkinen, 1983). The parents' indifference towards the child, physical punishment, and other indicators of a lack of child-centred guidance, were related to weak self-control, as well as to the number of offences. Results are not yet available to indicate the extent to which the earlier patterns of behaviour are predictive of persistent criminality in adulthood. Since peer nominations of aggression at age 8 and 14 correlated more highly with delinquency in adolescence than at a later age, as was shown above, one can assume that juvenile criminality is related to weak self-control, while persistent criminality is due to a multi-problem personality and antisocial values adopted from homes and institutions which are used for the treatment of juvenile delinquency.

Concluding comments

Delinquent development is a multi-faceted phenomenon. Delinquency emerges in several forms in males alone, and female delinquency has its own somewhat different features. In order to predict delinquent development, one should be able to formulate principles that selectively pick out those few multi-problem people who are at a high risk of developing a persistent criminal career. Accordingly, Farrington (1985, p. 150) suggests that 'it is more feasible to predict not delinquency in general but the most persistent or "chronic" offenders, who account for a significant proportion of all crime'. Since all multi-problem people do not develop a criminal career, statements on protective factors are also needed. To achieve a detailed knowledge of risk and protective factors in the development of criminal people, careful analyses of individual life courses should be carried out as suggested by Cairns (1986).

It should be obvious that causes of offending cannot be attached to a single factor. Delinquency has multiple causation. Therefore a mechanistic model is insufficient for explaining delinquent development. Furthermore, Rutter (see chapter 1) calls attention to the distinction between risk indicators and risk mechanisms. Risk indicators may be single factors, but risk mechanisms are individual and social–psychological processes that modify an individual's way of life.

An individual's delinquent behaviour cannot be explained solely on the basis of social factors or the development of an organism. An organismic model of development may add to the understanding of qualitatively different stages in human development which cause unique characteristics in the interaction between an individual and environmental factors. One of them is in puberty, another one in entering into adulthood. The former means searching for one's identity and experimenting with norms of an independent life, the latter establishing one's identity and a responsible adult life within accepted norms. These structural organismic changes may explain both changes in prevalence and incidence of delinquency, but they do not explain the maintenance or, in some few cases, the onset of criminal activity in adulthood. What is needed is a contextual model that explains how an individual affects his or her own development by being both a product and a producer of that development.

References

Cairns, R. B. (1986) Phenomena lost: issues in the study of development. In Valsiner, J. (ed.) *The individual subject and scientific psychology*. New York: Plenum Press, pp. 97–111.

Campbell, A. (1981) *Girl delinquent*. Oxford: Basil Blackwell.

Elliott, D. S., Huizinga, D. and Ageton, S. S. (1985) *Explaining delinquency and drug use*. Beverly Hills, CA: Sage.

Farrington, D. P. (1985) Predicting self-reported and official delinquency. In

Farrington, D. P. and Garling, R. T. (eds.) *Prediction in criminology.* New York: State University of New York Press, pp. 150–73.

(1986) Age and crime. In Torny, M. and Morris, N. (eds.) *Crime and Justice: an annual review of research.* Chicago: University of Chicago Press, pp. 189–250.

Farrington, D. P., Gallagher, B., Morley, L., Ledger, R. J. and West, D. J. (1986) Unemployment, school leaving, and crime. *British Journal of Criminology,* 26, 335–56.

Gibbons, D. C. and Krohn, M. D. (1986) *Delinquent behavior,* 4th edn. Englewood Cliffs, NJ: Prentice-Hall.

Hirschi, T. (1969) *Causes of delinquency.* Berkeley, CA: University of California Press.

Homans, G. C. (1967) *The nature of social science.* New York: Harcourt Brace Jovanovich.

Johnson, R. E. (1979) *Juvenile delinquency and its origins.* Cambridge: Cambridge University Press.

Joutsen, M. (1976) *Young offenders in the criminal justice system of Finland.* Reports from the Research Institute of Legal Policy No. 14. Helsinki.

Lerner, R. M. (1986) *Concepts and theories of human development,* 2nd edn. New York: Random House.

McCord, J. (1983) Family relationships and crime. In Kadish, S. H. (ed.) *Encyclopedia of crime and justice,* vol. 2. New York: Free Press, pp. 759–64.

Osborn, S. G. (1980) Moving home, leaving London, and delinquent trends. *British Journal of Criminology,* 20, 54–61.

Pulkkinen, L. (1982) Self-control and continuity from childhood to late adolescence. In Baltes, P. B. and Brim, O. G., Jr (eds.) *Life-span development and behavior,* vol. 4. New York: Academic Press, pp. 63–105.

(1983) Finland: the search for alternatives to aggression. In Goldstein, A. P. and Segall, M. H. (eds.) *Aggression in global perspective.* New York: Pergamon Press, pp. 104–44.

(1986) The role of impulse control in the development of antisocial and prosocial behavior. In Olweus, D., Block, J. and Radke-Yarrow, M. (eds.) *Development of anti-social and prosocial behavior.* New York: Academic Press, pp. 149–75.

Reese, H. W. and Overton, W. F. (1970) Models of development and theories of development. In Goulet, L. R. and Baltes, P. B. (eds.) *Life-span developmental psychology: research and theory.* New York: Academic Press.

Sarnecki, J. (1986) *Delinquent networks.* Stockholm: National Swedish Council for Crime Prevention. Report no. 1.

Silbereisen, R. K. and Noack, P. (1988) On the constructive role of problem behavior in adolescence. In Bolger, H., Caspi, A., Downey, G. and Moorehouse, M. (eds.) *Person and context: developmental processes.* Cambridge, MA: Cambridge University Press.

Sipilä, J. (1982) *Nuorten poikkeava käyttäytyminen ja yhteisön rakenne.* Reports from the Department of Social Politics no. 1. Jyväskylä: University of Jyväskylä.

West, D. J. (1982) *Delinquency: its roots, careers and prospects.* London: Heinemann.

11 School experiences as risk/protective factors

Barbara Maughan

By comparison with the extensive literature on family processes that may constitute risk or protective influences on children's development (Garmezy, 1985; Masten and Garmezy, 1985), the role of school experiences has received relatively little explicit consideration from this perspective. Indeed, it is only in recent years that there has been general acknowledgement that schooling can exert any significant independent impact at all. Less than twenty years ago Jencks, in a major study of education and inequality, concluded that 'differences between schools seem to have very little effect on any measurable attribute of those who attend them' (Jencks *et al.*, 1972). Longitudinal evidence, drawn from a number of different strands of research endeavour, has been important in challenging that view, but our picture of the range of possible school effects is still in many ways fragmentary, and our understanding of the processes involved largely tentative. Methodological issues remain the subject of debate if not dispute, and the cumulative process of building and refining on earlier findings is in its infancy. The issues involved, however, are clearly of both theoretical and practical relevance. Studies of non-family settings can make an important contribution to our understanding of environmental effects on development in general, and it has long been recognized that severe school difficulties constitute one of the mediating links between childhood and adult disorder (Robins, 1966). As one of the few branches of social policy reaching all children, at least in Western societies, education should be uniquely well placed as a focus for interventions if appropriate targets can be identified.

School experiences and the risk and protective paradigm

Before turning to look at some of the particular issues arising from recent research on school effects, it may be helpful to begin with a brief consideration of how the 'risk and protective' paradigm might be applied to school experiences in general. In the main, this perspective has been employed in investigations of the onset of particular disorders, or in studies of experiences that, prima facie, seem likely to be either deleterious – such as loss or separation – or potentially beneficial, such as the availability of social support. The model involved is an explicitly causal one, demanding experimental interventions, or a longitudinal, and ideally

200

a prospective, approach, for the hypothesized effects to be detected with any certainty. There is a considerable degree of specificity in the questions being posed, and the underlying assumption is of processes operating at the individual level.

Much recent research on schooling, by contrast, has had a very different point of departure: the more general question of establishing the existence of any environmental influence, among an array of potential candidates, in terms of both developmental outcomes and experiential factors. Many of the most fruitful findings have emerged from studies addressing the basic question of how far, and in what ways, school experiences can be shown to have significant implications for the generality of children. The concern has thus been as much with optimal development, and the role of schooling in facilitating or impeding this, as with the likelihood of developing specific disorders. The main 'at risk' groups studied systematically to date are those children likely to be educationally disadvantaged, and at risk of educational failure, by virtue of their social disadvantage. A massive literature points to the depressing and consistent links between poor educational performance and low social class (see, for example, Mortimore and Blackstone, 1982), and longitudinal data have illustrated clearly that a cumulative process is involved here, socially disadvantaged children falling progressively further behind their peers from the time of school entry onwards (Douglas *et al.*, 1968; Fogelman *et al.*, 1978). A more scattered series of investigations has focused on children who cause particular concern in the school setting: the disruptive, those with learning difficulties, the truant, and so on. These more individually focused studies have already begun to provide insights into the role of school experiences as risk and protective factors at the individual level. The broader-based research on the effects of schooling in general takes a complementary focus, on a perhaps wider definition of the concepts of both risk and protection.

Although the usual rubric for studies of this kind refers to 'factors', our eventual concern will of course be with the underlying processes that those factors reflect. It is at least plausible to think of individual variables that could show risk-type relationships in some circumstances and protective ones in others, so that a concentration on variables alone will not be enough. A range of different types of mechanism might be involved, some reflecting the effects of long-standing experiences, others traceable to particular turning points or changes in the developmental pattern, yet others representing the eventual outcomes of chains of interlinked events. Translating these to the realm of school experiences, we might anticipate that some of the mechanisms involved would be analogous with family processes, while others would be particular to the school setting. This second group might include peer group influences, effects associated with the in-built transitions and decision points in a child's school career, and the concomitants of experiences of success and failure.

With these general considerations in mind, we can turn to a more detailed examination of how longitudinal data have contributed to our understanding of the effects of school experiences. The aim will be to point up some of the conceptual and methodological problems arising from recent research, using illustrative findings to highlight particular issues. As noted earlier, the evidence currently available derives from two rather different bodies of work: first, studies that take the school as the unit of analysis, and attempt to identify variations in effects between *schools*; and second, studies that focus on particular groups of *children*, and set out to trace the implications of the school experience for them. We begin with the first of these approaches.

School effectiveness studies

The last decade has seen a proliferation of research in Britain, the US and Europe, all converging on issues of school effects and effectiveness. Two central questions have been pursued: first, can it be shown that schools do have an impact on their pupils' progress; and second, if so, which aspects of schooling and the school experience are most centrally involved? The ideal design to answer these questions would, of course, be an experimental one, with random allocation of children to different types of school. Since this is clearly not feasible, at least within the mainstream school system, the issues have been pursued using a variety of quasi-experimental designs, building on naturally occurring variations between schools to identify potential effects. A range of different strategies has been employed to provide the necessary contrasts: comparisons between school systems (e.g., Coleman *et al.*, 1982; and Steedman, 1983) and between groups of schools (e.g. Rutter *et al.*, 1979; Mortimore *et al.*, 1988), 'outlier' studies (e.g. Klitgaard and Hall, 1975), studies of schools with atypical outcomes (e.g. Weber, 1971), and studies of change (e.g. Brookover and Lezotte, 1979; and Ouston *et al.*, 1984). The aim has generally been to assess results for all pupils in a given school, and the outcome measures explored, although showing a relatively heavy bias towards academic attainment, have also included attendance, behaviour in school and delinquency outside, continuance in education, links with employment, and other non-cognitive attributes such as attitudes and self concept. A number of major reviews and commentaries have already been undertaken (Reynolds, 1982; Purkey and Smith, 1983; Rutter, 1983; Grosin, 1985; Reynolds, 1985).

Controlling for intake variations

Longitudinal strategies have been important in unravelling a number of the issues involved. First, and perhaps most central, has been the need to demonstrate that variations between schools in children's outcomes are more than simple reflections of comparable variations at the stage of intake. It is clear that, even within very local geographical areas, individual schools vary markedly in the range and types of pupil they admit. Since children's intellectual ability, social background, and a variety of other characteristics, will all have strong effects on their progress, it is essential to take adequate account of these before any conclusions can be drawn about possible school effects. To the extent that relevant variations at intake are omitted from, or underestimated by, the analyses, we are likely to overestimate the contribution of the school to effects on outcome.

A variety of different approaches have been taken to address this problem. Some have relied on general characteristics of school catchment areas, or group-based intake data, to select 'similar' schools for comparison, or to provide a basis for developing adjustment procedures to compare outcomes as if intakes were similar. Under certain constrained conditions – for example in studies of schools in severely disadvantaged areas that have markedly positive outcomes – these procedures may prove satisfactory. One of the most frequent criticisms of work in this field, however, has centred on the inadequacy of the intake measures used, in terms of either their range, their crudity, or the level at which they have been applied. As Rutter (1983) argued in relation to earlier studies, and Gray and his colleagues (1986) have pointed out in connection with the publication of examination results, in general, the use of aggregate measures is almost certain to result in ecological fallacies, and may in some circumstances give rise to highly misleading conclusions. To avoid these dangers, individually based longitudinal data, assessing the same pupils at both intake and outcome, and including as wide as possible a range of theoretically relevant variables, are effectively a *sine qua non*.

Some problems of analysis

Even within designs of this kind, a number of difficult analytic issues remain. Most are variants of problems common to all studies of intact groups. The first concerns the effects of unreliability – which will inevitably be present – in the intake variables. Since unreliability in predictor variables produces a bias towards zero in the estimates of their coefficients, a corresponding bias will also arise in estimates for other effects in the model. The result, in the present context, would be to underestimate the contribution of explanatory background variables, and so overestimate the contribution of schools. In some circumstances, where reliability is known, corrections can be introduced into the analysis. An alternative approach would involve the use of parallel measures of the explanatory variables, to allow for direct estimates of reliability, or for the fitting of structural equation models (Jöreskog and Sörbom, 1981).

The second issue concerns the appropriate unit of analysis. Since the eventual aim is to assess whether there are differences between *schools*, the simplest model is one with at least two levels: the individual pupil and the school. In many instances, a more complex model may be required, including, for example, classes within schools. The problem turns on how best to represent the school term in the analyses. The most usual approach has been to take the pupil as the unit of analysis, regress outcome measures on intake variables, and include school attended as a fixed effect in the model. The school contribution can then be assessed either in terms of proportions of variance explained, or in terms of departures from prediction for individual schools. One difficulty of this approach in its basic form is that it assumes that relationships between intake and outcome measures will be similar in all schools, and that variations between schools will essentially be evident in the form of differences in intercepts. This is clearly a limiting assumption, and one that may preclude investigation of some of the potentially most interesting features of the results. A more realistic model would be one that allowed for the possibility of different intake–outcome relationships between schools, and which in turn might provide important pointers to factors associated with relative effectiveness.

A further issue concerns the homogeneity or heterogeneity of the schools represented in any given sample. The general model described here assumes homogeneity, and a considerable degree of overlap in the range of intake characteristics represented in each school. In some circumstances, however, this assumption clearly will not hold. In studies contrasting different school systems, for example, the initial selection procedures involved in entry to one sector or another may result in only a very limited overlap between sectors in the groups of pupils served. In this case, regression estimates derived from the whole range on any measure will be based on inappropriate extrapolations in particular groups of schools. Here, alternative strategies are required which focus the analyses on areas of the range actually represented in the comparisons that are of interest (Willms, 1984; Maughan and Rutter, 1987).

Perhaps the most important difficulty in this type of analysis, however, is that the fixed-effects model fails to take account of the inherently 'nested' structure of the data in studies of this kind. It is implicit in this structure that, since pupils in the same class or school share common experiences, their results will be more homogeneous than those of a random sample of pupils drawn from the population of all schools; the resulting within-school (or within-class) correlations thus need to be modelled along with other parameters in the analysis. As Aitkin and Longford (1986) point out in a detailed discussion of these issues, the problem of design effects of this kind has been virtually intractable until recently. The development of multi-level variance components, or random-effects models (Goldstein, 1986), marks a major advance here, enabling researchers to take adequate account of the nested structure of the data in studies of this kind.

To date, the only major British studies published using multi-level as well as fixed-effects models are the Inner London Education Authority Junior School Project (Mortimore *et al.*, 1986; Mortimore *et al.*, 1988) and the Policy Studies Institute's report on factors associated with success in multi-ethnic secondary schools (Policy Studies Institute, 1987). Some examples from the ILEA study will serve to illustrate the differences found using these two types of approach. This carefully designed study has traced the progress of children in 50 junior schools over a three-year period, from the ages of seven to ten. Using a variety of measures of intake characteristics, the results indicate marked differences between schools in both cognitive and non-cognitive outcomes. As has been consistently reported in all studies of this kind, initial attainment accounted for by far the greater part of the individual variance explained. In relation to ten-year-old reading, for example, earlier reading levels accounted for 62% of the explained variance, background factors a further 2%, and school attended 9%. When assessments were made of the children's *progress* in reading over the period, school effects accounted for a much higher proportion of the variance (24% using the fixed-effects approach, 20% with the random-effects model). Significant effects were found on a range of other cognitive outcomes, on assessments of behaviour, attitudes to school and individual subjects, and on measures of self concept and attendance.

As has frequently been argued, however, (see, for example, Rutter, 1983), presenting results of this kind in terms of proportions of variance explained at the individual level fails to illuminate the prime interest of the analyses, namely the effects associated with membership of one or another *school*. In general, earlier attainment and other background factors will almost always account for by far the greatest proportion of variation between individuals; school effects, by comparison, are likely to be of importance to the extent that they raise or lower *levels* of performance across the board. Viewed from this perspective, factors that account for quite small proportions of individual variance may nevertheless have far from negligible effects, especially at certain points in the range.

Table 1 illustrates the range of school differences found in the ILEA study on just two measures, reading attainment and an overall index of behaviour in school (here, a higher score reflects poorer behaviour). On each measure, differences between the most and least effective schools in the sample were marked, and clearly of educational as well as statistical significance. Nevertheless, the results of these extreme schools must be seen in the context of findings for the sample as a whole. More detailed data in the report make it clear that across the majority of schools the range of school effects was more restricted. This has also been the pattern

Table 1 *ILEA Junior School Project: differences between schools in third-year outcome measures*

	Possible score range	Sample mean	School differences	
			Most effective	Least effective
Reading	0–100	54	+15	−10
Behaviour	27–135	60	−19	+ 9

Source: Data extracted from Mortimore *et al.* (1986, Part C).

in much earlier work. In studies of school effects for unselected groups of pupils, it seems likely that the most powerful influences, both positive and negative, will be accounted for by relatively small groups of schools in the extremes of the range.

Accounting for differences between schools

Once the existence of differences between schools has been established, a series of subsidiary questions arise. Are the effects stronger for some types of developmental outcome than for others? Do they persist beyond the end of schooling? Are they similar for all groups of children within a school, or are some schools effective for some children, less so for others? Are the same schools effective in different domains – for example the cognitive and non-cognitive? Are the same schools effective over time? And, perhaps most importantly, are there measurable characteristics of the schools themselves that appear to be related to variations in their effectiveness? On their own, findings of differences between schools in pupil outcomes can tell us nothing about *how* such effects come about. Evidence that outcome differences are consistently related to school-level factors would considerably strengthen the supposition that causal processes are indeed involved. This has been the second main concern of the school effectiveness work.

In general, three broad types of school-level factors have been investigated: first, what might be regarded as 'given' characteristics, such as size, administrative status and resource levels; second, aspects of policy and day-to-day practice that contribute to the nature of schools as social organizations; and, finally – a variant on the issue of intake factors – measures of the *group* composition of the intakes, or the balance of particular pupil groups represented in a school. Comparative or correlational approaches have then been used to relate differences in effectiveness with school characteristics. Once again, we see the importance of the accurate specification of the model for assessing effectiveness; if this is inadequately specified, we may not only derive biased estimates of school effects, but we may also be led to identify the wrong school-related factors as contributors to more or less successful outcomes.

The second general need at this stage is of course for appropriate data on school-level factors. Conceptualizing and quantifying the characteristics of institutions as complex as schools is a highly demanding enterprise, but it is probably fair to conclude that it has attracted a good deal less attention in the literature than the problems of statistical analysis outlined above. If we are to increase our understanding of why schools differ in their effectiveness, and eventually of how the school experience may influence the individual child, it is essential that this aspect of the equation be accorded equal status with others. Although some innovative and important steps have been taken here, the measures developed to date have been based largely on informed intuitions rather than on any well-developed theoretical framework.

School factors associated with differential effectiveness

What has emerged from a very diverse range of studies of this kind is a perhaps surprisingly consistent picture of what a 'good school' looks like. The importance accorded to 'given' factors varies, with features such as school size and resource levels showing associations with effectiveness in some contexts, but not in others. Within the range studied to date, however, it seems generally agreed that although advantaged status in such respects may facilitate good functioning, it will not necessarily ensure it. The factors showing consistently stronger links with progress have been those under the heads of intake balance, and school climate, ethos or process.

Summarizing very briefly, it appears that the general composition of pupil groups (in terms, for example, of the numbers and proportions of able children, or of those from disadvantaged backgrounds) is related to additional effects over and above those of individual pupil characteristics (Willms, 1985). More successful schools are also differentiated from their less successful counterparts by a number of features of their internal operations: these generally include purposeful leadership by the headteacher; the involvement of staff in decision-making; consistency and consensus amongst staff; and parental involvement. More directly in terms of the pupils' experiences, positive outcomes have been associated with a pleasant but work-oriented environment, both interpersonal and physical; effective classroom management; stimulating teaching; and, especially perhaps for older children, opportunities for them to be involved in, and take responsibility for, aspects of their lives at school (see Rutter, 1983; and Reynolds, 1985).

It is of course of interest in itself that individual schools do vary in all these aspects of their internal organization. One question that immediately arises is the causal direction of the influences involved. The assumption of the argument so far has been that variations in school characteristics lead to variations in effectiveness. Since the links involved are correlational, however, it remains at least plausible that the effects could arise in other ways.

It could be, for example, that the institutional climate of a school develops in response to the characteristics of its pupils, or that it follows on from, rather than contributes to, success. The literature on child effects on adults within the family might lead us to anticipate some reciprocal influences of this kind, but a number of different strands of evidence suggest that such relationships at the school level are far from deterministic. Brookover *et al.* (1979) found schools matched on intake characteristics nevertheless had quite different profiles on climate variables. In our own research, we were able to use the patterns of relationships between variables at different times to show that, for example, a combined measure of school process was only weakly (but nevertheless positively) correlated with assessments of the children's behaviour at entry ($r = .39$), but much more strongly with later behaviour ($r = .92$), (Maughan *et al.*, 1980). However, one of the clear implications of differences in the progress of children at selective and non-selective schools was that the much more homogeneous intakes in the academically selective schools may have enabled them to pursue a range and type of curriculum that would be difficult if not impossible to encompass with more varied pupil intakes (Maughan and Rutter, 1987). Although there are clearly some reciprocal influences at work here, the implication is that school characteristics may indeed make some independent contribution to children's progress.

Longitudinal studies of schools

The strategies outlined thus far have primarily been developed as a means of strengthening causal inferences in studies that combine longitudinal data on children with essentially cross-sectional data on schools. The pattern of findings points to the existence of causal links, but correlational evidence of this kind cannot of course entirely rule out potentially competing explanations. The picture would be strengthened further if we could include a longitudinal element in the study of *schools*, and demonstrate, for example, that both their relative effectiveness, and their characteristics as organizations, tended to show stability over time. There is indeed some evidence that this is the case (Reynolds *et al.*, 1980; Rutter *et al.*, 1979), but perhaps the most powerful approach would be one that tested the hypothesized links directly, by studying the effects of change in school-related factors. This might be done in a variety of ways: by observational studies of natural change, or by direct intervention, using an action research approach (Rapoport, 1985). Within education, there is a large literature in both of these areas, encompassing curriculum development, a wide variety of school improvement programmes, the major preschool interventions of the last two decades, and a plethora of smaller-scale projects focusing on developments at the classroom level.

The preschool programmes are of major importance to any discussion of educational experiences in a risk and protective framework, and we will come on to consider them in greater detail later. Much of the more general work on school improvement, however, has had a rather different emphasis from our prime concern here, concentrating less on the *effects* of change than on what might be regarded as the logically prior question of how best, and how far, schools can be encouraged to take on new ways of working (Lehming and Kane, 1981; Dalin and Rust, 1983). The results of these efforts suggest that major change is by no means easy to achieve. Many attempts at innovation have either failed to be maintained for any significant period after their introduction, or indeed have failed to be put into effect at all. Where changes have been taken on board, they have not infrequently been adapted so much at the local level that they bear little resemblance to their originators' conceptions, so causing considerable headaches for evaluators. Interventions in schools, as in many other practice settings, must clearly be designed to take adequate account of the professional value systems of the practitioners involved, and the organizational characteristics of the institutions themselves (Baldridge, 1975). It is almost certainly not by chance that many of the most successful interventions in the educational field have been centred outside the mainstream system, in special demonstration projects where the aims of the research could be given equal weight with the needs of practice.

Our own attempts to pursue these issues in an intervention study pointed up further challenges in this type of approach (Ouston *et al.*, 1984). Even in a situation where we were fortunate to have the full co-operation and active interest of the schools involved, and where we attempted to follow a pragmatic approach, planning changes jointly with staff, the process of change was a slow one. Across a five-year period, a number of specific changes were introduced which had measurable short-term effects in the expected directions. By the end of the project, however, the cumulative impact of these individual initiatives had not been such as to be reflected in longer-term measures of pupil outcome. In addition, as in all research in 'real world' settings, our interpretation of the findings was much complicated by other developments, many quite outside the remit or control of the research, that had taken place over the same period. Our conclusions at the end of this study were that, at least in our current state of knowledge, it is probably precipitate to assume that interventions at the whole-school level can contribute in any major way to

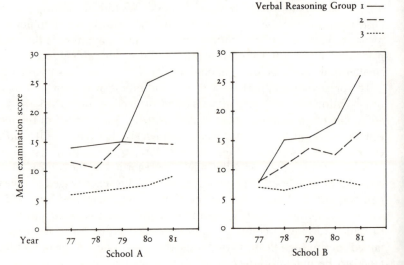

Figure 1   Changes in examination attainment at schools with new headteachers

our understanding of causal processes. This does not of course mean that we should abandon the study of change as a whole; rather, it should direct our attention to situations where interpretable change has taken place, or can be predicted to do so. More-focused interventions clearly can be of immense value from both a theoretical and a practical point of view (Tizard *et al.*, 1982).

As an alternative, naturalistic examples of change are not hard to seek. The arrival of a new headteacher might be one such situation. Our own work (Ouston *et al.*, 1984) included case studies of this kind, and provided examples of very considerable changes in outcomes over a five- to seven-year period in schools serving socially disadvantaged populations whose intakes had remained essentially the same over that time. Figure 1 shows mean scores on a weighted measure of attainment in public examinations for five successive cohorts of pupils at two schools where new headteachers had recently been appointed.

Data from interviews with staff suggested that where changes of this kind had occurred, they did indeed appear to reflect phased moves towards the development of many of the characteristics identified in the earlier literature – purposeful leadership, involvement of staff and pupils, clear expectations for all those involved in the institution, and an atmosphere that was both constructive and enjoyable. The timescale involved was considerable, with these more positive results for pupils only being evident some seven to eight years after the initial implementation of the new policies. The retrospective nature of the school measures means that we must be cautious in drawing strong conclusions, but the parallels with the earlier findings lend further weight to the likelihood of causal influences.

Possible mechanisms

What pointers to possible risk or protective processes can we draw from this general body of work? As we noted at the outset, the focus of much of the school effectiveness literature – on school-wide characteristics, and average outcomes for groups of children – cannot allow us to extrapolate directly to process at the individual level. To answer individually based questions, we need to concentrate more specifically on particular groups of children within schools. We know little as yet about how far schools that are successful for the majority of their pupils may also be successful with disadvantaged or disruptive children, or those at risk in other ways. What can be claimed on the basis of current research is that generally effective schools appear equally effective for some rather broad subcategories of children: both our own earlier work (Rutter *et al.*, 1979) and the ILEA (Mortimore *et al.*, 1988) study, for example, found that school effects were similar for working-class and middle-class children, for boys and girls, and in general (though there were exceptions here) for children of different ethnic backgrounds. If the principal effect of school differences is indeed to raise or depress general *levels* of progress, this might be of quite crucial significance for certain groups of children at sensitive points in the range. In the most and least effective schools, as we have seen, effects may be considerable across the board.

How are these effects mediated for the individual child? If we wish to explore school experiences as risk or protective factors, this ultimately must be the question of prime concern. The answers are inevitably speculative; most interpretations propose a cumulative model, in which the various dimensions of effectiveness identified combine to produce a climate or ethos in the institution as a whole that serves to increase or decrease children's involvement in, and identification with, schooling. When this works positively, it supports and enhances effective classroom teaching, and so contributes to optimum progress. Findings on the importance of intake balance point to another source of influences, those emanating from the peer group; these could also operate positively, to support school norms and values, or negatively, either to oppose or remain indifferent to them. The central processes seem to be those of engaging the child with the school and its aims, and promoting positive outcomes in a variety of areas.

These interpretations are essentially *post hoc*, derived from the general pattern of findings emerging from what might be regarded as the first generation of studies in this field. They provide a range of more specific hypotheses that might be tested in a more detailed way in future research.

To learn more about these processes at an individual level, we need to focus more closely on selected groups of children, or specific aspects of school functioning. Ideally we also need measures collected at more frequent intervals, to illuminate hypothesized mediating mechanisms as well as the basic intake–outcome framework described here. Pointers to some of the kinds of effect likely to emerge are already available from very different examples of school-related research.

Effects of preschool programmes

A more individually focused model of process has been derived from evaluations of the effectiveness of preschool programmes for disadvantaged children. Here the emphasis has been explicitly on at-risk groups, and the findings unequivocally point to long-term protective effects in some circumstances. The links involved, however, were by no means direct or immediate. Indeed, a major impetus in the development of the currently accepted model of process arose from apparent *discontinuities* in the findings from one stage of the research to another.

The most influential reports have emerged from an almost unique body of longitudinal data, tracing the progress of children involved in a number of the best-designed and most carefully evaluated US experimental preschool programmes of the late 1950s and early 1960s. From the mid-1970s onwards, a group of the original investigators on these studies combined together to form the Consortium for Longitudinal Studies, pooling results from earlier stages of their work and conducting further joint follow-ups when the ex-preschool children were in adolescence or early adulthood (Lazar and Darlington, 1982).

A consistent pattern of findings emerged. First, as many other early evaluations had concluded (see, for example, Bronfenbrenner, 1974), although impressive cognitive gains were recorded for these severely disadvantaged children during and immediately after the programmes, these were lost after three or four years in the ordinary school system. But a range of other more 'real world' measures, taken at various stages throughout the children's schooling and beyond, suggested the persistence of other effects. By comparison with controls, the programme children's general competence at school was considerably more satisfactory. Among a group of children all at major risk for educational failure, they were only half as likely to be referred for special education, and somewhat less likely to be retained in grade; instead, they were *more* likely to receive remedial help within the mainstream school system, suggesting that teachers perceived them as more competent. The children's mothers were more satisfied with their progress, and the children themselves were found to have stronger achievement motivation at later stages in their schooling. At the longer-term follow-ups, programme participants were found more

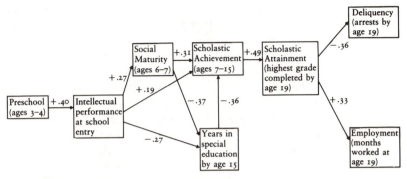

Figure 2   A causal model for effects of the Perry Preschool Program
(from Berrueta-Clement *et al.*, 1984)

often to have completed high school, and to have been more likely to have
found employment. More detailed reports from one of the Consortium
studies, the Perry Preschool Program (Berrueta-Clement *et al.*, 1984),
include results at age 19 in a much wider range of areas: these show
ex-preschool participants with lower rates of delinquency and crime, less
reliance on welfare benefits, and a lower incidence of teenage pregnancies
among the girls.

How had the pathways of the experimental children and the controls
come to diverge so widely? The researchers put forward a transactional
model, proposing a reciprocal mesh of attitudes and expectations
amongst the children, their teachers and parents which, in combination
with the children's performance, may have been of particular significance
at certain crucial decision points in their school careers. The model posits
a series of interlinked developments over time, each successively increasing or reducing the likelihood of successful adaptation at later stages. This
interpretation is supported by various causal path analyses, one of which
is shown in Figure 2.

On this formulation, the initial IQ gains made during the programme
were of importance not because they occurred at some sort of 'critical
period' in developmental terms (as had originally been assumed), but
because they enabled the children to cope successfully with what may well
be a critical period from the institutional point of view, that of entry into
school. It is suggested that preschool experience equipped the children
with both cognitive skills, and probably also with some non-cognitive
attributes, that enabled them to manage the transition to school more
effectively. They were better able to adapt to classroom procedures, and
to do schoolwork, and so developed both a belief in their own abilities to
achieve in school, and a positive attitude towards it. These were crucial
first steps in their engagement with what the researchers describe as the
'school success flow'. Their more positive orientation to both schooling

and their own competence was in turn seen as a vital mediating link with the later findings on more satisfactory functioning outside the school setting.

The findings on placement in special education, retention in grade, and involvement in remedial teaching, have been interpreted as suggesting expectancies on the part of the teachers that programme children could manage in mainstream schools, and indeed should receive additional support to do so. As Woodhead (1985) has pointed out, however, in a discussion of the generalizability of these results, referral to special classes and the like are not simply criterion measures of the effects of these programmes, but may have been important mediating variables, directly contributing in themselves to the transformation of the initial effects by amplifying both earlier success and failure. Placement in a special class may constitute a major turning point for a child, with long-term implications on the expectations of a succession of teachers. This could be just one of a number of branching points in children's school careers, many of which are institutionally structured, that may mark key divergences in the pathways of different groups. Any full account of the impact of school experiences must clearly take cognizance of effects of this kind.

Possible mechanisms

This sort of model begins to move us closer to an understanding of how school experiences might contribute to risk or protective mechanisms. Rutter (in press) suggests that the mediating mechanisms in protective processes might include (a) reduction in the impact of risk, (b) reduction of negative chain reactions, (c) the promotion of feelings of self-efficacy and self-esteem, and (d) the opening-up of new opportunities. The preschool findings clearly have parallels here. First, it is evident that although preschool experiences were associated with long-term effects, these did not arise in any simple linear fashion. The programmes had originally been designed in the hope of producing long-term cognitive gains. In practice, their effects seem more likely to have arisen through a series of much shorter-term links, each increasing or decreasing the likelihood of particular outcomes at the immediately succeeding stage. The reduction of negative chain reactions, and the promotion of more positive developments, was clearly central here. In a similar way, our study of the transition from school to work found a very comparable pattern of effects (Gray *et al.*, 1980). There was evidence of school effects on employment, but these were indirect, arising from prior influences on attendance and attainment, which in their turn opened up, or closed off, opportunities in the employment field. As in many other areas of environmental influence, it seems likely that school experiences may frequently have their effects – whether beneficial or less so – in this way.

Following on from this, the preschool findings highlight the importance of particular turning points in children's school careers. Factors of this kind are also attracting increasing atention in the literature on risk and protective mechanisms, as in, for example, Elder's study of the effects of military service in postponing other life transitions, and so enabling men otherwise at risk of disorganized adult lives to make considerably more stable adjustments (Elder, 1986). Schooling includes many such institutionalized turning points, from initial school entry onwards, which may be particularly sensitive stages at which poor adaptations may arise, or more positive functioning may be reinforced. In this sense, they may be especially illuminating as a focus for studies of risk or protective effects.

Finally, the results suggest that feelings of self-competence and self-worth among the children themselves, reinforced by the attitudes of their teachers and families, may have been central to the amplification of the effects of the preschool experience. Perceptions of competence and mastery (or the lack of them) seem likely to be especially important outcomes of school experiences. Rutter and Quinton (1984) provide evidence of this from a much later stage in the life course, in a study of the adult adjustment of institution-reared women. Positive school experiences (as reported by the women themselves), formed one of the key connecting links in a chain of influences contributing to their later functioning. Working backwards in this chain, one of the central features differentiating ex-care women with good and poor outcomes was the extent to which they 'planned' developments in various aspects of their lives, in particular in relation to work and marriage. One of the features that in turn distinguished 'planners' from others, was the recollection of positive school experiences. The authors suggest that the school experiences were influential via effects on the girls' sense of their own competence, and their ability to control events. This was in turn hypothesized to contribute to more positive planning strategies in their later lives. Perhaps the most interesting feature of the findings, however, was that these associations did not emerge in a comparison group of women brought up in their families of origin. It is suggested that for most girls in the comparison group, experiences in their homes and families would have provided ample sources of self-worth, so that any additional effects of positive experiences at school could only serve to reinforce these. For the ex-care women, however, success or a sense of accomplishment at school may well have been vital in compensating for a lack of opportunities in their main rearing environment. For them, school experiences may well have been necessary to *create* feelings of self-efficacy and esteem that then laid the foundations for better adult functioning.

For other groups, experiences at school may tend to lower self-esteem. Comparisons with peers may constitute an important influence here. Harter (1985) provides interesting evidence of this in relation to learning-disabled children. Comparing the perceived cognitive competence of learning-disabled and retarded elementary school children, all established in mainstream classes, she found an apparently paradoxical pattern. The retarded children perceived themselves as no less competent than their mainstream peers, but the learning-disabled group (whose IQs were within the normal range), nevertheless had *lower* perceived competence scores. The explanation seemed to lie in the reference groups each group of children chose in reaching appraisals of their own abilities, which in turn reflected the differing educational 'careers' of the retarded and learning-disabled children. The retarded group, identified as having problems at an early age and needing special educational placement, naturally selected other retarded peers as the basis for their social comparisons. The learning-disabled children, however, had much less clear-cut histories, and a generally much later identification of their specific difficulties. For them, other mainstream children would form a more natural reference group, with inevitably less satisfactory consequences for their self-esteem.

These findings point to the need to examine the particular social world experienced by the child in developing an understanding of the effects of experiential factors. It is worth noting here that very little of the research reported to date in relation to schooling really allows us to talk of 'school experiences' in this sense. There are, however, a number of lines of evidence suggesting that the quality of school life may differ considerably for children in apparently similar settings. One such picture comes from a prospective study by Nicol and his colleagues (1985), which contrasts a group of children eventually suspended from secondary school with both 'non-difficult' controls and with a comparison group matched on levels of behavioural difficulty soon after entering secondary school.

The longitudinal design of this study, which included very frequent assessments of disruptive behaviour, is illuminating in a number of ways. For the suspended children, the months immediately preceding suspension were marked by an increasing spiral of disruptive incidents, occurring at much higher frequency, and in different settings, than for the difficult controls. It seems likely that some self-amplifying process was at work here, in terms of both the childrens' behaviour and their teachers' reactions, finally crystallizing in the act of suspension. A very similar picture is suggested in a study of the links between early classroom behaviour and later police contacts and delinquency (Spivack *et al.*, 1986). Here we see possible parallels in the classroom setting with the dynamics in parent–child interactions proposed in studies of children with difficult temperament (Bates, 1980). Initial signs of difficult behaviour may result in negative adult perceptions and reactions, leading to less adaptive patterns of coping in the child, and so increasing spirals of difficulty that develop their own momentum.

In addition to this picture of events in the immediate run-up to suspension, it was clear from initial screening data, collected in some cases three years earlier, that the suspended children had inhabited a very particular personal world within the context of the school from the outset. Sociometric ratings showed that they were more likely than the difficult comparison group to be rated as tough, and as fooling around, by their peers, and that they were considerably more likely to be rejected. Within the overall environment of the school, these children clearly experienced a particular *individual* environment that was much less hospitable than that of their well-adjusted peers.

Conclusions

Studies of this kind, focusing on particular groups of children, and on particular aspects of the school experience, have taken us far from our original point of departure. In many ways, this is not an inappropriate reflection of the diversity of work in the field. Each of these very different threads of research interest provides differing, but persuasive, evidence of the potential of school experiences to function as either risk or protective factors. The models illustrated here have been by no means straightforward; as we have seen, such influences as do occur may arise from a variety of sources, and may have many different kinds of impact, in both the short and the longer term. In addition, we have already begun to see evidence, which will doubtless become more extensive as studies of this kind increase, of the importance of interactions between particular types of child characteristic and particular kinds of school experience.

Each of these various types of evidence moves us some way forward in understanding the nature of the underlying processes that are likely to be involved. In this sense, however, we are still very much at the beginning of the road. The challenge for the next generation of research will be to integrate these different perspectives, and to develop conceptual models, not dissimilar in their aims to the statistical ones described earlier, that can reflect the nested and layered structure of the school experience, and the ways in which the wider environment is articulated with the world of the individual child. The next steps must be to bring together findings from the broad-brushstroke approach of the school differences literature with the more detailed insights gained from studies of particular groups of children, in order to provide a more comprehensive mapping of the area that can in its turn be applied to a wider range of at-risk populations. In this endeavour, as in the work undertaken to date, a developmental perspective, reflected in longitudinal strategies, will continue to be an essential starting point in increasing our understanding of the unfolding impact of environmental influences on children's lives.

218 Barbara Maughan

References

Aitkin, M. and Longford, N. (1986) Statistical modelling issues in school effectiveness studies. *Journal of the Royal Statistical Society*, 149, 1–43.

Baldridge, J. V. (1975) Organizational innovation: individual, structural and environmental impacts. In Baldridge, J. V. and Deal, T. E. (eds.) *Managing change in educational organizations*. Berkeley: McCutchan, pp. 151–75.

Bates, J. E. (1980) The concept of difficult temperament. *Merrill-Palmer Quarterly*, 26, 300–18.

Berrueta-Clement, J. R., Schweinart, L. J., Barnett, W. S., Epstein, S. S. and Weikart, D. P. (1984) *Changed lives: the effects of the Perry Pre-school Program on youths through age 19*. Ypsilanti, MI: High Scope.

Bronfenbrenner, U. (1974) *Is early intervention effective?* Washington, DC: Department of Health, Education and Welfare.

Brookover, W. B. and Lezotte, L. W. (1979) *Changes in school characteristics coincident with changes in student achievement*. East Lancing: Institute for Research on Teaching, Michigan State University.

Brookover, W. B., Beady, C., Flood, P., Schweitzer, J. and Wisenbaker, J. (1979) *School social systems and student achievement: schools can make a difference*. New York: Praeger.

Coleman, J. S., Hopper, T. and Kilgore, S. (1982) Achievement and segregation in secondary schools: a further look at public and private school differences. *Sociology of Education*, 55, 162–82.

Dalin, P. and Rust, V. D. (1983) *Can schools learn?* Windsor: NFER-Nelson.

Douglas, J. W. B., Ross, J. M. and Simpson, H. R. (1968) *All our future: a longitudinal study of secondary education*. London: Davies.

Elder, G. H. (1986) Military times and turning points in men's lives. *Developmental Psychology*, 22, 233–45.

Fogelman, K., Goldstein, H., Essen, J. and Ghodsian, M. (1978) Patterns of attainment. *Educational Studies*, 4, 121–30.

Garmezy, N. (1985) Stress-resistant children: the search for protective factors. In Stevenson, J. (ed.) *Recent research in developmental psychopathology*, a book supplement to the *Journal of Child Psychology and Psychiatry*, 4. Oxford: Pergamon Press, pp. 213–33.

Goldstein, H. (1986) Multilevel mixed linear models analysis using iterative generalised least squares. *Biometrics*, 73, 53–64.

Gray, G., Smith, A. and Rutter, M. (1980) School attendance and the first year of employment. In Hersov, L. and Berg, I. (eds.) *Out of school: modern perspectives in truancy and school refusal*. Chichester: Wiley, pp. 343–70.

Gray, J., Jesson, D. and Jones, B. (1986) The search for a fairer way of comparing schools' examination results. *Research Papers in Education*, 1, 91–119.

Grosin, L. (1985) *School effects and pupil outcome: research findings and some theoretical considerations*. Research bulletins from the Institute of Education, University of Stockholm, vol. 11, no. 1.

Harter, S. (1985) Processes underlying the construction, maintenance and enhancement of the self-concept in children. In Suls, J. and Greenland, A. (eds.) *Psychological perspectives on the self*, vol. 3. New York: Erlbaum, pp. 137–81.

Jencks, C., Smith, M., Acland, H., Bane, M. J., Cohen, D., Gintis, H., Heyns, B. and Michelson, S. (1972) *Inequality: a reassessment of the effect of family and schooling in America*. New York: Basic Books.

Jöreskog, K. D. and Sörbom, D. (1981) LISREL, V. Analysis of linear structural relationships by maximum likelihood and least squares methods. Research Report, 81–3. Department of Statistics, University of Uppsala, Sweden.

Klitgaard, R. E. and Hall, G. R. (1975) Are there unusually effective schools? *Journal of Human Resources*, **10**, 90–106.

Lazar, I. and Darlington, R. B. (1982) *Lasting effects of early education: a report from the Consortium for Longitudinal Studies*. Monograph of the Society for Research in Child Development, vol. 47, nos. 2–3.

Lehming, R. and Kane, M. (eds.) (1981) *Improving schools: using what we know*. Beverly Hills: Sage.

Masten, A. S. and Garmezy, N. (1985) Risk, vulnerability and protective factors in developmental psychopathology. In Lahey, B. B. and Kazdin, A. E. (eds.) *Advances in clinical child psychology*, vol. 8. New York: Plenum Press.

Maughan, B. and Rutter, M. (1987) Pupil progress in selective and non-selective schools. *School Organization*, **7**, 50–68.

Maughan, B., Mortimore, P., Ouston, J. and Rutter, M. (1980) Fifteen Thousand Hours: a reply to Heath and Clifford. *Oxford Review of Education*, **6**, 289–303.

Mortimore, J. and Blackstone, T. (1982) *Disadvantage and education*. London: Heinemann.

Mortimore, P., Sammons, P., Stoll, L., Lewis, D. and Ecob, R. (1986) *The Junior School Project: Main report parts A, B, C and technical appendices*.London: ILEA.

(1988) *School matters: the junior years*. London: Open Books.

Nicol, A. R., Willcox, C. and Hibbert, K. (1985) What sort of children are suspended from school and what can we do for them? In Nicol, A. R., (ed.) *Longitudinal studies in child psychology and psychiatry*. Chichester: Wiley, pp. 33–49.

Ouston, J., Maughan, B. and Rutter, M. (1984) Innovation and change in six secondary schools. Final Report to the Department of Education and Science. Institute of Psychiatry, London.

Policy Studies Institute and University of Lancaster (1987) Factors associated with success in multi-ethnic secondary schools. Mimeographed report.

Purkey, S. C. and Smith, M. S. (1983) Effective schools: a review. *Elementary School Journal*, **83**, 427–52.

Rapoport, R. N. (ed.) (1985) *Children, youth and families: the action-research relationship*. Cambridge: Cambridge University Press.

Reynolds, D. B. (1982) The search for effective schools. *School Organization*, **2**, 215–37.

(ed.) (1985) *Studying school effectiveness*. London: Falmer Press.

Reynolds, D., Jones, D., St Leger, S. and Murgatroyd, S. (1980) School factors and truancy. In Hersov, L. and Berg, I. (eds.) *Out of school: modern perspectives in truancy and school refusal*. Chichester: Wiley, pp. 85–110.

Robins, L. (1966) *Deviant children grown up*. Baltimore: Williams and Wilkins.

Rutter, M. (1983) School effects on pupil progress: research findings and policy implications. *Child Development*, **54**, 1–29.

(in press) Psychosocial resilience and protective mechanisms. In Rolf, J., Masten, A., Cicchetti, D., Nuechterlein, K. and Weintraub, S. (eds.) *Risk and protective factors in the development of psychopathology*. New York: Cambridge University Press.

Rutter, M. and Quinton, D. (1984) Long-term follow-up of women institutionalised in childhood: factors promoting good functioning in adult life. *British Journal of Developmental Psychology*, **18**, 225–34.

Rutter, M., Maughan, B., Mortimore, P., Ouston, J. and Smith, A. (1979) *Fifteen thousand hours: secondary schools and their effects on children*. London: Open Books.

Spivack, G., Marcus, J. and Swift, M. (1986) Early classroom behaviours and later

220   Barbara Maughan

misconduct. *Developmental Psychology*, 22, 124–31.

Steedman, J. (1983) *Examination results in selective and non-selective secondary schools*. London: National Children's Bureau.

Tizard, J., Schofield, W. N. and Hewison, J. (1982) Collaboration between teachers and parents in assisting children's reading. *British Journal of Educational Psychology*, 52, 1–15.

Weber, G. (1971) *Inner city children can be taught to read: four successful schools*. Occasional paper, no. 18. Washington, DC: Council for Basic Education.

Willms, J. D. (1984) School effectiveness within the public and private sectors: an evaluation. *Evaluation Review*, 8, 113–35.

——— (1985) The balance thesis: contextual effects of ability on pupils' O-grade examination results. *Oxford Review of Education*, 11, 33–42.

Woodhead, M. (1985) Pre-school education has long-term effects: but can they be generalized? *Oxford Review of Education*, 11, 133–55.

12 School effects: the use of planned intervention to study causal processes

J. C. van der Wolf

Introduction

In this chapter I consider a number of conceptual and methodological issues that play a role in longitudinal research into school effects. First I take up a few points made by Barbara Maughan concerning the extent and nature of the effects of school on the development of children. Then I make several suggestions about theory with regard to the effects of internal school factors on the development of pupils.

Effects of the school on children's progress

At the end of the book *Fifteen thousand hours* Rutter and his research colleagues (1979, p. 204) concluded: 'our study necessarily was concerned with correlations and associations. These suggest mechanisms and causal influences, but only studies of planned change in schools can identify these with any certainty. Such investigations are needed.' The idea that insight into causal relationships can be obtained from correlations used to be fairly widespread. Tuckman, for example, (1972, p. 127) stated: 'While it is difficult to establish causality, it is possible to identify potential causes which often can then be tested more directly by manipulation.'

In her chapter, Maughan is pessimistic about the possibilities that this method offers for theory development. Instead, she argues for the study of change in schools as it occurs naturally through changes of staff or of policy. Rutter *et al.* (1986) tried to implement the findings from *Fifteen thousand hours* in three schools They found that 'some useful things were accomplished but it was an uphill struggle and the achievement was very modest indeed' (p. 41). I myself am inclined to see advantages in intervention research. I believe that people stop too soon, because there are few short-term results to be seen at pupil level, and furthermore that such studies are not sufficiently preplanned. I should like to illustrate this with some examples from my own research.

There are several key differences between our approach and that of Barbara Maughan and her colleagues. First, our interventions were focused on classrooms rather than on the school as a whole. I agree that it is often difficult to alter the functionings of a whole school and, even when you succeed, the very complexity of the changes makes it difficult to isolate the crucial elements in the intervention. Second, our interventions were both specific and closely related to the variables previously found to differentiate effective and less effective schools. Third, we sought to examine the effects on teacher and pupil attitudes rather than on pupil performance as such. Of course, the latter must be a main objective, but frequently it will be the case that performance improves because attitudes change for the better. This is what we tried to study. Our research had one essential element in common with that of Barbara Maughan, namely the use of individually based longitudinal data, a necessary feature if one is to study causal mechanisms.

In my Ph.D. research I showed that there was a connection between school dropout (at school level), pupils' school experiences, perceptions and attitudes, and the working methods of teachers. Because of the study design, no statements could be made about causal connections, so we followed the advice given by Rutter *et al.* (1979) to investigate the effects of planned change.

In our pilot research we concentrated on improving the school experience of pupils and the co-operation between teachers. Four of the schools involved in the empirical quantitative research were interested in research to study the effects of intervention (two other schools were used in the quasi-experimental pre-test/post-test design as controls). The research carried out in the school year 1983–4 consisted of a pre-test, a nine-month period of intervention, and a post-test.

At the beginning of the school year, pupils aged between 9 and 13 in the participating schools were given a pre-test, consisting of a pupil questionnaire and a sociometric test. In the questionnaire, pupils were asked how much they agreed with certain statements about the classroom situation in their school. These questionnaires contained scales that in my previous research had explained a considerable amount of the variation of school dropout (see Figure 1). Their reliability and validity were satisfactory. Using sociometric tests, we gained an overview of the relationships of children in the classroom.

The teachers were given a teacher questionnaire. These questionnaires

1.	Waiting and getting bored	When I've finished my work, I have to wait
2.	Support from classmates	In this class children tell each other about their problems
3.	Attitudes towards school	I think it's a shame when school's over
4.	Social adaptability	I don't have anyone to play with in break
5.	Image of self-functioning	I think I get on well at school
6.	Fear of school	I get all nervous when teachers ask things about my work
7.	Relationship with teachers	I think the teachers like me

Figure 1   Scales showing the pupil questionnaire with a sample comment

1.	Satisfaction with headteacher	I don't think much of the way the head does his job
2.	Reaction to work pressure	School staff meetings waste too much time
3.	Satisfaction with school curriculum	I think the teaching and general education in our school really need improving in several ways
4.	Satisfaction with colleagues	The teachers in this school don't discuss their work with each other
5.	General job satisfaction	I get a lot of satisfaction from my work

Figure 2 Scales showing the teacher questionnaire with a sample comment

contained a number of scales (see Figure 2) that had demonstrated differences between effective and non-effective schools in my Ph.D. research.

After administering the pre-test we developed several intervention strategies that aimed to improve the children's school experience and co-operation between teachers (Ponte and van der Wolf, 1986). These strategies dealt with specific problem areas that are connected with the subscales chosen from the questionnaire. The interventions were made at the classroom, rather than the whole-school, level in order to provide a better focus on the mechanisms that might be involved in the effects. At the end of the school year the post-test was carried out, using the same instruments as in the pre-test.

Results

In order to measure the effects of the intervention we carried out a covariance analysis at classroom level. The post-test pupil questionnaire was taken to be the dependent variable. The independent variable was the intervention strategy (experimental versus control group). The score of the pre-test concerned was the covariate. Table 1 summarizes the findings. The mean scores given in the table are unadjusted for pre-test level because none of the group differences before the intervention were either sizeable or statistically significant.

These results were disappointing. In general we saw no improvement in the classrooms that had taken part in the experiment. The only significant change (attitudes towards school) lies in the 'wrong direction'. From this we might conclude that such methods of working do not provide any positive results. However, is a clear result to be expected?

In the first place, it should be said that the intervention period was short (October to June). In the second place, both at pupil level and at classroom level the pre-test score eliminated much of the variance. The pre-test scores are all significant predictors of post-test scores at levels of 1%. In connection with the image of self-functioning, for example, 30.8% of the variance at pupil level and 47.9% at classroom level was determined by

Table 1 *Unadjusted mean scores for the experimental and control group on pupil measures*

Dependent variables	Experimental group	Control group	p	Explained variance
Waiting and getting bored	42.30	41.51	.260	3.2%
Support from classmates	35.45	36.16	.110	5.1%
Attitudes towards school	35.51	36.88	.043	12.2%
Social adaptability	33.29	33.80	.135	5.3%
Image of self-functioning	16.88	17.04	.847	0.1%
Fear of school	14.00	14.09	.129	0.3%
Relationship with teachers	17.03	16.92	.135	0.3%
Popularity	2.25	2.13	.076	2.7%

the pre-test score. These data are corroborated by the findings of Hox and de Leeuw (1986). They investigated the size of the effect of contextual characteristics (the teacher, the classroom, the school) during the period of one school year. This effect appeared to be small. The main determinants as regards both school achievement and experience of school at the end of the school year consisted of the pupil characteristics seen at the beginning of the school year. Only in the case of the variable 'popular' did it appear that the character of the teacher had a fairly strong impact on the position of the pupil. Here it was more a question of the group structure than a pupil characteristic. This does not mean, of course, that the school is an irrelevant factor. These analyses, as well as those from our intervention-oriented research, are directed towards assessing differences between pupils and classrooms as these manifest themselves in the course of a school year. The development that all pupils undergo (for example, that at the end of a school year they feel more secure) is not reflected in these analyses. We can, however, draw the conclusion that there is very high stability of individual differences during this short period. This implies that intervention is not likely to have much effect on such differences between children. However, it would still of course be possible to raise, for example, overall levels of pupil satisfaction without the intervention having much effect on variance.

If we now consider the effects of the intervention on teachers (see Table 2), a somewhat different picture emerges. We observe a distinct increase in the feeling of satisfaction with colleagues and the school head – probably as a result of the project. The experienced job pressure diminished (although the staff were working hard on the project!) while at the same time satisfaction with the way of working in the school increased. There were no changes with regard to general job satisfaction. This appeared to be a fairly stable characteristic of the teachers in question. 49.5% of the

Table 2 *Unadjusted mean scores for the experimental and control group on teacher measures*

Dependent variables	Experimental group	Control group	p	Explained variance
Satisfaction with headteacher	25.31	22.67	.044	16.4%
Reaction to work pressure	16.29	20.00	.064	12.3%
Satisfaction with school curriculum	23.07	18.56	.063[a]	11.9%
Satisfaction with colleagues	22.64	18.33	.021	14.6%
General job satisfaction	31.14	28.56	.245	0.6%

[a] This is the only variable for which there was a significant between-group pre-test difference ($E = 22.4$, $C = 18.2$; $p < .039$); its presence indicates that a treatment effect should not be inferred for this variable.

variance was determined by the score of the pre-test. This is understandable; in the course of one year people do not radically alter their attitudes to the job/profession they have chosen.

Discussion

We found a clear difference between the effects on teachers and the effects on pupils. The amount of explained variance at teacher level was considerably larger. This is probably explained by an effect that is well known in innovation literature. The innovation had reached the teachers, but not yet penetrated to the pupils.

Attempts at innovation cost blood, sweat and tears. Over the short term, the results are sometimes minimal. Thus, for example, team teaching – intended to reduce the negative effects of teachers' working in isolation – has the side-effect that it does not improve classroom teaching. Armstrong (1977) concluded that the results of team teaching are better in those teams that use this method over a longer period. The innovation or renewal is then given shape; the teachers have more time and energy for their classes.

We concluded in our study that school effects operate via the teachers. We distinguished two factors here:

1 A delay factor. The results of a change can be measured only after a considerable period at classroom and pupil level. Our results suggest that the effects are first apparent in changes in teacher attitudes. Presumably it may take longer for these changes to influence pupils. Our study did not last long enough to detect these (hypothesized) later effects, and more prolonged investigations are required.

2 A diffusion factor. When implementing interventions, teachers tend to make school- and classroom-specific variations. This is sometimes because the interventions have not been sufficiently specifically described. This makes it difficult to determine the causes of the differ-

ences that are found. It is not clear what causes we should ascribe changes to. This proves a hindrance in developing theories and models about risk and protective factors in schools and classrooms.

Two things need to be done. First, we need to spend more time trying to identify the important variables at pupil, classroom and school level (multi-level models). In the second place, we need to develop strategies at these levels that are sufficiently specifically described. These should be consistently applied and then assessed according to effect. For this, schools will have to be observed over a longer period. This combination of clear conceptualizing and intervention evaluation at all school levels may produce the well-developed theoretical framework that is needed.

References

Armstrong, D. G. (1977) Team teaching and academic achievement. *Review of Educational Research*, **47**, 65–86.

Hox, J. J. and de Leeuw, E. D. (1986) De invloed van individuele en contextuele kenmerken op schoolbeleving en prestatie. In van der Wolf, J. C. and Hox, J. J. (eds.) *Kwaliteit van onderwijs in het geding*. Lisse: Swets and Zeitlinger, pp. 44–56.

Ponte, P. and van der Wolf, J. C. (1986) Beinvloeding van de schoolbeleving van leerlingen; drie praktijken, een doel. In Lagerwey, N. A. J. and Wubbels, Th. (eds.) *Onderwijsverbetering als opdracht*. Lisse: Swets and Zeitlinger, pp. 63–73.

Rutter, M., Maughan, B., Mortimer, P., Ouston, J. and Smith, A. (1979) *Fifteen thousand hours: secondary schools and their effects on children*. London: Open Books.

Rutter, M., Maughan, B. and Ouston, J. (1986) The study of school effectiveness. In van der Wolf, J. C. and Hox, J. J. (eds.) *Kwaliteit van onderwijs in het geding*. Lisse: Swets and Zeitlinger, pp. 32–43.

Tuckman, B. W. (1972) *Conducting educational research*. New York: Harcourt, Brace, Jovanovich.

13   Normative life events as risk factors in childhood

Judy Dunn

How do young children respond to perturbations and change in their social and emotional lives? Why do some children appear to be more vulnerable than others to 'life events'? To what extent do the 'ordinary' stresses of transitions and change in childhood cast a long-term shadow over individuals' lives? The importance of gaining some clearer perspective on these questions is becoming increasingly urgent. Patterns of daily family life are changing dramatically in Europe and the US. With sharp increases in the employment of mothers of young children, in single-parent families, in divorce and separation of parents, and in the use of less-than-ideal substitute care that is forced upon parents by inadequate child-care provision, a large and growing proportion of young children face, in their early years, major and potentially stressful changes in their social lives. In addition to these experiences, children also have to cope with more 'expected' changes, such as starting or changing school, moving house or neighbourhood, and changes in family life with the birth of a sibling. These 'ordinary' events in a young child's life may well also be stressful, involving as they do major changes in the familiar architecture of children's lives and strenuous emotional and cognitive demands. Such 'normal' changes are indeed comparable to the experiences of life events that research has demonstrated to have significant effects in adulthood (Paykel, 1978; Rutter, 1983).

The grounds for studying the impact of such 'ordinary' events upon children are, then, two. First, such events may in themselves influence children's emotional adjustment and their future well-being; second, such study may help us to understand better the processes that link more obviously stressful events, such as parental separation and loss, to different outcomes for different children. In one respect, the study of these experiences that are common to most children has a methodological advantage over the study of more traumatic events, such as divorce. The imputation of causal links between such traumatic events and subsequent behavioural problems is problematic; as Robins (1983) has pointed out, there may be common causal factors that contribute both to the traumatic event and to the behavioural disturbance, and the need to search for such possible common antecedents is often overlooked in stress research. Since virtually all children in our society make the transition to school, and 80%

227

of first-born children experience the birth of a sibling, these events in themselves cannot be attributed to a certain kind of family background or parental disorder. Such family variables are indeed, as we will see, often implicated in the nature of the children's response to the 'ordinary' event, but since we can study the children's response and their families before and after the event we can begin to separate out how far the event itself represents a traumatic change that contributes to the children's problems.

In this chapter the nature of children's responses to these 'ordinary' life events will be considered, and the question of what implications they may have for our understanding of other possibly more stressful changes in children's lives will be discussed. First, the evidence that such ordinary events can be associated with disturbance in children's behaviour will be considered, taking as examples three changes – starting school, moving house and the birth of a sibling. Next the processes that may be involved in linking event to outcome will be discussed; I will draw here chiefly upon the study of the birth of a sibling. In the final section the implications of the findings on the impact of such 'ordinary' events for other stressful changes will be briefly considered.

Normative life events

Adjustment to school

When children first go to school they are faced by a wide range of new demands. They have to adjust to a large group of peers, a teacher, a long separation from their family, which may be a first-time separation, a strange environment with a whole array of unfamiliar rules, a set of expectations that they will sit still, concentrate, pay attention and listen without interrupting, as well as the intellectual demands of formal schooling. It seems quite likely that such demands will be overwhelming for some children, and the studies that have examined the prevalence of behaviour problems following children's entry to school report quite consistent rates of disturbed behaviour. Hughes and his colleagues, for instance, studying children in a London borough, found 13% to be having general difficulty in 'coping with school' and 25% to be having difficulties in concentration, in language or in fine motor control after half a term (Hughes *et al.*, 1979). These findings are very similar to those reported by Thompson (1975), while Chazan and Jackson (1971; 1974), from studies of 726 children in 'deprived', 'stable working-class' and 'middle-class' schools, report 15% to be 'somewhat' or 'very' disturbed in their first year, and 24% to be giving some indication of deviance. Emotional disturbances, especially problems with concentration, are consistently reported to be the most common.

Difficulties of adjustment to school are not, then, trivial; neither are they transient. Consistent findings on the persistence of these problems are reported. Together the studies show that while for the majority of children the difficulties of starting school are relatively short-lived, there is a small but important group whose problems persist. Thus Chazan and Jackson found that 43% of the children who were 'poorly adjusted' at five were still having problems at seven, and Hughes and his colleagues found between a quarter and a half of the children with difficulties at school entry were still having problems 18 months later. In Elizur's (1986) study of Israeli children, the children who were most disturbed at school entry *deteriorated* over the next two years. Chazan and his colleagues stress that the association between poor adjustment and learning difficulties is often established in infant school; and a significant minority of children continue to have behavioural and emotional problems throughout their school years and even into early adulthood (Glidewell and Swallow, 1969; Stennet, 1971). The data from the Berkeley Study by MacFarlane *et al.* (1954) indicate that there are substantial correlations between problems at school entry at 5–6 years, and problems at the later transition to junior high school at 10–12 years. Kohlberg and his colleagues have pointed out that such problems at school entry predict better to the later transition problems than they do to problems of adjustment in the period between transitions, a point to which we will return (Kohlberg *et al.*, 1972).

This point – that school entry is a critical period for later school performance and adjustment – is emphasized by Maughan (see chapter 11), and the empirical data from the Perry Preschool Project (Berrueta-Clement *et al.*, 1984) support her argument. Maughan puts forward, moreover, a persuasive case for the more general proposition that there is a chain of short-term links between adjustment and functioning in childhood and adulthood in which the transition to school, and then experiences during the school years, form a series of crucial 'turning points' in children's lives.

One such 'turning point' may be the experience of changing schools. Evidence here comes chiefly from studies of the change from junior to secondary schools; however, changing schools in the very early years may also present problems or opportunities. Here we have even less data, but one small-scale study of 3–5-year-olds who transferred to new preschools in the US examined the children's behaviour shortly before the move and reported substantial increases in agitated behaviour, including increases in illness, and difficulties in sleeping and feeding patterns (Field, 1984). We should note that even preschool children show anxious anticipation of a threatened change in their lives.

Moving house

It has been suggested by clinicians that for very young children, moving house may well be an upsetting experience (Stubblefield, 1955). For adults, house moves are high on the list of life events that are associated with stress. For a child, the change may of course also include alterations in financial circumstances, changes in family structure, separation from familiar friends *and* a change of school, as well as a parent under stress. Any or all of these may contribute to the stress of a house move for children. It appears, indeed, from clinical studies that 'mobile children' who are subjected to frequent changes of home and school do have special problems of adjustment and learning (Wattenberg, 1968). Again there is little systematic information on the extent to which house moves generally lead to disturbance. However, Moore (1969) reported from a longitudinal study of 223 individuals followed from birth to adolescence that 22% of house moves during the children's first eight years caused serious disturbance and a further 17% caused slight disturbance. The persistence of these problems was not reported.

Birth of a sibling

With the arrival of a sibling many first-born children show marked signs of disturbance (Dunn and Kendrick, 1982; Field and Reite, 1984; Legg *et al.*, 1974; Nadelman and Begun, 1982; Trause *et al.*, 1981). Increases in demanding and negative behaviour, in tearfulness and clinging, in withdrawal and lack of concentration, as well as changes in bodily function, such as increases in sleeping problems and breakdown in toilet-training, are all reported to be common in the first weeks following a sibling's birth. Follow-up studies showed that many of these disturbances in behaviour were relatively short-lived, for most children. In our Cambridge study the frequency of negative behaviour – 'deliberate naughtiness', excessive demands and sleeping problems, for example – had for most children substantially decreased by the time that the second child was eight months old, and were not dissimilar from their levels prior to the sibling birth. However, for some children, and some problem behaviours, the story was not so encouraging. The increase in worrying, anxious and fearful behaviour shown at the sibling birth by some children *increased* over the year that followed.

The persistence of these anxious behaviours takes on particular significance when we note that longitudinal epidemiological work has reported connections between such fearful and worrying behaviour in 3–4-year-olds and problems of neurotic behaviour in 8-year-olds (Richman *et al.*, 1982). And for some children – for instance those that responded to the sibling birth by withdrawing – the reaction to the birth was linked to the development of a very poor relationship between the siblings. Again, longitudinal studies show such poor relationships to persist over early childhood (Stillwell and Dunn, 1985) and to be associated with later anti-social behaviour (Richman *et al.*, 1982).

There are also suggestions from longitudinal studies that some effects of the sibling arrival may persist even longer. McCall (1984) reported data from the Fels longitudinal study showing that in the two years following the birth of a sibling the IQ performance of older children dropped ten points relative to singletons, and there was no evidence that the effect diminished over the ensuing years of adolescence. There is also some evidence that first-born but not only children have a slightly increased risk of emotional disturbance later in childhood (Osborn *et al.*, 1984; Rutter *et al.*, 1970).

These data on the prevalence and persistence of problems following these 'ordinary' events in children's lives indicate that *for some children* such changes involve significant stress, and merit our attention. How far do the studies clarify the questions of which children are most at risk from these changes, and what processes might be involved in linking such events to later problems and disturbances in children's behaviour? The detailed analyses of the behaviour of the children and their families in the sibling birth study (Dunn and Kendrick, 1982) allow us to move from the simple description of the prevalance of disturbance to a consideration of what processes might be involved in both disturbance and coping responses. These analyses have suggested a number of principles to be central to understanding the impact of such 'ordinary' life events upon children's well-being.

Links between event and outcome

Individual differences between children are of central importance
The first point that must be emphasized concerns the importance of considering individual differences in children's responses to stressful events, rather than discussing these events solely in terms of 'normative' prevalance rates of particular responses. Individual differences in the children's immediate responses to the constellation of events that surrounded the sibling birth were marked, both in the intensity and the nature of their reactions. Temperamental differences between the children, assessed several weeks before the sibling birth, were linked to differences in the children's reaction to the birth. Individual differences were also marked in the persistence of behavioural problems over the subsequent years, and again temperamental differences between the children assessed before the sibling birth accounted for whether or not such problems persisted. For example, there were strong links between the children's temperamental assessment before the sibling birth and the incidence of worries, fears, miserable moods, rituals, and sleep and feeding problems, eight months after the sibling birth. And children who had reacted to the sibling birth by becoming increasingly withdrawn or more clinging were one year later more likely to be 'frequent worriers' than the rest of the sample.

Other categories of individual differences, such as age, gender and intelligence, may also be important; however, their effects may well differ with different forms of stressful change. Age is likely, for instance, to be an important factor in children's adjustment to school, with the younger children having more problems than the older; we have, however, no systematic information on the matter, nor on how differences in intelligence relate to adjustment to school entry. With the birth of a sibling, there are age differences in the *form* of children's responses; however, the intensity and extent of disturbance are not clearly linked to age differences, at least for children under six years. Gender differences are reported for adjustment to school entry, and at follow-up in the school, with boys showing more aggressive and restless behaviour (see, e.g., Chazan and Jackson, 1974; Hughes *et al.*, 1979). Boys were also found in the Cambridge study of the sibling birth to be more likely to withdraw. The bases for these gender differences, which are also reported for other more acute stresses (Rutter, 1983), are not clear.

The notion of what is a stressful event in childhood is, as these results suggest, closely tied to the issue of individual differences in personality. But it is not simply that some children find particular experiences stressful and others do not. Rather, the findings of the sibling study indicate that differences in the responses of parents, and in that of each member of the family to the others' altered behaviour, are implicated, too.

Changes in family relationships are implicated

The second issue, then, concerns the role of the child's family relationships in the impact of stressful events. In the sibling study we examined the interaction between first-born child and mother before the sibling was born, in the immediate post-sib-birth period, and over the subsequent year. Two important points stand out from this analysis, in relation to the children's reaction to the sibling birth.

First, individual differences in the quality of the mother–child relationship before the birth were related to individual differences in the children's reaction to the birth. Difficult behaviour and escalation in confrontation between child and parent were particularly marked in children whose relationships with their mothers had been high in conflict before the sibling birth. Second, there were marked changes in the mother–child relationship at the time of the birth (see also Field and Reite, 1984; Taylor and Kogan, 1973), and these, too, were related to the children's reaction. Measures of sensitive maternal attention and play decreased after the birth, while measures of restrictive prohibiting and punitive behaviour increased. There was also a change in the balance of responsibility for communicative exchange between mother and child: after the sibling birth there was a sharp decrease in the frequency with which mothers initiated conversations with their first-born, and thus the children took greater responsibility for starting and maintaining communicative inter-action. It should be recalled that some children had reacted to the sibling birth by withdrawing; for these children the drop in interaction with their mothers after the birth was particularly marked. It was argued from these results that these experiences of a dramatic shift in the relationship with the mother should certainly be taken into account in attempting to explain children's disturbed reactions following the sibling birth.

It should be noted that many children (including some of those who were most disturbed at the sibling birth) showed not only increases in difficult behaviour but also great interest in, and affection and concern for, the new baby. This positive interest in, and affection for, the sibling showed considerable continuity over the years that followed (Stillwell and Dunn, 1985), and we should not leave the topic of the connection between the mother–child relationship and the children's response to the birth without noting that certain features of the mothers' behaviour at this time were systematically linked to the development of a particularly friendly relationship between the siblings. These will be discussed below when the connections between family relationships are considered.

What these results suggest is that the impact of the sibling birth may not only be critically linked to the temperament or personality of the first-born, but that changes in family relationships that accompany the change in family structure may also be implicated. It should be noted, too, that temperamental differences between children are not independent of the quality of the relationship between parent and child. Although temperamental differences are not simply attributable to differences in parent perception of the child, they are closely associated with differences in parental behaviour (Dunn, 1986; Stevenson-Hinde and Hinde, 1986). We cannot therefore assume that the connections between stressful event, child temperament and child outcome do not involve differences in parental behaviour.

Neither can we assume the direction of causal links between altered or difficult behaviour of one family member and disturbed relations between that member and others within the family. Such links are of course very likely to be two-way. Perturbation in the mother–child relationship may initially arise *either* because of increasingly difficult behaviour from the 'displaced' two-year-old, *or* because of the increased irritation of an exhausted mother coping with two young children on very little sleep; in each case the effect is likely to increase the other person's negative behaviour.

While we do not have detailed assessments of children's temperament or of changes in family relationships at school entry, it is clear that a focus on individual differences in children and on family relationships is relevant here, as in the sibling study. Chazan and Williams (1978), for instance describe the children who adjusted poorly in their large-scale study as coming from less secure, less settled and less happy homes, and having mothers who were less emotionally stable than the mothers of the children who had no problems adjusting to school. They link the persistence of problems over the next two years to a lack of parental encouragement and play (though they report only small differences associated with the emotional atmosphere of the home). Elizur's Israeli study examined more specifically how children's adjustment was linked to parental patterns of coping with their disturbed child, and his results clearly implicate both father and mother. Improvements in adjustment to school were linked to the father's coping ability, and to the mother's efforts to get the father involved. These findings alert us to the third principle – that relationships beyond the mother–child dyad are implicated in even the very young child's response to stressful events.

Relationships beyond the mother–child dyad are implicated

The third general issue highlighted by the analysis of the sibling birth was that of the significance of the relationships between child, mother *and others*, both within the immediate family and beyond, in relation to the child's reaction to the event. The relationship of the father with the first-born child was of particular importance in the sibling study. For instance, in families in which father and first-born had intense close relationships the escalation of conflict and confrontation between mother and child was less marked, and the decrease in maternal attention and play less extreme. It is not clear how this effect was mediated. It could be that fathers in these families were more directly involved with their children than the other fathers after the sibling birth, and that their children were in consequence less difficult towards their mothers, that is the affectionate relationship between child and father 'buffered' the child against tension with the mother. The connection could also be a less direct one in that such fathers may have been more supportive of their wives in other ways that did not directly involve the first-born child, and that their wives, less burdened, were then able to relate more happily to their first-born.

The difficulties that we face in making inferences about precisely how the father's relationship with the first-born was linked to the changes in the mother–child relationship draws attention to an important point. The links between different relationships involve connections of very different kinds, operating at very different levels of analysis. Which of these we choose to emphasize will depend in part upon the framework within which we describe and study relationships; it will also influence the kinds of prediction that we make about the consequences of changes in family relationships. For instance, some of the results of the sibling study suggest, as we have noted, that the perturbation in the mother–child relationship at the sibling birth causes a general emotional disturbance in the first-born children. If this interpretation is correct, we might predict that the child's relationships with a wide range of others – not solely the sibling – will be affected.

However, other results of the study indicate connections of a rather different kind: for instance, a particularly warm and affectionate relationship between the mother and her second child was found to be associated with a particularly hostile relationship developing over time between the siblings. Here the mediating connection between the relationships is, we would infer, a focused hostility towards a specific individual, rather than a generalized emotional disturbance; the predictions that we would make concerning the consequences for the child's adjustment might in this case be different from those in the first case when a general emotional disturbance was suggested. The direction of effects between the two relationships is, of course, likely to be two-way.

This set of connections, illustrating the way in which one family relationship is systematically linked to others within the family is one example of a much more general point: that to understand how family influences are mediated we need to broaden our framework of study from a focus upon the parent–child dyad. We need to include not only mother–child, father–child and sibling–child influences, but the effects of these upon the different children within the family. Comparisons of single children brought up within different families, up to now the accepted framework for studying family influence, cannot in fact expose what are the chief sources of family influence upon children. These are *within-family* sources of influence that act differently upon different children within the same family (Plomin and Daniels, 1987).

It appears very likely that other intimate relationships 'beyond the dyad' can play a significant part in supporting children through other kinds of stress. Elizur reports, for instance, that improvements in adjustment to school were associated with the parents' cooperation with one another, as well as with their individual relationships with the child. It is also likely that children's relationships *outside* the family may either play a supportive role or may increase stress for children at times of crisis. In beginning school, for example, the child's relationships with other children are probably very important in adjustment to the new world of school. The study by Hughes and his colleagues showed that the way in which the school was organized, particularly in relation to term of entry, influenced the prevalence of problems of adjustment. It is not clear from their results whether the crucial factor here was the way in which the teacher behaved to new entrants, or the behaviour of the other children. It seems very plausible that the children's relationships with the other children in the class (which were likely to differ in the two terms of entry) were of real significance in the way in which the new children adjusted. As Maughan (see chapter 11) points out, comparison with peers is likely to be of much importance in how children experience school, and in how the transition to school affects children's self-esteem and sense of self-efficacy. As a separate point, it appears likely that friendship and support from other children will be of significance during the period of adjustment to school. Unfortunately we know little of how the entry to school is experienced by children in these respects.

The evidence for the role that social support and intimate relationships can play in protecting adults from depressive feelings (Brown and Harris, 1978; Brown *et al.*, 1986) indicates that such factors are likely to be important in mothers' responses to events, such as house moves, that are known to be stressful for adults – and thus will be indirectly important for their children, too. In general, the evidence for the importance of the quality of the marital relationship and of social support (for the mother) in relation to differences in the mother–child relationship (Belsky and Isabella, 1985; Crockenberg, 1981) means that these factors are likely to have indirect but significant effects on how *children* experience other stressful changes, such as house moves and changes in job experience, that we know to be stressful for adults.

That stressful life changes are associated with changes in the stability and the security of the mother–child relationship has been shown in several studies (e.g. Vaughn *et al.*, 1980). These studies highlight the difficulties of elucidating which particular events are most centrally implicated in the development of troubled relationships or disturbed behaviour. It is an especially pertinent point in relation to the question of how maternal employment and mothers' work conditions affect the mother–child relationship. In low socio-economic status samples, maternal employment, and especially changes in maternal employment, are associated with high levels of life stress, with multiple changes in child care and with fathers' unemployment. It is not surprising that, for these samples, associations are reported between maternal employment and instability of attachment. In contrast with the results of such studies, the findings of research on maternal employment and mother–child attachment in middle-class samples report no consistent association between maternal employment and instability of the relationship. There is, as Owen and her colleagues report, no clear-cut evidence to support the notion that maternal employment *per se* diminishes the quality or disrupts the stability of the child's attachment to either parent (Owen *et al.*, 1984). However, their study, and those of others (e.g. Bronfenbrenner and Crouter, 1982), demonstrate that the effects of maternal employment, or of changes in maternal employment, do have complex effects on family relationships, and *these* may affect the children's adjustment. Until such 'family effects' and the impact of mothers' work conditions upon the mother and the father are carefully examined, conclusions on the consequences for children of their mothers starting to work or changing their employment will be premature.

Processes of cognitive appraisal, sense of self-blame and self-worth may be involved in 'normative life events' even with very young children

Other results of the sibling birth study suggest quite different processes linking the mother–child relationship with other family relationships and children's behaviour, in ways that may influence children's responses to stress and change. In families in which the mother talked to the child about the newborn sibling as a person with needs, wants and feelings, both children over time behaved in particularly friendly fashion towards each other. The implication was that even two-year-old children do attend to, and reflect upon, the needs and wants of others; the connection between mother–child and sibling–child relationships that these results suggest is a far more 'cognitive' link than the other two. Other current work on young siblings establishes that issues of blame and responsibility are of great interest and salience to children from 24 months onwards (Dunn, 1988). Another quite different set of research findings that reinforces the point that young children reflect on their own role and responsibility for stressful family crises is Sourkes' (1987) study of the siblings of chronically sick children. The proposition that maternal discussion of feelings, behaviour, blame and responsibility can profoundly affect children's behaviour – even at the preschool stage – is borne out by other studies (Zahn-Waxler and Radke-Yarrow, 1982; Dunn, 1988; Dunn and Munn, 1986). Its implications for helping children who are under stress, and for encouraging coping behaviour, clearly deserve further attention.

The significance of these different kinds of connection between relationships is discussed more fully elsewhere (Dunn, 1987). In the present context it is simply the general point that I want to emphasize: that the links between different family relationships at times of stress or change may be complex and of very different kinds – ranging from generalized emotional disturbance to cognitively mediated 'attributional' processes. Which of these is important may well differ for different children, at different developmental stages, faced with different life events.

'Life events' involve major changes in routine, and these have important effects on children

The response of first-born children after the sibling birth brought to our attention the significance to young children of routine or expectable patterns of daily life. It was apparent that even when mothers gave birth to their second child at home rather than in hospital, there were major changes in the children's lives. The mothers in the Cambridge sample attributed much of the children's distress to such changes, and felt that the eventual re-establishment of familiar routines was very helpful to the children. We have only indirect, rather than definitive, evidence to support such views; however, they seem extremely plausible, given that we know of the sensitivity of young children to a familiar structure in their lives. While some children thrive on change and the stimulation of new environments, many find change in routine difficult and upsetting, as the research on temperament has documented (Dunn, 1980). The 'life events' that we are considering here involve, by definition, sharp changes in children's routines. As 'turning points' these events could provide the foundations for new trajectories in children's development – either positive or negative.

The changes in children's lives that follow 'ordinary' life events are chronic in the long term

The notion of a stressful life event carries the connotation of a single occurrence. Yet with the arrival of a sibling, a house move, or beginning school, as well as with more traumatic crises such as divorce or death of a parent, the changes in children's lives are long-term and continuing. They are chronic rather than acute experiences. With the birth of a sibling, a child's relationship with his or her parents is never the same again. In attempting to understand the links between the sibling birth and the persistence of disturbance we must therefore take into account that the changes in the child's life do persist. It is possible that it is the continuing, altered patterns of his or her relationships that account for the persistence of problems. McCall's (1984) analysis of the continuing IQ differences that for years follow the sibling birth supports this argument.

Implications for other changes in children's lives

How far are these principles that are apparently significant in the response of children to 'ordinary' events in their lives also important in relation to other more clearly stressful changes? What 'models' for the effects of stressful experiences on children do these findings suggest?

In answer to the first of these questions, the evidence from studies of divorce, hospital admission or loss of a parent indicate that individual differences in children and family patterns of response may well contribute importantly to how children respond to these events. Hospital admission studies, for instance, suggest that temperamental differences between children assessed before the admission are linked to differences in the children's response to the experience. They also show that procedures to help children admitted to hospital may in fact be effective because they seek to allay *parental* anxiety (Ferguson, 1979; Wolfer and Vistainer, 1979). These procedures were not, incidentally, concerned with reducing parent–child separation, but with reducing anxiety about the procedures that lay ahead of the child. As Rutter (1983) comments, children may be affected as much by their parents' attitudes as by the hospital procedures. After divorce, the behaviour of both the parent who has custody of the child and the parent who does not, changes towards the child, and these changes are associated with disturbances in the children (Hetherington *et al.*, 1976).

The themes of the importance of relationships 'beyond the dyad', of changes in the children's daily lives, and of the long-term nature of changes in family relationships that follow the life event, are echoed, too, in studies of major stresses in childhood. Thus Rutter (1983) has argued that the explanation for the long-lasting effects of two hospital admissions in childhood probably lies in the nature of the child's experiences in the family after reunion. Long-term effects are more likely if the child comes from a deprived family, or if the previous parent–child relationship was poor. In studies of attempted suicide, the association between early loss of parent and suicidal ideation is strongly linked to the long-term consequences of the change in family organization (Adam, 1982). Furthermore, the suggestion that 'ordinary life events' that involve major changes in the daily structure of children's lives and experiences can act as 'turning points' with either positive or negative consequences is receiving increased support from systematic research, such as that into children's progress through secondary school (see chapter 11).

In these ways, therefore, the principles suggested by the studies of children's responses to 'ordinary' events appear significantly relevant to more traumatic events. However, in answer to the second question – concerning models of the effects of life events – two points must be made.

First, it is important that we should move away from very general claims about the importance of changes (long-term or short-term) in family relationships for later disturbance in children towards a more specific and clearer understanding of such connections. Rutter (1983) has argued that different life events – bereavement, divorce, separation, and so on – have different effects on children, and that these different effects are probably mediated by differences in the changes in family interaction patterns that accompany the events. If we are to understand why some children cope well with stressful change, and even make developmental advances at such times, while others become disturbed, then closer attention to the nature of the changes in family interaction, and a finer grasp of what kinds of connection there may be between the different family relationships, will be essential.

Second, the work on sibling birth raised the possibility that one such connecting process might involve cognitive appraisal and reflection about the event. Research on adult depression has shown just how significant such appraisal can be. It has been plausibly argued that an individual's conceptualization of the cause and consequences of an event, and the relation of this appraisal to his own sense of self-worth, play an important part in the genesis of depression (Brown and Harris, 1978; Seligman and Peterson, 1986). Seligman and his colleagues, for example, have proposed that the attributional style with which someone interprets events, both good and bad, is closely bound up with the probability that a crisis will lead to depression. They report findings that suggest that a mother's attributional style is linked to her children's attributional style, and that both are linked to the incidence of later depression in children. In the research into the links between life events and adult disorders it has been shown that the impact of different kinds of event is very different, and it has been argued that in explaining why there should be such specific links between certain events and certain disorders it is crucial to take into account the *meaning* of the event to the individual (Brown and Harris, 1978; Brown *et al.*, 1986). There are of course obvious difficulties in deciding what the 'meaning' of life events is to young children; our inferences will depend upon our assumptions about the nature of children's understanding of the world and themselves, and this is a contentious issue.

Much more work, then, is needed to clarify how far processes of attribution and cognitive appraisal are implicated in the sequelae of different 'life events', but the evidence that children are intensely interested in issues of blame, responsibility, transgression and psychological causality from their third year onwards suggests that such work would be worthwhile. Anticipation of an event, as was noted from the evidence on children's behaviour before a change of school, clearly can be important from the preschool period onwards. It is possible, then, to interpret the evidence that *two* hospital admissions in childhood have a significant long-term association with later disorder in terms of a 'sensitization' of the child, produced by the first admission, that predisposes the child to react very adversely to a second admission; cognitive anticipation and conceptualization of the event might play a central part in such sensitization. Note that such a process is very different in kind from the idea of a general 'emotional disturbance', caused by the event, as a mediating link.

Indeed, very different models could be proposed for the mediating links in the consequences of the 'ordinary' events we have discussed here, each of which might be relevant for *some* life events. Consider first a 'developmental stage model', Kohlberg's phase-specific reaction model. Kohlberg and his colleagues, discussing the links in the Berkeley study between problems at school entry and problems at junior high school transition, suggest that there are connections that are 'phase-specific' reactions to developmental problems (Kohlberg *et al.*, 1972). The idea is that individuals who have experienced problems with certain developmental crises will have problems with similar later developmental crises. (It is not clear whether this pattern is attributed to a sensitization process.) Such a model is contrasted by Kohlberg and his colleagues with what we could term a 'personality model', in which problems are attributable to temperamental traits, such as a lack of adaptability to new situations, oversensitiveness, irritability, or shyness.

In this model, the genesis of disturbance, it is argued, does not relate to the age or stage of the individual. Such personality-related difficulties, according to the Berkeley study, are the best predictors of problems over the long term. In neither model are social relationships with other people seen as playing a significant part (though they are not necessarily excluded from them), in contrast with the model suggested by the sibling birth data – a 'social relationships model' – in which both the precipitation of the problem and its persistence are attributable in part to changes in important family relationships. Under this model the processes mediating the connections could include either general emotional disturbance, generated by the perturbation in the relationship, or more specific or cognitive links.

It remains, then, an empirical question as to how far the response of children to different 'normative' life events, or to more stressful events, approximates to these different models. It is probable that some combination of the elements of each model is important in the problems caused by life events in the real world, but such combinations may differ for different 'normative' life events, faced by children at different ages. The challenge for the researcher is to specify these differences. Support for children vulnerable to such events will be more effective when we have gained a better grasp of the nature of such combinations.

Conclusions

In summary, the following points should be emphasized:

1. 'Ordinary' life events have serious consequences for some children.

2. In examining *who* is vulnerable, and *who* copes with these 'ordinary' events, we come to Garmezy's (1983) triad of protective factors – the importance of individual differences in children, in supportive family relationships, and in supportive relationships outside the family. Further, the results highlight the importance of cognitive appraisal even in very young children, of supportive relationships 'beyond the dyad' not only for the parent but for the child, and of the familiar expected architecture of the child's usual life. One research strategy that is likely to be fruitful is to study more than one child within a family faced with such events, to elucidate the links between individual differences in children and the role of family relationships in their different vulnerability to stressful change.

3. Differentiating general from specific consequences of such life events will be important if we are to grasp the implications of the response of children to such ordinary events for their vulnerability to more obviously stressful events.

4. The documentation of the disturbance experienced by some children

faced with 'ordinary' events, together with the knowledge that stressful changes are increasing in frequency in young children's lives, highlights the urgency of our pursuing these questions and gaining a better understanding of the processes linking such events to disturbance. Longitudinal research strategies that employ a variety of techniques at different levels of analysis are likely to be most fruitful; detailed study of family interaction as well as child outcome will be a necessary part of such research if we are to reach a clearer understanding of the processes involved.

References

Adam, K. S. (1982) Loss, suicide and attachment. In Murray-Parkes, C. and Stevenson-Hinde, J. (eds.) *The place of attachment in human behavior*. New York: Basic Books, pp. 89–103.

Belsky, J. and Isabella, R. A. (1985) Marital and parent–child relationships in family of origin and marital change following the birth of a baby: a retrospective analysis. *Child Development*, 56, 342–9.

Berrueta-Clement, J. R., Schweinart, L. J., Barnett, W. S., Epstein, A. S. and Weikart, D. P. (1984) *Changed lives: the effects of the Perry Pre-school Program on youths through age 19*. Ypsilanti, MI: High Scope.

Bronfenbrenner, U. and Crouter, A. C. (1982) Work and family through time and space. In Kamerman, S. and Hayes, C. (eds.) *Families that work: children in a changing world*. Washington, DC: National Academic Press, pp. 39–83.

Brown, G. W. and Harris, T. O. (1978) *Social origins of depression*. London: Tavistock.

Brown, G. W., Harris, T. O. and Bifulco, A. (1986) Long-term effects of early loss of parent. In Rutter, M., Izard, C. E. and Read, P. B. (eds.) *Depression in young people*. New York: Guilford Press, pp. 251–96.

Chazan, M. and Jackson, S. (1971) Behaviour problems in the infant school. *Journal of Child Psychology and Psychiatry*, 12, 191–210.

(1974) Behaviour problems in the infant school: changes over two years. *Journal of Child Psychology and Psychiatry*, 15, 33–46.

Chazan, M. and Williams, P. (1978) *Deprivation and the infant school*. Oxford: Blackwell.

Crockenberg, S. (1981) Infant irritability, mother responsiveness, and social support influences on the security of infant attachment. *Child Development*, 52, 857–65.

Dunn, J. (1980) Individual differences in temperament. In Rutter, M. (ed.) *Scientific foundations of developmental psychiatry*. London: Heinemann, pp. 101–9.

(1986) Commentary: issues for future research. In Plomin, R. and Dunn, J. (eds.) *The study of temperament: changes, continuities and challenges*. Hillsdale, NJ: Erlbaum, pp. 163–71.

(1987) Relations among relationships. In Duck, S. (ed.) *Handbook of social relationships*. Chichester: Wiley.

(1988) *The beginnings of social understanding*. Cambridge, MA: Harvard University Press.

Dunn, J. and Kendrick, C. (1982) *Siblings: love, envy and understanding*. Cambridge, MA: Harvard University Press.

Dunn, J. and Munn, P. (1986) Sibling quarrels and maternal intervention:

individual differences in understanding and aggression. *Journal of Child Psychology and Psychiatry*, 27, 583–95.

Elizur, J. (1986) The stress of school entry: parental coping behaviours and children's adjustment to school. *Journal of Child Psychology and Psychiatry*, 27, 625–36.

Ferguson, B. F. (1979) Perparing young children for hospitalisation. *Pediatrics*, 64, 656–64.

Field, T. (1984) Separation stress of young children transferring to new schools. *Developmental Psychology*, 20, 786–92.

Field, T. and Reite, M. (1984) Children's responses to separation from mother during the birth of another child. *Child Development*, 55, 1308–16.

Garmezy, N. (1983) Stressors of childhood. In Garmezy, N., and Rutter, M. (eds.) *Stress, coping and development in children*. New York: McGraw Hill, pp. 43–84.

Glidewell, J. C. and Swallow, C. S. (1969) *The prevalence of maladjustment in elementary schools*. Chicago: Chicago University Press.

Hetherington, E. M., Cox, M. and Cox, R. (1979) Family interaction and the social, emotional and cognitive development of children following divorce. In Vaughn, V. and Brazelton, T. (eds.) *The family: setting priorities*. New York: Science and Medicine, pp. 71–87.

Hughes, M., Pinkerton, G. and Plewis, I. (1979) Children's difficulties on starting infant school. *Journal of Child Psychology and Psychiatry*, 20, 187–96.

Kohlberg, L., Lacrosse, J. and Ricks, D. (1972) The predictability of adult mental health from childhood behavior. In Wolman, B. B. (ed.) *Manual of Child Psychopathology*, New York: McGraw Hill, pp. 1217–84.

Legg, C., Sherick, I. and Wadland, W. (1974) Reaction of preschool children to the birth of a sibling. *Child Psychiatry and Human Development*, 5, 3–59.

McCall, R. B. (1984) Developmental changes in mental performance: the effect of the birth of a sibling. *Child Development*, 55, 1317–21.

MacFarlane, J., Allen, L. and Honzik, N. (1954) *A developmental study of behavior problems of normal children between 21 months and fourteen years*. Berkeley: University of California Press.

Moore, T. (1969) Stress in childhood. *Human Relations*, 22, 235–49.

Nadelman, L. and Begun, A. (1982) The effect of the newborn on the older sibling: mothers' questionnaires. In Lamb, M. and Sutton-Smith, B. *Sibling relationships: their nature and significance across the lifespan*, Hillsdale, NJ: Erlbaum, pp. 13–37.

Osborn, A. F., Butler, N. R. and Morris, A. C. (1984) *The social life of Britain's five-year-olds*. London: Routledge and Kegan Paul.

Owen, M. T., Easterbrooks, M. A., Chase-Lansdale, L. and Goldberg, W. A. (1984) The relation between maternal employment status and the stability of attachments to mother and to father. *Child Development*, 55, 1894–1901.

Paykel, E. S. (1978) Contribution of life events to causation of psychiatric illness. *Psychological Medicine*, 8, 245–54.

Plomin, R. and Daniels, D. (1987) Why are children within the same family so different from one another? *Behavioral and Brain Sciences*, 10, 1–59.

Richman, N., Stevenson, J. and Graham, P. J. (1982) *Preschool to school: a behavioural study*. London: Academic Press.

Robins, L. N. (1983) Some methodological problems and research directions in the study of the effects of stress on children. In Garmezy, N. and Rutter, M. (eds.) *Stress, coping and development in children*. New York: McGraw Hill, pp. 335–46.

Rutter, M. (1983) Stress, coping and development: some issues and some questions. In Garmezy. N. and Rutter, M. (eds.) *Stress, coping and development in children*. New York: McGraw Hill, pp. 1–41.

Rutter, M., Tizard, J. and Whitmore, K. (eds.) (1970) *Education, health and behaviour*. London: Longman.

Seligman, M. E. P. and Peterson, C. (1986) A learned helplessness perspective on childhood depression: theory and research. In Rutter. M., Izard, C. E. and Read, P. B. (eds.) *Depression in young people*. New York: Guilford Press, pp. 223–50.

Sourkes, B. M. (1987) Siblings of the child with a life-threatening illness. *Journal of Children in Contemporary Society*, **19**, 159–84.

Stennet, R. G. (1971) Emotional handicap in the elementary years: phase or disease? In Bower, E. M. (ed.) *Orthopsychiatry and education*. Detroit: Wayne State University Press.

Stevenson-Hinde, J. and Hinde, R. A. (1986) Changes in associations between characteristics and interactions. In Plomin, R. and Dunn, J. (eds.) *The study of temperament: changes, continuities and challenges*. Hillsdale, NJ: Erlbaum, pp. 115–29.

Stillwell, R. and Dunn, J. (1985) Continuities in sibling relationships: patterns of aggression and friendliness. *Journal of Child Psychology and Psychiatry*, **26**, 627–37.

Stubblefield, R. L. (1955) Children's emotional problems aggravated by family moves. *American Journal of Orthopsychiatry*, **25**, 120–6.

Taylor, M. K. and Kogan, K. L. (1973) Effects of the birth of a sibling on mother–child interactions. *Child Psychiatry and Human Development*, **4**, 53–9.

Thompson, B. (1975) Adjustment to school. *Educational Research*, **17**, 128–36.

Trause, M. A., Voos, D., Rudd, C., Klaus, M., Kennell, J. and Boslett, M. (1981) Separation for childbirth: the effect on the sibling. *Child Psychiatry and Human Development*, **12**, 32–39.

Vaughn, B. E., Gove, F. L. and Egelund, B. (1980) The relationship between out-of-home care and the quality of infant–mother attachment in an economically disadvantaged population. *Child Development*, **51**, 1203–14.

Wattenberg, W. (1968) Mobile children need help. *Education Forum*, **12**, 335–45.

Wolfer, J. A. and Vistainer, M. A. (1979) Prehospital psychological preparation for tonsillectomy patients. *Pediatrics*, **64**, 646–55.

Zahn-Waxler, C. and Radke-Yarrow, M. (1982) The development of altruism: alternative research strategies. In Eisenberg, N. (ed.) *The development of prosocial behavior*. New York: Academic Press, pp. 109–37.

14 Studying the impact of ordinary life: a developmental model, research plan and words of caution

Dale F. Hay

Life can have kaleidoscopic properties; at times, it seems all the pieces have been rearranged. In her essay on normative events in childhood (see chapter 13), Dunn has drawn our attention to three such kaleidoscopic changes in a child's life: the birth of a sibling, entering school for the first time, and moving house. These are all ordinary experiences that nonetheless entail drastic changes in a child's physical and social world.

Dunn has brought these three diverse experiences together under the general rubric of 'life events' (see Brown, *et al.*, 1987). She has argued that these three experiences not only have features in common, but also share communalities with other, less frequently encountered sorts of life events, including hospitalization, bereavement in childhood, and so on.

This is a strong claim that is as yet untested. Investigators of life events in adulthood have attempted to contrast the effects of events that are statistically normative with those of events that occur less frequently. It appears that normative and non-normative events pose different risks for physical health and psychological well-being, largely as a function of the availability of adequate social support; one's family and friends are usually better equipped to provide support in familiar situations (Schulz and Rau, 1985). Nonetheless, Dunn's choice to begin the study of life events in childhood with an analysis of normative events represents a powerful strategy. It assures her of a reasonable sample size, and she is sampling from a heterogeneous population, in which individual differences are matters of interest, not confounds. This permits an analysis of different sorts of children's reactions to normative events.

In addition, the events she has chosen for analysis are not simply statistically normative; they are predictable in advance. The very predictability of these events of course raises certain problems of generalizability. Even infants react differently in predictable as opposed to unpredictable situations (Gunnar *et al.*, 1984). Nevertheless, studying experiences that can be predicted in advance conveys important methodological advantages, in that the power of prospective longitudinal designs can be exploited. Dunn's own work on the effects of the birth of a sibling illustrates the strength of this approach.

Thus the study of normative events in childhood needs no defence, though the question of generalization to other classes of life event remains. If, for the time being, we disregard that question, in what direction should the study of ordinary life experiences proceed? In particular, what longitudinal analyses should be contemplated with respect to the study of any such class of ordinary event?

A developmental model of children's responses to their life experiences

The study of experience

At its most general level, the study of life events in human development is part of the more general study of behavioural epigenesis, that is, how active organisms develop as a function of their own characteristics and experiences (e.g. Kuo, 1967). This implies that the study of normative events in childhood takes up some of the same issues that arise when the embryologist studies the impact of events prior to birth or hatching (e.g. Gottlieb, 1976) or when the developmental psychobiologist studies the effects of early stressors (e.g. Levine, 1982). General principles identified in such investigations may be usefully applied to the analysis of human life events. For example, Gottlieb (1976) has noted that experiences may affect development in terms of facilitation of an existing trajectory, maintenance of that trajectory, or induction of a new course of development. In assessing the outcomes of particular events in childhood or adult life, it is quite helpful to keep such distinctions in mind.

Nonetheless, the study of life experiences in human childhood poses particular problems, the most central of which is the problem of meaning. I am not convinced that the problem of meaning is absent when one studies non-human lives; for example, Kuo's (1930) classic comparisons of cats reared with their rat-killing mothers as against those who grew up companionably with rats highlight the importance of social meaning up and down the phylogenetic scale. The difference is that the embryologist *can* ignore the problem of meaning, but the investigator of life events in childhood simply cannot.

The study of adult life events indeed confronts the problem of meaning at every turn, and this confrontation is fraught with methodological problems. Since a person's psychological well-being may influence the meaning he or she ascribes to particular events, a statement about what experiences mean cannot be taken at face value. A solution has been for investigators to rate the meaning a particular event would have to a hypothetical person with the respondent's history and circumstances (e.g. Brown *et al.*, 1987). That indirect approach, however, has its own limitations (see Rutter, 1986). Yet another strength of Dunn's choice to study normative events lies in the fact that meaning itself can be a dependent variable whose construction and transformations can be charted longitudinally.

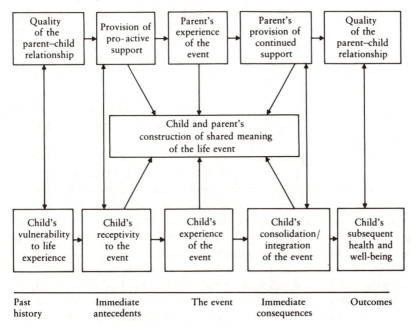

Figure 1   The processing of life events

Components of the proposed model

A model of children's processing of the meaning of life events is presented in Figure 1. I now describe particular dimensions of the model.

The time line. The construction of the model rests on the assumption that a child's responses to a life event represent a developmental progression in its own right that is embedded in the child's overall developmental history. Thus one must map a sequence of events immediately surrounding the target event's occurrence, but also seek evidence both of earlier determinants of the child's reactions and of long-term consequences. For the sake of convenience, in Figure 1 I have subdivided the time line into five periods: past history, immediate antecedents, the event's occurrence, its immediate consequences, and subsequent outcomes. Determining the precise time of onset and offset of the event itself of course requires some thought.

Reactions and social support. Against this standard time line one can then chart the child's reactions to the event and the social support he or she receives. Dunn's analysis of normative events reminded us that a proper longitudinal analysis of the impact of life experiences must incorporate assessments of an individual's personal characteristics, focal relationships and the larger social context. For simplicity's sake, in developing the model in Figure 1, I have restricted the analysis of social support to one focal relationship, that between parent and child. This relationship was chosen largely on the grounds that, throughout most of childhood, the parent or other primary care-giver serves as a paramount source of support and interpreter of experience. Dunn's recommendation to move beyond the parent–child dyad is, however, a point that cannot be ignored, and eventually the model would have to be expanded.

In tracing the parent's provision of support in parallel to the child's responses to the event, we must ask, 'Whose life event is it, anyway?' and examine how a particular child's experience ripples through the life of his or her family. Indeed, the parent is no anonymous, independent source of social support, but rather is simultaneously experiencing the event. Furthermore, the parent may have been, at least in the child's eyes, the perpetrator of the event. Thus, when studying the impact of life events in childhood, an attempt completely to disentangle social support from mutual experience would seem foolish. Rather, one must try to specify the particular interactions between a child and his or her source of support that influence the processing of the event in question, on both parts. Hence, in Figure 1, bidirectional pathways between the child's reactions and the parent's provision of support are depicted.

Past history. In the model, events in the past are summarized in terms of two general constructs, the child's vulnerability to life experience and the overall quality of the parent–child relationship, in terms of its capacity to function as an ongoing source of support. Particular variables that contribute to the child's general level of vulnerability (i.e. particular risk and protective factors) include dispositional characteristics such as temperament and intellectual ability, past experiences with other stressors, both chronic and acute, and the child's emerging world view, with respect to the nature of self, companions and the world at large. The latter, of course, is partly a product of the first two, but may prove to be a useful mediating variable between the individual difference variables identified by Dunn and the child's reactions to particular experiences. World view would encompass the child's self concept and self-esteem, as well as his or her person perception, and understanding of the basic regularities, including causal relationships, in the physical and social world. Traits such as generalized optimism or pessimism (e.g. Fischer and Leitenberg, 1986) are closely related to this notion of a world view.

With respect to the quality of the parent–child relationship, similar sets of variables may be seen as contributing, including the parent's dispositional characteristics, experiences with other stressors, and world view. The latter would of course subsume the parent's views about this particular child, as well as children in general, which in turn may influence the nature and extent of support offered in a particular situation.

Immediate antecedents to the event. The various phenomena that may be observed immediately prior to the occurrence of a target event, and may be seen to predict the way in which it is processed, are similarly subsumed under two general constructs, the child's receptivity to the event and the parent's provision of proactive support. The child's receptivity reflects his or her expectations, hopes and fears about the likely occurrence of the event, the degree of control the child has over the event's occurrence, timing and impact and the presence of other stressors and compensatory experiences. Current receptivity could of course be expected to be influenced by all the factors contributing to prior vulnerability.

Similarly, the parent's capacity to provide proactive support (i.e. preparation for anticipated experiences) depends upon the parent's degree of control over the occurrence of the event, his or her expectations, hopes and fears, and his or her experience of other stressors. Proactive support is of course only possible for the type of events Dunn describes, where the event's occurrence is predictable and to a certain extent under the parent's control. Obviously, in the case of completely unexpected events, proactive support could not be offered. (One might characterize 'overprotective' parents as those who expect untoward occurrences and offer proactive support when it is not necessarily needed, but that is another matter.)

Experiencing the event. Both child and parent experience the event itself along several different dimensions; furthermore, the parent experiences the event both as a person and in the role of source of support to the child. Both child and parental reactions include perception of the event, arousal and affective reactions, labelling and interpretation of the event, in the light of general knowledge and past experiences, and immediate defensive and coping strategies designed to ameliorate the impact of the event. These would include physical and physiological, as well as psychological, ones.

Immediate consequences. The occurrences that follow next are summarized in terms of two general constructs, the child's consolidation and integration of the event into his or her overall life experience, and the parent's provision of continued support. The latter obviously requires some effort at consolidation and integration on the parent's part as well. Those efforts by child and parent are a function of delayed arousal and affective reactions, reconstructive memory processes, and perception and comprehension of a fundamentally changed world. The latter point underscores a fact drawn attention to by Dunn, namely that ordinary life events are nonetheless capable of inducing kaleidoscopic change.

Subsequent outcomes. The longer-term outcomes to be examined may similarly be summarized in terms of the general constructs of the child's health and psychological well-being and the supportive quality of the parent–child relationship. Both are likely to be affected by what has gone before; both are expected to affect the child's and parent's responsiveness to future life events. Thus, for example, the processing of the second occurrence of an event may depend on what happened when that type of event first occurred, which may partly account for such observations as the cumulative impact of repeated hospitalization (see Rutter, 1986).

The impact of life events on the child's health and well-being may usefully be described in terms of the presence of defined physical illness and psychiatric disorder (see, for example, Rutter, 1986); however, psychological outcomes that do not meet the threshold for 'caseness' may profitably be assessed as well. Such outcome variables would include the child's ability to regulate and deploy behaviour, expression and regulation of emotion, intellectual capacity and achievement, responsivity to novel or repeated stressors, and, perhaps most importantly, readjustment of world view. The last follows directly from the consolidation and integration efforts made immediately after the event in question; it incorporates the child's readjusted expectations and sense of control over, as opposed to hopelessness about, the occurrence of future problems.

The quality of the parent–child relationship is clearly affected by the child's current health and psychological well-being, but also by the parent's experience of the event and his or her degree of success in providing support for the child. Self-perceived failure in serving as a source of support may deflate the parent's own self-esteem, which in turn might affect the parent–child relationship deleteriously.

Among the outcomes to be examined is the child's own capacity to provide support for others, including the parent. Such an assessment paves the way for an analysis of the effects of a child's own life experiences on his or her later capacities for parenting. At present, it is not completely clear whether the experience of extended or repeated stress would inhibit or facilitate a person's capacity to minister to others, and evidence for both possible outcomes should be sought.

The construction of shared meaning. Figure 1 also depicts a central dyadic construct that summarizes the developments taking place for both child and parent before, during and after the event, namely their mutual assignment of shared meaning to the event. This is clearly a dynamic, interactive process, and one with consequences for their subsequent relationship and the child's later health and well-being. Success or failure in the task of establishing shared meaning may itself constitute a protective or risk factor with respect to later outcomes. For example, parents and children are known to disagree about the children's psychological state (e.g. Angold *et al.*, 1987); such fundamental disagreement may be a manifestation or outcome of a more general failure on the part of parents and children to attain consensus about the meaning of the child's life. Such a departure of views, which lessens the parent's effectiveness as an informed source of support, may, in turn, exacerbate the child's problems.

Developmental and social constraints on the model
Each of the components of the model depicted in Figure 1 may be expected to be influenced by the child's (and, for that matter, the parent's) developmental status and by their wider social context. For example, although expectations of forthcoming events can be documented as early as three months of life (Fagen *et al.*, 1984), the nature and power of an individual's expectations surely change with age, and thus receptivity to anticipated life events would be expected to change as well.

Similarly, as Dunn has pointed out, to understand the impact of life events in childhood, one must move beyond the parent–child dyad. For example, the parent's capacity to provide support for the child is clearly affected by the parent's own access to social support from partner, friends and community (Brown *et al.*, 1987). In any tests of this model, particular developmental and social constraints should be identified and investigated.

A plan for research: cross-sectional and longitudinal experiments

Dunn's own work on a normative event in childhood, the birth of a sibling, exemplifies the finest tradition of naturalistic, longitudinal observation. In any tests of the model I have proposed here, such a study would be a method of choice. At the same time, her chapter makes a compelling case for the adoption of supplementary experimental methods.

Cross-sectional experiments on contributing processes
Dunn rightly points out that, to understand the impact of life events, we must determine just how children themselves perceive, interpret, and generally try to make sense out of their worlds. Such cognitive processes are critical components of the model I have sketched out here. There is a need for smaller-scale, intensive cross-sectional experiments on selected processes that complement the longer-term longitudinal observations. Investigators of life events in childhood would do well to consult the existing literature on children's understanding of causality, immanent justice, and the like, but they should also design experiments that address the specific issues they are studying. The choice of measures for the larger longitudinal studies could be narrowed down in these associated experiments.

Longitudinal experiments
The fact that normative events do happen to many children opens up the possibility for mild, ethical, but nonetheless carefully controlled, experiments on children's lives. In such longitudinal experiments, children sampled from the general population would be randomly assigned to different levels of selected independent variables; the dependent variables of choice would be measured repeatedly over time. For example, with respect to the topics of school entry or sibling birth, one could compare different intervention techniques to ameliorate possible school adjustment problems, or different ways of teaching parents to reduce displays of jealousy over the birth of a sibling. In such studies, where all treatment conditions are potentially beneficial, or at least no different from normal life, random assignment and controlled experimentation are perfectly possible. The study of discrete, potentially stressful events that are likely to happen to almost everybody provides an important arena for such experimentation.

With the support of an ethics committee, I would probably be willing to go even further and test my proposed model by actually randomly assigning certain children to experience predefined life events in predefined ways. Such an experiment would not be directed to the study of any particular class or event, such as school entry or hospitalization, but rather to the analysis of particular variables that are present in diverse classes of events.

For example, a critical variable in school entry, sibling birth and hospitalization is separation from parents. I would suggest that one could study children's processing of short-term separation experiences directly by returning metaphorically to the Robbers' Cave (Sherif *et al.*, 1961) and setting up an experimental camp. Children whose parents were willing to send them to the camp for a week (which of course would not be a representative example from the general population, and might exclude the children who would have the hardest time coping) could then be randomly assigned to different experiences beforehand and at the camp itself, which would allow us to test various hypotheses about the processing of this life event. For example, with respect to my proposed model, one could manipulate the forms of proactive support parents were encouraged to provide or the ways in which children themselves were shown how to prepare. One could also manipulate various dimensions of the separation experience, such as the extent of separation (day camp or overnight camp? parents permitted to visit on Wednesday or not?). The experiment would indeed be a longitudinal one, in that the period of study would extend from an antecedent period to a follow-up assessment some months later. Such an experiment would simulate complete, kaleidoscopic change in a child's daily routine; it should, however, also provide a fairly pleasant experience with no long-term threat. Information about the processing of life events gleaned in such a simulation exercise cannot replace that obtained in studies of the actual phenomena, but may constitute an important supplement.

Some words of caution

Both Dunn and I have suggested strategies for uncovering general principles of development – factors that modify or regulate life experiences. But is this quest for generality always so admirable? Are we in danger of forgetting that the life forest is made up of varied and uniquely important trees? Is it at all meaningful to combine across the category of life events?

I have tried to outline a general model for children's processing of anticipated life experiences; however, I think we must acknowledge divergences among classes of life event as well as communalities. Experiencing the birth of a sibling has some things in common with experiencing the first day at school or a grandmother's death, but it also differs in non-trivial ways. Investigators of life events have tried to place events along a common scale, for example the level of threat they offer the model individual (e.g. Brown *et al.*, 1987), but when does calibration become undesirable homogenization? When do we begin to ignore the unique importance of the particular things that happen to us?

I have already called attention to the existence of developmental and social constraints on the processing of life events. At the simplest level, to the extent that events are 'temporally normative' (Schulz and Rau, 1985), that is that they happen most often at particular times in life, the developmental constraints operating on different classes of event are sure to be different. For example, if many children experience the birth of a sibling as two-year-olds but go to school for the first time as five- or six-year-olds, their abilities to interpret and prepare for those two events are going to be quite different.

Thus, in general, I have my doubts about the wisdom of studying anonymous, characterless masses of life events. I applaud Dunn's success in explaining the important general implications of her work on siblings for the study of the effects of experience throughout the life span. At the same time, I remain impressed with the beauty of her descriptive approach and with the power of a research strategy that focuses on a socially, as well as a theoretically, meaningful phenomenon like the growth of a relationship between siblings, and analyses that particular phenomenon in loving, careful detail.

References

Angold, A. C., Weissman, M. M., John, K., Merikangas, K. R., Prusoff, B. A., Wickramaratne, P., Gammon, G. D. and Warner, V. (1987) Parent and child reports of depressive symptoms in children at low and high risk of depression. *Journal of Child Psychology and Psychiatry*, **28**, 901–15.

Brown, G. W., Bifulco, A. and Harris, T. O. (1987) Life events, vulnerability and onset of depression: some refinements. *British Journal of Psychiatry*, **150**, 30–42.

Fagen, J. W., Morrongiello, B. A., Rovee-Collier, C. and Gekoski, M. J. (1984) Expectancies and memory retrieval in three-month-old infants. *Child Development*, **55**, 936–43.

Fischer, M. and Leitenberg, H. (1986) Optimism and pessimism in elementary school-aged children. *Child Development*, **57**, 241–8.

Gottlieb, G. (1976) Conceptions of prenatal development. *Psychological Review*, **83**, 215–34.

Gunnar, M. R., Leighton, K. and Peleaux, R. (1984) Effects of temporal predictability on the reactions of 1-year-olds to potentially frightening toys. *Developmental Psychology*, **20**, 449–58.

Kuo, Z. Y. (1930) The genesis of the cat's responses to the rat. *Journal of Comparative Psychology*, **11**, 1–35.

—— (1967) *The dynamics of behavior development: an epigenetic view*. New York: Random House.

Levine, S. (1982) Comparative and psychobiological perspectives on development. In Collins, W. A. (ed.) *The concept of development: the Minnesota symposia on child psychology*, vol. 15. Hillsdale, NJ: Erlbaum, pp. 29–35.

Rutter, M. (1986) Meyerian psychobiology, personality development, and the role of life experiences. *The American Journal of Psychiatry*, **143**, 1077–87.

Schulz, R. and Rau, M. T. (1985) Social support throughout the life course. In Cohen, S. and Syme, S. L. (eds.) *Social support and health*. Orlando, FL: Academic Press.

Sherif, M., Harvey, O. J., White, B. J., Hood, W. R. and Sherif, C. W. (1961) *Intergroup conflict and cooperation: the Robber's Cave experiment*. Norman: University of Oklahoma Press.

15 Intergenerational longitudinal research: conceptual and methodological considerations

M. E. J. Wadsworth

Introduction

We live in times of relatively rapid change both of the physical environment and in many aspects of social circumstances in terms of behaviour, attitudes and beliefs. Many changes have also been made in recent years in national programmes of health, education and welfare. Some of these changes are monitored by official statistics or by research projects that allow comparisons to be made between the *status quo* at different social times. Social change is of particular interest in research in psychosocial development, where the processes of interaction between the individual and the social environment are important parts of the topic of study. For many purposes the preferred method of investigation of such processes is the longitudinal study, in which development and change in these processes are observed over time in order, for example, to investigate effects of environmental factors, experience, and increasing age and maturity, on individuals' reactions to, and coping with, events. Opportunities to compare such processes between generations allow us also to evaluate the effects of a change in social circumstances on the processes of development and on reactions to events.

Studies of vulnerability to illness and of the habits and experiences that may increase risk of illness or protection against it have become increasingly complex. These investigations are concerned not only with indicators of vulnerability, but also with its origins and aetiology, and they therefore take into account increasing lengths of life span, which may now include intergenerational time (Emanuel, 1986). As life expectancy increases and research into ageing develops, many kinds of research have an interest in studies of the individual's physical and mental change over time. Research design is therefore often concerned with methods of handling the problem of time. Since it is not usually possible or practical to follow up the same individuals over the long time spans now of interest, other methods have been developed. It is rarely sufficient to compare the experience of different cohorts in order to develop a picture of likely changes in characteristics over time (Bakketeig and Hoffman, 1979; Rodgers, 1986), and there is often no alternative but to study the same group of individuals over a period of time. Indeed, many aspects of questions about, for instance, the length of time during which the effect of a particular experience may be detected can be answered by sampling affected populations and controls at an appropriate later time. Questions about the effect of environmental change over time, however, require different strategies. It is, for instance, useful to look for opportunities that may be provided by environmental or social change, when such changes include factors that are thought to be part of the process of risk development or maintenance: for example, changes in ideas about child-rearing (Wadsworth, 1981a) or changes in medical and educational services, or national experience of catastrophe (Elder, 1974).

This chapter is concerned with longitudinal research strategies for intergenerational investigations of risk and protective factors and with a consideration of the advantages and disadvantages of continuous follow-up as compared with catch-up study design.

Risk and protective factors

Risk may be considered both in terms of experience and of individuals' reaction to experience. Originally it was usually conceived of as experience, perhaps because many of the earlier studies were concerned with screening out children with difficulties in early life. There was a particular emphasis on experience of events thought to be damaging, notably the death of, or separation from, a parent or close relation or friend (Bowlby, 1973; Brown and Harris, 1978; Rutter, 1981), and with similar types of experience, for example admission to hospital (Douglas, 1975). Studies of these kinds of experience make it clear that not all those who encountered the experience would have the same or similar, or indeed any reaction, and in many instances the best guide to the risk of later outcome associated with such experiences was found in intrinsic aspects of the study population and in their circumstances at the time of the experience. Clearly the same experience might mean different things in different cultures, and different things within one culture according to life stage, family circumstances and individual commitments. Risk may also therefore be seen as a dynamic concept varying within individuals according to their circumstances, and their reactions to an event will depend on these factors and on their stock of previous experience and of the temperament that they have to contend with experience. Many potentially adverse life events occur apparently by chance, and in the face of an adverse experience the individual degree of vulnerability or invulnerability depends on the nature of coping or reacting (Rutter, 1985). This in turn will be associated with the individual's own attributes and previous experiences. Thus, as age increases, relative vulnerability or invulnerability to a particular type of experience will change, as previous experience acts as a constant source of modification. The developing child's coping or reacting will be associated with his/her achieved stage of maturity, and in adults the life stage will be important for reasons that are both intrinsic (such as accumulation of experience, temperament, the evaluation of self-worth) and extrinsic (such as the existence and, if so, the age of offspring, spouse and parents). Scarr and Weinberg (1983) found evidence of a process of change in the influence of intrinsic and extrinsic factors during the life course in their adoption studies:

Younger children, regardless of their genetic relatedness, resemble each other intellectually because they share similar rearing environments. Older adolescents, on the other hand, resemble one another only if they share genes. Our interpretation is that older children escape the influences of the family and are freer to select their own environment. Parental influences are diluted by the more varied mix of adolescent experiences.

The results support the idea that older children and adolescents fill their own niche, which can be seen as an active genotype environment correlation (Plomin, de Fries and Leohlan 1977). Different people select different aspects of their environments that they find compatible. Choices of environment are influenced by genetic differences in what individuals enjoy and at which they are competent.

Such fluid notions of risk, and therefore of protective factors, have to be studied in the individual over time, and therefore longitudinal research techniques are necessary.

Reaction to a potentially adverse experience may also be, in some important respects, conditioned not only by age, life stage and experience, but also by cultural factors. For instance, it is clear from contemporary research (Bowlby, 1951) and from books of comment (Watson, 1950) that during the years immediately following the Second World War the childhood experience of parental divorce or separation was thought to be a very serious source of risk for the child's moral and emotional development. In one contemporary study, comparisons of teachers' and community nurses' assessments of the behaviour and life chances of children who had this experience with those of children who did not, showed that teachers and community nurses had significantly lower expectations of children's life chances if their parents had divorced, and in due course these expectations were associated with lower achievements (Douglas, 1964; Wadsworth, 1979). This sharply critical view of divorce and separation is much less intense now, however, and is a cultural factor that has changed. Similarly, very great changes in expert and professional assessments of the 'risks' of being a first-born child took place during the 1920s and 1930s in comparison with the period immediately after the Second World War. In the pre-war years the first-born child was felt, and indeed reported, to be at much greater risk of being 'spoilt', and therefore at greater risk of neurotic behaviour in later life, and parents were advised to be restrained in their behaviour with their first-born children. In post-war times this advice was reversed, as experts felt that displays of affection were not risk factors but a healthy part of development (Wadsworth, 1981a).

Such changes provide a natural experiment for research workers, who can compare the effect of changes in social circumstances on childhood by using intergenerational studies. These look for differences in the development and behaviour in later life of children brought up, for example, with parents who restrained their displays of affection as compared with those brought up by more expressive parents, or between children whose parents divorced at a time when such an experience was considered a serious risk compared with children whose parents divorced when this risk was no longer considered to be especially great. Such investigations may be carried out using a relatively simple sampling frame of two cohorts of adults, one comprising those who had been children before the change in predominant ideas about upbringing and the other those who had been children at a later date. However, an intergenerational form of study could make greater use of such natural experiments. By being intergenerational, that is by being an investigation of the same individuals in childhood and in adult life, such a longitudinal study could (a) ask whether relative vulnerability or invulnerability to the perceived source of stress in one generation was associated with similar relative vulnerability or invulnerability in the following generation, and (b) investigate the aetiology of vulnerability and invulnerability in the individual. There are, therefore, several ways in which intergenerational studies may be undertaken. At their simplest they can take the form of a comparison of cohorts born at different social times, but they may comprise follow-up of individuals from one generation into the next, or the linking of more than two generations in a research design that combines follow-up through two generations with recollection of an earlier generation as well.

The following sections consider different possibilities for the design of intergenerational longitudinal studies.

Design of intergenerational studies

Intergenerational studies that rely wholly on records are of great interest (Hareven, 1978) but are not considered here. Designs of intergenerational studies that are based on data collected from subjects can be grouped into two types, and these are considered below under the headings 'Catch-up design' and 'Continuous follow-up design'. It is, however, first worth considering three particular methodological problems that are common to both designs, namely population sampling, recollection, and comparability of measures over time.

Population sampling

Plans for the continuation of an existing longitudinal study to include investigation of the following generation will be constrained by the scale of the original sample and the purpose for which it was taken. Studies of a subsequent generation that wish, for example, to compare individuals' rates of change on some indicator or experience of a particular risk factor may very well be carried out on a relatively small sample. However, in these circumstances only very exceptionally will a control group also be available on whom the same data have been collected at the same time(s) in the past (Quinton and Rutter, 1984).

A much larger sample in the first generation will be required for research concerned both with analysis of individuals' experience and with the intergenerational comparison of their attainments, health and experiences in relation to social factors. This larger population base will offer the additional advantage of readily available control groups for many purposes (Douglas, 1981a; 1981b). Much larger samples are also generally required as a basis for continuous longitudinal follow-up of studies that begin when their subjects are children, since losses that will occur through death are particularly heavy in childhood, and losses through geographical mobility and emigration are likely to be heaviest when parents are young (Wadsworth, 1987). In the longitudinal study of a cohort of children born in 1946, for instance, losses through death amounted to 5.6% by the time study members were 30 years old, but three-quarters of these deaths had occurred by the age of five years. The value of a relatively large study population for the purposes of analysis is discussed further below.

Whatever the scale of the first generation of the study population the selection of sample members for a second generation study has to be made according to the purposes of the continued follow-up. If the study is to be of a group of adults who were themselves, as children, the original study population, then the sampling has, in effect, already been carried out, but if the investigation is to be concerned with their offspring, then the questions arise of which child to study, and whether it is necessary to study the offspring at a particular age. If the intention is to study the parenting styles of cohort members, then it must be decided whether it would be most appropriate to collect data at a fixed time in family life, for example at a particular age of the first-born child, or at the ages when data collection took place with the cohort member parent (Wadsworth, 1981b), or both. In a study of how members of a birth cohort went about bringing up their first-born children (e.g. Wadsworth, 1981b) data were collected in the last year before offspring went to school full-time in order to compare certain aspects of preschool parenting in the two generations. Data were again collected at the age of eight years, this time in order to compare verbal attainment in the two generations, and to compare the associations of preschool experience with verbal scores on tests taken four years later at the age of eight years, in each generation (Wadsworth, 1986). In this instance it was also necessary to select for study only the offspring of the same ordinal position as the cohort member parent.

Decisions must also be taken about whether or not to include multiple births (they are, in practice, almost always too few, unless the sample has been specially enriched with them) and whether the follow-up of offspring will continue for those who eventually do not live with the parent who is the original cohort member. Thus basic decisions have to be taken about whether a proposed intergenerational study aims primarily to compare aspects of childhood in two generations or to investigate the parenting behaviour of a population already studied. The study of parenting behaviour makes the greatest use of earlier data collection, and this is itself one of the most important criteria for decisions about longitudinal study design. For example, when weighing relative merits of data collection strategies or deciding whether or not to include a particular question at the time of new follow-up contacts, those aspects that make better use of data already collected are usually to be favoured.

Whichever strategy is chosen for the design of an intergenerational study it is almost always necessary to have some information on the family circumstances of the child's life at each data collection. This involves collecting information on what may be quite a large population, since children of divorced parents will probably have a network of relevant other adults in addition to those with whom they live. For the purposes of some intergenerational investigations it may be appropriate to have both the cohort member parent and their partner as informants, but this may prove quite impractical because of the expense of making what may often be more than one visit to each family.

Recollection

When studies either continue over long periods of time or are concerned with asking questions about long periods of time, recollection inevitably plays an important part in the study design. It is in many ways a limiting factor whose dimensions are not particularly well known.

It is clear that some kinds of information either cannot be recollected or are likely to be unreliable if collected in retrospect. For example, asking study subjects to recall reactions to earlier experiences, or attitudes, or feelings of self-worth at earlier times, is not likely to yield useful information. Some things may not be recollected in this way at all because they were not known at the time, for instance weight or blood pressure. But experiences themselves may be usefully recalled (Robins, *et al.* 1984; 1985) as a way of collecting some sorts of data about earlier life. In a longitudinal study they can also be used to assess reliability; Cherry and Rodgers (1979), for instance, report that in the longitudinal study of a birth cohort of 1946 Douglas (1975) found that mothers' reports of deterioration in children's behaviour after a period in hospital in the first five years of life were associated with teacher ratings of the children as troublesome at the ages of 13 or 15. The smaller the extent of deterioration reported by mothers at the time of the event the lower the rate of troublesome behaviour reported in due course by teachers. Cherry and Rodgers (1979, p. 35) conclude that 'retrospective reporting by mothers of troublesome teenagers would have held little weight in assessing this relationship'.

Failure to recall will vary between subjects even of the same age, but will also vary with age. In a continuous follow-up study of the same population over a long period of time this would be a source of interest, since an increase in the length of the time the study continues also increases chances of evaluating the extent of loss or failure of memory in individuals, and provides opportunities for the study of its prevalence and severity, perhaps as part of a more general investigation of cognitive decrement.

Distortion of recollection is more complicated. It may be the result of an inability to differentiate own recall from recall of reports of others: for instance, recollection of some childhood experience may in part or in whole rely on what others have said, and the degree to which this is so may possibly not be known to the subject. Yarrow *et al.* (1970, p. 67) concluded that 'mothers have a significant role in determining the folklore of the family and, by extension, in shaping the nature of the findings in retrospective investigations.' Distortion may also occur, perhaps deliberately or perhaps unconsciously, in the recollection of painful past events. Yarrow *et al.* (1970, p. 37) report that mothers 'recalled infancy generally as an easier, happier, healthier period than was the case in baseline reports', but 'from contemporaneous measures of the preschool period the father–child relationship ... was characterised by a slightly greater warmth than the mother–child relationship ... whereas recall of this period showed an almost perfect reversal, with the father–child relationship presented as less warm than the mother–child relationship'. Distortion may also occur because of changes in social values: now, for example, that much more participation in the care of young children is generally expected from fathers, recollections of such activities in a previous generation might be exaggerated. It can also happen that reaction to recent circumstances in an individual's life may distort recollection of that person at an earlier time. A chronically sick adult, for instance, may be inclined to recall childhood, unduly, as dominated by illness. At some point in a longitudinal study, where there is contemporaneously collected data on the earlier event which study members are now asked to recall, distortion may itself usefully be seen as data, in the sense that comparison of individuals' tendencies to distort, and the kind of distortion that occurs, can be informative about the interpretation of past and current events.

Recollection is of great importance in longitudinal research design not only because of the potential for the data to be unreliable, but also because distortion of memory or failure to recall may distort the sequencing of past events and, as Robins *et al.* (1984) note, when recall is of an illness that carries a risk of death, then the prevalence rate reported by older persons will have been reduced compared with that of younger persons, giving a false impression that the rate of the disorder is increasing in the younger generation.

Therefore when recall periods cannot be minimized in the study design, reports should wherever possible be checked by reference to records, and questions asked at interview should provide the maximum possible assistance to aid recall, for example by asking for recollection of a sequence of events or other information from the time in question.

Comparability of measures over time
Longitudinal studies that use coding schemes that are publicly available, such as in Britain the social class classification (Registrar General, 1971) or the World Health Organization International Classification of Diseases (World Health Organization, 1977), find this of benefit for comparison with other investigations, but often have problems in the longer term as schemes are changed and reclassified during the life of the study. Social class is especially difficult, since both the coding scheme and the individual's classification on it often change over long periods of time. For many purposes there is little alternative but to recode the original data, as well as keeping the old code, as a way of coping with changes in coding schemes (Britten, 1981), and this can often be done largely by computer. It is, however, sometimes also necessary to construct static indicators. For example, Douglas *et al.* (1968) found that in the study of social-class differences in children's attainment scores it was valuable both to examine the effects of social-class change on attainment score, and also to make a static indicator of class comprising social class of family of origin and achieved level of education of each parent, and the family social class when the child took the tests. In general in such studies recoding is necessary from time to time, since coding schemes designed for previous analyses may well not sufficiently encompass all the aspects of meaning required in current work.

Many kinds of indicator of social position and social circumstances, and even of illness, are difficult to compare at their face value over long periods of time. This can be because of changes in the definition of what constitutes the social position or the illness, when changes in necessary qualifications or perceived status or diagnostic criteria have taken place. For example, intergenerational comparison of the apparent effects on children of parental divorce or separation should take into account the contemporary perceptions of the possible effects, since they may well constitute a mechanism of a self-fulfilling prophecy; however, this kind of social-context data is hard to acquire, and has generally not been collected in longitudinal studies. Comparison over long time periods of apparently similar indicators may also be misleading because of changes in attitudes towards those regarded as disadvantaged, for example those with epilepsy (Britten *et al.* 1986) or the divorced. Changes in perceptions of the sufferer of a chronic illness may also take place over time. For instance, in a study of members of the birth cohort who had experienced epilepsy in childhood, Britten *et al.* (1986) found that the self-perceived stigma apparently increased with increasing age.

Elder's concern (Elder *et al.*, 1984) about the relatively narrow range and small number of measures available from the original contacts with his study population is a feature of all long-term research. Elder's study shows the great advantage in the catch-up design of longitudinal research in having an indicator of experience that does not, *per se*, change its meaning over time and which provides a relative ranking of all members of the study population, in this instance in terms of percentage income loss. McCord (1979) was less fortunate in her follow-up of an American population first studied in 1939. In this work a key population selection factor that might also have been used as an indicator of experience, was the receipt of social-work advice and counselling, but this was not well documented. However, counsellors' reports of family circumstances, especially marital harmony, have proved invaluable in later follow-up work with this population, after systematic recoding of their reports (McCord, 1979). Thus, in such later follow-up work with a population studied at earlier times, there is a need for care and discernment about the validity of indicators of all kinds, and recoding of earlier information may be necessary.

Few studies can enjoy the benefits of having comparable measures of particular attributes, for example biological or behavioural ones, of each member of their study populations in two generations. Generally, the problem is that the measure of interest is available on the current generation and not on its forebears, either because it was simply not carried out in the first generation, or because such a measure did not exist at the earlier time. There are many kinds of behavioural and biological measure, commonly used with children today, that were not available 20 years ago. For example, it was until recently thought that measures of height, growth rate and the absence of illness provided an adequate assessment of physical health in childhood, but measures of blood pressure and of respiratory function are now thought, together with other indicators of the level of biological functioning, to be of importance. However, even though the data collected at earlier times may not match up to present-day requirements, there may well still be useful analyses to be carried out with existing data. For instance in the investigation of earlier life precursors of relatively raised blood pressure at the age of 36 in members of the cohort of British children born in 1946, Wadsworth *et al.*

(1985) found that, even without data on childhood blood pressure, disorders in the father that related to low birth weight and high blood pressure were significant risk factors.

It may happen that a measure of current interest was carried out in the first generation, but is no longer in use. In this instance comparability of measures may be achieved by comparing individual scores or positions in one generation in relation to those of others in the next generation, for instance to see whether relative ranking in terms, say, of deciles of scores has changed between generations. Alternatively, the current generation can be measured using both the technique employed in the earlier generation and that of present-day choice. In some instances the measures used at early times may be updated. In a study of verbal attainment at the age of eight years in two generations, for example, Wadsworth (1986) made tests of word reading and pronunciation generation fair by replacing out-of-date words with others that were found on testing to have comparable facility value, and by reordering the facility value of all the words as necessary.

Thus intergenerational longitudinal studies have to contend with the problems of generation and age equivalence of measures. These difficulties are part of the powerful argument for the retention of all original material in longitudinal investigations, both for the purposes of recoding and reclassification, and also for the case-by-case examination of records that is inevitable at some point in most analyses.

The catch-up design. In this design a study population once investigated in a previous generation is used as the basis of a study of their offspring. This is becoming increasingly possible, since during the years before the Second World War in the United States, and after the war in Europe and the United States, a large number of longitudinal studies of children were carried out. An overview of studies is given in Mednick and Baert (1981) and in Mednick *et al.* (1984). More recent English work of various catch-up designs includes that of Quinton and Rutter (1984), of Miller *et al.* (1985) and of Zeitlin (1986). A striking example of such work is that of Elder (1974). During 1969–70 Elder and his colleagues recontacted members of the Berkeley Guidance Study, who comprised a sample of families whose first child was born in 1928 or 1929 and who were regularly studied up until 1945; a comparison sample was also used from the Oakland Growth Study cohort of children born between 1920 and 1921. Elder and his colleagues made ingenious use of cultural or social time passing by recontacting the cohorts who had been studied before and during the experience of extensive social catastrophe, namely the American Great Depression that took place in the early 1930s. They used this experience that occurred to all members of the Berkeley Guidance Study to ask whether it affected their health, self-confidence, work, marriage and parenthood, and whether and by what means individuals seemed to have mitigated its effects.

The overwhelming advantage of this design is that in comparison with the continuous follow-up method a great deal of time, possibly 20 years, is not spent in frequent follow-up studies of a cohort before the birth of their offspring population in order to carry out intergenerational study. Compared with studies that rely wholly on recollection the catch-up design has the benefit of providing contemporaneously collected information both about the social conditions of the time as seen through the eyes of the study population and about their reactions to current circumstances. The catch-up design may also provide information about the individual's reaction to earlier life experience, about processes such as coping with emotional disruption, and about states, for instance self-esteem, none of which could be reliably collected, in retrospect. But there are also some disadvantages.

The first disadvantage is that of the risk of population loss. Losses will inevitably have occurred through death, and for some research purposes the study of a survivor-only population can be a problem. It is also more difficult to deal with the problem of recontacting members of the original study population in the catch-up design, and although some remarkable achievements have been made in finding study population members after many years without contact (e.g. McCord, 1979) this is a potential risk in the catch-up design (Miller *et al.*, 1985). In Elder's study 57.8% of the original population of 211 individuals were contacted for the follow-up (Elder *et al.*, 1984).

This period without contact is important, since information about this time will mostly be available only through recollection. Unfortunately in the catch-up design this recall period often includes adolescence and a certain amount of early adult life, when many changes in circumstances occur and when perceptions of life chances will influence the many decisions that individuals take, as well as those that others take about them. These are difficult things to remember in detail, and they are subject to all the problems of recollection that were discussed above. This may be particularly a problem in studies of vulnerability, since investigations that are concerned with hypothesized causal chains or with patterns of experience over time, as well as a range of possible manifestations of vulnerability, will lose some of the necessary information from the recalled period.

In the catch-up design researchers who collect information on the second generation are to a great extent constrained in their work by the choice of population in the first generation, by that population's age at points of contact, and by the choice of measures used in the original investigation. This last constraint affects not only the direct intergenerational comparisons that may be made, but also the range of information that can be interpreted as indications of vulnerability or otherwise, and the range of experiences reported that may be seen as risk or protective factors. For Elder these difficulties were minimized not only by the existence of good and detailed data on child-rearing in the first generation, but especially also by the existence of a control population who did not experience what Elder hypothesized as a risk, namely the American Depression.

Continuous follow-up design

Although when considering the continuous follow-up design for purposes of intergenerational studies it is appropriate to think of the time before the birth of offspring as a long waiting period, data collection that takes place during this time is of great importance. Not only will data collected during these years be available in its own right, for example for providing outcome measures during these years before parenting begins, but it also provides information on the important life stages of adolescence and the early adult years, which will in due course be of great relevance in the study of partner choice and later parenting behaviour. Much of this information cannot be collected in retrospect, for reasons discussed above. The continuous study design also minimizes the problems associated with recollection over long periods of time.

This design, therefore, provides the best kinds of information for the study of causal chains in view of its relative frequency of data collection throughout life stages (Essen and Wedge, 1982). For instance, in a continuous follow-up study of a national sample of children begun at the time of their birth in 1946, Douglas (1964, p. 118) found that:

Children who come from well kept homes and who are themselves clean, well clothed and shod stand a greater chance of being put in the upper streams [in schools] than their measured ability would seem to justify. Once there they are likely to stay and improve in performance in succeeding years. This is in striking contrast to the deterioration noticed in those children of similar initial measured ability who are placed in the lower stream. In this way the validity of the initial selection appears to be confirmed by the subsequent performance of the children.

In this instance Douglas found that a constellation of information on home physical circumstances and the cleanliness and clothing of the child, the parents' interest in education, teachers' assessments, and measures of educational attainment, all combined together to indicate, when negative, the long-term risk of poor educational attainment and, when positive, the likelihood of educational success. It is fair to say that Douglas almost certainly did not foresee all aspects of the relevance of the assessments that health visitors (community nurses) made of the state of physical care, possibly including these associations with later educational attainment, but the predictive value of these assessments was far-reaching. Measured attainment and parental interest in education during the school years were associated with the child's ultimate educational achievements, and therefore with socio-economic achievements in adult life. When in due course these children themselves became parents, high-attaining children whose parents had had high aspirations showed, significantly more often than others, signs of considerable interest in the educational progress of their own first-born offspring (Wadsworth, 1986). This particular example illustrates a difficult aspect of the design of continuous follow-up studies, where the aim is to investigate human development, both physical and mental, in its social and family setting. Such research must plan and obtain funding for each data collection, usually only one step at a time, and under these circumstances it can be difficult to justify and to be appropriately perceptive about collecting information, both for possible long-term future analysis and for immediate use.

Continuity of data collection makes it easier to seek and assess the value of what may be indicators of individual vulnerability by using data collected at various times before the outcome measure under consideration. For example, signs of disturbance in children, such as bed-wetting or sleep disturbance, were found in the 1946 birth cohort children in significant excess after their experience of the loss of a parent through divorce or separation before the age of five (Douglas, 1973). But these signs did not significantly discriminate those at risk of later delinquency. However, data on pulse rate reaction to a somewhat stressful experience collected six years later, when the same children were 11 years old, was a good discriminator of criminal behaviour, particularly violent offences committed by boys on average six years later, at the age of 17 or older (Wadsworth, 1976). Men and women who experienced parental divorce whilst they were aged 0–14 years achieved significantly lower educational qualifications when compared with others from similar socio-economic families, and men with a background of this nature who were gainfully employed were found, both at the age of 26 and at the age of 36 to be paid a significantly lower average wage than others (Wadsworth and Maclean, 1986). Men and women from such families were themselves more likely to have divorced by the age of 36. There was thus a chain of increased risk across the generations. The comparable chain of protective factors is dominated by educational achievement, which was in turn closely associated with parental concern for the child's progress. However, without greater detail of information than was collected in this study on the quality of parents' marital relationships and on the knowledge that teachers had of the childrens' family circumstances it is not possible to go into a great deal of detail about the workings of these observed associations, except by internal cross-checking of hypotheses.

Because of the range of data collected during the various life stages encompassed in such a study, in terms, that is, of topic areas, this design is at a particular advantage not only in the study of sequence of events and experiences but also in the internal cross-checking of hypotheses. For example, an outcome indicator that it is associated with a negative experience can be examined further to see whether its variation with positive experience varies in accordance with the hypothesis being tested. In the 1946 birth cohort study boys who before the age of five experienced a disruption of relationships with their parents because of parental divorce had a significantly increased likelihood of delinquent behaviour in adolescence. Amongst the population of those who did not experience parental divorce the disruption caused by the birth of two siblings during these first five years of life was associated with the greatest chance of delinquency, one sibling birth being associated with a lesser chance of delinquency and no sibling births with the least chance of delinquency (Wadsworth, 1979). In this same study internal cross-checking of hypotheses was also carried out through the case-by-case examination of those false positives predicted to be delinquent when using the data on parental divorce. This revealed significantly higher rates of emotional disturbance and of some illnesses of probable psychosomatic origin in the false positives group when compared with others (Wadsworth, 1979; 1984).

These advantages of a continuous design may be used to further advantage if the study's population is in some way representative of a national population, since the specificity and sensitivity of prediction of risk in subpopulations or even amongst individuals may be tested, and will therefore show the likely value of risk indicators in other populations (Wadsworth, 1984).

Conclusion

Studies of aetiology in mental and physical illness are increasingly concerned with the development of conditions over long periods of the individual life span (Barker and Osmond, 1986; Berenson, 1986), and with reasons for individual vulnerability and robustness in the face of extrinsic and intrinsic risk factors (Rutter, 1985). Longitudinal studies of risk and protective factors that begin in childhood are concerned with how the child develops resources and is influenced by experience, and the feedback of effects of such experience, within the social context of home, school and historical time. Comparison of generations, either by comparison of cohorts or the continuous study of one cohort, asks how these resources and influences are manifest in parenting and other adult behaviour and whether, and if so how, individuals change or escape from patterns of behaviour and particular circumstances in one generation as compared with another. The existing longitudinal studies of various kinds offer opportunities to examine many aspects of these processes. But where there is not now appropriate information for such work, or where there is not a sufficient case for beginning a new longitudinal study, it may be worth using a method of flagging individuals thought to be at particular risk and comparing these with controls, so that later study, with perhaps some form of one-off contemporary data collection, may be possible. This would help to perpetuate the fund of studies carried out at different historical times, studies that are invaluable for comparison of the effects of changes in social factors on the risk of illness and emotional difficulties.

Longitudinal and intergenerational studies are thus increasingly likely to be required and, although they are relatively complex and time-consuming to carry out, there are techniques that enable research to take place relatively rapidly. Many of the questions now raised in studies of risk and protective factors require such longitudinal investigation since these studies are designed to contend with many aspects and interactions of personal and historical time passing.

References

Atkins, E., Cherry, N., Douglas, J. W. B., Kiernan, K. E. and Wadsworth, M. E. J. (1981) The 1946 British birth cohort: an account of the origins, progress and results of the National Survey of Health and Development. In Mednick, S. A. and Baert, A. E. (eds.) *Prospective longitudinal research: an empirical basis for the primary prevention of psychosocial disorders.* Oxford: Oxford University Press, pp. 25–30.

Bakketeig, L. S. and Hoffman, H. J. (1979) Perinatal morbidity by birth order within cohorts based on sibling size. *British Medical Journal*, 2, 693–6.

Barker, D. J. P. and Osmond, C. (1986) Childhood respiratory infection and adult chronic bronchitis in England and Wales. *British Medical Journal*, 292, 1271–5.

Berenson, G. S. (1986) (ed.) *Causation of cardiovascular risk factors in children.* New York: Raven Press.

Bowlby, J. (1951) *Mental care and mental health.* Geneva: World Health Organization.
  (1973) *Attachment and loss*, vol. 2, *Separation, anxiety and anger.* London: Hogarth Press.

Britten, N. (1981) Models of intergenerational class mobility: findings from the National Survey of Health and Development. *British Journal of Sociology*, 32, 224–38.

Britten, N., Wadsworth, M. E. J. and Fenwick, P. B. C. (1986) Sources of stigma following early-life epilepsy: evidence from a national birth cohort study. In Whitman, S. and Hermann, B. P. (eds.) *Psychopathology in epilepsy: social dimensions.* Oxford: Oxford University Press, pp. 228–44.

Brown, G. W. and Harris, T. (1978) *Social origins of depression.* London: Tavistock.

Cherry, N. and Rodgers, B. (1979) Using a longitudinal study to assess the quality of retrospective data. In Moss, L. and Goldstein, H. (eds.) *The recall method in social surveys.* University of London Studies in Education no. 9. London: University of London Institute of Education, pp. 31–47.

Douglas, J. W. B. (1964) *The home and the school.* London: MacGibbon and Kee.
  (1973) Early disturbing events and later enuresis. In Kolvin, I., MacKeith, R. C.

and Meadow, S. R. (eds.) *Bladder control and enuresis*. London: Spastics International Medical Publishers, pp. 109–17.

(1975) Early hospital admissions and later disturbances of behaviour and learning. *Developmental Medicine and Child Neurology*, 17, 456–80.

(1981a) The contribution of long-term research to social medicine. In Schulsinger, F., Mednick, S. A. and Knop, J. (eds.) *Longitudinal research: methods and uses in behavioral science*. Boston: Martinus Nijhoff, pp. 277–84.

(1981b) The value of birth cohort studies. In Schulsinger, F., Mednick, S. A. and Knop, J. (eds.) *Longitudinal research: methods and uses in behavioral science*. Boston: Martinus Nijhoff, pp. 176–86.

Douglas, J. W. B., Ross, J. M. and Simpson, H. R. (1968) *All Our Future*. London: Peter Davies.

Elder, G. H. (1974) *Children of the Great Depression*. Chicago: Chicago University Press.

Elder, G. H., Liker, J. K. and Cross, C. E. (1984) Parent–child behaviour in the Great Depression: life course and intergenerational influences. In Baltes, P. B. (ed.) *Life-span development and behavior*, vol. 6. New York: Academic Press, pp. 109–58.

Emanuel, I. (1986) Maternal health during childhood and later reproductive performance. *Annals of the New York Academy of Sciences*, 477, 27–9.

Essen, J. and Wedge, P. (1982) *Continuities in childhood disadvantage*. London: Heinemann.

Hareven, T. (1978) *Transitions: the family and the life course in historical perspective*. New York: Academic Press.

McCord, J. (1979) Some child-rearing antecedents of criminal behavior in adult men. *Journal of Personality and Social Psychology*, 37, 1477–86.

Mednick, S. A. and Baert, A. E. (1981) (eds.) *Prospective longitudinal research in Europe*. Oxford: Oxford University Press.

Mednick, S. A., Harvey, M. and Finello, K. M. (1984) (eds.) *Handbook of longitudinal research*, vol. 1, *Birth and childhood cohorts*, vol. 2, *Teenage and adult cohorts*. New York: Praeger.

Miller, F. J. W., Kolvin, I. and Fells, H. (1985) Becoming deprived: a cross-generation study based on the Newcastle-upon-Tyne 1000-family study. In Nicol, A. R. (ed.) *Longitudinal studies in child psychology and psychiatry*. Chichester: Wiley, pp. 223–40.

Quinton, D. and Rutter, M. (1984) Parents with children in care. *Journal of Child Psychology and Psychiatry*, 25, 211–50.

Registrar General (1971) *Classification of occupations*. London: HMSO.

Robins, L. N., Helzer, J. E., Weissman, M., Orvaschel, H., Gruenberg, E., Burke, J. D. and Regier, D. A. (1984) Lifetime prevalence of specific psychiatric disorders in three sites. *Archives of General Psychiatry*, 41, 949–58.

Robins, L. N., Schoenberg, S. P., Holmes, S. J., Ratcliff, K. S., Benham, A. and Works, J. (1985) Early home environment and retrospective recall: a test for concordance between siblings with and without psychiatric disorders. *American Journal of Orthopsychiatry*, 55, 27–41.

Rodgers, B. (1986) Change in the reading attainment of adults: a longitudinal study. *British Journal of Developmental Psychology*, 4, 1–17.

Rutter, M. (1981) *Maternal deprivation re-assessed*, 2nd edn. Harmondsworth: Penguin.

(1985) Resilience in the face of adversity. *British Journal of Psychiatry*, 147, 598–611.

Scarr, S. and Weinberg, R. A. (1983) The Minnesota adoption studies; genetic differences and malleability. *Child Development*, 54, 260–7.

Wadsworth, M. E. J. (1976) Delinquency, pulse rates and early emotional deprivation. *British Journal of Criminology*, 16, 245–56.

(1979) *Roots of delinquency: infancy, adolescence and crime.* Oxford: Martin Robertson; New York: Barnes and Noble.

(1981a) Social change and the interpretation of research. *Criminology*, 19, 53–75.

(1981b) Social class and generation differences in pre-school education. *British Journal of Sociology*, 32, 560–82.

(1984) Early stress and associations with adult health behaviour and parenting. In Butler, N. R. and Corner, B. D. (eds.) *Stress and disability in childhood.* Bristol: John Wright, pp. 100–4.

(1986) Effects of parenting style and preschool experience on children's verbal attainment: a British longitudinal study. *Early Childhood Research Quarterly*, 1, 237–48.

(1987) Follow-up of the first British national birth cohort: findings from the MRC National Survey of Health and Development. *Paediatric and Perinatal Epidemiology*, 1, 67–89.

Wadsworth, M. E. J. and Maclean, M. (1986) Parents' divorce and children's life chances. *Children and Youth Services Review*, 8, 145–59.

Wadsworth, M. E. J., Cripps, H. A., Midwinter, R. A. and Colley, J. R. T. (1985) Blood pressure at age 36 years and social and familial factors, cigarette smoking and body mass in a national birth cohort. *British Medical Journal*, 291, 1534–8.

Watson, J. D. (1950) *The child and the magistrate.* London: Cape.

World Health Organization (1977) *Manual of the international standard classification of diseases, injuries and causes of death.* Geneva: WHO.

Yarrow, M. R., Campbell, J. D. and Burton, R. V. (1970) *Recollections of childhood: a study of the retrospective method.* Monographs of the Society for Research in Child Development 138, vol. 35, no. 5.

Zeitlin, H. (1986) *The natural history of psychiatric disorder in children.* Institute of Psychiatry, Maudsley Monographs no. 29. Oxford: Oxford University Press.

16 Longitudinal approaches to intergenerational studies: definition, design and use

David Quinton

The term 'generation' is used in a number of ways, all of which, by definition, contain some reference to similarity in age, but which otherwise define groups or categories of individuals somewhat differently. Thus the definition may involve social age ('the younger generation') or reference to a particular cultural or historical period ('the Beat Generation'). These usages locate people in social or historical time and imply a process of succession – of one generation following another – but not necessarily of descent – with the members of one generation necessarily all being the parents of, or generating, the other.

The term 'intergenerational' can share these overlapping usages in a way that causes some confusion. Comparisons may be made between children and adults on some characteristics, with these described as differences between generations, or correlations may be established between childhood and adulthood and referred to as 'intergenerational continuities'. This is the sense in which the term is used by Wadsworth (see chapter 15), but comparisons between childhood and adulthood, either at the same point in time or within the sample of individuals, cannot be called 'intergenerational' without removing from that term its distinctive meaning. The former are better described simply as age cohort studies and the latter as panel studies (Glenn, 1977), with the term 'intergenerational' used only when the component of descent is present, that is when referring to studies of associations on particular variables between parents and their children (Quinton, 1985).

'Intergenerational transmission' has been used to describe the passing-on by parents of behaviours, characteristics or circumstances to *dependent* children. The definition is used in this way by Kolvin and his colleagues in the Newcastle Thousand Families Study (see chapter 5). However, this is unnecessarily confusing because, for example, it groups studies concerned with the *immediate* effects of child-rearing practices (family studies) with studies examining whether those practices are repeated by the children when they themselves become parents.

It is preferable to restrict the phrase 'intergenerational studies' to the investigation of continuities or discontinuities between parents and children on particular variables at the same chronological or social age. This is in order to distinguish a field of investigation whose distinctive feature is an interest in the reappearance or otherwise in subsequent generations of characteristics or circumstances the features of which can only with certainty be comparable when people are of roughly the same developmental age, that is the field is concerned with intergenerational *transmission*. For example, psychiatric disorder in children is associated with disorder in their parents, but the *form* of the childhood disorder is not strongly related to the form of the parental illness, with the possible exception of depression. Childhood disorders associated with schizophrenia in parents show some specific interpersonal and neurodevelopmental features (Rutter, 1984) and there is some tendency for personality disorder in parents to be associated with conduct disorder in sons (Rutter and Quinton, 1984), but in both cases the childhood symptoms appear as precursors of the adult illness rather than as the disorder in its adult form. We do not yet know whether other childhood emotional and behavioural disorders commonly associated with parental illness are precursors of the parental type of disorder *in adulthood* or whether the continuities between disorders in childhood and adulthood are different depending on whether parental disorder is implicated or not (Rutter and Quinton, 1984). The intergenerational question is whether the parental disorder leads to problems in the next generation of adults and how such a link might be mediated. Of course, although intergenerational studies are concerned with continuities between parents and children this does not imply that the links are necessarily forged through family features, whether these be behavioural, attitudinal or genetic. Intergenerational continuities may also arise through social forces outside the family, as is the case with the transmission of earnings. For example, Atkinson and his colleagues (Atkinson *et al.*, 1983) have shown that parental earnings are strongly related to their children's educational level and this in turn to the children's earnings at a comparable stage in the life cycle. However, even when these educational differences are taken into account the children of higher-income earners have a clear advantage in the earnings market.

The term 'intergenerational' can be used to refer to continuities between the generations at any comparable age, for example in comparing experiences in childhood in both generations as Wadsworth has done for preschool education (Wadsworth, 1981), but should not be used to refer to intragenerational links between childhood and adulthood, or adulthood and old age. Intragenerational continuities are of central importance for understanding intergenerational ones but should not be confused with them. Particularly important in this regard are those processes where *experiences* in childhood affect development in such a way as to lead to *behaviours* in adulthood that reproduce for the next generation the childhood environment of the parents. In understanding these processes both the study of individual development and the study of sociological process is essential.

Association or process?

The definition of intergenerational studies proposed here implies that the focus of research should be on the processes linking behaviours and circumstances in two or more generations rather than on the size of the associations between them, or the extent to which certain population characteristics are increasing or decreasing in successive age cohorts. Such trends are central to demographic studies but, on their own, measures of intergenerational continuity tell us little about the extent or nature of intergenerational links. This is so for two reasons. First, if analyses are confined to reporting the proportion of adults with a particular characteristic who have parents or children with the same characteristic, the findings mean little. Changes in base rates within the population can readily create a quite misleading picture of continuity or discontinuity. For example, during a period when crime rates are rising, many more criminal adults will have criminal children than had criminal parents. Secondly, low correlations across generations may disguise quite strong associations in small subpopulations. For example, early loss of parent is weakly and inconsistently associated with depression in adulthood. However, Brown and his colleagues (Brown *et al.*, 1986) have shown that early loss is a key variable in setting in train a chain of circumstances leading to adult disorders of this kind.

Design and sampling

Real-time prospective studies (panel studies) have been argued to be the best design for longitudinal research, predominantly on the grounds that they avoid the problems inherent in other designs, which arise out of an inevitable reliance on long-term retrospective reporting. Within this approach age cohort studies, like the National Survey of Health and Development and the National Child Development Study (Fogelman, 1985), have been strikingly successful in tracking their samples to a point where intergenerational questions can be tackled. The advantages of national cohort studies lie in their large sample sizes and their representativeness. This latter feature is important where the nation is the appropriate focus for sampling, that is where data are required to answer questions on the distribution of characteristics across a national population or when the nation is a homogeneous or distinct cultural entity. However, the usefulness of national age cohorts depends a great deal on the kind of research question being posed. By their nature they are practically difficult to maintain, heterogeneous in character, and may undersample characteristics of research interest.

The advantages of size are further offset by inevitable limitations in data quality and coverage. This is a central problem in studies of intergenerational process because detailed assessments of both functioning and environment are often required. This is further complicated, as Wadsworth points out, by the fact that measures taken at one point in time may be inappropriate for later phases, or that variables relevant to theoretical interests at the time of follow-up may not have been adequately measured in earlier waves. Finally, it has to be realized that for intergenerational studies even this design will be retrospective for the parent who is not in the age cohort.

All these considerations mean that despite its apparent advantages this design should be avoided unless it is essential to the research question or to measurement (Robins, 1980). The intergenerational associations established by such studies are important starting points for research but the level of measurement makes the understanding of process problematical. Of course, where such samples have been collected, every effort should be made to use them to tackle intergenerational questions, although the studies may then come more to resemble the catch-up prospective design. The problems of missing data, either because their need was not initially realized or because of sample attrition during the course of the study, means that even this design is likely to need to use retrospective reporting to tackle many questions. In addition, as Wadsworth mentions, issues of intergenerational continuities always require data on both parents and ideally on all four grandparents, and whatever the sampling frame, recall is almost bound to play a part in data collection on many important family variables. The issue of 'retrospective recall' is discussed in the next section.

One further limit of the cohort approach for intergenerational studies is that, although the sample is representative of the age group of children selected and therefore also of their parents, their own children will be a progressively more unrepresentative sample of the population at any particular point of follow-up as the cohort selection age band narrows. For example, with a follow-up of a one-week birth cohort into their early thirties all the teenage children in the second generation will be children of teenage parents, and thus their behaviour may be unrepresentative of the behaviour of teenagers in the population as a whole. The whole cohort would need to be followed until all the offspring were through their teenage years before intergenerational comparisons on adolescent issues could be approached, but with the complication that period effects could not then be addressed.

An alternative to the real-time study is the catch-up prospective investigation, in which a group on whom systematic records exist from some time in the past are recontacted for further study. This can be a particularly effective method when the original data are directly relevant to the type of continuity of interest, as was the case in Robins' study of sociopathic personality (Robins, 1966) or Kolvin's follow-up of the Newcastle Thousand Families Study (Miller *et al.*, 1985). Such studies can answer questions concerning the outcome from particular behaviours or experiences, but, unless there are adequate comparison samples, they cannot explain the full range of the expression of a problem since they are likely to omit links due to background variables and also to omit current cases where problems do not have an intergenerational component.

A third approach is the retrospective study, in which a sample identified through the current occurence of some characteristic is chosen and life history data collected to examine intergenerational links. This approach has immense advantages in that the sample can be chosen on the basis of the *outcome* variable of interest, and the data on the previous generation can be collected with a specific research question in mind. However, this method can provide an estimate of the strength of an intergenerational link only if the selected sample is representative of the full range of outcomes on the variable of interest. In addition, on its own it is likely to be a risky procedure for the study of intergenerational processes unless it can be assumed that a particular characteristic is also well distributed in the previous generation. If this is not the case, an excessively large sample may need to be drawn in order to obtain a satisfactory number of cases on certain childhood variables.

Heterotypic continuity

Wadsworth lays strong emphasis on the need for intergenerational studies to make allowance for heterotypic continuity, and suggests that we provide for as many hypothesized outcomes as possible. In the present state of knowledge it is, of course, important to know the range of outcomes with which particular experiences or behaviours are associated. An understanding of intragenerational links of this kind is necessary also for the understanding of intergenerational processes. The ability to give leads on heterotypic continuity is seen to be a distinct feature of longitudinal age cohort studies and, indeed, such investigations are particularly valuable in this regard. The problem is whether they are also able to advance knowledge on the nature of the associations and here the measurement issue becomes crucial. It seems likely that when data are required on a more focused association, for example psychiatric disorders or parenting problems, other strategies are more informative. As yet combined retrospective–prospective strategies have been little used, but they have a number of distinct advantages.

Retrospective–prospective strategies

In order to circumvent the problems of both unanticipated antecedents and unanticipated consequences of some behaviour or experience a combined strategy can be particularly effective (Quinton and Rutter,

1984; Quinton, *et al.*, 1984). This approach is, in effect, a combination of catch-up prospective and follow-back investigations. In our studies of transmitted parenting difficulties, for example, parenting outcomes were examined for a high-risk group defined in terms of the experience of poor parenting in a group institutionalized in childhood as against a general population comparison sample; and the antecedents of poor parenting were examined in a follow-back study of adults showing poor parenting currently, that is having children currently in residential care, again in comparison with a general population group. This strategy allowed both an estimate of the extent of continuity looking backwards, the possible antecedents of poor parenting not occurring in the high-risk group, and the extent to which such problems arose anew in each generation unassociated with intergenerational factors. The point here is that relatively small samples could be used with the advantage of better quality data on family variables.

Retrospective reporting

It has been argued that even within the real-time prospective study the investigation of intergenerational questions will require some recourse to long-term retrospective reporting. The more inclusive term 'reporting' is to be preferred to 'recall' because in work of this nature we are often more interested in what individuals know about themselves from whatever source than in whether they remember particular events or experiences. Retrospective methods are needed for collecting data on life history over the years between waves in the data collection, for collecting data missing from particular waves because individuals were not interviewed then, and for collecting data on features of history and development that have only become of theoretical or practical interest since the study was first begun. Where life history data are important, retrospective methods will also be a major part of catch-up prospective designs, and are the necessary data collection method in follow-back approaches. A striking example of this is provided by Elder's follow-ups of the Oakland and Berkeley samples, (Elder *et al.*, 1984), where second- and third-generation data were initially collected in intensive short-term follow-up direct assessments, first-generation data from recall by the second generation, and some key third-generation data – on parenting – by recall by the fourth generation in adulthood.

The best-known evidence against the retrospective method is the study by Yarrow and her colleagues (Yarrow *et al.*, 1970), which compared mothers' reports of their children's development with systematic clinic and nursery school records, the reports being given up to 30 years after the children's births. In general, correlations between maternal reports and clinic records were low. More importantly, systematic biases were found, with mothers reporting fewer problems in their children's development than appeared in the records and also overestimating their children's abilities. These reports were influenced by the child's developmental history and by current child-rearing fashions.

However, before accepting that retrospective reports are necessarily flawed, we need to consider the possible sources of error and how these might be minimized. The first point to make is that in examining the reliability of reporting it is necessary to be sure that the data against which recall is being tested are themselves reliable. This assumption cannot usually be made except where the events recorded have a particular significance or finality, for example a date of death. Data on the variability in even good-quality clinic records are well illustrated in Tilley's recent study of mothers whose daughters were exposed *in utero* to the sex hormone diethylstilboestrol (Tilley *et al.*, 1985). As might be expected, clinics keeping centralized records had the most complete records, clinic records kept by individual physicians had more missing data, and mailed questionnaire responses from family physicians had the most omissions. But there was also evidence that *within* the centralized clinic group, missing data were more likely amongst the group exposed to the hormone. Because these variations existed in the quality of the criterion data, the authors concluded that the degree of agreement between the subjects and the records could be taken as an indication only of the reliability of accounts and not of their validity.

The majority of studies that have compared subjects' reports with written records have used hospital or clinic data. Two general conclusions can be drawn from these investigations: first, that reliable recall is more likely for events that carry some importance for the individual (Cannell, 1977), and secondly, *whether* events have happened is more accurately recalled than *when* they occurred. This can be so even for major happenings. For example, approximately 20–30% of women in two separate studies were more than one year out in the reporting of the date of a hysterectomy (Paganini-Hill and Ross, 1982; Bean *et al.*, 1979). In the dating of events there is a tendency for time periods, ages and quantities to be rounded. This process involved both interviewer and respondent effects (Baddeley, 1979).

The distinction between recall and reporting has already been drawn. As yet no studies have been published that assess recall of family relationships or reactions to events against systematic criterion data. As a consequence it is not possible to estimate the extent of unbiased forgetting. It may be that there are quite major losses of information in retrospective studies due to such processes, although it seems likely that a saliency rule will apply here also. Support for this comes from studies that have addressed the third issue in reporting: namely, whether there are *systematic* biases in recall. Here the question is whether a person's current circumstances or mental state affect the reporting of events or relationships. Some studies have suggested that this is the case. Wolkind and Coleman (1983) found that women currently anxious or depressed reported more parental marital problems than women who had been depressed but were now well. Robins (1966) found that adverse childhood events (as noted in clinic records) were more reliably reported by those with current psychosocial problems than by those who were now not disturbed. However, in a more systematic evaluation of the recall of childhood events after 30 to 50 years by siblings with and without current psychiatric problems, Robins has not replicated the biasing effect of current mental state (Robins *et al.*, 1985). Agreement between siblings was good for factual data such as the number of homes they lived in, schools attended and family socio-economic circumstances. Agreement was also good for parental behaviours such as marital disputes or involvement in community activities. Robins drew the important conclusion that what might be thought to involve 'forgetting' is attributable to the fact that what concerns us about family histories are feelings and attitudes that are intrinsically dependent on an individual interpretation and assessment of behaviour.

A number of important issues concerning retrospective reporting still remain to be investigated. Foremost amongst these is the comparison of accounts of family relationships and feelings against good criterion data, and the extent to which different data collection approaches are responsible for poor 'recall' or are effective in improving it. However, the overall level of agreement between siblings and the lack of major biases established by the Robins study make the method acceptable for scientific studies. Until the question of individual experiences, memories and reactions to childhood experiences are better understood it is preferable to place most weight on discrete events located within broad time periods, to concentrate on obtaining clear descriptions of events and relationships rather than on generalized recollections, and to use the reconstructive nature of memory (Bartlett, 1932) to locate events within a coherent life history framework.

Appropriate measures

Wadsworth raises a number of issues as to the quality and appropriateness of measurement and most of these problems are familiar: Do you use the same test as in the previous generation? How do you balance sample size and measurement adequacy? He rightly concludes that measurement decisions can only be made on the basis of the question you are trying to answer. However, I would like to discuss one other major conclusion that he comes to, and that is that continuous measures are better than categorical ones because the ability to rank individuals is a central advantage of intergenerational studies. Allowing for the fact that these remarks apply to his discussion of intragenerational continuities, I think that this view is mistaken. Whether ranking or absolute level is the more appropriate measurement strategy depends entirely on the question being asked. This can be illustrated with two examples, one concerning continuities in housing disadvantage and one concerning continuities in income. In McDowell's (1983) reanalysis of data for the National Survey of Health and Development, housing disadvantage in childhood was compared with that in adult life, an analysis of the change from 1948 to 1972. Whereas in 1948 some 45% of the sample were overcrowded and lacked at least two basic amenities, by 1972 this applied to fewer than 1%. However, all those ranked in the deprived group in 1972 had had a similar rank in 1948. Thus, although the quality of housing changed markedly, people's ranking was much more stable. Whether this should be considered an intergenerational continuity depends entirely on the question being asked. It is reasonable to ask whether status differences are maintained intergenerationally, but it is a different matter to conclude that those differences have the same *meaning* in each generation. If the focus of interest is the contribution of transmitted housing deprivation to intergenerational continuities in psychiatric problems, then the quality of housing is likely to be a more important variable. If the interest is in the structure of society, then considerations concerning continuities in ranking may be more important.

The example of continuities in income and earnings comes from Atkinson's follow-up (Atkinson *et al.*, 1983) of Rowntree's earlier study of poverty in York (Rowntree and Lavers, 1951). Here the authors used national assistance or social benefit definitions in each generation to produce a basis for examining intergenerational continuities. These again are sensible measurement decisions for examining this issue. However, the measures would have been problematical if the main interest was in intergenerational continuities in the level of resources that might affect the transmission of other problems, such as in parenting, where some measure of the relative value of benefit might be more appropriate.

Intergenerational process

Much has been made in this chapter of the importance of using intergenerational studies to investigate linking processes. Some observations are therefore in order on the complexities of these and what is required to understand them. Let me take one of Wadsworth's central examples – that of parental divorce and separation (Wadsworth, 1984; Wadsworth and Maclean, 1986). This is one of those cases where an experience in childhood may become a behaviour in adulthood, that is where the continuity is one that is likely to involve both the impact of the experience of divorce on personality development and also a negative effect on family income, educational opportunity and the like.

In this example the data from the British National Study show that the experience of parental marital breakdown is associated with a whole series of adult problems, including stomach ulcers, colitis and criminality in men, and divorce and illegitimate births in women. When these outcomes are *aggregated* the rates are twice as high amongst those with the experience of divorce as amongst those without. The findings for crimes against the person and 'psychosomatic' illness were particularly related to the experience of divorce under the age of five. In comparison, the experience of divorce after the age of five was related to poorer educational attainment and lower income at the age of 26 for men from working-class families. Two separate processes are hypothesized to explain these differences: the early experience of divorce is seen to work through effects on personality development and the later experience of divorce through disruption in school life, reduced expectations amongst teachers, and effects on self concepts.

It is not, of course, that these findings are inherently implausible – they certainly are not – but just that there are insufficient data to support such conclusions in competition with other hypotheses. The differential effects shown in his data of later family breakdown by social class suggest that complex links exist via the environment and not just through impacts on self-esteem. Secondly, in studies where more data are available it is clear that the links from early adverse experiences to the re-creation of this experience for others in adult life also take multiple routes, but they are routes in which environmental continuities and personality development are intertwined. For example, in our study of institution-reared children the experience of early family disruption was strongly related to the re-creation of disturbed family relationships in early adulthood. There were undoubtedly some continuities associated with disturbances in personality functioning but this was by no means the whole story. Earlier experiences also predicted later adverse experiences irrespective of the girls' functioning in early adolescence, at least as measured. Thus those coming from disrupted homes were more likely to return to them, more likely to leave home early because of this disruption, and more likely to become pregnant under the age of 19 regardless of whether they showed disorder in their teens or not. As a group the institutionalized women were much more likely to set up home with deviant men, but this link, too, was not related to their earlier functioning. The link did not relate to the degree of early family disruption nor to functioning in early adolescence either. In this case the risk applied to the group as a whole as a consequence of their early experience independent of any effects on their development (Quinton and Rutter, 1988).

It is clear from this example that the processes mediating intergenerational continuities can be exceedingly complex. For these women they involve environmental continuities independent of functioning, environmental continuities consequent upon their behaviour, whether related to psychopathology or not, as with early pregnancy, and links formed through restricted life opportunities applying to the group as a whole, as with the availability of spouses. Moreover, it was these linked environments that provided the contexts in which individual vulnerabilities were manifest, thus when the women, for one reason or another, were in currently satisfactory marital and material circumstances their functioning as parents was of the same quality as the general population sample, but when they were not so well placed they showed a substantial excess of difficulties.

The only data tracing comparable links across four generations come from Elder's follow-ups of the Berkeley cohort, where the interlinking of unstable/volatile personalities and unstable relationships (as instanced by marital problems and poor parenting) has been tracked (Elder *et al.*, 1984). Here the within-generation association between marital problems and personality difficulties seemed predominantly explained by the impact of personality problems on relationships. However, personality problems in one generation had no direct association with personality difficulties in the next when they did not also lead to marital problems, and it further seemed likely that marital problems had their effect on personality development for the next generation primarily through their association with parenting deficits. This is consistent with other findings that emphasize the ameliorating effects of good parent–child relationships in the presence of discord (Rutter, 1981). Strikingly, also, Elder was able to show the complex nature of the linking process. Some links via the environment arose independently of the actions of individuals, and others as a consequence of individual behaviour. An example of the first kind of link was when income loss in the Depression – which did not affect families selectively – exacerbated parenting problems and marital difficulties. An example of the second was a tendency for ill-tempered behaviour in childhood to be associated with more erratic, and therefore more stressful work records for men, and for women the probability of marrying lower-status husbands.

Conclusions

Wadsworth's chapter is valuable in pointing up the advantages of real-time longitudinal studies for the study of intergenerational links and the limitations of this approach for addressing particular intergenerational issues. My own preference is to restrict the use of the intergenerational label to studies that examine the nature of links between generations at the same stage in the life cycle, although it is clear that intragenerational studies are necessary for understanding these. The major problem in the choice of research design is the need for adequate measurement of family, developmental and environmental variables to enable the unravelling of intergenerational processes. Large-scale studies are important in showing the extent and range of continuity inter- and intragenerationally, but for many questions the measurement requirements necessitate more-focused studies with smaller samples. In both approaches it seems likely that reliance on retrospective reporting will remain inevitable. Efforts should therefore be made to understand better both the limits of this method of data collection and the contribution of instrument or interviewer error to inaccuracies in reporting.

References

Atkinson, A. B., Maynard, A. K. and Trinder, C. G. (1983) *Parents and children: incomes in two generations.* SSCR/DHSS studies in deprivation and disadvantage no. 10. London: Heinemann.

Baddeley, A. (1979) The limitations of human memory: implications for the design of retrospective surveys. In Moss, L. and Goldstein, H. (eds.) The recall method in social surveys. University of London Studies in Education no. 9, London: University of London Institute of Education, pp. 13–27.

Bartlett, F. C. (1932) *Remembering.* Cambridge: Cambridge University Press.

Bean, J. A., Leeper, D. P., Wallace, R. B., Sherman, B. M. and Jagger, H. (1979) Variations in the reporting of menstrual histories. *American Journal of Epidemiology*, **109**, 181–5.

Brown, G. W., Harris, T. and Bifulco, A. (1986) Long-term effects of early loss of parent. In Rutter, M., Izard, C. E. and Read, P. B. (eds.) *Depression in young people: developmental and clinical perspectives.* New York: Guilford Press, pp. 251–96.

Cannell, C. F. (1977) A summary of studies of interviewing methodology. *Vital and Health Statistics*, series 2, **69**, 1–78.

Elder, G. H., Capsi, A. and Downey, G. (1984) Problem behavior and family relationships: a multi-generation analysis. In Sorensen, A., Weinert, F. and Sherrod, L. (eds.) *Human development: interdisciplinary perspectives.* New York: Springer.

Fogelman, K. (1985) Exploiting longitudinal data: examples from the National Child Development Study. In Nicol, A. R. (ed.) *Longitudinal studies in child psychology and psychiatry: practical lessons from research experience.* Chichester: Wiley, pp. 241–61.

Glenn, N. D. (1977) *Cohort analysis.* Beverly Hills: Sage.

McDowell, L. (1983) Housing deprivation: an intergenerational approach. In Brown, M. (ed.) *The structure of disadvantage.* London: Heinemann, pp. 172–91.

Miller, F. J. W., Kolvin, I. and Fells, H. (1985) Becoming deprived: a cross-generation study based on the Newcastle upon Tyne 1000-family study. In Nicol, A. R. (ed.) *Longitudinal studies in child psychology and psychiatry: practical lessons from research experience.* Chichester: Wiley, pp. 223–40.

Paganini-Hill, A. and Ross, A. K. (1982) Reliability of recall of drug use and other health-related information. *American Journal of Epidemiology*, **116**, 114–22.

Quinton, D. (1985) Measuring intergenerational change: a view from developmental psychopathology. In *Measuring socio-demographic change.* Office of

Population Censuses and Statistics Occasional Paper, no. 34. London: OPCS, pp. 26–38.

Quinton, D. and Rutter, M. (1984) Parents with children in care, I. Current circumstances and parenting skills. *Journal of Child Psychology and Psychiatry*, 25, 211–29.

(1988) *Parenting breakdown: the making and breaking of intergenerational links*. Aldershot: Gower.

Quinton, D., Rutter, M. and Liddle, C. (1984) Institutional rearing, parenting difficulties and marital support. *Psychological Medicine*, 14, 107–24.

Robins, L. N. (1966) *Deviant children grown up*. Baltimore: Williams and Wilkins.

(1980) Longitudinal methods in the study of normal and pathological development. In Earls, F. (ed.) *Studies of children*. New York: Prodist, pp. 34–83.

Robins, L. N., Schoenberg, S. P., Holmes, S. J., Ratcliff, K. S., Benham, A. and Works, J. (1985) Early home environment and retrospective recall: a test of concordance between siblings with and without psychiatric disorders. *American Journal of Orthopsychiatry*, 55, 27–41.

Rowntree, B. S. and Lavers, G. R. (1951) *Poverty and the welfare state*. London: Longman Green.

Rutter, M. (1981) *Maternal deprivation reassessed*, 2nd edn. Harmondsworth: Penguin.

(1984) Psychopathology and development, I. Childhood antecedents of adult psychiatric disorder. *Australian and New Zealand Journal of Psychiatry*, 18, 225–34.

Rutter, M. and Quinton, D. (1984) Parental psychiatric disorder: effects on children. *Psychological Medicine*, 14, 853–80.

Tilley, B. C., Barnes, A. B., Bergstral, H. E., Labarthe, D., Noller, K. L., Colton, T. and Adam, A. (1985) A comparison of pregnancy history recall and medical records. *American Journal of Epidemiology*, 121, 269–81.

Wadsworth, M. E. J. (1981) Social class and generation differences in pre-school education. *British Journal of Sociology*, 32, 560–82.

(1984) Early stress and associations with adult health behaviour and parenting. In Butler, N. R. and Corner, B. D. (eds.) *Stress and disability in childhood*. Bristol: John Wright, pp. 100–4.

Wadsworth, M. E. J. and Maclean, M. (1986) Parents' divorce and children's life chances. *Children and Youth Services Review*, 8, 145–59.

Wolkind, S. N. and Coleman, E. Z. (1983) Adult psychiatric disorder and childhood experiences: the validity of retrospective data. *British Journal of Psychiatry*, 143, 188–91.

Yarrow, M. R., Campbell, J. D. and Burton, R. V. (1970) *Recollections of childhood: a study of the retrospective method*. Monographs of the Society for Research in Child Development 138, vol. 35, no. 5.

17 Causal paths, chains and strands

George W. Brown

Plenty of people would rather declare an event incredible than follow the sequence of cause and effect, measure the strength of links in a chain, each arising from the one before it and inseverably joined with it, secretly, in the mind.

Honoré de Balzac, Eugénie Grandet

The role of causality in human development is indisputable, and yet as we focus on trying to establish how an event at one point in time is linked to another some time later it may begin to seem arbitrary, if not irrelevant. As an alternative to tidy temporal progression, studies have begun to emphasize how human organism and context are embedded in each other and 'because organisms influence the context that influences them, they are products of their own development' (Lerner, 1983, p. 279). As long as the constraints of the wider social structure on the outcome of such interplay are not underestimated, it is difficult to deny the cogency of this, nor the force of the assertion that, because of this embeddedness, developmental analysis should deal with this intimate relation between organism and context, and not look on them as separate or independent 'entities' or 'elements' (Lerner, 1983, p. 279). Such fidelity to our lives as they are lived is not, however, necessarily the only, or even always the best, way to proceed. While I do not doubt the essential truth of this interactional perspective, it may be useful to start from the opposite position, that is to accept that we are probably dealing with non-existing 'entities' and 'elements', and yet to consider how far their coming-together appears to result in something else. The faith required is that the associations that emerge will be found eventually to parallel processes occurring in the individuals involved.

If we choose this route, it is essential to proceed in stages. Ideally we should establish elements quite widely dispersed in time and then go on in new studies to fill in some of the 'gaps'. The potential gain is some early glimpse of a larger picture. Inevitably as research progresses we will be forced to take into account some of the reciprocal processes of the interactional perspective. The success of the initial mapping is, however, not to be judged in terms of describing these, but in establishing experiences at widely spaced points of time that are relevant to some final outcome – albeit probably by processes of the utmost complexity.

285

My own predilection has been not to start with questions of development at all, but to establish in causal terms something about what is going on in the present. And because it is the present, research is able to have some of the characteristics of an interactional perspective, particularly a concern with context. We can then proceed to link this present with its past. It is this mapping of key points in a causal chain or series of chains that I propose to discuss. The platform provided by the initial intensive research is important to the extent that it provides a kernel of a theory about mechanisms and in this way a guide in our search for relevant 'entities' in the past. The initial research can also be important in so far as it uncovers the presence of subgroups in which effects of the past are potentiated. Thus the past loss of a mother may lead to depression only among those in current adverse conditions. In this way the present can act as a magnifying glass for the past and may allow quite complex causal models to be built despite relatively small numbers.

The approach nevertheless is schematic and exploratory. One could hardly embark on such an undertaking without some measure of voluntary blindness to the true complexity of things. Nonetheless there is a possible counterbalancing advantage: some chain of influence may emerge that a smaller and more intensive concentration on individual biographical details might miss. The fact that the analyst will be forever on the edge of dealing with complexities that are not readily encompassed in his schematic models does not seem to matter as long as these models are seen as pointers to other things.

Survey research provides one of the intellectual models of such an approach and here Lazarsfeld's account of the elaboration of variables through the creation and interpretation of partial tables has had a profound effect on social research, and a grasp of its principles is still immensely important for the consideration of causal relationships (e.g. Rosenberg, 1968). But during the 1970s a number of more sophisticated variations under the general title of path analysis were introduced, and one of the major purposes of this essay will be to contrast these with the traditional Lazarsfeldian approach to causal analysis. Path analysis is by no means always used in longitudinal research concerned with developmental issues and I want also to consider the implications of this, particularly for intensive studies with relatively small numbers. Two such recent intensive studies in London that dealt with relating early experience to current behaviour did not use path analysis. The first study, using a specially selected sample of 139 women living in Walthamstow with an early loss of a mother (by death or separation of at least 12 months before the age of 17) and a comparison series from the same population, confirmed that such a loss relates to a considerably increased risk of clinical depression in adult life (Brown *et al.*, 1986a; Harris *et al.*, 1986; 1987a). The experience of marked rejection, or indifference, or marked lack of control, on the part of key care-takers – called 'lack of care' – was a critical link between such loss and later depression. A study by Quinton and his colleagues (Quinton and Rutter, 1984a, b; Quinton *et al.*, 1984; Rutter *et al.*, 1983) based on 81 women who had been taken into care in childhood, and a comparison series of children from the same area of London, isolated somewhat comparable effects, but their major emphasis has been on the quality of parenting in adulthood.

At this early point I should note that in order to simplify my presentation I will deal only with variables expressed as dichotomies and will ignore altogether the question of statistical significance. I do not believe this simplification affects any of the conclusions I reach.

In discussing the two approaches I will deal with a number of related issues. The most important of these are (a) the role of statistical interaction, and whether to consider so-called additive or multiplicative forms; (b) the use of categorical variables; (c) the problem of small numbers; (d) the need to specify all variables of importance and the role of good measurement if this is to be done; and (e) the potential clash of a path analytic approach with a thorough exploration of survey material and the tension between 'exploratory' and 'confirmatory' approaches to data. In general I conclude that path analysis has a role, perhaps at times an important one, in developmental research, but that it is essential to see it as only one of a number of approaches to analysis, and one that can be expected to play a less central role as we approach more closely the kind of interactional perspective outlined earlier.

I will follow Hellevik's (1984) terminology and call the first of these broad approaches prediction analysis, that is how variables combine to predict a particular outcome, irrespective of whether they are causally interrelated. Its importance lies in the fact that it deals with interactive effects. Lazarsfeld discussed it in terms of various ways of 'specifying' the conditions under which an outcome occurred (e.g. Galtung, 1967; Rosenberg, 1968, chapter 6). Path analysis, by contrast, although it can also be used to predict, typically ignores the presence of any interactive effects and builds on the degree to which the non-outcome variables are causally interrelated.

Although the structural equation and causal modelling literature make clear that such interactive effects can be dealt with in the path analytic tradition (e.g. Macdonald, 1977; Asher, 1983), there is a good deal of conceptual and methodological disagreement as to how they should be analysed and interpreted (e.g. Cleary and Kessler, 1982). Much of the point in what follows is that the inclusion of such effects is not easily achieved and that in practice they are usually ignored in path diagrams and in the calculation of causal effects from them. It is the implications of this practice that I will explore rather than deal with criticisms of path analysis in any fundamental sense.

Two approaches to the analysis of causal effects

Prediction analysis, the first of the approaches, considers the rate of an outcome variable in terms of the various possible combinations formed by the non-outcome variables, and this was the approach used in the two London Studies. Interaction is seen in a traditional sense and this should perhaps be spelt out. In terms of a 2 × 2 × 2 table let 1 and 2 represent two independent factors and a, b, c and d represent proportions of a third dependent factor in the four cells formed by a combination of 1 and 2:

$$
\begin{array}{ccc}
 & \multicolumn{2}{c}{1} \\
 & \text{yes} & \text{no} \\
\text{yes} & a & b \\
2 & & \\
\text{no} & c & d \\
\end{array}
$$

The effect of variable 1 is $(c - d)$ and 2 is $(b - d)$; d is subtracted in each instance as it represents a state of affairs when neither 1 nor 2 occur. This is also known as a partial or conditional association. Thus a simple additive effect of 1 and 2 will be $(b - d) + (c - d)$. Interaction represents the excess in terms of a proportion when these terms plus what could be expected in any case without them (i.e. d) is subtracted from the effect when 1 and 2 occur together (Galtung, 1967, p. 415):

$$\text{Excess (interaction)} = a - [(b - d) + (c - d) + d]$$

Therefore we have the possibility of variable effects, an interactive effect and a constant. The approach has the conceptual advantage of extracting any interaction from the 'main effects' of the non-outcome variables. (In the terminology of analysis of variance, variable effects could be considered 'main effects' when interaction is not present). In order to illustrate prediction analysis I anticipate some of the Walthamstow material and give in Table 1 the proportion depressed among those with loss of mother in terms of the eight possible combinations formed by the three dichotomous variables lack of care in childhood, current social class status, and low intimacy or undependability of husband. The causal effects are based on differences in proportions.

There is clearly a strong interactive effect in both the left- and right-hand parts of Table 1, distinguished by whether or not there is 'low intimacy or undependability of husband'. If the proportion of .68 experiencing depression when all three factors are present is divided into its component parts, much the largest is due to statistical interaction (.53) (see Table 1B). The calculations involved in obtaining the effects in Table 1B are straightforward. For example, the effect of lack of care (.10) is obtained by subtracting the proportion depressed (.07) when none of the three factors are present from the proportion depressed (.17) when only

Table 1 *Proportion depressed among women with early loss of mother in Walthamstow by lack of care, current class status and low intimacy or undependability of husband*

	A. Low intimacy or undependability of husband				
Lack of care	Yes		No		
	Working class	Middle class	Working class	Middle class	Total
Yes	.68 (13/19)	.27 (4/15)	.31 (4/13)	.17 (4/24)	.35 (25/71)
No	.17 (1/6)	.06 (1/16)	.06 (1/17)	.07 (2/29)	.07 (5/68)

B. Decomposition of proportion depressed (.68)

1.	Lack of care	.10	
2.	Low intimacy or undependability of husband	−.01	.08
3.	Social class	−.01	
1 × 2		.11	
1 × 3		.15	
2 × 3		.12	.53
1 × 2 × 3		.15	
Constant		.07	
Total		.68	

lack of care is present. The various interactive effects are obtained by subtracting such variable effects from the proportion depressed when different combinations of the variables are present (Galtung, 1967; Hellevik, 1984, p. 162). For example, the interaction of lack of care (1) with working-class status (3) is calculated as the change in the effect of lack of care when the value of social class moves from absent (middle class) to present (working class) with the other variable, low intimacy (2), absent. Only the right-hand subtable is therefore involved and the calculation has the same form as in the 2 × 2 × 2 table discussed earlier. That is:

Interaction 1 × 3 = .31 − [(.17 − .07) + (.06 − .07) + .07] = .15

To calculate the interaction involving all three independent variables, one considers the changes in the interaction between variables 1 and 3 as the second changes from absent to present. This is done by calculating the interaction of 1 and 3 based on the left-hand subtable where 2 is present (i.e. .30) and subtracting from it the interaction already obtained (i.e. .15).

In terms of the results in Table 1B, 89% of the rate of depression due to all three factors occurring together (i.e. .68 − .07 = .61) is due to some form of statistical interaction. Only lack of care shows an effect on its own and this is modest compared with the overall importance of the interactive effects.

It can be easily overlooked that additive rather than multiplicative interaction is used in such calculations. If, by contrast, effects are multiplied, the size of interactive effects can be reduced or may even disappear altogether (see Brown and Harris, 1986, pp. 152–7; Brown, 1986; Rutter, 1983). Logistic regression in recent years has provided a powerful method of analysing such tables. However, in its usual hier-archical form, it deals only with multiplicative interaction. The issue of what kind of interaction to use has led to a good deal of controversy. It is probably useful, therefore, to bear in mind that a multiplicative interactive approach runs counter to the straightforward hypotheses usually con-sidered in terms of the various interactions in the table just discussed (Rutter, 1983). I will use only an additive approach (which is, for example, provided by the binary regression used in this essay), but I will return later to some of the implications of this choice.

The second of the two approaches, path analysis, as already noted, takes a quite different approach and one in which the time order of variables is critical – in prediction analysis it is strictly only necessary to establish that the outcome variable occurs after the others. Unlike prediction analysis it is concerned with causal links between non-outcome variables, that is not only with the link of lack of care to depression, but whether, for example, low intimacy intervenes between lack of care and depression, and whether social class can explain the association between the two in the sense of bringing about a spurious link. To do this the association between every pair of factors is considered in the light of the other factors occurring prior to the latest one of a pair. In terms of the epigraph it follows Balzac's view that a causal chain involves events that are 'inseverably joined'. As just seen, an alternative view is inherent in prediction analysis. This depends, as in Table 1B, on decomposing the proportions of an outcome variable in a multivariable table into variable effects, interaction effects and a constant. These can be then used to predict the proportion of the outcome variable for any combination of the non-outcome variables whether or not they are causally linked. Path analysis, by contrast, is concerned with decomposing a particular outcome, say the development of depression, into causal components. In Table 1B it would be concerned with calculating the relative contribution of lack of care, low intimacy and social class to bringing about depression.

The approach is usually associated with regression and the use of non-categorical measures, but a recent stimulating discussion by Hellevik (1984) makes clear that it is possible to utilize differences in proportions as the basis for calculating path coefficients. While there is always a possibility that the use of dichotomies will lead to an important loss of information, this is by no means always the case. Effects dealt with in the social sciences are surprisingly often well represented by dichotomies, and their use has the advantage of being readily understandable.[1] However, if proportions are used, it is desirable to employ a quite sophisticated weighting procedure to combine effects in the partial tables, particularly if interaction effects are present. In fact, using a weighting scheme that takes account of how near to the extremes of 0.0 or 1.0 the proportions involved are, and hence to an undesirable lowering of variance (Boyle, 1966), gives results that in most instances are close to those obtained by using binary regression (Hellevik, 1984, chapter 9).[2] I give only an elementary introduction that concentrates on the decomposition of basic associations between variables in a path diagram. I have not attempted to deal systematically with the underlying structural equations that are calculated for each factor, which include the coefficients for variables having a direct impact on a particular variable, and also an intercept. I have avoided more complex issues, such as reciprocal effects, altogether (Macdonald, 1977).

Of the various path analytic techniques the most straightforward is effects analysis since it deals only with that part of a path diagram showing direct effects on an outcome variable (Davis, 1985). In a simple three-variable situation, as in Figure 1, where variable Y intervenes in time between variables X and Z, the path coefficient reflecting the *direct* effect of X and Z is obtained by controlling for Y.

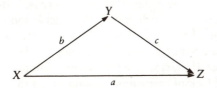

Figure 1   Simple three-variable path model (direct effects)

Given that the variables are all positively associated, it will be less than the association between X and Z because of the *indirect* effect of X on Z via Y. In the same way the direct effect of Y on Z is obtained by controlling for X to give Z. This is less than the association between Y and Z because a part is spurious, that is brought about by the link of X with Y, and X with Z. The overall causal effect of X *and* Y on Z can be obtained by adding these two direct effects.

A second step involves considering a *full* path diagram that takes

[1] The use of proportional differences does not entirely rule out using non-dichotomies (see Hellevik, 1984; and Davis, 1975; 1976).
[2] However, binary regression does not supply the important partial tables given by the proportional difference approach of prediction analysis and in this sense one is kept more distant from the actual data – an issue to be discussed later. Hellevik (1984, p. 169) also notes that under certain circumstances binary regression may give more accurate results and in the present account, therefore, coefficients from bivariate regression have been given if there is any divergence between the two methods.

account of all possible paths. In the present example this involves calculating b, which is simply the association of X and Y, since with only three variables there is no other variable prior in time to X and Y that needs to be controlled for. With more variables the size of effects may be calculated through any number of distinct paths. In the three-variable case there is only one indirect effect, that of X on Z via Y, which is calculated by multiplying the two relevant path coefficients b and c. An alternative way of conceiving this effect is to see it as the association of X and Z minus the path coefficient representing the direct effect of X upon Z.

Before proceeding it may be useful to summarize the differences between the two approaches used to describe the data in Table 1. In prediction analysis the proportion depressed when all three factors are present (.68) can be reproduced by adding together all the effects as long as a constant (.07) is included to take account of the rate of depression when none of the three factors are present. This breakdown is shown in the left-hand column of Table 2.

In the right-hand column, by way of contrast, are the three direct effects of factors derived from path analysis with a total causal effect of .56. Therefore both methods give much the same overall assessment of the predictive power of the factors as a whole. But in the case of path analysis interactive effects are not isolated as such. The indirect effects are given separately in Table 2: they cannot be included in the total causal effect as their contribution has already been included in the calculation of the direct effects – see the foot of the right-hand column. However, the indirect effects have two important functions. First, they can be used to estimate the *total* causal effect of a factor. They show, for example, that in addition to a direct effect of lack of care on depression of .24 there is an indirect one of .04 via other factors. Nonetheless, in this instance the total effect of lack of care of .28 (i.e. .24 'direct' + .04 'indirect') still falls well short of that of .51 obtained by prediction analysis (i.e. .10 'variable effect' + .11 'interaction' + .15 'interaction' + .15 'interaction'). The reason for this is that the path analysis only took account of other factors in relation to the effect of lack of care in so far as lack of care had a causal effect on them, that is while in the two approaches the total causal effect of *all* variables will be much the same, the total causal effect of *individual* factors will be a good deal lower in path analysis if interactive effects are present among variables that are not strongly correlated. The second important function of indirect effects is that they can be used to calculate the strength of a particular indirect path, say of lack of care on depression via social class.

Path analysis and the Walthamstow study on early loss of mother

Following this general introduction, I shall now turn to a more detailed consideration of the Walthamstow material, and for the first time consider

Table 2. *Contrasting results of two approaches to causality based on the data given in Table 1*

		ADDITIVE MODEL Variable effects	PATH ANALYSIS Direct effects
1.	Lack of care	.10	.24
2.	Low intimacy or undependability of husband	−.01	.15
3.	Social class	−.01	.17
		Interactive effects	
1 × 2		.11	
1 × 3		.15	
2 × 3		.12	
1 × 2 × 3		.15	
Total		.61	.56
Constant		.07	
Proportion associated with the experience of all three factors		.68	
			Indirect effects
1.	Lack of care (via class)		.04
2.	Class (via low intimacy or undependability of husband)		.01
3.	Undependability		.00
	Total		.05

them in terms of path analysis. The model that my colleagues and I have developed on the basis of prior analyses is complex and its general structure best characterized by two distinct strands that link experiences surrounding early loss of mother with later clinical depression (Brown *et al.*, 1986b; Harris *et al.*, 1986; 1987a). The first deals with experiences in the woman's external world, for instance with quality of care by parents or parent substitutes before and after the loss of mother, circumstances surrounding leaving home, premarital pregnancy and severe life events occurring to her in connection with marriage or motherhood. Although external characteristics are emphasized in this strand, the assumption is that their importance will tend to lie in their impact on a woman's idea of herself and her future. By contrast, the second strand deals directly with the internal characteristics of the woman, particularly salient attitudes about her self and her world, and styles of attachment that would be likely to influence the way she tackles problems concerning core relationships in her life and the quality of the relationships she forms. In dealing with strand 2, particular emphasis has been placed on the cognitive sets of low self-esteem and 'helplessness'. Of course, in so far as such a cognitive set is present it is likely to relate in a significant way to some aspects of self on which the experiences of strand 1 are also likely to impinge. Implicit in the very idea of such strands is some sense of continuity. We have likened strand 1 to a conveyor belt that will tend to carry a woman into increasing difficulties – but at the same time there is nothing inevitable about it. The most we wish to suggest is that in general it proves increasingly difficult to get off the conveyor belt. A further complication is, of course, that strand 1 and strand 2 will inevitably influence each other over time and therefore reflect something of the interactional perspective discussed in my opening paragraph. Any failure, for example, at the level of strand 1 will tend to influence feelings of helplessness, a strand 2 phenomenon, and this will tend to feed back onto the impact of experience of the external world.

Our research strategy has been to establish evidence for strand 1 effects in terms of critical experiences that are not only 'hard', but also readily dateable in time, for instance clear evidence of marked rejecting behaviour on the part of key care-takers, experience of institutions, premarital pregnancy, and so on. And given that links are established between such experiences, and between them and later depression, it is possible to feel more confident about incorporating 'softer' variables into the model in as much as they correlate with the structure provided by the 'hard' material.

The number of women we could study with our investigator-based approach to measurement was limited. Of the women we studied 139 had lost a mother before the age of 17 and such numbers meant that in our main analysis we had to proceed by slowly working through the mass of material we had collected, trying to isolate factors of key importance through none too complex cross-tabulations. And even when we had settled on factors of likely importance there were many contenders. We therefore proceeded by concentrating on major parts of the two strands in the hope that the various partial perspectives they gave would in the end convey a picture that made some overall sense.

Our small comparison group was specially matched with the 139 with early loss of mother on factors such as current social class, and we were therefore not dealing with a representative sample of the Walthamstow population. In order to avoid the complexities of trying to 'weight' such a series, two types of analysis were carried out. The comparison series was first used to establish certain key results concerning loss of mother, for example that loss of mother roughly doubled the risk of depression in adult life. We also utilized the comparison series to rule out possible confounding factors. Once this had been done we moved to an analysis that dealt only with those with loss of mother, and in this way we explored the pathways by which such loss had had its long-term effect. Clearly, circumspection must be shown about evidence emerging from such a restricted analysis. Fortunately, the results of a recent survey in Islington, not primarily designed to look at the impact of early loss, have broadly confirmed the basic findings (see Bifulco *et al.*, 1987).

This traditional approach to analysis did provide us with a comprehensive model and, since it is on the basis of this that I have embarked upon the present path analytic exercise, I will say a little more about it in substantive terms. The key initial links in terms of strand 1 start with loss of mother, move to lack of care by parent or surrogate parent figures and then to premarital pregnancy. At this point matters become more complex. Failure to cope adequately with premarital pregnancy is associated with subsequent working-class status, and in this way with an eventual increased risk of depression. However, in addition, premarital pregnancy, irrespective of any inadequacy in coping with it, is associated with an increased risk, but only among working-class women, that is there is interaction between premarital pregnancy and social class.

The situation for middle-class women is more straightforward. Here lack of care simply relates to an increased risk of depression with no role for premarital pregnancy, although risk is increased for a woman with lack of care if she also marries early. Any understanding of the failure of premarital pregnancy to relate to depression among middle-class women relies on the fact that those who successfully cope with it tend more often to rise in class status compared with their father. Unfortunately, in the current environment, no systematic measurement was made of life events and difficulties as we were restricted by time and we wished to devote most attention to the past, but it should be noted that having poor support, judged by, for example, undependability in a husband or lack of an intimate close tie with him, was related to an increased risk of depression.

The present path analytic exercise began by considering the following variables that had the highest zero-order associations with depression – childhood lack of care, premarital pregnancy, current working-class status, current low intimacy or undependability of spouse, current situational helplessness, helplessness in childhood, current lack of employment, and having three or more children under 15 at home. Numbers were too small to cope with the analysis of eight variables, so I started by using the first four of these, with current depression as the outcome variable. In making the choice of these four I had in mind that the helplessness variables were too 'soft' to include at an early stage and the last two variables had rather less strong associations than the rest. With the dependent variable, depression, included, each possible pair of the five variables was considered in terms of time order, and the difference in proportions between the earlier and the later variable has been adjusted for the effects of all other variables prior in time to either of them (see

Table 3 *Causal interpretation of path effects and depression shown in figure 2: first analysis of women with early loss of mother in Walthamstow*

	Causal effects in terms of proportion depressed			
	Lack of care	Premarital pregnancy	Working-class status	Low intimacy or undependability of husband
Basic difference in proportions – bivariate associations	.28	.27	.21	.21
Total causal effect[a]	.28	.20	.15	.13
Direct causal effect[b]	.21	.14	.15	.13
Indirect causal effect[c]	.07	.06	.00	.00
Spurious effect	.00	.07	.06	.08

[a] i.e. net prior variables.
[b] i.e. net of all other non-outcome variables.
[c] i.e. due to intervening variables.

Figure 2). Loss of mother itself does not appear as we are only dealing with those women with such a loss, but it will be recalled that its entire effect on depression is mediated by lack of care. With such a diagram it is possible to use the coefficients (based on differences in proportions) to work out the direct effects on depression of each factor. The contribution to depression of lack of care is greatest (.21), followed by working-class status (.15), premarital pregnancy (.14) and finally low intimacy or undependability of husband (.13). The comparable original zero order associations are .28, .27, .21 and .21 respectively, and therefore the effect of each variable was reduced when allowance was made for the influence of others.

As already discussed, actual paths between any number of variables can also be calculated. (As there is no link between working-class status and low intimacy or undependability of husband this path has not been included.) Table 3 gives the contribution of each factor in terms of direct effects (already presented), and indirect and spurious effects. For example, the indirect path from premarital pregnancy is calculated by multiplying the path coefficient linking it and class status by that linking class status and depression (.21 × .15 = .03), and adding the result to a similar calculation with coefficients linking premarital pregnancy, low intimacy and undependability of husband, and depression (.23 × .13 = .03). This gives, as shown in Table 3, a total indirect effect of .06. The total causal effect (row 2) is the sum of the direct (row 3) and indirect (row 4) effects. The difference between total causal effect and the original bivariate association gives the spurious effect. The main message appears to be that

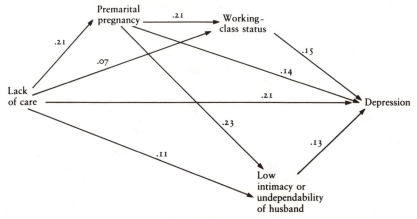

Figure 2   Path diagram for 139 women in Walthamstow with early loss of mother

the direct effect of lack of care is far more important than its indirect effects, and the basic association between the other variables and depression contain moderately large spurious components.

The large direct effect of lack of care was surprising. Perhaps influenced by the prediction analysis, I had expected it to be mediated to a far greater extent through other factors in the model. The most likely explanation seemed to be that the model had two rather poorly measured factors immediately before depression. The measure of support by husband had been influenced by the Camberwell research and ignored support from anyone close who was not a man. Recent work in Islington has made it clear that support from other close ties can also be protective, particularly if the woman is neither married nor cohabiting (Brown *et al.*, 1986a). Furthermore, current social-class status is at best a crude indicator of current adversity. A more comprehensive measure of support ('poor support') was therefore created by the additional consideration of close ties with someone other than a husband or boyfriend. Also a *post hoc* estimate was made of the occurrence of severe events and major difficulties before the onset of the depression. Although this must be an approximate estimate, we had collected a good deal of material about each woman in our lengthy interviews and we felt in most instances that our material was good enough to make this rating.

When these refined data were first examined in terms of a prediction analysis (see Table 4), it did indeed seem as if the picture might have changed as a result of improving the two measures. Table 4 shows that lack of care has *no* effect on its own; as many as one-third of those with lack of care have neither a provoking agent nor poor support and none of these is currently depressed (0/24) compared with 53% (25/47) of those

Table 4 *Proportion depressed among women with early loss of mother in Walthamstow by lack of care, presence of provoking agent in year before onset/interview and refined measure of poor support*

| | A. Refined measure of poor support | | | | |
| | Yes | | No | | |
Lack of care	Provoking agent	No provoking agent	Provoking agent	No provoking agent	Total
Yes	.63 (15/24)	.50 (2/4)	.42 (8/19)	.00 (0/24)	.35 (25/71)
No	.20 (1/5)	.00 (0/10)	.25 (3/12)	.02 (1/41)	.07 (5/68)

	B. Decomposition of proportion depressed (.63)	
1.	Lack of care	−.02 ⎫
2.	Poor support	−.02 ⎬ .19
3.	Provoking agent	.23 ⎭
1 × 2		.52 ⎫
1 × 3		.19 ⎬ .42
2 × 3		−.03 ⎪
1 × 2 × 3		−.26 ⎭
Constant		.02
Total		.63

Table 5 *Causal interpretation of path effects and depression: second analysis of women with early loss of mother in Walthamstow*

| | Causal effects in terms of proportion depressed | | | |
	Lack of care	Premarital pregnancy	Poor support	Provoking agent
Basic difference in proportions – bivariate associations	.28	.27	.29	.38
Total causal effect[a]	.27	.19	.19	.31
Direct causal effect[b]	.13	.07	.13	.31
Indirect causal effect[c]	.14	.12	.06	.00
Spurious effect	.01	.09	.10	.07

[a] i.e. net prior variables.
[b] i.e. net of all other non-outcome variables.
[c] i.e. due to intervening variables.

others with lack of care and at least one of these other agents. Decomposition of the proportion depressed shows the same: lack of care only has an effect in interaction with factors in the current environment (see Table 4B).

The path analysis, however, again gives a quite different impression. The results did not diverge from the first path analysis (see Table 2) nearly as much as had been expected. The direct effects of the new factors on depression were, as predicted, a good deal larger than the original factors of the first analysis they had replaced, with a coefficient of .29 for poor support and .38 for provoking agent. Yet despite this improvement about half the causal effect of lack of care remained direct and not via other factors in the model (see Table 5).

What, then, can be made so far of the three sets of results, and in particular how should the important role of lack of care be interpreted in terms of causal chains? The large direct effects of lack of care shown by path analysis follows from its concern with the causal links between non-outcome variables; in this way it usefully underlines our ignorance of the mechanism by which lack of care manages to have an important long-term effect – not by causing provoking agents and poor support, but by potentiating their effects, that is in interaction with them. The strict implication is that the lack-of-care experience is in some way continuing into the present and then interacting with poor support and provoking agent. It is a message that might easily be overlooked if we used only prediction analysis. But can more be said?

The concept of causal chain

The causal chains I have dealt with so far consist of a series of linked paths. But perhaps this usage is too limited. Might there be something to be said for including *any* factor that potentiates an earlier experience, even if the two factors are not linked in a causal sense? Since the subsequent experience will be bound to occur in some of the population, the interplay between the two should perhaps be seen in terms of a causal chain, in the sense of reflecting a set of experiences that have a certain probability of occurring together and which together serve to influence a particular outcome. (Such an influence may to be increase or decrease risk.) By definition any such effect must be interactive in a statistical sense. In terms of the current environment it has already been shown that powerful statistical interactive effects are present in the case of early lack of care and depression (see Table 2). However, it is probably useful here to distinguish contemporary from other intervening experiences. For instance, for middle-class women lack of care is *only* related to a raised risk of depression in those instances where they married early (see Table 6). Although the lack of care is quite unrelated to the marrying early, the two do have the hallmarks of an interactive causal chain in the sense that in some way the experience of early marriage is associated with an especially marked reaction among those with lack of care, and that some of those with lack of care will inevitably be caught up in such an experience.

Table 6 *Proportion depressed among middle-class women in Walthamstow with early loss of mother by experience of lack of care and early marriage*

	Lack of care	
Early marriage	Yes	No
Yes	.38 (6/16)	.00 (0/12)
No	.09 (2/23)	.09 (3/33)

It may be useful to conceive of at least three types of causal chain, partly on theoretical, partly on heuristic, and partly on practical grounds:

1. A 'related' chain, which is formed by an indirect path from an early factor to an outcome variable. The linking, intervening factors may involve only the past, only the present, or past and present. If there is more than one intervening factor, the chain may be conceived either in terms of a series of related causal links or in terms of their total effect. Thus the total 'related' effect of variable 1 in the following would be the sum of the indirect paths $1 \rightarrow 2 \rightarrow 3 \rightarrow 5$, $1 \rightarrow 3 \rightarrow 5$, and $1 \rightarrow 4 \rightarrow 5$, ignoring $1 \rightarrow 5$:

$$2$$

$$1 \qquad\qquad 3$$

$$5$$

$$4$$

2. This kind of related complex is what is meant by the term chain and is usually assumed to exist in path diagrams. But the word also has a second meaning: it can convey that two factors are linked even if one does not actually lead to the other, but once linked they form a unity which leads on further. In this sense an 'early interactive' chain is one in which the impact of a factor in the past on outcome is potentiated in an interactive sense by a following factor or factors also in the past, but which are not related to the first (e.g. lack of care, early marriage, and depression, among middle-class women).

3. A 'late interactive' chain is in every way comparable to this, but involves factors in the present interacting with earlier ones from either the past or the present. An extreme example of this occurs when the interaction involves only a factor in the distant past and one in the present (e.g. lack of care, provoking agent, and depression).

These three types can obviously combine in various ways, but only the first is a causal chain in the traditional sense. Indeed, it might be useful to use the more generic term 'strand', an interweaving of chains, to convey that in practice they may occur together. Evidence for such causal chains should in any case only serve as a backdrop for more intensive inquiry. There is, for example, an interesting alternative interpretation of the early interactive chain of lack of care, early marriage, and depression, among middle-class women. It is possible that only some of the lack of care experienced had been harmful – either because the measure encompasses a range of experience and some of the women fell at the more benign pole, or because of some basic resilience in the girl. Given this, early marriage might have no causal effect in itself, but may have served to highlight the women whose early experience had been the most harmful. For example, this might arise because early marriage among those most affected was associated with a greater need to leave home or to be 'looked after'. The variable 'early marriage' would then have provided a form of *refinement* of the lack of care measure. I give this example, not to argue for it, but to illustrate the likely need for more detailed research. The urgency to isolate intervening experiences of importance would, of course, be increased if early marriage merely served to improve the measurement of lack of care.

So far, therefore, only a part of the effect of lack of care on depression (i.e. the .14 indirect effect in Table 5) has been shown to be part of a related chain of effects. Some of the remaining influence is certainly due to an early interactive effect because of the way early marriage increases the impact of lack of care among middle-class women. However, a good deal of the direct effect of lack of care left when the related chain is allowed for is accounted for by later interactive effects of factors such as poor support and the provoking agents associated with a working-class position.

However, it would be foolhardy to use the idea of interactive chains to avoid altogether the challenge of these path analyses. In particular, the idea of a pure late interactive effect must be suspect. Although there are influential aetiological theories in psychiatry that argue something of the sort – Beck's cognitive model of depression for instance – it does not seem particularly likely that an effect would remain dormant for so long. Therefore the presence, as in the Walthamstow results, of the strong late interactive effects of lack of care is bound to be felt to demand urgent attention – either to establish that there are earlier intervening links, or, at least, to start to spell out something of the mechanisms involved in the delay.

Fortunately, it is now possible to supplement the Walthamstow data with new material from a study of a random sample of women with children at home living in Islington in north London. The two populations have certain differences – in particular the Islington women were almost entirely working class, they lived in a more deprived area of London, and they were born approximately ten years later. All three differences probably contributed to the fact that premarital pregnancy was much more common among the women in Islington who were followed up one year after the initial interview – 49% (174/353) versus 24% (33/139) among the Walthamstow women with loss of mother – and it therefore follows that premarital pregnancy may well have a somewhat different significance in Islington. Nonetheless, despite such differences, the basic finding concerning lack of care was repeated: among those followed up 41% (26/63) with lack of care were either cases of depression at the time of our first contact, or developed such a depressive condition in the following year, compared with 20% (56/290) of other women ($p < .001$) (Bifulco *et al.*, 1987).

Path models of the Islington material

The Islington study involved two contacts with the women roughly one year apart and was especially designed to tackle the issue of onset of depression. The longitudinal design meant that 'softer' factors, such as self-esteem, could be measured at the time of first contact, that is well before any onset of depression in the follow-up year that we wished to explain. Henceforth, I will concentrate on those women developing depression in the follow-up year, excluding those with depression at the time of our first contact, as this adds to the precision of a causal analysis.

Two path analyses have so far been carried out. In the first, the second Walthamstow analysis was followed quite closely using an index reflecting negative experiences during the three months before our first interview with the women and also a direct measure of provoking agents occurring in the follow-up year. (For women with an onset of depression only those events occurring before onset were included.) The 'negativity of core relationship index' was designed as an overall measure of quality of life and was developed by selecting 'objective' measures of daily life that were related to low self-esteem, once women suffering from clinical depression had been excluded. It includes, for instance, three measures of negative interaction – with husband, with children and with persons outside the home. The overall results are broadly similar to Walthamstow, although premarital pregnancy plays a less significant role, but even with this tighter design a path analysis still shows that the greater part of the impact of lack of care is a direct one and not part of a *related* causal chain. The basic proportional association of .13 between lack of care and onset is only reduced to .09 when premarital pregnancy, provoking agents and negative context are taken into account, that is a reduction of just over a quarter. It is a result, therefore, that remains not very different from that in Walthamstow (see Table 7 for further details).

Second path analysis of Islington women

Due to changing societal values premarital pregnancy as such may well have had a somewhat different significance in Islington than in Waltham-

Table 7 *Causal interpretation of path effects on depression (first analysis of Islington women: onset cases of depression N = 303)*

	Causal effects in terms of proportions depressed			
	Lack of care	Premarital pregnancy	Negative context	Provoking agent
Basic difference in proportions – bivariate associations	.13	.04	.09	.19
Total causal effect[a]	.13	.02	.08	.18
Direct causal effect[b]	.09	−.03	.04	.19
Indirect causal effect[c]	.04	.05	.04	.00
Spurious effect	.00	.02	.01	.01

[a] i.e. net prior variables.
[b] i.e. net of all other non-outcome variables.
[c] i.e. due to intervening variables.

stow, and since it only served to link lack of care with provoking agents a further analysis has been carried out without it and including instead a measure of self-esteem. This is a variable that seemed eminently qualified to act as the type of factor intervening along the more cognitive/emotional strand 2 of the Walthamstow model between lack of care and adult depression, and which might clinically reduce the direct effect of lack of care by reducing its indirect effect. Failure to measure a cognitive set like low self-esteem, which started with lack of care and continued through the person's life span to interact with provoking agents and poor support in adulthood, could exaggerate the direct effect of lack of care.

Our theory dealing with the aetiology of depression places a good deal of weight on the role of low self-esteem, suggesting that its presence increases the risk of depression, but only when a provoking agent has occurred, that is that it acts as a vulnerability factor. This was confirmed by the longitudinal material in Islington: of those experiencing a provoking agent, 33% (18/54) with negative evaluation of self, and 13% (12/96) without, developed depression in the follow-up year, whereas practically none in either group without a provoking agent did so (Brown *et al.*, 1986a). (The term 'negative evaluation of self' is used rather than 'low self-esteem' to convey that the measure is based only on the woman's negative comments about herself, excluding any consideration of positive comments.)

Surprisingly, however, the inclusion of negative evaluation of self in the model did not change the basic result concerning the effect of lack of care on onset – the greater part of its impact is still direct (.08 direct versus .05 indirect – see Figure 3 and Table 8).

Since negative context and negative evaluation of self were measured at the time of the first interview, it is possible to question the time order

Table 8 *Causal interpretation of path effects and depression (second analysis of Islington women: onset cases of depression* N = 303). *Based on path model in Figure 3*

	Causal effects in terms of proportion depressed			
	Lack of care	Negative context	Negative evaluation of self	Provoking agent
Basic difference in proportions – bivariate associations	.13	.09	.18	.19
Total causal effect[a]	.13	.07	.15	.16
Direct causal effect[b]	.08	−.01	.13	.16
Indirect causal effect[c]	.05	.08	.02	.00
Spurious effect	.00	.02	.03	.03

[a] i.e. net prior variables.
[b] i.e. net of all other non-outcome variables.
[c] i.e. due to intervening variables.

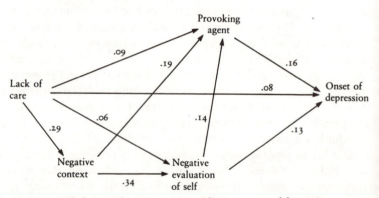

Figure 3   Path diagram for 303 women in Islington: onset of depression

assumed in the path diagram, where negative context precedes negative evaluation. However, this assumption does not effect the conclusions drawn about lack of care. (A more conservative analysis in terms of the diagram as a whole would treat negative context and negative evaluation as a 'block' in which no time order is assumed, that is the block could be given an unambiguous time order in terms of the total model – the non-recursive element would have been eliminated from the model.)

Therefore, although the path diagram is clearly informative about some of the processes leading up to the onset of depression, in the light of the strong interactive effect of provoking agent and low self-esteem it would be essential to supplement it with the kind of predictive analysis illustrated in Tables 1 and 2.

Further analysis of Islington material

It is, of course, not possible to stop here. The problem of interpreting the direct effect of lack of care arising from the path analysis remains and it is important to go on looking for possible intervening factors. For example, there are grounds for believing that, along Bowlbyan lines, certain styles of attachment play some part in the basic lack of a care–depression link. (In terms of the Walthamstow model they would involve strand 2.) Unlike self-esteem, however, they would have an impact upon the tendency towards generalization of hopelessness by affecting the subject's beliefs about other people's ability, not just about her own unaided ability, to help restore something of what was lost after the intervention of the provoking agent (Harris, 1988). With this in mind we have recently explored the Islington material to look for any evidence that personality factors may play a role in the link established between receiving support from a core tie at the time of a crisis and a much reduced risk of depression (Brown *et al.*, 1986a). We were particularly concerned with the possibility that the woman herself may often have played a key role in the development of the relationships that proved to be inadequate in terms of support once a crisis occurred. For this exploration we concentrated on the 150 women who experienced a provoking agent during the follow-up year, but who were not cases of depression at the beginning of the year. In this way we identified a group of 13 who had early lack of care *and* who had shown 'non-optimal' confiding at the time of our first contact, that is who had developed relationships in whom they confided (in a fashion), but in which confiding did not elicit support and which often let them down in a crisis (Andrews and Brown, 1988).[3] Lack of care was highly related to such non-optimal confiding – 28% (13/47) and 4% (10/256) respectively of those with and without lack of care had non-optimal confiding. The 13 women with lack of care and such non-optimal confiding at first contact had a particularly high risk of depression during the following year – 69% (9/13) compared with 15% (21/137) among the rest of the 150 women with a provoking agent. It should be noted that there were a further 10 women with non-optimal confiding who had not experienced lack of care and these had quite a low rate of depression (3/10). Therefore early lack of care is both highly linked to non-optimal confiding and acts synergistically with it to raise the risk of depression. (For a speculative account of how this happens, see Andrews and Brown, 1988). We strongly suspect, but as yet have no systematic evidence, that the pattern of non-optimal confiding goes back some way in time.

There is therefore some possibility that the high risk of depression among this small group of women once a provoking agent has occurred is

---

[3] In the paper referred to we used a somewhat broader concept of 'inadequate parenting', but to be consistent I have kept the same factor 'lack of care' in the present analysis.

related to a persistent style of attachment which in turn is related to experiences of rejection in childhood. The importance of the finding for my concern is that it might in the future resolve the issue of the puzzlingly high direct causal effect of lack of care which so far I have only been able to interpret in terms of a late interactional causal chain. If non-optimal confiding is introduced into the path diagram as an intervening variable with provoking agents and negative evaluation of self, the indirect effect of lack of care upon depression may increase, with a resulting decline in the direct effect. Indeed, when the occurrence of a provoking agent, negative evaluation of self, and non-optimal confiding, are considered in terms of a path analysis, the direct link of lack of care with onset largely disappears (the direct effect reduces from .08 to .01), that is much of the impact of lack of care on the onset of depression appears to be mediated through its indirect links via provoking agents and non-optimal confiding. To sum up: early lack of care is highly linked to non-optimal confiding and the two then act synergistically greatly to raise the risk of depression. Of course this link via non-optimal confiding is, as yet, speculative, but with this relatively optimistic assessment of the possibility of progress I will return to the main methodological theme of this essay and deal with two final points.

Auxiliary analyses

In pursuing the role of lack of care I have ignored some of the links we had established in our main analysis of the Walthamstow material. One of interest is that involving inadequacy of coping with premarital pregnancy, and final class status. If a woman coped well with premarital pregnancy, she was more likely to move from a working-class status (based on father's occupation) to a middle-class one, and this, as already seen, had implications for current depression.[4]   A simple path diagram in Figure 4 sums up the relevant effects. There is a linking chain from lack of care → premarital pregnancy → inadequate coping → working-class status which finishes with a final direct link between coping with premarital pregnancy and current class of .41. This compares with a path coefficient of .19 linking father's class and current class. Unfortunately, as already emphasized in the discussion of the main analyses, the path diagram also fails to convey that there is an important interactive effect, that is that inadequate coping with premarital pregnancy in practice only contributes to final

---

[4] The index developed to reflect coping was based upon the idea that such pregnancies may act as a trap in which a woman may become ensnared by marrying a man she would not otherwise have chosen. It grouped together on the one hand reactions such as seeking a termination, only marrying the father if he had already been intended as the future spouse, or choosing as a husband a man who was not the father of the child, and on the other marrying the father only because of the illegitimate conception, becoming a long-term single mother, or bearing the child only to have it adopted later (Harris *et al.*, 1987a).

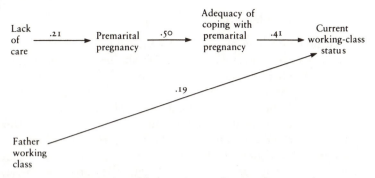

Figure 4   Auxiliary path model: determinants of current class status for women in Walthamstow with early loss of mother

Table 9 *Father's class background, adequacy of coping with premarital pregnancy and proportion currently working class (Walthamstow sample: 139 with loss of mother)*

Coping with premarital pregnancy	Proportion currently working class with father's social class	
	Working class	Middle class
Inadequate	.92 (11/12)	.40 (2/5)
Adequate – or no premarital pregnancy	.39 (31/79)	.26 (11/43)

class position when the woman *also* had a working-class father (see Table 9).

The main path diagrams presented earlier should ideally also have taken into account the combined effect on current class status of adequacy of coping with premarital pregnancy and father's class status. However, any increase in the number of variables is likely to cause problems and there is in any case no easy way to incorporate interaction effects in path models. Investigators are usually content to see them averaged out by the particular weighting procedure employed – assuming they are aware of them. In general, when faced by a situation of small numbers the presentation of a parallel or auxiliary analysis that supplements the basic model should be considered. One possible way of dealing with interactive effects is to perform a 'comparative analysis' presenting two distinct path diagrams in terms of only those with one particular factor involved in the interactive effect – in the present instance according to whether the father was working class or middle class (Hellevik, 1984, pp. 150–2).[5]

---

[5] Wheaton (1985) gives an excellent introduction to a possible alternative approach.

The need for exploration of data

So far no compelling reason has been given for rejecting path analysis – indeed, I have illustrated how it may sharpen our perspective on the results of other approaches. In practice there has been, however, a tendency to use it to test a limited range of hypotheses rather than to come to terms with the plethora of possibilities inherent in a complex data set. This practice is worrying and runs counter to the spirit of the Durkheim–Lazarsfeld tradition of analysis and often appears to reflect a misunderstanding of the delicate balance between getting and testing ideas, between the imaginative and the critical, in research (Medawar, 1969). There is an element of this interplay in path analysis in the sense that it might well reveal that certain paths can be excluded, but the possibilities for exploration are limited and I doubt whether its use alone will usually have the necessary depth of contact with material to provide an effective mode of analysis. Path coefficients obtained more or less routinely from a computer-based program are no substitute for getting to know material by puzzling over it in its innumerable manifestations for months, if not years. It does not, for example, supply the all-important partial tables of the traditional Lazarsfeldian approach. Given the flawed measures, the emphasis on 'factors' and the primitive state of knowledge in most fields of inquiry, path analysis is probably best seen primarily as an aid to exploring material and as providing a useful method of summarizing the results of a broader and more complex analysis.

Perhaps an example of the kind of exploration I have in mind would be helpful. Fairly early in the analysis of the Walthamstow material it became clear that premarital pregnancy was an important link between lack of care and later depression. Once this had been established the possible role of 13 other teenage experiences, such as age at leaving school, were considered. Among the women with early loss of mother only three of these showed a relationship with later depression. But in the course of the analysis we still tabulated all 13 tables of premarital pregnancy and depression and here something interesting emerged. None of the 13 types of experience showed any suggestion of a link with depression once premarital pregnancy had been controlled for. And yet, to our surprise, among those not experiencing premarital pregnancy, leaving home before the age of 20 related to a *decreased* rate of depression (Harris *et al.*, 1987a, Table 2, row 4). This was one of the first indications in the data of the notion of a 'trap' and of how it was apparently important for women to have been masterful enough to extricate themselves. Such interactive effects are rarely considered in routine regression-based inquiries and are easily missed if, as in this instance, one of the factors involved shows no basic bivariate relationship with the outcome variable when considered alone. And if it had been missed we would have lost an opportunity to arrive at an insight about the critical role of escaping from 'traps'. Such clues can often be missed even when the effect itself is made clear enough in tabular or diagrammatic form. Because of this common lack of perceptiveness, it is highly desirable for a worker to give him- or herself the opportunity of arriving at the same insight from as many different directions as possible. This I suspect best comes from muddling through data, moving from one thing to another as ideas occur and reworking analyses over and over again as new factors emerge. It is perhaps unnecessary to add that this should be done in the spirit of developing and testing ideas of what might be going on in causal terms. Mere looking for interesting things should probably be done, if at all, very early in an analysis. In this context many will point out the problems of data 'dredging' and the danger of uncovering associations occurring by chance. In my experience this can be greatly exaggerated. It needs to be borne in mind that in a focused analysis one is often not looking at, say, two unrelated results, but one hypothesized to occur in the light of the earlier result. For example, in the analysis of the Walthamstow data the intervening role of low intimacy was predicted in the light of the importance of lack of care. In some instances such hypotheses will be the result of specific theoretical ideas developed in the course of the research and, of course, in so far as this occurs, the likely validity of findings is strengthened (see Brown, 1986). There is a good deal of difference between data dredging and the kind of focused exploration of material that I have in mind, and between this and more formal testing of hypotheses. In practice, of course, some element of all three approaches may well be involved in a larger-scale analysis and the real issue is the relative size of their contribution.

Final comments

As my main theme, I have contrasted the different pictures that may emerge from two approaches to causal inquiry. The first, prediction analysis, is akin in general approach to the new loglinear methods, and particularly logistic regression. It concentrates on predicting outcome in terms of the various combinations formed by the non-outcome factors. It takes into account variable effects, interactive effects and a constant, and ignores the degree to which there are links between the non-outcome variables. Instead of dealing with such links it focuses on how the factors may come together mutually to bring about outcome. Path analysis, by contrast, typically ignores interaction as such and deals with the joint effect of the non-outcome variables only in so far as they are causally interrelated. This means that although the two approaches give much the same result in terms of the *overall* predictive strength of the total variables on outcome, they can give quite different estimates of the strength of the effects of *individual* factors. In the course of a series of detailed analyses prediction analysis conveyed the overwhelming importance of lack of care among women with early loss of mother in the sense that depression was rarely present without it also occurring, almost always in combination with some other factor such as working-class status or poor support (see Table 2, column 1). However, path analysis ignores this potentiation of lack of care by other factors in so far as they were not causally interrelated (see Table 2, column 2). The picture that emerged from path analysis placed greater emphasis on the direct causal effect of lack of care in depression not mediated by other factors. In addition, as a corollary of ignoring interactive effects as such, the overall predictive strength of lack of care was also a good deal smaller. However, the key issue concerned the emphasis placed by path analysis on the role of lack of care as a direct causal effect on depression. One consequence of this was that the results of the various path analyses stimulated our search for further intervening factors, which in the Islington material finished with isolating non-optimal confiding as a factor of possible importance.

Both perspectives are undoubtedly important and three types of causal chain have been discussed that help to take both into account – related, early interactive and late interactive chains. Only the first is a causal chain as usually understood in path analysis and I have emphasized that the term 'chain' itself is best seen as having less narrow causal implications – that it may refer to factors that although not causally linked do have an effect on a further factor. The term strand is even more general and can be used to take account of all chains and their possible complex interplay as long as they have some common theoretical focus – as in strands 1 and 2 in the Walthamstow research. I left open how far the two interactive effects could be included in a traditional path analytic approach, and have been content to asume that once the issues are recognized there will be some way forward. I have also noted the role of auxiliary analyses (see also Wheaton, 1985). Given the somewhat untidy and *ad hoc* quality of such analyses, I am unclear about their effectiveness in tackling more complex models and, in any case, with them the attractive simplicities of an ordinary path diagram are left behind.

In addition to this general theme, I have dealt with a number of more specific problems that might arise. One concerns numbers. The ability to carry out an effective path analysis will be threatened to the degree to which there are cells with zero entries. Five factors, or at the most six, seemed to be about all that could be reasonably tackled with sample numbers ranging between 150 and 300, although just how the variables are interrelated will be relevant. However, it is possible that small numbers may not prove an insuperable problem. The number of clearly distinct factors of importance that are revealed even in an intensive inquiry is likely to be quite limited. Furthermore, it is probably possible to do analyses in stages, dropping variables that have the lowest coefficients or those having a purely intervening role between two factors. But attention would need to be given to the possibility that the variable dropped relates in a significant way to the one added. One way of tackling this might be to consider only the interrelationship of the non-outcome variables. Another would be to carry out auxiliary analyses of the kind that considered the roles of father's social class and coping with premarital pregnancy in determining eventual class position (see Figure 4), that is variables such as father's class and coping with pregnancy need not be included in the central model, but could still be considered in any overall view of the processes involved.

The need to specify all relevant factors in a path model is widely recognized. The failure to specify a model adequately can, of course, occur even if all relevant factors are included, if these are poorly measured. One example is the increase in the size of the path coefficient with depression for the variable of poor support when it was refined in the second Walthamstow analysis (see Tables 3 and 5; see also the way in which working-class status had acted in the earlier of these two tables as a proxy variable for provoking agents in Table 5). Unfortunately, adequate specification is not easily achieved. The possible role of non-optimal confiding among Islington women illustrates the likely subtlety of some of the factors involved in long-term effects and the difficulty that may be experienced in isolating them.

While I do not see these problems as insuperable, their possible presence, not least the problem of specifying all relevant factors with adequate measures, does warrant a certain humility in attempts at model building. In other words, I see the particular strength of path analysis as likely to be 'exploratory' rather than 'confirmatory'.

I have also conveyed a more general scepticism about whether all the intricacies of causal processes we are likely to uncover in developmental research can be represented in terms of path diagrams. Rutter (1983), for example, has discussed various kinds of interactive effect and their heterogeneous nature, and how each should be examined in terms of its own features and not be pooled under any umbrella category. I continue to be surprised at the complexities – statistical, theoretical and practical – that can emerge in analysing even a $2 \times 2 \times 2$ table and I can only endorse his view concerning the need to utilize more than one statistical procedure (Rutter, 1983, p. 315). Nor can I see that there should be any great concern if path models are supplemented by auxiliary accounts presented in a different manner, or even if path models are bypassed altogether. Prediction analysis and logistic regression have much to offer and in any case at times it will be necessary to deal with issues primarily in terms of their wider theoretical or logical implications. For instance, I have become convinced that the choice between using additive and multiplicative models of interaction cannot be resolved by statistical arguments alone – in the sense that there is no argument that would convince sceptics on either side. However, it may be possible to produce convincing evidence for an additive model once it is realized that the two approaches to interaction have important implications that can be tested quite independently of the statistical techniques. This kind of evidence can be straightforward to present, can be persuasive and can bypass completely the niceties of the statistical arguments (see Brown (1986) for an example).

It may also be helpful to keep in mind, in terms of my opening discussion, that the very notion of causal chain as exemplified by the path analytical tradition may prove to be most relevant at fairly early stages of a research programme, particularly when the mapping of quite crude 'factors' is under way. As we move to fill in intervening links and begin to concern ourselves with possible mechanisms, the picture will certainly become more complicated. Indeed, as mechanisms underlying such links become clearer, the very language of 'factors' utilized in such models may become something of a handicap. For example, to return to the issue of causal factors in depression, a provoking agent (e.g. separation from husband) may in a matter of months turn into a vulnerability factor (e.g. lack of an intimate tie and general loneliness). This in turn may serve to increase the risk of new provoking agents occurring (e.g. as the woman enters somewhat dubious new sexual relationships in an attempt to deal with her loneliness.) And one such crisis may prove to be enough to bring about a severe depressive disorder – perhaps because of the way it underlines the hopelessness inherent in the developing situation. Rutter has referred to such complex processes as a reason for a move from a concern with 'factors' to a concern with 'mechanisms' (Rutter, in press). While I agree with the need to consider mechanisms, I do not believe this should be taken too far too soon. The language of 'factors' is quite able to cope with the kind of situation I have just outlined if time is taken into account and as long as one does not fall into the naive trap of taking indicators too literally. There should be no problem in accepting that separation from husband can be an 'event' when it occurs and sometime later can reflect a vulnerability factor in so far as it has had an impact on support. Indicators need to be seen in context, though this is not to say that in doing so a good deal more does not need to be done in improving the sensitivity of our measurement of 'factors'. Therefore I see the need for a certain tension between working with factors and a move towards dealing with mechanisms, that is to a full-blown interactional perspective. And here I return for a final comment on path analysis. Perhaps one of the main dangers is that its use will delay any move beyond the 'factors' of a particular model. It will delay it both in the sense that some processes can at best only be incorporated with difficulty in such analyses and because some sense of their importance may only emerge from a more traditional method of analysing material. Just what the solution will turn out to be I must confess I have no clear idea. But I suspect that like Lazarsfeld's general approach to methodology it will be necessary to build recommendations around what proves to be successful in our practice rather than try too hard to fit practice into what is desirable in a formal statistical or a methodological sense. Of course, I somewhat beg the question by talking about what is successful, but high on my list would be the ability to convey findings with a reasonable degree of clarity to those with little technical expertise. We are fortunate to work in an area with a wide and disparate audience concerned with both scientific and practical issues, and a major task must be to communicate effectively – even if at times this means giving up some of the statistical and methodological niceties which it can be rewarding to surround our work with.

Acknowledgement

I am extremely grateful to Tirril Harris for her illuminating criticisms of this paper and for her help with the analyses.

References

Andrews, B. A. and Brown, G. W (1988) Social support, onset of depression and personality: an exploratory analysis. *Social Psychiatry*, 23, 99–108.
Asher, H. B. (1983) *Causal modeling*, 2nd edn. Beverly Hills: Sage.
Bifulco, A., Brown, G. W. and Harris, T. O. (1987) Childhood loss of parent and adult depression: the Islington study. *Journal of Affective Disorders*, 12, 115–28.
Boyle, R. P. (1966) Causal theory and statistical measures of effect: a convergence. *American Sociological Review*, 31, 843–51.
Brown, G. W. (1986) Statistical interaction and the role of social factors in the aetiology of clinical depression. *Sociology*, 20, 601–6.
Brown, G. W. and Harris, T. O. (1986) Establishing causal links: the Bedford college studies of depression. In Katschnig, H. (ed.) *Life events and psychiatric disorders*. Cambridge: Cambridge University Press, pp. 107–87.
Brown. G. W., Andrews, B., Harris, T., Alder, Z. and Bridge, L. (1986a) Social support, self-esteem and depression. *Psychological Medicine*, 16, 813–31.
Brown, G. W., Harris, T. O. and Bifulco, A. (1986b) Long-term effects of early loss of parent. In Rutter, M., Izard, C. E. and Read, P. B. (eds.) *Depression in young people*. New York: Guilford Press, pp. 251–96.
Cleary, P. D. and Kessler, R. C. (1982) The estimation and interpretation of modifier effects. *Journal of Health and Social Behavior*, 23, 159–69.
Davis, J. A. (1975) Analyzing contingency tables with linear flow graphs: d-systems. In Heise, D. (ed.) *Sociological methodology 1976*. San Francisco: Jossey-Bass, pp. 111–45.
(1976) Background characteristics of the US adult population 1952–1973: a survey-metric model. *Social Science Research*, 5, 349–83.
(1985) *The logic of causal order*. Quantitative Application in the Social Sciences 55. London: Sage.
Galtung, J. (1967) *Theory and methods of social research*. London: Allen and Unwin.

Harris, T. O. (1988) Psycho-social vulnerability to depression: the biographical perspective of the Bedford College studies. In Henderson, A. S. and Burrows, G. D. (eds.) *Handbook of social psychiatry*. Oxford: Blackwell.

Harris, T. O., Brown, G. W. and Bifulco, A. (1986) Loss of parent in childhood and adult psychiatric disorder: the role of lack of adequate parental care. *Psychological Medicine*, 16, 641–59.

(1987a) Loss of parent in childhood and adult psychiatric disorder: the Walthamstow study. The role of social class position and premarital pregnancy. *Psychological Medicine*, 17, 163–83.

(1987b) Loss of parent in childhood and adult psychiatric disorder: the Walthamstow study. The role of situational helplessness. MS

Hellevik, O. (1984) *Introduction to causal analysis*. London: Allen and Unwin.

Lerner, R. M. (1983) The 'goodness of fit' model of person. Context interaction. In Magnusson, D. and Allen, V. L. (eds.) *Human development: an interactional perspective*. London and New York: Academic Press, pp. 279–92.

Macdonald, K. I. (1977) Path analysis. In O'Muircheartaigh, C. A. and Payne, C. (eds.) *Model fitting: the analysis of survey data*. London: Wiley, pp. 87–104.

Marsh, C. (1982) *The survey method: the contribution of surveys to sociological explanation*. London: Allen and Unwin.

Medawar, P. B. (1969) *Induction and intuition in scientific thought*. London: Methuen.

Quinton, D. and Rutter, M. (1984a) Parents with children in care, I. Current circumstances and parenting. *Journal of Child Psychology and Psychiatry*, 25, 211–29.

(1984b) Parents with children in care, II. Intergenerational continuities. *Journal of Child Psychology and Psychiatry*, 25, 231–50.

Quinton, D., Rutter, M. and Liddle, C. (1984) Institutional rearing, parenting difficulties and marital support. *Psychological Medicine*, 14, 107–24.

Rosenberg, M. (1968) *The logic of survey analysis*. New York: Basic Books.

Rutter, M. (1983) Statistical and personal interactions: facets and perspectives. In Magnusson, D. and Allen, V. L. (eds.) *Human development: an interactional perspective*. London and New York: Academic Press.

(in press) Psychosocial resilience and protective mechanisms. In Rolf, J., Masten, A., Cicchetti, D., Nuechterlein, K. and Weintraub, S. (eds.) *Risk and protective factors in the development of psychopathology*. New York: Cambridge University Press.

Rutter, M., Quinton, D. and Liddle, C. (1983) Parenting in two generations: looking backwards and looking forwards. In Madge, N. (ed.) *Families at risk*. Heinemann Educational.

Wheaton, B. (1985) Models for the stress-buffering functions of coping resources. *Journal of Health and Social Behavior*, 26, 352–64.

18 Data gathering and data analysis for prospective and retrospective longitudinal studies[1]

Lee N. Robins

The nature of prospective studies

The classic longitudinal study that seeks to understand the causes of a particular behaviour pattern or disorder is the prospective study. A sample is identified and at first contact its members' histories are assessed with respect to ever having experienced the behaviour or disorder of interest and its presumed predictors. Those who have not yet had the outcome of interest are then followed at a later date or several later dates to learn who develops it. If the sample is selected so early in life that none of the sample has entered the age of risk for the outcome, or if the outcome is one that precludes falling into the sample – suicide, for example – every member initially seen may be eligible for follow-up.

There is no standard criterion for how long the follow-up should continue, but clearly, to allow meaningful statistical analysis, it must not terminate before a sufficient segment of the sample has demonstrated the outcome. The researcher can then look back at earlier assessments to see how those who developed the outcome could have been distinguished at an early age from those who did not.

One flaw in this design is that some of those who have not developed the outcome at the final assessment may develop it later. This can result in a loss of power, because the characteristics of the 'negative' cases are muddied by the characteristics of those who will later be positive. Results may also be generalizable primarily to those with unusually early onsets, since all early-onset cases will enter the group of the 'positives', but only part of the later-onset cases will have appeared as positives by the end of the study. One solution is to study only outcomes with a fixed early-terminating period of risk, such as being adjudicated a juvenile delinquent or failing to complete secondary education, or else to continue the follow-up so long that virtually all cases will have emerged.

Long-term follow-up appears the more attractive alternative, since it allows studying a broad range of outcomes. But the longer the follow-up, the greater the risks of attrition of subjects *and* investigators, and of changes in focus of interest to which the original assessments may be

[1]This work was supported by USPHS Grants MH 00334, MH 31302 and MH 17104, and by the MacArthur Risk Network.

315

irrelevant. Long-term follow-ups are also unlikely to include multiple cohorts, since the study would have to continue until the youngest cohort was followed through the period of risk. Restriction to a single cohort raises a question about whether results generalize to other eras. As expense increases with duration, the longer the follow-up period, the more likely it is that there will be long intervals between assessments.

To be certain that no new causal variables appearing since the last assessment are overlooked, as well as to compensate for omissions in the earlier assessments of questions needed to test new causal hypotheses, researchers generally ask for historical information about causal variables at each successive contact, thus bridging the interval since the last contact and correcting previous omissions. They must also ask whether the outcome occurred during the interval since the last assessment, even if it is not currently in evidence. If the outcome of interest has occurred and new potentially causal factors have occurred as well, the investigator must try to date the first occurrence of each so that the order of their appearance is known and causes and consequences of the outcome of interest will not be confused.

The need for a retrospective survey of events during intervals between assessments is more obvious when the interval between assessments is long than when it is short. However, failing to get histories for short intervals can lead to error. If assessment is only cross-sectional, some episodes of the outcome may be missed, leading to a confusion between factors predicting first onsets of the outcome with factors predicting its relapse. Our own research (Helzer *et al.*, 1985, Robins, 1977) has shown that these predictors may be quite different. The chance of finding either the precursor or the outcome present cross-sectionally depends not only on the frequency of follow-up, but also on the duration of the event and its consequences. Thus, if police contacts are the outcome of interest, an arrest leading to a long sentence is sure to be noted because the respondent will be in prison cross-sectionally, while an arrest on the same date that led to no conviction will be missed. If early separation from a parent is to be investigated as a possible causal variable, parental deaths would be evident cross-sectionally because they are irreversible, but the chance of detecting temporary separations, desertions and hospitalizations would vary with their frequency and duration. Failure to take histories of the interval leads to an underestimation of the prevalence of milder causal events and briefer outcome episodes.

The nature of retrospective studies

Since prospective studies generally require retrospective review at each contact of the interval since the previous contact, and even of earlier intervals if there was any deficit in previous data collections, it is apparent that simple retrospective studies can be viewed as a prospective study in reduced form. There is but a single contact, at which the interval from birth to the date of interview is covered with respect to both causal and outcome variables.

By a 'retrospective' study, we shall mean a study in which the sample is chosen by area survey or other procedure intended to select a random sample of the general population. We are not including case-control studies, even though they also have a single contact with respondents during which respondents are asked for a lifetime history of possible causal factors. Case-control studies determine the presence of the outcome variable prior to first contact in order to select two matched samples, one of persons known to have the outcome and the other of persons known to be free of the outcome. They then look for events present prior to the onset of the disorder being studied that distinguished the two groups at that time. Cases in case-control studies are usually selected from treatment rosters. This means that they do not represent the whole affected population, which includes untreated cases as well, and that causal variables identified may be either causes of the disorder or causes of coming to treatment once the disorder is present. Further, any variable used for matching controls to cases is unavailable for investigation as a possible cause of the disorder. These restrictions do not apply to retrospective studies using area samples or other samples unselected for the outcome. Cases in these studies include both those known and unknown to treatment, and the controls occur spontaneously, for they are those subjects that do not have the outcome of interest.

Since a retrospective study makes only a single contact with its subjects, the problem of attrition does not arise, and it is feasible to study large samples and multiple-birth cohorts. Weighing against these advantages is the fact that if the outcome of interest biases access to the sample by leading to death, institutionalization, or mobility to other regions, the affected interviewed sample will not be representative of all persons who suffered the outcome. This is a serious issue, for which no obvious solution is at hand.

Recall error in retrospective and prospective studies

The criticism of retrospective studies that has concerned researchers more than the representativeness of the sample is the question of recall error. Recall error can be of three kinds: forgetting, reversals and invention. Forgetting leads to denial of outcomes or precursors that actually occurred; reversals exchange the order in memory between the cause and the outcome, leading to reporting as causes events that may have been consequences; invention has to do with 'retrospective falsification' – either reporting events that did not occur or exaggerating their seriousness in an effort to explain the outcome. It is worth noting that the same type and degree of error is caused by 'inventing' memories on the part of those who experience an adverse outcome as by selective denial of adverse early experiences by persons who do not have the adverse outcomes. In both cases falsely positive results are produced, whether by the positive cases overreporting the causal variable or by the negative cases underreporting it.

Forgetting

Prospective studies have a clear advantage over retrospective studies in being able to establish the sequence of causal variables and outcomes when events are sufficiently widely separated in time that the potential cause first appeared at an earlier assessment than the outcome did. But when cause and outcome occupy the same follow-up interval, the order, even in prospective studies, can be established only by retrospection, and the advantage over the retrospective study is only that the recall is requested for somewhat more recent events.

While the longer interval over which events must be recalled in retrospective studies is of concern, little is known about how much difference the longer interval makes nor what strategies can improve recall. The loss in accuracy has been assessed for a few topics by asking subjects of prospective studies in their final interview to recall topics covered earlier, and then comparing the results with the earlier responses. One such study (Robbins, 1963) showed a considerable loss. A recent study by Sorenson *et al.* (1987), however, shows surprising agreement between the ordering of delinquent behaviours as recalled by adults reporting on their behaviours many years earlier and adolescents reporting on recent behaviours, suggesting that the loss in accuracy may not be great.

In our experience, forgetting can be reduced and dating improved by careful question design. Respondents are greatly helped in dating events when they are asked to consider them in terms of major life changes, such as whether they had yet entered school, whether they were still living at home, whether they were in military service at the time, whether they had yet married, etc. But even without such props, recall of memorable events may be excellent. In our previous study of Vietnam veterans and matched controls (Robins, 1974), we thought the vivid recall of the sequence of illicit drugs used by veterans was made easy by their being able to associate their introduction to particular drugs as being prior to entering the military, in the military before going to Vietnam, or in Vietnam. However, the civilian controls also found it easy to date their first use of specific drug categories in a sequence that was remarkably consistent across users. Others (e.g. Kandel, 1978) have found the same kind of consistency across subjects in the sequence in which they report first using different categories of drugs.

Even when these aids to memory do not enable respondents to recall the date of an event, they are often able to recall the order in which two events occurred. Therefore, when investigators get an 'I don't know when' response, they should ask about the order of first occurrence between pairs of positive events, rather than settling for missing information about sequences.

Reversals

Forgetting earlier events that actually preceded an outcome can reduce the associations found between causes and outcomes, but is unlikely to lead to erroneous positive findings. Reversing the order of events in memory to better fit causal stereotypes can lead to positive error. When studies do not date onsets, they commonly assume that the associated events preceded the outcome. But relationships between two events that typically occupy the same time period are often reciprocal. For example, first delinquency and school dropout, both common around age 16, are events that are probably reciprocally causal. Since the problem of reciprocal relationships only applies to events occurring in the same time interval, this is equally a problem for prospective and for retrospective studies, since both events may begin between the same pair of prospective study assessments, making their sequence uncertain.

Methods for determining the order of events that both occurred within a short time have not been evaluated. The common method is to ask the age at first occurrence of each event of interest, and to drop as potential causes events that occurred in the same year as the outcome, because the order is indeterminate (Robins and Wish, 1977). We should explore the accuracy with which respondents can order events that occurred in the same year by validating their responses in record sets. Changes in school grade point averages as related to school disciplinary experiences might be a good pair of events to test, because both can be scored from the same data sets.

Invention

Invention or exaggeration of false memories can also create falsely positive results. We have a modest amount of evidence that retrospective revision of the prior history is not a major problem when the time separation between potential cause and outcome is great (Robins *et al.*, 1985). We interviewed pairs of siblings, only one of whom had a psychiatric disorder, about their recall of the childhood home environment, and found no bias towards greater criticism of the parents or the home on the part of the affected sibling. We would have expected such bias if the affected sibling had been trying to 'explain' his psychiatric disorder in terms of exposure to inferior parenting or if the control sibling was now denying the bad environment in which both were reared. This was reassuring after our finding in an earlier study (Robins, 1966) that former child guidance clinic patients who were psychologically healthy as adults described their parents' behaviour less adversely than their childhood records did. If our finding that adult disorder does not bias childhood memories is correct, there may be little difference between prospective and retrospective studies in the risk of exaggeration of predictors of outcome.

Since retrospective longitudinal studies have still not been carefully evaluated in terms of the loss attributable to their requiring recall over longer periods, it is difficult at present to decide when the less costly retrospective study design can suffice. One clue that might be helpful is whether the information to be gathered is likely to be readily accessible in the respondent's memory. The literature provides abundant evidence that reliability is greater when the information requested is something already in the respondent's memory rather than having to be constructed on the spot. Thus opinion polls that ask about topics on which the respondent has no strong opinion get unreliable results, as shown by the fact that these opinions are unstable over time and affected by the way the question is asked (Schuman and Presser, 1981). One can see why this must be so. If someone is asked to make up a story and then asked to repeat it a week later, he will probably not reproduce it as accurately as if he had been asked to tell and later repeat the story of Little Red Riding Hood. The latter story has been frequently rehearsed and can be 'read out of the memory' at any time, making it unnecessary for the testee to recall precisely how he narrated it on the previous occasion. This also explains why recall for common events like what one had for dinner last week tends to be poor, as is recall of the age at which children passed certain developmental milestones (Robbins, 1963); both lack rehearsals. Developmental milestones become datable when connected to some more memorable life event (perhaps a child's first steps were taken on his first birthday) or eagerly anticipated because there had been a significant developmental delay.

We would assume, therefore, that asking about events well known to the respondent, such as whether or not he was arrested, repeated a grade, had a child, ran away from home, can be successfully asked in a retrospective study. Reporting that requires making a judgement not previously made about past events, such as whether he experienced 'severe' insomnia, the quality of the relationship between his parents, whether he fought more than most other youngsters, are probably not reliably ascertained many years later unless at the time they led to memorable events, such as seeing a doctor or being sent to the principal's office, events which the respondent had previous occasion to explain to himself or others. Thus Brown's decision (see chapter 17) to restrict questions in his retrospective study on depressive symptoms and quality of relationship with the spouse to the current year, while accepting recall of maternal loss in early childhood, is probably a sound choice.

Recall problems, in short, exist for both prospective and retrospective studies. For some areas of recall, there may be little to choose between the two, but overall there is a clear advantage to prospective studies. We have suggested some ways of assessing the degree of handicap retrospective studies suffer in recall and some possible ways of reducing that handicap. If these are insufficient, recall error in retrospective studies can be compensated for in part by supplementing interviews with reviews of school and police records, and those of Departments of Vital Statistics.

Data analysis in retrospective and prospective studies

Whichever longitudinal study design is used, a variety of possible causal factors, often highly intercorrelated, will usually be identified, the relative power of which we would like to quantify. When these events are not dated, a limited selection of multivariate statistical methods are available for retrospective studies. The commonly used methods are multiple regression, logistic regression and path analysis. Of these, only path analysis requires making explicit one's hunches about the sequential order. The other two can test sequential models if the stepwise pro-gramme option is not used, but instead independent variables are entered into the analysis in the order in which the investigator believes they occur. When a factor found significant early in the analysis becomes non-significant when another variable is added to the analysis, the second variable can be interpreted as the mechanism through which the first variable affects the outcome.

In prospective studies, even when events occurring within the same interval between assessments were not dated nor their order determined, rough empirical information on sequence is available because the analyses can be done from one assessment point to the next. This makes it possible to test empirically some of the hypotheses about the sequential order that in a cross-sectional study can be tested only by seeing whether the relationships between variables are consistent with the investigator's a priori model.

Both retrospective and prospective longitudinal studies that attempt to date the first appearance of each behaviour have available the powerful statistical tools that use life tables, and are referred to as 'survival analysis'. These methods use not only the sequence between presumed causes and presumed outcome, but the length of the interval between their respective first occurences, information ignored by other techniques. These methods were devised for clinical studies where the subjects are selected for study because they are already known to be at risk, but are followed for different lengths of time because some drop out of the study before its conclusion, or enter the study after it is already in progress. However, these methods are equally appropriate for epidemiological longitudinal studies, where the variation in length of follow-up is caused by the fact that the exposure to risk factors can occur at any time during the follow-up interval. The most commonly used life table method for studying the contribution of multiple-risk factors simultaneously is the Cox Proportional Hazard method. Instead of producing information about the risk of occurrence, it produces a risk rate, that is what the increase in annual risk attributable to the presumed cause is. Estimates can be for multiple variables, each net of the other variables, or the net effects of some variables can be estimated, stratifying on the others (e.g. the analysis in Brown's Table 2, chapter 17, would involve stratification on sex and maternal loss to estimate the net effects of quality of care, class, and confidante on depression). The ability to control on some variables and stratify on others relieves the problem of small cells faced in Brown's $2 \times 2 \times 2$ tables, although even substantial samples, such as Brown's, might produce unstable beta weights were all six of his variables (sex, maternal loss, quality of care, social class, spouse relationship and depression) to be entered simultaneously.

Furthermore, since survival analysis is equally applicable to prospective and retrospective studies, given dated events, it would be an excellent tool for measuring the cost in precision suffered by using a single rather than multiple points of data collection.

As Brown's work shows so clearly, relationships between life events and later outcomes differ between various categories of the population. To discover such variation, analyses selected to analyse longitudinal studies, whether prospective or retrospective, must look for interactions. Interactions can be obtained routinely in loglinear analyses, but they can also be sought in other types of analyses by stratification of the sample.

Once the relative strength of the dated predictors of the outcome of interest is determined by survival analysis, both prospective and retrospective studies allow calculating the prevalence of the various risk factors at each age for the various subpopulations. When it comes to making decisions about how to use results of studies of the cause of adverse outcomes, one wants to know not only how powerful each predictor is but which parts of the population are most affected by it, how common it is among them, and how early it can be detected in them. The greatest pay-off comes from selecting the most vulnerable populations for intervention, and designing interventions likely to reduce the risk factors that are common among them, detectable early, and highly associated with the unwanted outcome.

The role of experiments

Even if we solve the problem of dating events so that we can unequivocally state that for some part of our population the appearance of some event is associated with the subsequent appearance of a particular outcome, we have to remember that our results are still only correlational, and may suggest, but cannot prove, a causal relationship. Beginning in early childhood, and increasingly thereafter, one's life events are influenced by one's predispositions. Thus any correlation between disorder and preceding events must be looked at sceptically. We have done two studies that should show how psychiatric disorder is affected by life events which are independent of individual predispositions – if any such exist. The first is a study of the effects of being in combat in Vietnam (Helzer *et al.*, 1979), and the second studies the effects of suffering flood damage (Robins *et al.*, 1986). Both revealed that much of the excess symptomatology in persons with these experiences could be explained by the kinds of people who had the experiences. Soldiers in Vietnam who saw a great deal of combat had had on average more behaviour problems and learned fewer occupational skills before they came to Vietnam than those who were not in combat, reflecting the fact that they were younger than other soldiers, many having enlisted as high school dropouts before reaching draftable age. Presumably those volunteers saw combat because they had none of the occupational skills that might have kept them behind the lines as cooks, or clerk/typists, or medical aids. Those who lived in areas that were flooded were poorer and less well educated than those who lived on higher (and more expensive) land. In both cases, controlling on social class and school achievement virtually erased the initial correlations between experience and symptoms.

To demonstrate the correctness of any causal hypothesis derived from either prospective or retrospective studies, it remains necessary to carry out a true experiment, with subjects randomly assigned to experimental and control categories. Therefore any interventions based on these findings should be so designed that they test the hypotheses on which they are based. Even after random assignment of cases, this requires compensating as far as possible in final statistical analysis for any deviation from initial equivalence that may result from statistical accident or from attrition that is imbalanced between experimental and control groups. It also means selecting subjects as typical as possible of the target high-risk population, and verifying that the intended intervention has actually taken place as planned and produced a real change in the prevalence of the risk factors. An intervention that fails to accomplish the intended modification of the risk factors allows a negative assessment of the intervention, but tells us nothing about the soundness of the causal hypothesis on which the intervention was based.

References

Helzer, J. E. and Robins, L. N. (1985) Specification of predictors of narcotic use vs addiction. In Robins, L. N. (ed.) *Studying drug abuse*. Rutgers University Press Series in Psychosocial Epidemiology, ed. A. E. Slaby. New Brunswick: Rutgers University Press, pp. 173–97.

Helzer, J. E., Robins, L. N., Wish, E. D. and Hesselbrock, M. (1979) Depression in Vietnam veterans and civilian controls. *American Journal of Psychiatry*, **136**, 526–30.

Helzer, J. E., Robins, L. N., Taylor, J. R., Carey, K., Miller, R. and Combs-Orme, T. C. (1985) The extent of long-term moderate drinking among alcoholics discharged from medical and psychiatric treatment facilities. *New England Journal of Medicine*, **312**, 1678–82.

Kandel, D. B. (1978) Convergences in prospective longitudinal surveys of drug use in normal populations. In Kandel, D. B. (ed.) *Longitudinal research on drug use*. Washington, DC: Hemisphere, pp. 3–38.

Robbins, L. C. (1963) The accuracy of parental recall of aspects of child development and of child rearing practices. *Journal of Abnormal and Social Psychology*, **66**, 261–70.

Robins, L. N. (1966) *Deviant children grown up: a sociological and psychiatric study of sociopathic personality*. Baltimore: Williams and Wilkins. Reprinted Robert E. Krieger: Huntington, NY (1974).

(1974) *The Vietnam drug user returns*. Special Action Office Monograph, series A, no. 2. Washington, DC: US Government Printing Office.

(1977) Estimating addiction rates and locating target populations: how decomposition into stages helps. In Rittenhouse, J. D. (ed.) *The epidemiology of heroin and other narcotics*. National Institute in Drug Abuse Research Monograph Series, no. 16, Department of Health, Education and Welfare Publication no. 1 (ADM) 78–559.

Robins, L. N. and Wish, E. (1977) Childhood deviance as a developmental process: a study of 223 urban black men from birth to 18. *Social Forces*, **56**, 448–73; errata, **56**, 999 (1978). Reprinted in part in Bloom, M. (ed.) (1980) *Life span development: bases for preventive and interventive helping*. New York: Macmillan; abstracted in *Current Abstracts, Child and Youth Services*.

Robins, L. N., Schoenberg, S., Holmes, S., Ratcliff, K., Benham, A. and Works, J. (1985) Early home environment and retrospective recall: a test for concordance between siblings with and without psychiatric disorders. *American Journal of Orthopsychiatry*, **55**, 27–41.

Robins, L. N., Fischbach, R., Smith, E. M., Cottler, L. B. and Solomon, S. D. (1986) The impact of disaster on previously assessed mental health. In Shore, J. H. (ed.) *Disaster stress studies: new methods and findings*. Washington, DC: American Psychological Association, pp. 21–48.

Schuman, H. and Presser, S. (1981) *Questions and answers in attitude surveys*. New York: Academic Press, pp. 253–73.

Sorenson, A. M., Brownfield, D. and Carlson, V. (1987) Methodological considerations in the comparison of adolescent self reports and adult retrospective reports of delinquency. Paper presented at the annual conference of the American Sociological Association, August.

19 Structural equation modelling of measurement processes in longitudinal data

D. M. Fergusson and L. J. Horwood

Introduction and background

Introduction

The purpose of this chapter is to provide an introduction to the use of structural equation modelling methods in dealing with problems of measurement which recur in longitudinal data. Since the emphasis is upon the application of these methods, a full formal account of the mathematical basis of structural equation models will not be offered. However, the reader is referred to the available sources for an account of the mathematical basis of structural equation models. Good introductions to this area may be found in Duncan (1975), Heise (1975), Kenny (1979), Long (1983a,b) and Everitt (1984). More advanced treatments may be found in Aigner and Goldberger (1977), McDonald (1978), Jöreskog and Sörbom (1979), Browne (1982) and Jöreskog and Wold (1982). Accounts of the application of structural equation models to longitudinal data have been provided by Jöreskog and Sörbom (1977), Rogosa (1979) and Jöreskog (1979).

The logic of structural equation models

Structural equation models provide a method of describing some pre-specified causal theory of the structure of a set of variables of interest in terms of an explicit and solvable set of linear equations which encapsulate and summarize the key causal assumptions of the theory. It is important to recognize that seldom do structural equation models provide any direct test of the causal assumptions on which these models are based. In general, it is wisest to think of structural equation models as being a formal statement of the investigator's beliefs about the causal structures that underlie a set of observed variables. These beliefs may be based on evidence of varying strength. At one extreme, structural equation models may be formulated on the basis of little more than common sense and intuition, whereas at the other extreme the investigator may have strong evidence (such as that provided by controlled experimentation) about the causal structure of his/her data.

While the causal assumptions of a structural equation model are seldom amenable to direct testing, there are often many indirect tests of the plausibility of a model. In particular, informative models tend to summarize the observed variances and covariances of a set of variables in terms of a smaller number of parameters. Such models are said to be overidentified and are amenable to testing since there is no guarantee that the model parameters will provide an adequate account of the observed data. Thus it is possible to reject inadequate overidentified models on the basis of poor goodness of fit to a set of observations, while at the same time the failure of a model to be rejected does not imply that the model is the true structural model that generated the observed data. This, of course, is the logic of falsification set out by Popper (1961), who has argued that while it is possible to reject false scientific theories on the basis of evidence that contradicts these theories we can never be sure that a theory that has survived testing is the correct theory of the observed data.

In addition to the possibility of testing structural models using goodness-of-fit methods, there are often sources of external evidence that can be used to judge the plausibility of the causal assumptions of the model. The various criteria for making causal judgements on the basis of correlational evidence have been discussed in the epidemiological literature (e.g. Susser, 1973). By bringing these external criteria to bear on a model it is often possible to determine whether the model assumptions are consistent with all that is known about the causal structure of a set of variables.

In summary, structural equation models should be seen as convenient mathematical fictions that describe the investigator's beliefs about the causal structure of a set of variables of interest. Seldom are the causal assumptions of these models amenable to direct test. However, models can be subject to indirect tests through attempts to falsify the model on the basis of model fit. Additionally, the plausibility of model assumptions may be examined using various external criteria. Good models are those that summarize the structure of a set of variables in a realistic, informative and parsimonious way, and which are able to withstand concerted attempts at falsification using both goodness-of-fit criteria and external evidence of the plausibility of model assumptions.

The LISREL model

While there have been many attempts to specify the general form of structural equation models, (see, for example, McDonald, 1978; and Jöreskog and Wold, 1982), probably the most useful formulation has been given in the LISREL model described by Jöreskog and his associates (Jöreskog, 1973; Jöreskog and Sörbom, 1984). LISREL, which is an acronym for Linear Structural Relationships, provides a body of statistical theory and a computer program that makes it possible to fit a wide range of structural models to observed variance/covariance matrices.

Model specification. A full account of the mathematical basis of the LISREL model may be found in Jöreskog and Sörbom (1979) and more accessible accounts for non-mathematical readers have been given by Everitt (1984) and Long (1983a,b). Here only the major features of this model will be described.

The point of departure for the LISREL model is the variance/covariance matrix Σ of a set of observed variables. These variables are assumed to be measured on interval scales and are scaled to have a mean of zero. If these variables are standardized to have unit variance, Σ is the matrix of correlations between variables.

The LISREL model distinguishes between two types of observed variable:

1 Variables that are indicators of latent independent or exogenous variables. These variables are denoted by a vector $x = (x_1, \ldots, x_q)$.
2 Variables that are indicators of latent dependent or endogenous variables. These variables are denoted by a vector $y = (y_1, \ldots, y_r)$.

The LISREL model represents the relationships between the x and y variables by two sets of equations which are described as the measurement model and the structural equation model. The measurement model describes the relationships between the observed variables and the latent variables that these observed variables represent. The structural equation model describes the relationships between the latent variables.

The measurement model for the x variables is:

$$x = \Lambda_x \xi + \delta$$

where Λ_x is a parameter matrix of regression coefficients that describe the relationships between the observed variables x and the latent independent variables ξ, and δ is a vector of disturbance terms reflecting errors of measurement in the x variables.

The measurement model for the y variables is:

$$y = \Lambda_y \eta + \varepsilon$$

where Λ_y is a parameter matrix of regression coefficients that describe the relationships between the observed variables y and the latent variables η, and ε is a vector of disturbance terms reflecting errors of measurement in the y variables.

In effect, these equations partition the variance in the observed variables into components attributable to the latent variables of the model and to errors of measurement. The reader will notice the close affinity of the measurement model equations to the equations of the conventional common factor model. However, there is an important difference between these two models. In the common factor model, the elements of the factor loading matrices (Λ_x, Λ_y) are permitted to be free and have values assigned by the application of statistical methods. In the LISREL model the elements of these matrices are usually restricted to imply a particular factor structure of the latent variables. This difference is important since conventional factor analysis aims to *discover* the latent structure of variables by data analytic methods, whereas in the LISREL model this structure is specified on the basis of prior theory. The distinctions between the conventional factor model and the confirmatory factor model of LISREL have been discussed in greater detail by Long (1983a).

While the measurement model equation of LISREL resolves the issue of the relationships between latent and observed variables, often concern will be with the structural relationships which exist between the latent variables. These relationships are represented by the structural equation model of LISREL:

$$\eta = \Gamma\xi + \beta\eta + \zeta$$

where η, ξ are defined by a prespecified measurement model, Γ is a parameter matrix of regression coefficients describing the relationships which exist between the exogenous variables ξ and the endogenous variables η, β is a matrix of regression coefficients which describe the relationships between the endogenous variables η, and ζ is a vector of disturbances reflecting the components of η which are not explained by the model. In this general form the structural equation model permits all exogenous variables ξ to influence all endogenous variables η, and all endogenous variables to be related to each other. In practice, however, it is necessary to set some of the elements of the parameter matrices Γ, β to zero to ensure that the model is identified (see section on identification below).

The equations of the LISREL model contain a number of non-observed variables. These non-observed variables are the latent variables ξ, η and the disturbance variables δ, ε, ζ. This implies the existence of a number of variance/covariance matrices which describe the relationships between these non-observed variables. In the LISREL model the following matrices are permitted to be non-zero:

1 The matrix Θ_δ, which represents the variances and covariances of the disturbance terms δ for the measurement model for the x variables.
2 The matrix Θ_ε, which represents the variances and covariances of the disturbance terms ε for the measurement model for the y variables.
3 The matrix Φ, which represents the variances and covariances of the non-observed latent variables ξ.
4 The matrix Ψ, which represents the variances and covariances of the disturbance terms ζ.

The LISREL model makes it possible to specify a wide range of structural equation models in terms of the parameter matrices Λ_y, Λ_x, B, Γ, Φ, Ψ, Θ_δ and Θ_ε. This may be achieved by imposing various constraints on the parameter matrices to satisfy a given model specification. Model parameters may be of three types:

1 Fixed parameters, which are assigned given values.
2 Constrained parameters, whose values are unknown but which are equal to other model parameters.
3 Free parameters, which are unknown and not constrained to be equal to other parameters.

Identification. While it is possible to specify a wide range of models in terms of the standard LISREL parameter matrices, it is not the case that all such models can be solved. For some model specifications the information in the observed variance/covariance matrix will not be sufficient to secure estimates of some or all model parameters. Such models are said to be underidentified and cannot be solved without either reformulating the model to overcome the sources of the identification problem or introducing additional information to solve the identification problem.

Models that are not underidentified are identified, which means that it is possible to estimate all model parameters on the basis of the observed variance/covariance matrix. Exactly identified models are those in which all model parameters are identified and the number of the model parameters is equal to the number of observed variances and covariances. Such models are not amenable to falsification through goodness-of-fit methods since the fitted model must exactly reproduce the observed variance/ covariance matrix as a matter of mathematical necessity.

Models which are identified and have fewer parameters than observed variances and covariances are said to be overidentified. Overidentification is a desirable feature of a model since overidentified models do not fit the observed data as a matter of mathematical necessity and thus can be subject to test on the basis of goodness-of-fit measures.

The problem of identification in structural equation models is perhaps the most difficult part of model formulation since ideally it is necessary to show that each model parameter can be expressed as an explicit function of the observed variances and covariances. However, even in simple models this may require the solution of large numbers of non-linear equations. A good introduction to the problem of assessing identification is provided by Long (1983a,b). To overcome some of the problems of assessing identification, a number of *ad hoc* tests for assessing identification have been proposed. These include the use of so-called counting rules (see, for example, Duncan, 1975), which provide necessary but not sufficient conditions for identification, and the use of computer-based methods for detecting underidentified models (Jöreskog and Sörbom 1984).

Model fitting. While the LISREL model makes it possible to specify complex structural models, this formulation does not provide any account of the way in which model parameters are to be estimated. LISREL resolves this issue by using a generalized method of maximum likelihood estimation. This method assumes that the observed variables have a multivariate normal distribution, and the values of the parameters are estimated by maximizing the likelil:ood of observing a given matrix Σ conditional on a set of parameter values Θ and the assumption of multivariate normality. For situations in which the assumption of multivariate normality is unrealistic, LISREL provides an unweighted, least-squares method of estimation. This method minimizes the sum of the squared deviations between the observed variances and covariances and those predicted by the model.

Goodness of fit. For overidentified models the problems of assessing the fit of the model to the observed data arises. There is no single test of goodness of fit that will prove to be adequate in all circumstances, but there are a number of approaches that may be used in assessing model fit:

1. Perhaps the most useful general test is through visual inspection of the residual variances/covariances obtained from taking the differences between the observed variances/covariances and the variances/covariances estimated from the model. If these residuals are small, relative to the original variances/covariances and are distributed in a random or haphazard way with respect to sign, this can be taken as good evidence of model fit. Jöreskog and Sörbom (1984) provide a number of ways of examining the properties of such residuals to detect systematic deviations between the fitted model and the observed data.

2. The maximum likelihood method of estimation yields a formal goodness-of-fit test in the form of a log likelihood chi-square statistic. This statistic, which is analogous to the conventional chi-square goodness-of-fit statistic, provides a measure of the fit of the model to the observed data. However, this test is known to be sensitive to large sample size and departures from multivariate normality and for this reason is seldom used as a formal test of fit. More often the log likelihood chi-square is used for comparing the fit of competing models of the data (Jöreskog and Sörbom, 1984).

3. A variety of indices have been suggested to measure the differences between the observed data and the fitted model. These indices are discussed by Jöreskog and Sörbom (1984) and Bentler and Bonnet (1980) and may be used to assess various aspects of model fit.

The justification for LISREL-type models. The LISREL model provides a highly abstract account of the way in which covariance matrices of observed variables may be analysed to obtain estimates of the parameters of linear equations. It is by no means immediately obvious from this abstract account why one would choose to analyse longitudinal data or other social data using this approach in preference to using less complex methods of data analysis. There are three major justifications that may be proposed for choosing this type of approach.

1. Explicitness of model formulation. A feature of the LISREL model is that it requires the theorist to make explicit all of the assumptions that are required to impose a given causal interpretation on a set of data. These assumptions are of two types:

(a) The underlying assumptions of LISREL about linearity of relationships, distributional forms of variables and certain fixed assumptions about the disturbance terms of exogenous and endogenous variables (see Jöreskog and Sörbom, 1984).

(b) Restrictions on the LISREL parameter matrices which serve to specify the causal linkages that the theorist is prepared to assume and, more importantly, those which are assumed to be non-existent.

In contrast, in causal analysis based upon statistical interrogation of data, these assumptions are often left implicit, opening the way for them to be ignored or overlooked. In turn, this lack of an explicit model can easily lead to faulty inference. A simple example of such faulty inference is given for illustration.

Let us assume that we are concerned to study the relationships between three variables: annual rainfall, annual pasture growth and the live weight of sheep at the point of slaughter. The causal model that links these three variables is intuitively clear:

Rainfall → Pasture growth → Sheep weight

Next let us assume that appropriate data are available to examine this issue and, to estimate the contribution of rainfall and pasture growth, an investigator elects to examine these relationships by the application of a multiple regression equation in which sheep weight is regressed upon pasture growth and rainfall. The results of this analysis are predictable and will show that pasture growth is a significant predictor of sheep weight but rainfall is not. Since the analysis is based on a statistical method rather than a prespecified causal model, the next step is likely to be the conclusion that while pasture growth is an important causal factor, rainfall is not. Taking the argument one step further, one could then argue that farmers have no grounds for complaint during periods of drought. The conclusions are, of course, totally specious and arise from a failure of the analysis method to recognize the underlying causal structure of the data and the failure of the investigator to recognize that data analysis alone cannot answer questions of causal inference. This point has been stated elegantly by Fisher (1946, p. 191), who noted: 'If we take a group of social phenomena with no antecedent knowledge of the causation or absence of causation among them, then calculation of correlation co-efficients total or partial will not advance us a step towards evaluation of the importance of the causes at work.'

Given the central role of theory in causal data analysis, it seems an entirely reasonable step to integrate such theory into the statistical technology used to analyse data and this, in effect, is what is provided by LISREL-type models.

2. Latent and observed variables. Most of the variables by which social scientists choose to describe the world do not refer to directly observable properties; rather they are hypothetical constructs or latent variables which describe the dispositional properties of observations. Examples of such latent variables are intelligence, personality, social class and permanent income. The distinction between latent and observed variables raises the important issue of establishing the rules of correspondence or epistemic correlations that exist between latent variables and the observed variables which purportedly represent these variables (Costner, 1985). In this respect LISREL makes a major contribution by drawing a clear distinction between what the investigator has observed (i.e. fallible indicator variables) and what he/she would like to observe (i.e. errorless measures of latent constructs), and by providing a technology to estimate the relationships between these variables subject to a given model specification.

This feature is not simply a matter of conceptual clarity, it also has very important implications for the estimation of the coefficients of a causal model. For the most part, data analysis in the social sciences has tended to resolve the issue of the distinction between latent and observed variables by assuming that the structural relationships between observed variables will in some way reflect the structural relationships that exist between the latent variables which are represented by the observed variables. In general, this article of faith is almost completely groundless. As Costner (1985) has pointed out, what is needed is a subsidiary theory that links the observed variables to the latent variables which they represent and thus permits estimation of the structural relationships between latent variables. The measurement model components of LISREL provide this subsidiary theory.

3. Testability. An important feature in establishing the plausibility of a causal model is to examine the testable predictions that follow from this model. In methods of causal analysis based on data analytic techniques such predictions are usually tested by determining whether certain coefficients are significantly different from zero. However, well-specified causal models will often contain predictions about data other than whether certain coefficients are non-zero. By expressing causal theories as LISREL models it is possible to evaluate all of the predictions of a causal model rather than simply those suggested by intuition.

Examples of structural equation models applied to longitudinal data

Introduction

This section of the chapter is intended to provide an introduction to the process of specifying, interpreting and testing structural equation models using LISREL. Two examples are presented. The first concerns the estimation of the reliability and stability of measures of depression collected during the course of a longitudinal study, and the second deals with the estimation of the trait and method components of longitudinal maternal and teacher reports of child conduct disorder. Both examples emphasize the ways in which conceptualizing measurement problems as causal processes may lead to insights into the nature of the measurement process. This emphasis upon measurement models has been chosen for two reasons. First, despite the extensive literature on test reliability relatively little attention has been given to the estimation of errors of measurement in survey variables (Alwin and Jackson, 1980). Secondly, measurement models are relatively easy to describe and depict by path diagrams, which makes them ideal examples to illustrate the process of model formulation and interpretation.

To maintain the presentation at an introductory level, the account of model specifications and identification will largely be based on a consideration of path diagrams rather than the formal LISREL model specifications. The conventions used in the path diagrams presented in this section are summarized in Figure 1. However, to introduce the reader to the way in which models may be specified in LISREL, a simple introductory example which shows the full model specification and the identification of the model is given.

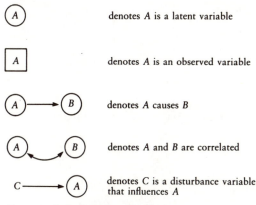

Figure 1   Path diagram conventions

True-score models and the stability of depressive symptoms
True-score models are an important class of models in psychometrics and form the foundation of most indices of test reliability (Lord and Novick, 1968). The essential feature of a true-score model is that the variation in an observed variable is attributed to two components: a true score and an error score. The true scores and error scores are assumed to be uncorre-

lated. A simple true-score model applied to longitudinal data is shown in Figure 2. In this diagram it is assumed that the same construct, ξ, has been measured on two occasions. At each occasion two indicators of ξ have been obtained and these are labelled x_i. The variation in the observed variables x_i is attributed to the causal effects of two non-observed variables: the true-score variables ξ_1, ξ_2 and errors of measurement δ_i. The latent constructs and the errors of measurement are assumed to be uncorrelated and the errors of measurement are assumed to be mutually uncorrelated. The latent constructs ξ are assumed to be correlated between times with a correlation of ϕ_{12}.

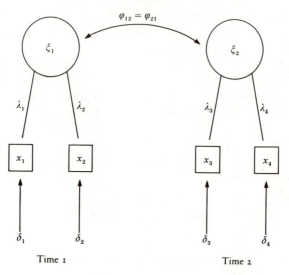

Figure 2   A two-variable, two-wave, true-score model

The model in Figure 2 may be written as the following equations:

$$x_1 = \lambda_1 \, \xi_1 + \delta_1$$
$$x_2 = \lambda_2 \, \xi_1 + \delta_2$$
$$x_3 = \lambda_3 \, \xi_2 + \delta_3$$
$$x_4 = \lambda_4 \, \xi_2 + \delta_4$$

where the coefficients λ_i are the regression coefficients that describe the relationships between the observed variables x_i and the non-observed variables ξ_1, ξ_2. If these coefficients are expressed in standardized form they are analogous to the factor loadings of a model in which x_1, x_2 load on the factor ξ_1, and x_3, x_4 load on the factor ξ_2. The terms δ_i denote the component of the observed variables x_i which is attributable to errors of measurement. This model may be expressed in terms of the parameter matrices of LISREL as follows:

$$x = \Lambda \quad \xi + \delta$$

$$\begin{bmatrix} x_1 \\ x_2 \\ x_3 \\ x_4 \end{bmatrix} \begin{bmatrix} \lambda_1 & 0 \\ \lambda_2 & 0 \\ 0 & \lambda_3 \\ 0 & \lambda_4 \end{bmatrix} \begin{bmatrix} \xi_1 \\ \xi_2 \end{bmatrix} \begin{bmatrix} \delta_1 \\ \delta_2 \\ \delta_3 \\ \delta_4 \end{bmatrix}$$

The model implies that the non-observed variables ξ_1 ξ_2 have variances and covariances. The variance/covariances of these variables are given by:

$$\Phi = \begin{bmatrix} 1 & \phi_{12} \\ \phi_{21} & 1 \end{bmatrix}$$

It will be noted that in this specification the variances of the latent variables have been set to unity, implying that these variables are measured in standardized form. Under these circumstances the covariances $\phi_{12} = \phi_{21}$ become the correlations that exist between the non-observed latent variables.

It is also assumed that the disturbance terms δ_i of the model are uncorrelated with each other. This implies that the variance/covariance matrix of these variables is:

$$\theta_\delta = \begin{bmatrix} \theta_{11} & & & \\ 0 & \theta_{22} & & \\ 0 & 0 & \theta_{33} & \\ 0 & 0 & 0 & \theta_{44} \end{bmatrix}$$

where the non-zero elements θ_{ii} denote the variances of the disturbance terms. The variances θ_{ii} have the interpretation of being the amount of random error variation in the observed variables (subject to the assumptions of the model).

The relative simplicity of the model in figure 2 makes it an ideal example to illustrate the issue of model identification. To show that the model is identified it is necessary to show that each parameter can be expressed as an explicit function of the observed variances and covariances (Long, 1983a). Denoting the variance of x_i as σ_{ii} and the covariance of x_i, x_j as σ_{ij} the relationships between the observed variances and covariances and the model parameters may be expressed as follows:

$$\sigma_{12} = \lambda_1 \lambda_2$$
$$\sigma_{13} = \lambda_1 \lambda_3 \phi_{12}$$
$$\sigma_{14} = \lambda_1 \lambda_4 \phi_{12}$$
$$\sigma_{23} = \lambda_2 \lambda_3 \phi_{12}$$
$$\sigma_{24} = \lambda_2 \lambda_4 \phi_{12}$$
$$\sigma_{34} = \lambda_3 \lambda_4$$
$$\sigma_{11} = \lambda_1^2 + \theta_{11}$$
$$\sigma_{22} = \lambda_2^2 + \theta_{22}$$

$$\sigma_{33} = \lambda_3^2 + \theta_{33}$$
$$\sigma_{44} = \lambda_4^2 + \theta_{44}$$

The rules for deriving such equations are described in detail by Long (1983a,b).

Inspection of the above shows that the ten observed variances and covariances are functions of nine model parameters (λ_1, λ_2, λ_3, λ_4, θ_{11}, θ_{22}, θ_{33}, θ_{44}, ϕ_{12}). This property demonstrates that the model satisfies a necessary but not sufficient condition for identification: the number of model parameters to be estimated is not greater than the number of variances and covariances available to estimate these parameters (Everitt, 1984). However, to produce sufficient conditions for the model to be identified it is necessary to show that each parameter can be expressed as an explicit function of the observed variances and covariances (Long, 1983a,b).

At first sight this looks to be a daunting task involving the solution of ten non-linear equations in nine unknowns. However, in this instance there is a major simplification which aids in establishing the identification of the model. It is easy to show that providing the covariance ϕ_{12} is identified and a single parameter λ_i is identified, then all other parameters are identified. This follows from the fact that once ϕ_{12} and λ_i are known it is easy to estimate the other parameters by substituting these values into the above equations. Thus a sufficient condition to establish the identification of the model is to show that ϕ_{12} and λ_1 (say) are identified.

The coefficient ϕ_{12} may be estimated as follows:

$$\sigma_{12} = \lambda_1 \lambda_2$$
$$\sigma_{13} = \lambda_1 \lambda_3 \phi_{12}$$
$$\sigma_{24} = \lambda_2 \lambda_4 \phi_{12}$$
$$\sigma_{34} = \lambda_3 \lambda_4$$

$$\Rightarrow \phi_{12}^2 = \frac{\sigma_{13}\sigma_{24}}{\sigma_{12}\sigma_{34}}$$

Similarly an estimate of λ_1 may be obtained as follows:

$$\sigma_{12} = \lambda_1 \lambda_2$$
$$\sigma_{14} = \lambda_1 \lambda_4 \phi_{12}$$
$$\sigma_{24} = \lambda_2 \lambda_4 \phi_{12}$$

$$\Rightarrow \lambda_1^2 = \frac{\sigma_{14}\sigma_{12}}{\sigma_{24}}$$

With these conditions established, it can be concluded that at least one estimate of the model parameters can be obtained and thereby the model is identified. Note, however, that the model is only identified empirically if $\phi_{12} \neq 0$ (see Rindskopf, 1984).

It is fairly easy to see that since all parameters are identified and there are fewer parameters than observed variances and covariances, the model is over-identified. This overidentification can be expressed by the following restriction on the covariances:

$$\sigma_{14}\sigma_{23} = \sigma_{13}\sigma_{24} = \phi_{12}^2\lambda_1\lambda_2\lambda_3\lambda_4$$

Thus, if the above restriction is satisfied by the observed data (within the limits of sampling variability) this provides a necessary but not sufficient condition for the model to be the 'true' account of the data. The model is thus falsifiable to the extent that the overidentifying restriction above may not be satisfied and that this will lead to the rejection of the model.

The true-score model described above can be employed to estimate the stability of depressive symptoms over time. It is well known that measures of emotional symptoms tend to be correlated over time, reflecting the tendency for such conditions to both persevere over time and to recur. It is often useful to describe the stability of such measures by computing the correlations between symptom scores at different times. However, in general, the correlations between observed measures will underestimate the true stability of depressive symptoms. This arises because observed measures may contain random errors of measurement which lead to a downward bias in the observed correlations. To estimate the stabilities of measures of depression it is therefore necessary to take into account the effects of such measurement error (i.e. unreliability). A model designed to produce such estimates is described below.

This model is based on data collected on the frequency of depressive symptoms in a sample of over 1,000 New Zealand women with school-age children who were studied over a four-year period using a modified version of the Levine Pilowsky Depression Inventory (Horwood and Fergusson, 1986). Table 1 shows the matrix of correlations between split half measures of this test at each of the four measurement periods. Split half measures were used to provide the two indicator measures at each period, which provide the minimum information needed to solve a true-score model. Inspection of Table 1 suggests the following conclusions:

1 Within each measurement period split half measures are strongly correlated, with coefficients ranging from +.86 to +.89.
2 Between measurement periods the indicator variables are moderately correlated, with coefficients ranging from +.37 to +.53.

The intuitive impressions conveyed by Table 1 are that:

1 The measures are of good reliability as indicated by the high within time correlations.
2 There is moderate stability in symptom scores between measurement periods.

Table 1 *Matrix of correlations between split half measures of depression at four measurement periods*

Time	Split half	x_{11}	x_{12}	x_{21}	x_{22}	x_{31}	x_{32}	x_{41}	x_{42}
1	1 (x_{11})	1							
	2 (x_{12})	.87	1						
2	1 (x_{21})	.47	.44	1					
	2 (x_{22})	.46	.43	.86	1				
3	1 (x_{31})	.38	.38	.51	.51	1			
	2 (x_{32})	.37	.38	.52	.53	.86	1		
4	1 (x_{41})	.41	.42	.41	.41	.52	.50	1	
	2 (x_{42})	.37	.40	.38	.38	.49	.49	.89	1

A model to describe the within- and across-time structure of the eight split half measures is shown in Figure 3. This model assumes that:

1 At each measurement period the split half test scores are influenced by two non-observed variables: the subject's true but non-observed symptom level and random errors of measurement. The true scores and the errors of measurement are assumed to be uncorrelated.

2 Between measurement periods the true-score variables are assumed to be correlated, reflecting the across-time stabilities of these variables.

The coefficients shown in Figure 3 are estimates of the standardized model parameters and may be interpreted in the following way:

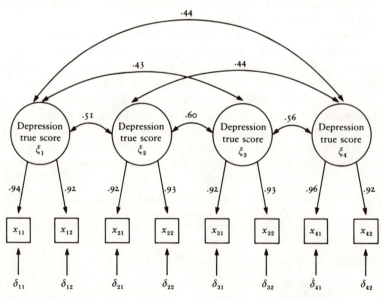

Figure 3 A four-wave, true-score model of depressive symptom measures (all model coefficients are expressed in standardized form). x_{ij} denotes the jth indicator of depression at the ith measurement period. δ_{ij} denotes errors of measurement influencing x_{ij}

1 The coefficients linking the true-score variables to the indicator variables give estimates of the correlations between the true-score variables and the observed variables. Equivalently, the square of these coefficients gives an estimate of the reliability of the split half measures as indicators of the true-score variables (under the assumptions of the model). The coefficients range from .92 to .96, implying that the split half measures have reliabilities in the region .86 to .92. This is consistent with the reliability of the full-length test, which is in the region of .93 (Horwood and Fergusson, 1986).

2 The coefficients linking the latent true-score variables between measurement periods give estimates of the across-time stabilities of the true scores. Between adjacent measurement periods these correlations range from +.51 to +.60, implying moderate to good stability in symptom levels between adjacent years. Between non-adjacent years the correlations are in the region of +.44. It will be noted that these stability coefficients tend to be slightly higher than those suggested by a simple inspection of Table 1.

The model in Figure 3 is heavily overidentified since there are 36 observed variances and covariances of the 8 variables and these are represented by 22 model parameters, implying the presence of 14 overidentifying restrictions in the model. Thus the model does not fit the observed data as a matter of mathematical necessity and an inadequate model can be rejected on the basis of a poor fit between the observed and predicted variance/covariance matrices. In fact, the fit of the model was very good, as may be seen from Table 2, which shows the matrix of residual correlations obtained by subtracting the original correlations from those implied by the standardized model parameters. It may be seen that the model accounts for the observed data with a high degree of accuracy. This result provides evidence that the observed data are consistent with a true-score model, although of course the good fit does not 'prove' that in reality the data were generated by a true-score model.

The common-factor model and the method–trait problem

The true-score models in Figures 2 and 3 assume that the variation in observed variables can be ascribed to the causal effects of non-observed true-score and random-error variables. In many situations these assumptions may be unrealistic and often it is more reasonable to assume that the observed data have been generated by a common-factor model rather than a true-score model. The differences between the common-factor and true-score models have been described by Alwin and Jackson (1980). Essentially, the difference between these models rests with the way in which the disturbance or error terms of these models are conceptualized. In the true-score model the disturbance terms are assumed to reflect random errors of measurement, whereas in the common-factor model these disturbances are assumed to reflect variation arising from two non-observed sources: (a) random errors of measurement; and (b) systematic variance in the observed variables which is not explained by the

Table 2 *Matrix of residual correlations for model in Figure 3*

	x_{11}	x_{12}	x_{21}	x_{22}	x_{31}	x_{32}	x_{41}	x_{42}
x_{11}	.00							
x_{12}	.00	.00						
x_{21}	.01	.00	.00					
x_{22}	.00	−.02	.00	.00				
x_{31}	.00	.01	−.01	−.01	.00			
x_{32}	−.01	.01	.00	.02	.00	.00		
x_{41}	.00	.01	.00	.00	.01	.01	.00	
x_{42}	−.02	.01	−.01	−.01	.01	.00	.00	.00

latent constructs of the model. This systematic variance is often described as the specificity of the variable (Harman, 1976).

The presence of specificity in observed variables introduces complications into the process of model specification and fitting. In particular, it is often not unreasonable to assume that the specificities of variables may be correlated. This is particularly likely to happen in longitudinal studies in which measures of the same variable are obtained at different times (see, for example, Wheaton *et al.*, 1977). To account for such correlation, models for the factor analysis of longitudinal data which permit correlated disturbances have been devised (see, for example, Corballis and Traub, 1970; Long, 1983a).

The problem of correlated disturbance variables also arises in the context of the so-called Multi Method Multi Trait (MMMT) model. The basis of this model was first described by Campbell and Fiske (1959) in their formulation of the MMMT matrix. In this analysis, Campbell and Fiske emphasized the need to compare different measures derived from the same source and the same measurements derived from different sources to examine the discriminant and convergent validities of measures. In its original form the MMMT matrix was conceptualized as a semi-formal way of examining the validities and reliabilities of observed variables. However, Jöreskog (1971) recognized that the ideas implicit in the MMMT matrix could be formalized as a causal model which ascribed variation in observed variables to non-observed trait and method factors. The issues of identification in such models were dealt with in detail by Alwin (1974).

A particular example of the method–trait problem arises in the measurement of child behaviour, where it has been observed that measures of children obtained from different measurement sources are often only weakly correlated. This lack of correlation between measures of allegedly the same trait variables raises important issues about the validity and interpretation of these measures. It seems reasonable to suggest that the lack of correlation between measures of the same

Table 3 *Correlations of measures of conduct disorder observed at three measurement periods*

Time	Source		M_1	T_1	M_2	T_2	M_3	T_3	C_3
Time 1	Maternal	(M_1)	1.00						
	Teacher	(T_1)	.35	1.00					
Time 2	Maternal	(M_2)	.66	.34	1.00				
	Teacher	(T_2)	.38	.57	.42	1.00			
	Maternal	(M_3)	.60	.35	.69	.39	1.00		
Time 3	Teacher	(T_3)	.31	.54	.39	.65	.42	1.00	
	Child	(C_3)	.17	.20	.18	.21	.24	.20	1.00
Standard deviation			2.52	3.12	2.29	2.94	2.31	3.36	4.51

behaviour derived from different sources may arise because the observed behaviour measures are functions of three sets of non-observed variables:

1 The latent trait variable that the measure of behaviour purports to represent.
2 Method-specific factors which reflect both the method used to obtain a given measure and other systematic situational factors related to this method of measurement.
3 Random errors of measurement

If method factors and random errors of measurement in child behaviour variables are relatively large, then one would expect only weak correlations between observed variables derived from different measurement sources. The issue raised by these considerations is that of constructing models that describe the relationships between observed measures of behaviour and the underlying method and trait factors which give rise to the variability in these measures. An example of such a model is given in Table 3. This shows the matrix of correlations between measures of conduct disorder for a sample of over 800 New Zealand children studied at seven, eight and nine years. At ages seven and eight measures of conduct disorder were obtained from mothers and the child's class teacher using the Rutter Behaviour Questionnaire (Rutter *et al.*, 1970). At nine years similar maternal and teacher reports were obtained, but these were supplemented by child reports using the Child Psychiatric Rating Scale described by Beitchman *et al.* (1985).

Inspection of Table 3 suggests that the structure of the observed correlations is not consistent with a true-score model in which all observed variables are generated solely by underlying trait measures of conduct disorder and random error. In particular:

1 Correlations between measures of conduct disorder obtained at the same time but from different sources tend to be modest. The correlations between maternal and teacher ratings range from +.34 to +.42 whereas

the correlations between child and adult ratings range from +.17 to +.24.

2 However, correlations of variables from the same source but at different times are much higher. The across-time correlations of maternal ratings range from +.60 to +.69, whereas the across-time correlations for teacher ratings range from +.54 to +.65.

The fact that the data in Table 3 did not fit a true-score model of the type shown in Figures 2 and 3 was confirmed by the extremely poor fit of this model to the observed data. The value of the log likelihood chi-square statistic for this model was 420.32 ($df = 11; p < .0001$). Given this result it is necessary to consider the ways in which the model might be modified to produce a more accurate account of the data. An alternative model is shown in Figure 4. This model assumes the following:

1 That the variation in the observed measures of conduct disorder is assumed to arise from two sources: the non-observed trait variables of conduct disorder (ξ_1) and a disturbance term δ that reflects both random errors of measurement and systematic (i.e. method) variance in the observed variable.

2 The disturbance terms δ of variables measured from the same source but at different times are permitted to be correlated. These correlations reflect the effects of common method-specific factors on the observed variables.

3 The trait variables are permitted to be correlated between measurement periods, reflecting the stabilities of these variables.

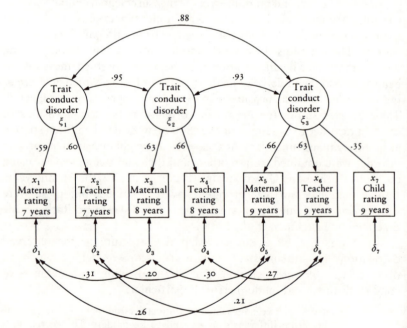

Figure 4   A common-factor model with correlated disturbances

This model can be shown to be identified without further restrictions on the model parameters. There are 28 observed variances and covariances and these are represented by 23 model parameters. By solving out the model in a way that is analogous to the example in Figure 2 it is possible to show that all model parameters are identified and that the model contains five overidentifying restrictions.

The fitted model in Figure 4 may be interpreted as follows:

1. The standardized coefficients linking the latent-trait measures of conduct disorder to the observed variables give estimates of the correlations between the latent traits and the observed variables. Equivalently, the squares of these correlations give estimates of the proportions of variance in the conduct disorder measures which are explained by the latent-trait variables. For maternal ratings these coefficients range from .59 to .66, implying that in the region of 40% of the variation in the observed measures can be explained by variation in the levels of trait conduct disorder in the child. The loadings for teachers are similar to those for mothers. The loading for the child measure (.35) is somewhat lower and this is to be expected since one would not expect nine-year-olds to be able to describe their general behavioural tendencies with great accuracy.

2. The fitted model shows that the disturbance terms of measures derived from the same source are moderately intercorrelated. The correlations for maternal ratings are in the region +.26 to +.31 whereas the correlations between teacher ratings range from +.20 to +.27. These correlated disturbances clearly suggest the presence of systematic method-specific variance in the ratings derived from a given measurement source.

3. An unexpected result from a model is the high correlations that exist between the trait variables between measurement periods. These correlations range from +.88 to +.95, suggesting that the trait component of the conduct disorder score is a highly stable attribute of the child. This high stability of the trait component of the measure is not at all apparent in the observed data (see Table 3), which suggests that the observed conduct disorder measures have stabilities which range (depending on the source of measurement) from as low as +.31 to as high as +.69. It is only when sources of measurement error and test specificity are taken into account that it becomes apparent that concealed within the observed data there is a highly stable attribute of the child.

The overall fit of the model was found to be good on the basis of direct examination of residuals and the goodness-of-fit indices of the LISREL model. This is reflected in the value of the log likelihood chi-square value of 8.46 with 5 df ($p > .10$) for the fitted model.

While the model in Figure 4 provides a statistically adequate account of the observed data, it is theoretically inadequate to the extent that it fails to account explicitly for the sources of correlation between the disturbance terms of the model. It is clear, intuitively, that these correlations arise from method- or situation-specific factors which introduce systematic variation into the observations derived from a given source. A more theoretically defensible model would be one in which the observed variances were modelled as functions of non-observed trait and method factors. Such a model is depicted in Figure 5, which assumes that the correlations between the disturbances in the model in Figure 4 can be represented as method-specific factors reflecting the presence of systematic sources of variation in maternal and teacher ratings which are uncorrelated with the trait variables.

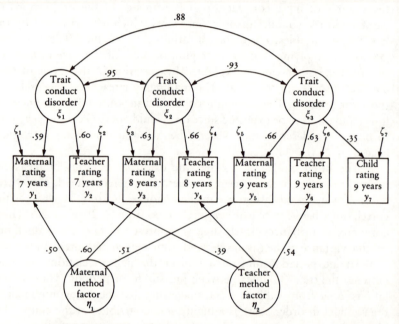

Figure 5   A Multi Trait Multi Method model of maternal and teacher ratings of conduct disorder ζ_k denotes the disturbance term (uniqueness) on the kth observed measure

The identification status and interpretation of this model are identical to the model in Figure 4, a result which reflects the fact that the MMMT model in Figure 5 may be thought of as a way of reparameterizing the model in Figure 4 to represent the correlated disturbances by common method factors. However, the model does make explicit the contribution of method factors to the variability in maternal and teacher ratings. The fitted model suggests that in the region of 25–36% of variance in maternal reports of child behaviour arises from method-specific factors and that in the region of 16–30% of the variance in teacher ratings arises from method-specific factors. In this way the model provides an explanation of the perplexing lack of correlation which is typically found between maternal and teacher accounts of child behaviour. This lack of correlation arises because a substantial amount of the variance in teacher and maternal reports reflects either method-specific factors or random-error variation. The effect of this (non-trait) component of the observed score is to lead to modest correlations between observed measures. It is important to note that the method factors in Figure 5 are not simply 'nuisance' variation but are likely to reflect real factors that influence the mother's and teacher's reporting behaviour. These factors are likely to include general differences in the ways in which mothers and teachers perceive children and real differences in child behaviour at home and school.

The advantages and limitations of structural equation models

The examples presented previously emphasize the use of structural equation models for exploring the measurement properties of longitudinal data. However, it is relatively easy to generalize the approach to model specification, identification and fitting to more complex situations in which both the measurement processes and the structural relationships between latent variables are described by systems of identified linear equations. (The LISREL manual (Jöreskog and Sörbom, 1984) contains a large number of worked examples which illustrate this process in greater detail.) The advantages of the structural equation modelling approach are almost self-evident. Providing that the investigator has a well-specified theory, providing that this theory can be expressed as an identified set of linear equations, and providing that data of sufficient quality and quantity exist, then structural equation models can provide a powerful tool for exploring the fit and implications of causal models. The limitations of the method arise from the failure of one or more of these conditions to be satisfied in practice.

Perhaps the least well described aspect of model building is that of devising an adequate theoretical framework on which to base a model specification. Typically in the social sciences (with the possible exception of economics) theoretical accounts are not specified with sufficient precision for one to argue that a given model specification is implied by a particular theoretical perspective. This situation places the model builder in the situation of having to make some form of 'inductive leap' from existing theory, evidence and conjecture to the postulation of a model. The nature of this inductive leap is often unclear but no doubt reflects the elusive process of scientific creativity. At the same time it seems likely that compelling structural equation models are most likely to be formulated in areas in which there is substantial prior evidence and theory on the causal structure of data, and are likely to be least effective in areas in which both theory and evidence are sparse. For this reason it seems likely that the major role of structural equation models will be to provide explicit and testable models in areas that have been well researched and that accordingly the role of structural modelling as an exploratory data analysis method is likely to be limited.

An important decision to be made in the early stages of model formulation concerns the metric on which the latent constructs of the model are measured. The vocabulary of the social sciences deals with two distinct types of latent entity. The major tradition in psychometrics, and particularly test theory, has been to treat latent constructs as continuous latent variables. In other disciplines (and notably those aligned with medicine) latent constructs are conceptualized as discrete latent classes. The formal differences between latent-class and latent-variable models have been described by Everitt (1984). These differences are, however, often blurred in applied data analysis, in which investigators may move from forms of analysis that assume latent-variable models to forms of analysis that assume latent-class models. For example, continuous variables may be dichotomized to represent the population as discrete classes of 'cases' and 'non-cases', or discrete variables may be treated as representing some underlying continuous variable. While these conventions may be useful for purposes of data display and description, at the point at which causal interpretations of data are offered some clear decision must be made as to whether the observed data are generated by a latent-variable or a latent-class model. In general, analysing data generated by a latent-class model by methods such as LISREL which assume continuous underlying latent variables is likely to produce meaningless results. Similarly, treating data that have been generated by a latent-variable model as though they were generated by a latent-class model is likely to result in a reduction of precision and confused interpretation.

One of the dangers of an uncritical use of structural equation models is that these models can lead to procrustean attempts to force existing causal theories into systems of linear equations. This tendency may vitiate the assumptions of the original causal theory and distort the process of inference. For example, it may be argued that many theories in social science presuppose the existence of non-linear or interactive relationships between variables (Rutter, 1983). If such theories are correct, attempts to represent data using linear and additive models may distort the interpretation of data in quite unpredictable ways. It is, however, possible to build structural equation models that take into account possible non-additive structures. These models and the issues of interpretation they pose have been discussed by Stolzenberg (1980). In addition, the recent versions of the LISREL program incorporate an option for multi-group analyses which may be a powerful tool for testing some types of interactive theory. For example, common interactive assumption in social science theory is that the behaviours of different groups of subjects are described by different causal laws: Brown and Harris (1978) argued that exposure to adverse life events only precipitates depressive responses in 'vulnerable' subjects. Such theories can be readily explored using the multi-group option of LISREL since it is possible to use this option to determine whether the covariance structure that describes the behaviour of one group of subjects is identical to the covariance structure which describes the behaviour of other groups of subjects. Despite the availability of these refinements, issues relating to linearity and interaction are likely to present persistent sources of uncertainty in the interpretation of structural equation models and a counsel of perfection would be that such models should only be devised in the light of strong theory and evidence which justifies the assumptions of linearity and additivity.

At the same time, as a matter of scientific strategy it may be useful to consider the properties of additive linear models of data before embarking on the development of interactive models. It is apparent from the models described here that even relatively simple models may involve considerable complexity in establishing the identification of the model. It is likely that this complexity will be far greater in models that assume interactive structures. Thus in the interests of simplicity of presentation and parsimony it is probably wisest to begin the process of model formulation with simple additive models which may be used to form the foundations of the more complex interactive models.

Additionally, establishing that observed data have been generated by an interactive latent-variable model is by no means a straightforward task. The problems involved can be illustrated by considering current practices in applied data analysis. A frequent method for detecting interaction is to dichotomize variables to form 2^k contingency tables which are then interrogated to detect interactive relationships. Presumably, this strategy is motivated by the belief that the presence of an interaction in a 2^k table is indicative of the fact that the observed data are generated by an interactive process. In fact this assumption is ill-founded, since it is easy to show that data that are generated by a perfectly additive and linear model in continuous variables can appear to be strongly interactive when these variables are dichotomized. Strictly, the presence of interaction in 2^k tables only implies that the data are generated by an interactive latent process if it is believed that the data are adequately described by a 2^k latent-class model. If the data are, in fact, generated by a continuous latent variable, then the presence of interaction in 2^k tables may reflect little more than the capricious effects of the decision rules used to dichotomize the data. Because of this, establishing whether data are generated by interactive processes requires the pitting of models that assume the latent structure of the data is interactive against models that assume additive and linear latent structures; evidence that the observed data are interactive does inevitably imply that the latent processes that generated the observed data are interactive.

However, models that assume interactive relationships between latent variables are very uncommon. As late as 1983, Busemeyer and Jones were able to conclude that there were no adequate methods for solving these models. Kenny and Judd (1984) have suggested a method of modelling interactive latent variables by defining product terms of latent variables which are indicated by product terms of observed variables. This method is appealing in the sense that it can be estimated using relatively simple extensions of existing structural-modelling methods. At the same time, Kenny and Judd noted that fitting the model raises a number of complex issues relating to variable distributions and stress that the model should be seen as being in a developmental stage. Despite these *caveats*, the general approach seems a promising solution to the problem of testing the extent to which observed data are generated by linear additive structures and the extent to which it is necessary to introduce non-linear or interactive assumptions.

The process of translating a causal theory to a causal model also requires that the investigator confronts the issue of the identification status of the model. It is not the case that all causal theories can be expressed as identified models. For example, it is often tempting to assume theories in which all variables are related to each other simultaneously. Such models will invariably be underidentified, and Duncan (1975) has described these models as 'hopelessly underidentified' to underline the point that theory rather than data analysis is needed to identify the causal structure of variables. The effects of confronting the identification problem are usually to force the investigator to make certain simplifying assumptions which, in effect, impose the condition that certain causal relationships do not exist. The result of this process is to make structural equation models approximations, perhaps caricatures, of the complex reality they represent.

It is important to recognize that underidentification in a structural equation model is symptomatic of logical rather than statistical problems. In effect, underidentification reveals that the proposed causal theory does not contain sufficient information, or assumptions, to lead to estimation of the causal linkages assumed by the theory. By consideration of this problem it may be possible to determine the additional information, or assumptions, that are needed to overcome these logical problems. An example of this approach is Alwin's (1974) analysis of the identification status of the general MMMT model. In this analysis Alwin was able to show that the most general version of this model was only identified if data for at least three variables measured from at least three measurement sources were available. This fact is by no means intuitively obvious.

Almost invariably, attempts to build structural equation models will be compromised by the fact that the data available to test such theories are limited in both quantity and quality. The major quantitative limitation on data is usually that the model or process of data collection may omit some variables which are of theoretical relevance. The omitted-variable problem has been a fertile ground for research criticism since it is possible to take almost any causal model and postulate the presence of omitted variables that impugn the validity of the causal interpretation. Such criticism has both constructive and destructive aspects. The constructive aspect of the argument is that the suggestion that certain variables are omitted leads to the development of more elaborate models which contain the omitted variables and that this leads to the development of tests of the difference between the original model and the revised model containing the previously omitted variables. The destructive aspect of this approach is the belief (which is apparently held by many research critics) that the act of listing omitted variables automatically impugns the validity of a causal model.

Under the ideal circumstances structural equation models should be solved on the basis of interval scale data which have a multivariate normal distribution. In practice, many variables measured by social scientists are likely to be non-normally distributed and measured on ordinal-level scales. This raises the knotty issue of the extent to which measurement level and distributional violations in observed data can lead to faulty interference. Despite extensive debate on this topic it is unlikely that the use of ordinal variables in structural equation models will pose serious problems. Duncan (1975) pointed out that providing the relationships between alleged ordinal variables are linear (a fact which should be established prior to modelling these variables), then we should feel little trepidation about using these variables since the ordinal scaling may be thought of as linearizing transformation imposed on the non-observed interval scale variables. More generally, Duncan (1975, p. 160) emphasizes the point that it is the substantive interpretation of the variable in the context of the model that is important rather than the issue of whether the variable is 'really' measured on an ordinal or an interval scale: 'the issue with regard to measurement is not resolved before a variable is entered into the model but in the process of entering it. Those scales that "work" in the sense of providing measurements which are well behaved ... are those which we come to accept as natural.' The problems of distribution are more complex and relatively little is known about the conditions under which violations of multivariate normality will lead to serious errors in model estimates (Bentler, 1980). However, judging from the frequency with which structural equation models are applied to non-normally distributed variables, there is a widespread assumption that these models are robust to violations of the normality assumption.

This practice has been partially supported by recent research which has devised methods of estimation that do require the strong assumption of multivariate normality. These estimators include the asymptotically distribution-free estimators developed by Browne (1984) and the latent-variable approach developed by Muthen (1979; 1983; 1984) for the analysis of dichotomous and categorical variables. Comparisons (e.g. Everitt, 1984; Huba and Harlow, 1987) of these robust estimation methods with the results of maximum-likelihood estimates suggest two major conclusions. First, the parameter estimates from robust estimators and from maximum-likelihood estimates are usually very similar, suggesting that typically the use of maximum-likelihood estimates with non-normally distributed data is unlikely to produce misleading parameter estimates. At the same time, there are differences between the results of robust estimation and maximum-likelihood in both measures of goodness of fit and estimates of standard errors. This work tends to suggest that while the application of maximum-likelihood estimation to non-normal data is unlikely to produce parameter estimates that are substantially in error, measures of goodness of fit of models and tests of significance should be approached with caution (Huba and Harlow, 1987). Hopefully, as methods for computing robust estimates become more widely available and widely used, many of the problems raised by the distribution of variables will be eliminated or at least reduced.

Even when problems of model specification, identification, variable scaling and estimation have been overcome, there may still be problems with the interpretation of the parameters of structural equation models. Usually these models are fitted to data from relatively large samples, with the result that the parameter estimates describe the relationships which exist 'on average' between variables. However, such models do not take account of inter-individual variations in responsiveness (Herzog and Nesselroade, 1987) and implicitly assume that the parameters of the model apply with equal force to all subjects. It is possible, however, that substantial inter-individual variation may exist, with the result that while the parameters of structural equation models may adequately describe the relationships which exist between variables, these parameters do not describe the behaviour of individuals represented by these variables. This view represents an extreme case of the issue of interaction discussed earlier, since it may be argued that an adequate structural equation model should include parameters that are specific to each individual and describe that individual's specific response characteristics. There have been suggestions (e.g. Herzog and Nesselroade, 1987) that estimates of such inter-individual variation can be incorporated into structural equation models through the use of longitudinal designs in which the behaviour of subjects is measured on many occasions. From such time series data, models of individual responsiveness can be estimated. Further inter-individual differences in responsiveness may then be modelled as functions of variables (e.g. socio-economic status) that describe differences between individuals. This proposal poses two major problems. First, obtaining data on many occasions is likely to involve expensive and highly time-consuming methods of data collection. Second, the problem of estimating both individual parameters and parameters that describe differences between individuals is likely to pose complicated statistical issues. However, an approach to the problem of estimating parameters in research designs involving such multi-level data has been described by Mason *et al.* (1984).

Consideration of the problems of specifying, fitting, testing and interpreting structural equation models suggests that there are many points at which this process may fail. Existing theory may not be sufficiently precise to suggest compelling causal models; in the process of model specification and identification compromises may be made that vitiate the assumptions of the original theory; observed data may be of insufficient quality or quantity to sustain the model-fitting process; and the use of parameter estimates based on sample data rather than individual data may misrepresent the causal processes which are occurring in populations. These problems are, of course, not peculiar to structural equation models and any serious attempt to construct compelling causal models of correlational evidence needs to confront such problems of model specification, identification, estimation, measurement and interpretation. In the final analysis the major contribution of current structural equation modelling methods to the social sciences may not be in the area of developing substantive models but rather in the area of sensitizing research workers to the theoretical, formal and empirical problems which must be confronted when causal accounts of correlational evidence are offered.

References

Aigner, D. J. and Goldberger, A. S. (eds.) (1977) *Latent variables in socio-economic models.* Amsterdam: North-Holland.

Alwin, D. F. (1974) Approaches to the interpretation of relationships in the multitrait–multimethod matrix. In Costner, H. L. (ed.) *Sociological methodology, 1973–1974.* San Francisco: Jossey-Bass, pp. 79–105.

Alwin, D. F. and Jackson, D. S. (1980) Measurement models for response errors in surveys. In Schuessler, K. F. (ed.) *Sociological methodology 1980.* San Francisco: Jossey-Bass, pp. 68–119.

Beitchman, J. H., Raman, S., Carlson, J., Clegg, M. and Kruidenier, B. (1985) The development and validation of the child's self-report psychiatric rating scale. *Journal of American Academy of Child Psychiatry,* 24, 413–28.

Bentler, P. M. (1980). Multivariate analysis with latent variables: causal modelling. *Annual Review of Psychology,* 31, 419–56.

Bentler, P. M. and Bonnett, D. G. (1980). Significance tests and goodness of fit in the analysis of covariance structures. *Psychological Bulletin,* 88, 588–606.

Brown, G. W. and Harris, T. (1978) *The social origins of depression.* London: Tavistock.

Browne, M. W. (1982). Covariance structures. In Hawkins, D. M. (ed) *Topics in applied multivariate analysis.* Cambridge: Cambridge University Press, pp. 72–141.

(1984) Asymptotically distribution free methods for the analysis of covariance

352   D. M. Fergusson and L. J. Horwood

structures. *British Journal of Mathematical and Statistical Psychology*, **37**, 62–83.

Busemeyer, J. R. and Jones, L. E. (1983) Analysis of multiplicative combination rules when the causal variables are measured with errors. *Psychological Bulletin*, **93**, 549–63.

Campbell, D. T. and Fiske, D. W. (1959). Convergent and discriminant validation by the multitrait–multimethod matrix. *Psychological Bulletin*, **56**, 81–105.

Corballis, M. C. and Traub, R. E. (1970) Longitudinal factor analysis. *Psychometrika*, **35**, 79–98.

Costner, H. L. (1985) Theory deduction and rules of correspondence. In Blailock, H. M. (ed.) *Causal models in the social sciences*. New York: Aldine, pp. 229–50.

Duncan, O. D. (1975) *Introduction to structural equation models*. New York: Academic Press.

Everitt, B. S. (1984) *An introduction to latent variable models*. London: Chapman and Hall

Fisher, R. A. (1946) *Statistical methods for research workers*, 10th edn. Edinburgh: Oliver and Boyd.

Harman, H. H. (1976) *Modern factor analysis*. Chicago: University of Chicago Press.

Heise, D. R. (1975) *Causal analysis*. New York: Wiley.

Herzog, C. and Nesselroade, J. R. (1987) Beyond auto-regressive models: some implications of the trait–state distinction for the structural modelling of developmental change. *Child Development*, **58**, 93–110.

Horwood, L. J. and Fergusson, D. M. (1986) Neuroticism, depression and life events: a structural equation model. *Social Psychiatry*, **21**, 63–71.

Huba, G. J. and Harlow, L. L. (1987) Robust structural equation models: implications for developmental psychology. *Child Development*, **58**, 147–67.

Jöreskog, K. G. (1971) Statistical analysis of sets of congeneric tests. *Psychometrika*, **36**, 109–33.

— (1973) A general method for estimating a linear structural equation system. In Goldberger, A. S. and Duncan, O. D. (ed.) *Structural equation models in the social sciences* New York: Seminar, pp. 85–112.

— (1979) Statistical estimation of structural models in longitudinal developmental investigation. In Nesselroade, J. R. and Baltes, P. B. (eds.) *Longitudinal research in the study of behavior and development*. New York: Academic Press, pp. 303–51.

Jöreskog, K. G. and Sörbom, D. (1977) Statistical models and methods for the analysis of longitudinal data. In Aigner, D. J. and Goldberger, A. S. (eds.) *Latent variables in socio-economic models*. Amsterdam: North-Holland, pp. 285–325.

— (1979) *Advances in factor analysis and structural equation models*. Cambridge, MA: Abt Books.

— (1984) *LISREL VI: analysis of linear structural relationships by the method of maximum likelihood*. Mooresville, IN: Scientific Software.

Jöreskog, K. G. and Wold, H. (eds.) (1982) *Systems under indirect observation: causality, structure, prediction*. Amsterdam: North-Holland.

Kenny, D. A. (1979) *Correlation and causality*. New York: Wiley.

Kenny, D. A. and Judd, C. M. (1984) Estimating the non linear and interactive effects of latent variables. *Psychological Bulletin*, **96**, 201–10.

Long, J. S. (1983a) *Confirmatory factor analysis*. Beverly Hills: Sage.

(1983b) *Covariance structure models: an introduction to LISREL.* Beverly Hills: Sage.

Lord, F. M. and Novick, M. R. (1986) *Statistical theories of mental test scores.* Reading, MA: Addison-Wesley.

McDonald, R. P. (1978) A simple comprehensive model for the analysis of covariance structures. *British Journal of Mathematical and Statistical Psychology,* 31, 59–72.

Mason, W. M., Wong, G. Y. and Entwistle, B. (1984) Contextual analysis through the multilevel linear model. In Leinhardt, S. (ed.) *Sociological methodology, 1983–1984.* San Francisco: Jossey-Bass, pp. 72–103.

Muthen, B. (1979) A structural probit model with latent variables. *Journal of the American Statistical Association,* 74, 807–11.

(1983) Latent variable structural equation modelling with categorical data. *Journal of Econometrics,* 22, 43–65.

(1984) A general structural equation model with dichotomous, ordered categorical and continuous latent variable indicators. *Psychometrika,* 49, 115–32.

Popper, K. (1961) *The logic of scientific discovery.* New York: Science Editions.

Rindskopf, D. (1984) Structural equation models: empirical underidentification, Heywood cases, and related problems. *Sociological Methods and Research,* 13, 109–19.

Rogosa, D. (1979) Causal models in longitudinal research. In Nesselroade, J. R. and Baltes, P. B. (eds.) *Longitudinal research in the study of behavior and development.* New York: Academic Press, pp. 263–302.

Rutter, M. (1983) Statistical and personal interactions: facets and perspectives. In Magnusson, D. and Allen, V. (eds.) *Human development: an interactional perspective.* New York: Academic Press, pp. 295–319.

Rutter, M., Tizard, J. and Whitmore, K. (eds.) (1970) *Education, health and behaviour.* London: Longman.

Stolzenberg, R. M. (1980) The measurement and decomposition of causal effects in non-linear and non-additive models. In Schuessler, K. F. (ed.) *Sociological methodology 1980.* San Francisco: Jossey-Bass, pp. 459–88.

Susser, M. (1973) *Causal thinking in the health sciences.* London: Oxford University Press.

Wheaton, B., Muthen, B., Alwin, D. and Summers, G. (1977) Assessing reliability and stability in panel models. In Heise, D. (ed.) *Sociological methodology.* San Francisco: Jossey-Bass, pp. 84–136.

20 Modelling reality: some comments[1]

Lars R. Bergman

I found Fergusson and Horwood's discussion (see chapter 19) of the uses and limitations of structural equation models of longitudinal data informative and intriguing. They give an account of the key features of linear structural equation modelling using the LISREL program and they also point to important application areas relevant to longitudinal risk research. In the following, I will concentrate on four points that I think are important to consider when deciding on a suitable method of analysing one's data in longitudinal risk research. To provide a more balanced picture, I will also discuss the limitations of (structural) regression models as statistical tools in longitudinal risk research.

The scaling properties of the variables to be studied

Sometimes important *observed* variables in a study are discrete; this can limit the choice of possible methods of analysis. If the discrete variables can be assumed to stem from normally distributed variables, it may be possible to handle them within the LISREL system, using the PRELIS program (Jöreskog and Sörbom, 1985). For instance, polyserial correlations can be estimated between continuous variables and ordinal variables, and polychoric correlations can be computed between pairs of ordinal variables. PRELIS can also handle censored variables, that is variables that are truncated, such as a test variable exhibiting ceiling effects. Somewhat simplified, provided certain assumptions are met, in all the cases mentioned above PRELIS estimates a correlation matrix that corresponds to the one that would have been obtained if all the observed variables had been measured on continuous scales. This matrix is then the input for an ordinary LISREL analysis.

In structural equation modelling, the concept of a latent variable is central. Consider now the case when there is reason to believe that the key *latent* variables in a study cannot be assumed to follow continuous distributions or to be on an interval scale. For instance, consider Fergusson and Horwood's model for the growth of conduct disorder, a model that also takes method variance into account. As I see it, the

[1] I am grateful to Dr Sigrid Gustafson, Professor David Magnusson, and Professor Georg Rudinger for many useful suggestions.

structural model they apply is one possible way of analysing such data. However, this approach reflects a specific view of the nature of conduct disorder. It is seen as a latent trait exhibiting nice continuous properties. Depending on your theoretical position, this assumption may or may not be reasonable.

Another view would be that forces in society strive to reduce the kinds of behaviour that are included in conduct problems. Children on the border line of what is considered unacceptable behaviour will experience a strong pressure to conform. However, once they pass that border line, other forces that could draw them even deeper into conduct problems may start to operate: for instance, being rejected by a normal peer group and joining a peer group of children with conduct problems. In this case one would perhaps have a bimodal distribution of conduct problems. It could also be argued that the psychological significance of the phenomena under study would not be reflected by the variable values (latent or observed) on an interval scale, a situation that would make structural modelling less appropriate. The need for choosing statistical methods that match the scaling properties of the variables involved has been explicated by Busemeyer (1980) and Townsend and Ashby (1984).

If this last theoretical view of conduct problems is taken, categorical methods for analysing longitudinal data may be preferable. For instance, the conduct problem variables could be dichotomized at what was believed to be the critical cut-off points and one of the following methods could be used:

1 One could concentrate on analysing the proportion of children with a conduct problem, employing a higher-order contingency table analysis along the lines shown by Brown (see chapter 17).
2 Each separate occasion and rating could be treated as a dichotomous variable that, for each individual, could take the value 'does not exhibit a conduct problem' or 'does exhibit a conduct problem' (more categories than two are, of course, possible). This method would result in seven dichotomous variables; the frequencies of the different value patterns in the sample could then be studied within the framework of configural frequency analysis (CFA) (Krauth and Lienert, 1982; Lienert, 1969). CFA has been extended to handle longitudinal data in different ways and is a fairly simple, robust methodology (Lienert and Kohnen, 1987; Lienert and Bergman, in press). The observed frequencies associated with different hypothesized typical and atypical value patterns can in this way be investigated.

Undoubtedly, the alternatives to structural modelling offered here are not as elegant; for example, they provide no explicit model for the errors of measurement. However, a categorical kind of analysis need not be purely descriptive since specific value configurations can be hypothesized as being overrepresented or underrepresented, and these hypotheses can be empirically tested. If one wants to stay closer to the kind of theoretical thinking that usually lies behind the formation of a structural model but use a categorical kind of analysis, some kind of loglinear modelling might be appropriate (Bishop *et al.* 1975; Goodman, 1978).

Problems introduced by errors of measurement

The importance of seriously considering errors of measurement is pointed out by Fergusson and Horwood and they show how certain kinds of error can be modelled using LISREL. In this section I will try to approach the issue of errors of measurement from a broader perspective.

It is, almost by definition, difficult to discuss the effects of errors of measurement in general terms, partly because errors of measurement, in a wide sense, incorporate disturbances of which one has very little knowledge and partly because, to a certain extent, errors of measurement are specific to a particular study in that they may be attributable to unmeasured factors. Indeed, what is considered as error variance by one researcher can be variance attributed to the independent variables in another study (Cronbach *et al.*, 1972). Thus the interpretation of errors of measurement and the process by which they are generated are inextricably tied to a specific study.

Furthermore, reliability, as it is usually measured, is not a fixed property of a measurement instrument; it depends on the properties of the study in which the instrument is to be used. For instance, if school satisfaction is studied by analysing answers to a questionnaire from a sample of school children, the reliability of a school satisfaction score would differ depending on the following factors:

1 The heterogeneity of the sample (large inter-individual differences in true scores would give a higher reliability than small differences would).
2 The exact definition of the theoretical construct that one wants to study. For example, if the purpose is to study school satisfaction as a *state* that changes from day to day, a test-retest coefficient with a one week's time interval must be given quite a different interpretation than if school satisfaction is to be studied as a *trait*. A low coefficient would, in the latter, but not in the former case, indicate a disturbing lack of reliability. It is obvious that in a longitudinal study a reasonable test–retest reliability is often a prerequisite for the involved indicators.

That errors of measurement can be troublesome in the study of change is well known (Bergman, 1972; Cronbach and Furby, 1970; Harris, 1963). This problem is intuitively apparent from the following argument. Assume one has a pre-test score X and a post-test score Y as indicators of the value of a theoretical construct at two different ages. Assume further that each observed score can be divided into a true score and an error score, that is $X = X_t + e_x$ and $Y = Y_t + e_y$. If change is the focus in the study, we are interested in $Y - X$, which can be written as:

$$Y - X = (Y_t - X_t) + (e_y - e_x).$$

If we are studying a stable characteristic, the variance of the true-score differences will tend to be small, with the result that a large part of the variance of the observed change score will consist of systematic error variance and/or random error variance. For instance, in a Swedish study concerning change in intelligence, it was found that the reliability of IQ change was .45 in spite of the fact that each of the IQ scores individually had a reliability of .90 (Berman, 1972). For this reason the use of change scores was avoided.

Even if the errors of measurement can be assumed to be benign, in the sense that the ordinary test theoretical assumptions hold, many difficult methodological problems are encountered in this field of research when conventional correlational and regression methods are used (Bergman, 1972; Harris, 1963). Thus that such errors can be incorporated in the model is a very useful property of LISREL.

Nevertheless, one must still question the frequency of situations in which the errors of measurement are, indeed, benign. Obviously, the process of error generation and interpretation is highly specific to the particular study under consideration, but the following two properties of longitudinal risk research may be relevant in the present connection:

1 The study may include repeated measures using the same instrument. In this case correlated errors may well occur. Fergusson and Horwood (see chapter 19) discuss the incorporation of such errors into a LISREL model of conduct problems. However, the correlation of errors and true scores may still be problematic in the above case if, for example, there is reason to believe that a specific subgroup of mothers underreport conduct problems of particularly troublesome children.
2 The study may include measures that reflect extreme manifestations of phenomena and may therefore be subject to ceiling or floor effects that lead to systematic errors. For example, in a longitudinal study of criminality a standard measure of aggression may lack the power to discriminate among different groups of criminals because many subjects obtain the maximum score.

A case study of errors

To be a little more concrete in my discussion of errors, I have analysed an old Swedish data set originally collected by Beckne (1966). The data set comprises the answers to a pupils' questionnaire concerning various aspects of the pupils' school experience. The sample consisted of $N = 154$ subjects, aged 13, who were given the questionnaire twice, with three to four weeks' interval between the testings.

Partly by using factor analysis, the following six scales were constructed by summation of the relevant items: V1 – School Satisfaction, V2 – Psychosomatic Reactions, V3 – Experienced Work Load, V4 – Bad Peer

Relations, V5 – Anxiety at Appearing in front of the Class, and V6 – Not Interested in the School Subjects. For all scales, a high score indicates a positive attitude or good adjustment. For the purpose of analysing the errors, all scales were retained as raw scores to enable the study of systematic shifts between the test and retest with regard to means and standard deviations.

Before continuing with the analyses of these data I would like to mention certain trivial sources of error that might have affected the present analysis (but which, of course, were avoided): (a) summing the scores of the items belonging to a factor without coding the factor score as missing for those few children with a partial dropout; (b) summing the scores of the items without correcting for the fact that a few items have a reversed meaning, with a high score indicating a positive attitude; (c) summing the scores without correcting for the fact that a few items with response alternatives 'yes', 'no' and 'maybe' were originally coded yes = 1, no = 2 and maybe = 3. These potential sources of error represent just a few possibilities of the kinds of error that may creep into one's data. Many such errors are avoided by careful documentation, which is especially important in a longitudinal study in which time weakens memory and the persons conducting the original investigation may leave the project.

For each subject, the difference between the test and the retest score was formed for each of the six scales. In a longitudinal setting, one would like to treat scores referring to the same age, as the test and retest scores used here do, as having the same true value. The test–retest difference, under standard test theoretical assumptions, can then be represented as normally distributed error with a mean of zero. In Table 1 the basic information is given concerning the difference scores.

Table 1 *Basic information concerning the test–retest difference scores (error scores)* (N = 154)

Scale	*t*-value difference	Skewness	Kurtosis	Test–retest correlation	
V1	0.654	0.48*	0.83	0.69	Seven correlations
V2	2.07*ᵃ	1.17**	4.26**	0.57	between difference
V3	−1.50	0.39	0.24	0.59	scores were significant
V4	−0.66	0.80**	2.84**	0.53	at the 5% level.
V5	−1.06	0.05	0.84	0.70	
V6	−1.67	0.07	−0.14	0.80	For V1 only there was a significant ($p < .001$) increase of the standard deviation.

ᵃ $p < .05$.
* or ** attached to a measure of skewness or kurtosis means that a significant deviation from normality is found at the 5% and 1% level, respectively.

The results in Table 1 may be interpreted as follows:

1 For Psychosomatic Reactions (V2) there is an increase in the proportion of children admitting symptoms.

2 Three out of six difference scores exhibit a departure from the normal distribution, indicating that the corresponding distributions are positive skewed and/or leptokurtic (Kendall and Stuart, 1963, p. 86; Snedecor and Cochran, 1967, pp. 85–8). The main feature appears to be that extremely high values and values close to the mean are more common than would be observed for a normal distribution. This finding may indicate that for Psychosomatic Reactions (V2) the systematic decrease in scores is not a general phenomenon caused solely by constant change with a moderate random error added. In addition, there may be, among other things, a subgroup of persons who alter their ratings substantially for some reason.

3 The correlations among the difference scores were significant in seven cases, ranging from .17 to .24, leading to the inference of correlated errors in these data.

A further comment on errors of measurement

The most important action to take with regard to handling measurement errors is, of course, to design the measurement process carefully so as to minimize the errors. One possible source of error variance that may be underestimated by many researchers is the variance introduced by the interviewer. Survey research indicates that this variance component can explain as much as 10% of the variation for certain attitude items (Collins, 1980; Kish, 1962). Experiments performed on the effect of question order on the answers to attitude items, the wording of questions, and the response format, should give us a healthy respect for the importance of also seriously considering these possible sources of bias and the tools available to minimize them (Bergman and Wärneryd, 1982; Schuman and Presser, 1981). This issue may be especially pertinent in a longitudinal study, where one must sometimes use slightly different indicators of the same theoretical construct, based on data referring to different ages, in order to study development.

Complicated errors make the choice of an appropriate model of analysis difficult. Categorical analyses of the kind indicated above normally carry the disadvantage of having no explicit model for the errors of measurement. Nevertheless, they may in some situations be more robust as compared to methods that assume the variables to be on an interval scale. This is exemplified by a story told by R. V. Jones in his book about scientific intelligence during the Second World War (Jones, 1979). He described how two scientists were assigned the problem of deducing the characteristics of German magnetic mines laid at sea. The data consisted of reports of the position of mines relative to that of the minesweeper at the time of the explosion. One scientist treated the data as accurate and did not solve the problem. The other went out minesweeping. He found that 'the reports from the minesweeping crews were wildly inaccurate as regards both range and bearing, and the only item of data on which one could rely was whether the mine had exploded to port or starboard. Simplifying all the later reports down to this extremely limited observation, he nevertheless succeeded in deducing the answer' (pp. 478, 479).

The problem of interactions between the variables

As has been pointed out, for instance by Rutter (1983), the word 'interaction' has many different connotations. I will here use the word in the following restricted sense:

There exists an interaction in a data set if, depending on the value in one or more variables, the relationships between other variables change.

Certain kinds of interaction can be handled using structural equation modelling, and, within the LISREL system, Fergusson and Horwood point to the possibility of using a specification analysing several populations. Other methods are also possible (Kenny and Judd, 1984).

However, more complicated interactions can be very troublesome to handle within the context of linear models as suggested by, for instance, Magnusson (1985), Hinde and Dennis (1986) and by Magnusson and Bergman (see chapter 3). Rogosa and Willett (1985a, b) have also pointed to the lack of modelling of *individual* growth as a problem in using standard structural regression models for studying change.

I will try to make the statement about complicating interactions more concrete by focusing on one aspect, namely the concept of pairwise relationships. To simplify, when applying regression analytic methods and linear structural equation models, one often uses a covariance or correlation matrix as the input data for the analysis. The results can then be valid only as far as the relevant relationships are reflected by the pairwise relationships summarized by that matrix.

The following example, using artificial data, is given here as an illustration of the fact that pairwise relationships do not always reflect the interactions present in the data. Let us assume that two dichotomous criteria are to be predicted from two dichotomous predictors. For the sake of concreteness, the criteria can be thought of as outcomes and the predictors can be thought of as risk factors. The value '−' can be thought of as being 'negative', that is indicating the presence of a risk factor or of a negative outcome. Let us assume that the data consist of 400 cases and that the pairwise relationships shown in Table 2 are obtained.

As can be seen in Table 2, there is no relationship at all between any pair of variables. If a measure of association were computed, the value would be zero for each pair of variables. What kind of multivariate distributions can generate the relationships shown in Table 2? In Table 3 three

Table 2 *Pairwise relationships for a set of four variables for* N = 400 *cases*

	P_2 +	P_2 −			C_1 +	C_1 −			C_2 +	C_2 −
P_1 +	100	100		P_1 +	100	100		P_1 +	100	100
P_1 −	100	100		P_1 −	100	100		P_1 −	100	100
	400				400				400	

	C_1 +	C_1 −			C_2 +	C_2 −			C_2 +	C_2 −
P_2 +	100	100		P_2 +	100	100		C_1 +	100	100
P_2 −	100	100		P_2 −	100	100		C_1 −	100	100
	400				400				400	

Table 3 *Three different aritifical data sets that generate the zero correlations found in Table 2 (*N = 400 *cases)*

	C ++	C +−	C −+	C −−			C ++	C +−	C −+	C −−			C ++	C +−	C −+	C −−
P ++	5	35	35	25		P ++	25	25	25	25		P ++	50			50
P +−	35	25	25	15		P +−	25	25	25	25		P +−		50	50	
P −+	40	20	20	20		P −+	25	25	25	25		P −+		50	50	
P −−	20	20	20	40		P −−	25	25	25	25		P −−	50			50
				400						400						400
	Data set 1						Data set 2						Data set 3			

multivariate data sets are given, each of which generates the absence of pairwise correlations found in Table 2.

The interpretation of the existing interactions in these three data sets could be summarized as follows:

> *Data set 1.* Two strong types exist that are highly significant, namely −+ by ++ and −− by −−. The last type indicates that the presence of both risk factors leads to an increased frequency of experiencing both negative outcomes as compared to what could be expected from a random model (an observed frequency of 40 as compared to an expected frequency of 25).
>
> *Data set 2.* No interactions whatsoever are present.
>
> *Data set 3.* An abundance of interactions exist, some of which are very strange.

Clearly, the pairwise correlations would be very misleading as indicators of the relationships for two of these three artificial data sets – the strong interactions that exist there would not show up in the pairwise correlations.

The above discussion should not be interpreted as a plea for constantly looking for complicated interactions. In many cases the ordinary practice of focusing on pairwise relationships appears to be well-founded.

However, one should not always take for granted that such complicated interactions can safely be ignored. In some situations it constitutes sound procedure to at least perform a complementary analysis that focuses on higher-order interactions. Moreover, under certain conditions one may choose to concentrate on this aspect, for instance by using a pattern approach as advocated by Magnusson and Bergman (see chapter 3).

Naturally, the need to take complicated interactions into account will vary among research areas and will depend on the specific problem under study. It might be that longitudinal risk research needs to take these problems seriously. It often concerns events and processes that can be viewed as lying outside the normal variation, and highly specific factors can sometimes be assumed to start operating at certain levels of risk factors. Furthermore, a high value in a risk factor can be thought of as indicating a *qualitatively* different internal functioning (e.g. a neurological disturbance) rather than a higher value on a continuum.

For instance, Cronbach (1975) has strongly argued the importance of including the study of interactions within many fields of psychology. However, he has also, somewhat pessimistically, pointed to the ever-increasing complexity that is encountered when more and more complicated interactions are introduced: one enters a hall of mirrors with new images emerging at every turn. Here, as elsewhere in science, it is probably wise to apply Morgan's canon and only introduce as many interactions as are necessary to account for the data. Nevertheless, it is then essential to study the relevant data; obviously it is not a sound application of the canon to try to explain data that do not reflect the relevant properties of reality.

Exploration versus confirmation

I agree with Fergusson and Horwood that one attractive property of structural modelling is that assumptions and prior knowledge have to be made explicit when constructing the structural model. It adds clarity to one's way of thinking and enables one to test many of these explicated aspects empirically. It was an important achievement of Jöreskog and other statisticians when they solved the problems of incorporating, in the same model, both a measurement model and a structural model for the relationships among the latent variables (for a review of this topic, see Bentler, 1986).

As Fergusson and Horwood point out, it is also possible to compare the fit of different models. For instance, using LISREL on a longitudinal data set, Olsson and I compared several different models for the growth of abilities with a very general model to see if any of the more parsimonious models fitted the data almost as well as the general model did (Olsson and Bergman, 1977). The aim of the study was to investigate the age differentiation hypothesis. Sometimes the most attractive approach would be to derive two (or more) different model specifications, each reflecting specific theoretical implications, and then compare the fit of the different models. From a statistical/technical viewpoint it is difficult to make this kind of comparison if the models do not fulfil certain statistical criteria for how they are related. An example of the comparison of six nested models of the development of fluid and crystallized intelligence is given in Rudinger (1985). He used LISREL and let the different models impose different degrees of invariance on the measurement model over time.

In practice, structural equation modelling is often used in a rather exploratory fashion, testing successive approximations of an initial model until a good fit to the data set is obtained. Indeed, the unsophisticated user may be encouraged in this approach by the LISREL program, in that rather detailed information is provided by each program run concerning which aspects of the fitted model are associated with a lack of fit. An option also exists whereby the program performs automatic model modification iteratively and stops when a fitting model has been found.

There is, of course, nothing wrong with exploring to find a model that fits; it can often be a very sensible procedure. But it is important to recognize the limitations of such a process. It does not provide a test of the model that is finally found; rather, it is the outcome of a search procedure, the results of which must be replicated on another sample. The search is a kind of model hunt, and it should be recognized that if a hunter happens to shoot a white rabbit, that occurrence is no strong support for a theory that all rabbits are white.

The importance of avoiding excessive exploration has, of course, been emphasized many times. For instance, regarding LISREL, Jöreskog and Sörbom (1984) pointed to the importance of combining the automatic model modification with careful judgement. One aspect of this judiciousness is to use the 'never free' specification to fix parameters such that the model search is restricted to those models that make sense according to one's theoretical expectations.

The issue of hypothesis testing versus exploration in (structural) modelling of the phenomena under study has a particular bearing on longitudinal risk research. Normally such data take a long time and considerable effort to collect. Therefore they are usually only collected after a careful decision process through which the researcher forms a theoretical basis on which to base expectations and hypotheses. Thus a confirmatory approach appears to be natural in many cases. Nevertheless, it is important to be flexible and not to adhere rigidly to the principle of testing only a single model constructed beforehand which will be accepted or rejected. Such rigidity may underuse the data, leading one to focus solely on the limited aspect of the reality that is modelled.

From a pragmatic point of view, longitudinal risk data are too precious a commodity to be used mainly for a theoretical one-shot. It is also important to use the data exploratively and to be prepared to notice the unexpected result that may point to a new theoretical formulation. This new formulation could then be tested, preferably on another sample, but perhaps using information from the same sample, as illustrated by Brown (see chapter 17). Of course, from a formal hypothesis-testing perspective, the approach advocated above raises many problems which in some way must be addressed. In some situations, a division of the sample into two split halves, with one half used for exploration and the other half used for cross-validation, might be useful. The orientation advocated here can perhaps be described as result-centred, in the context of Greenwald *et al.* (1986).

Conclusions

In this chapter I have not attempted to discuss the issue of causal inferences. This issue has received much attention in the literature concerning (structural) regression modelling. From a substantive point of view it is also discussed in several chapters in this book (see, for example, chapter 1). It has repeatedly been pointed out that even an application of the most sophisticated tools, such as LISREL, offers no golden road to causal inferences (see, for example, Cliff, 1983). For instance, even though a certain theoretical model of causal relations may lead to the formulation of a statistical model that fits the data, this finding does not rule out the possibility that another theoretical model, making different causal assumptions, would also fit the data. Thus the interpretation of the results with regard to causal relationships can never be a statistical matter; it is fundamentally an interpretation made by the researcher on the basis of psychological theory and common sense.

In spite of the complications, discussed above, in analysing longitudinal data, it is my belief that important aspects of reality can be modelled reasonably successfully. Nonetheless, it is important to be aware of the problems. Many of the measurement problems can be solved, or at least alleviated, by a careful design of the study (see, for instance, the careful discussion of how to measure offending in a longitudinal perspective, as given by Farrington in chapter 9).

With regard to the choice of a statistical model for analysing the data, I would like to see more combining of parametric and non-parametric procedures applied to the same sample: for example, exploration looking for higher-order interactions, and hypothesis-generating and confirmatory analyses using structural modelling (maybe using a division of the sample into split halves for purposes of cross-validation). A multitude of analytical possibilities exist, and in many cases longitudinal research alone can carry the torch to light up the paths of development.

References

Beckne, R. (1966) En analys av data från elevenkäter (An analysis of data from pupils' questionnaire). Ph. D. thesis, University of Stockholm.

Bentler, P. M. (1986) Structural modeling and Psychometrika: an historical perspective on growth and achievements. *Psychometrika*, 51, 35–51.

Bergman, L. R. (1972) *Change as the dependent variable.* Reports from the Psychological Laboratories, the University of Stockholm, supplement no. 14.

Bergman, L. R. and Wärneryd, B. (1982) *Om datainsamling i survey-undersökningar* (Data collection in survey research) Stockholm: Liber.

Bishop, Y. M. M., Feinberg, S. E. and Holland, P. W. (1975) *Discrete multivariate analysis: theory and practice.* Cambridge, MA: MIT Press.

Busemeyer, J. R. (1980) Importance of measurement theory, error theory, and experimental design for testing the significance of interactions. *Psychological Bulletin*, 88, 237–44.

Cliff, N. (1983) Some cautions concerning the application of causal modeling methods. *Multivariate Behavioral Research*, 18, 115–28.

Collins, M. (1980) Interviewer variability: a review of the problem. *Journal of the Market Research Society*, 22, 77–95.

Cronbach, L. J. (1975) Beyond the two disciplines of scientific psychology. *American Psychologist*, 30, 116–27.

Cronbach, L. J. and Furby, L. (1970) How should we measure 'change' – or should we? *Psychological Bulletin*, 74, 68–80.

Cronbach, L. J., Gleser, G. C., Nanda, H. and Rajaratnam, N. (1972) *The dependability of behavioral measurements: theory of generalizability for scores and profiles.* New York: Wiley.

Goodman, L. A. (1978) *Analyzing qualitative/categorical data.* London: Addison-Wesley.

Greenwald, A. G., Pratkanis, A. R., Leippe, M. R. and Baumgardner, M. H. (1986) Under what conditions does theory obstruct research progress? *Psychological Review*, 93: 2, 216–29.

Harris, C. W. (1963) (ed.) *Problems in measuring change.* Madison, Milwaukee: University of Wisconsin Press.

Hinde, R. A. and Dennis, A. (1986) Categorizing individuals: an alternative to linear analysis. *International Journal of Behavioral Development*, 9, 105–19.

Jones, R. V. (1979) *Most secret war.* London: Hodder and Stoughton.

Jöreskog, K. G. and Sörbom, D. (1984) LISREL VI. University of Uppsala, Department of Statistics.

(1985) PRELIS – a preprocessor for LISREL. University of Uppsala, Department of Statistics.

Kendall, M. G. and Stuart, A. (1963) *The advanced theory of statistics*, vol. 1. London: Charles Griffin.

Kenny, D. and Judd, C. (1984) Estimating the nonlinear and interactive effects of latent variables. *Psychological Bulletin*, 96, 201–10.

Kish, L. (1962) Studies of interviewer variance for attitudinal variables. *Journal of the American Statistical Association*, 57, 92–115.

Krauth, J. and Lienert, G. A. (1982) Fundamentals and modifications of configural frequency analysis (CFA). *Interdisciplinaria*, 3, 1–14.

Lienert, G. A. (1969) Die 'Konfigurationsfrequenzanalyse' als Klassifikationsmittel in der klinischen Psychologie. In Irle, M. (ed.) *Bericht über den 26. Kongress der Deutschen Gesellschaft für Psychologie.* Tübingen, Göttingen: Hogrete, pp. 244–53.

Lienert, G. A. and Bergman, L. R. (in press) Longisectional interaction structure analysis (LISA) in psychopharmacology and developmental psycho-pathology. *Neuropsychobiology.*

Lienert, G. A. and Kohnen, R. (1987) Interactional research in human develop-ment approached by interactive configural frequency analysis. In Mag-nusson, D. and Öhman, A. (eds.) *Psychopathology: an interactional perspec-tive.* New York: Academic Press.

Magnusson, D. (1985) Implications of an interactional paradigm for research on human development. *International Journal of Behavioral Development,* 8, 115–37.

Olsson, U. and Bergman, L. R. (1977) A longitudinal factor model for studying change in ability structure. *Multivariate Behavioral Research,* 12, 221–42.

Rogosa, D. R. and Willett, J. B. (1985a) Understanding correlates of change by modeling individual differences in growth. *Psychometrika,* 50, 203–28.

(1985b) Satisfying a simplex structure is simpler than it should be. *Journal of Educational Statistics,* 10, 726–42.

Rudinger, G. (1985) Intellectual development in a longitudinal perspective. In Mussen, P., Munnichs, J. and Olbrich, E. (eds.) *Life-span and change in a gerontological perspective.* New York: Academic Press, pp. 63–74.

Rutter, M. (1983) Statistical and personal interactions: facets and perspectives. In Magnusson, D. and Allen, V. L. (eds.) *Human development: an interactional perspective.* New York: Academic Press, pp. 295–319.

Schuman, H. and Presser, S. (1981) *Questions and answers in attitude surveys.* New York: Academic Press.

Snedecor, G. W. and Cochran, W. G. (1967) *Statistical methods,* 6th edn. Ames, IA: Iowa State University Press.

Townsend, J. T. and Ashby, F. G. (1984) Measurement scales and statistics: the misconception misconceived. *Psychological Bulletin,* 96, 394–401.

21 Continuities and discontinuities: conceptual issues and methodological considerations

Robert A. Hinde

Introduction

Science has involved innumerable attempts to force the natural world into categories. For the most part, nature is not like that. Physical versus biological, living versus non-living, plant versus animal, unicellular versus multicellular, normal versus pathological – these are just a few of the dichotomies that seemed clear-cut, but proved to be misleading. We must beware of the same dangers in studying continuities and discontinuities in development. When discussion about their relative importance becomes an argument *for* one or the other, it becomes silly. Individuals are neither infinitely malleable, hostages of whatever winds of fortune they may encounter, nor are they rigidly consistent, maintaining an identical psychological structure as they pass through life's successive stages. The contrast between continuity and discontinuity is useful only as a descriptive tool that opens the way to questions about process: What psychological changes formed the basis for the sudden change in behaviour? What mechanisms underlie the consistency from time 1 to time 2?

The issue of continuities versus discontinuities has been much discussed in recent years, in part because of the growing acceptance of the complexity of developmental processes. Thus Hinde and Bateson (1984) argued against a too easy acceptance of apparent discontinuities as indicating basic changes in the underlying mechanisms, and Rutter (1987) has provided an extensive review. Many of the contributions in the present volume, and perhaps especially those of Kalverboer and Brown (see chapters 7 and 17), underline the potential complexity of developmental interactions, and thus by implication indicate the naivety of any simple dichotomy between continuity and discontinuity. The present contribution briefly reviews the evidence that has been used to postulate continuities/discontinuities, and then discusses some difficulties in its interpretation. It is concluded by a few general remarks about mechanisms.

The nature of the evidence

Evidence for 'continuities' and 'discontinuities' usually comes from assessments of behaviour at different points in time: usually, but not invariably, the behaviour is of the same type at each time point. In addition, long-term effects of experience are taken as evidence for continuity. In practice, the evidence used can be categorized as follows:

1. Evidence concerned with consistencies or with marked changes in the behaviour of an individual or a group of individuals. Here several types of data may be involved. For instance, the appearance of a qualitatively new pattern of behaviour, especially if it replaces a pre-existing one, may be taken as evidence for a discontinuity: the change from sucking to eating solid food is an obvious example. Or the data may concern a sudden change in developmental rate, such as the growth spurt at puberty. Or again, a third type of evidence refers to marked changes in the correlations between different types of behaviour (Barrett and Bateson, 1978).

A related type of evidence concerns the persistence of the effects of experience. This involves comparison between two groups, one having the experience and the other lacking it. Thus one may ask whether the differences between infants born after obstetrical complications and infants who have had easy births persist over time (Sameroff and Chandler, 1975); or whether the gains produced by special educational techniques are lasting (see below).

2. Evidence based on comparisons between different types of behaviour in the same individual. Such ('ipsative') data concern changes (or consistency) in the relative frequencies (or some other measure) of different types of behaviour in the same individual.

3. Evidence based on comparisons between individuals. This usually involves changes in the rank order of individuals on a particular measure. For instance, the finding that the scores of babies on a number of measures at two months fail to predict their relative scores on the same measures at four months has been used as evidence for a discontinuity between these two ages (Kagan, 1978). Such a discontinuity is referred to as 'normative' change.

Problems with the evidence

Data of the types discussed above raise a number of problems.

Heterogeneity
The types of evidence listed above are distinct from each other, so that evidence implying continuity/discontinuity in one sense does not imply a similar conclusion in another (Emmerich, 1964; Sackett *et al.*, 1981; Kagan, 1978). For example, Engfer (1986b), studying mother–infant relationships at 4 and at 18 months, found that feeding and sleeping routines showed high 4–18-month correlations (indicating continuity) but a marked change in the group means (indicating discontinuity). By

contrast, night waking showed low 4–18-month correlations but little change in the group mean. One must conclude that examples of continuity or of discontinuity may have diverse causal bases.

Misinterpretation of correlational evidence

Evidence for discontinuities based on changes in rank order of individuals, or in correlations between items of behaviour, can be explained in a number of ways, some of which are trivial (Bateson, 1978; Hinde and Bateson, 1984; Rutter, 1987):

1 Ceiling or floor effects. Correlations can diminish because scores approach a common value. Such a possibility can be discounted given information about the scores and their variances. Quinton (see chapter 16) uses an explanation of this type to account for the absence of an effect of positive school experiences in a control group of women, when such an effect was found in an ex-care group.

2 Individual differences in timing of development. A change in the rank order of individuals may be due to some individuals undergoing a developmental change (e.g. puberty) earlier than others. The change in rank order may then be merely temporary, the original order being restored when all individuals have passed through the stage in question. This issue is emphasized by Magnusson and Bergman (see chapter 3).

Other statistical issues

Continuity may be difficult to prove simply because of the impossibility of proving the null hypothesis of no change. Where group data are used, apparent continuity may conceal marked changes in subgroups: for instance, individuals may differ markedly in their susceptibility to environmental agents (e.g. Gloag, 1980). Alternatively, apparent continuity may depend upon a small group of extreme individuals (see chapter 3).

The question of pooling measures

It is a reasonable presumption that each item of behaviour represents the expression of numerous psychological mechanisms and environmental influences, and that any identifiable psychological mechanism may find expression in numerous aspects of behaviour. If measures of behaviour change over time, it remains possible that the underlying psychological mechanisms display greater continuity than the overt behaviour. One possibility, then, is to aggregate measures that are presumed to relate to the same psychological mechanism. This can help in two ways. First, every measure is inevitably subject to error, and aggregation is likely to give a more stable and representative estimator than any simple measurement. The validity of this principle has been demonstrated in diverse areas of psychology: low correlations are often improved by aggregating measures (Rushton *et al.*, 1983). Second, aggregation may provide an index of a more basic mediating variable that predicts inter-subject differences (e.g. Block, 1981). This would be more appropriate the more the measure reflected an individual characteristic rather than a relationship one (Stevenson-Hinde, 1987). Estimates of the reliability of the measures can be used to improve the estimate of the (presumed) mediating variable (Fergusson and Horwood, chapter 19). Of course even then, however, such a variable would not necessarily predict behaviour in particular situations accurately: that might or might not be a matter of concern, according to the aims of the investigator. Another approach to the study of continuity is introduced by Magnusson and Bergman (see chapter 3), with the suggestion that *patterns* of symptoms may be better than simple or aggregated measures in predicting later behaviour.

Environmental effects
A major issue in longitudinal studies arises from the fact that they always involve simultaneous changes in both the individual(s) under study and in the situation. Indeed the two are interdependent, since a developing individual may come to perceive an objectively similar situation differently. Thus apparent continuities may have a fragile dependence on consistency in the environment and apparent discontinuities may in fact depend on changes in the effective environment.

For example, infant rhesus monkeys separated from their mothers for a few days were found to behave quite normally in their home cages a year or two later, but their behaviour in mildly stressful situations was markedly affected (Hinde and Spencer-Booth, 1971; Hinde et al., 1978). More importantly, the persistence of the effects of early experience may lie in the individual's relationships with important others. Thus programmes of intervention in the preschool years were earlier thought to lead to some immediate IQ gains but to no substantial long-term consequences. As discussed by Maughan, however (see chapter 11), it has recently become apparent that there are longer-term sequelae involving some increases in academic achievement and a reduction in the proportion of children requiring special educational treatment (e.g. Clarke and Clarke, 1982; Clarke-Stewart and Fein, 1983; Lazar and Darlington, 1982). However, the evidence suggests that such effects depend on a variety of social factors, including continued parental support for education, positive personality characteristics and supportive teachers. The long-term effects are thus not just due to an immediate effect of the initial experience, but stem from a sequence of effects involving relationships in both home and school (Rutter, 1987).

Sometimes environmental consistency may be due to, or be created by, the individual. The consequences of early institutional rearing on the social behaviour of children subsequently adopted or fostered appear to be more marked than those on cognitive development. Clarke and Clarke

(1976, p. 13) suggest that 'the disturbed institutional child, placed in foster care, may elicit from the foster mother antagonistic responses which strengthen the child's instability ... [thus] the child may become the unwitting agent of his own later difficulties'.

Contrariwise, just as consistencies may depend on the presence of persisting experiential factors, so apparent discontinuities in the behaviour of an individual may be due to changes in his or her environment, and especially to changes in important relationships. In the case of dramatic discontinuities, this is often obvious enough: every schoolteacher knows that the appearance of problems in school may reflect trouble at home. Perhaps of more general importance, many parents adjust their parental behaviour to the requirements of their children more easily at one age than at another. Thus Dunn *et al.* (1985) found that parents behave with considerable consistency to successive children of the same age, but parental behaviour often changes dramatically as children grow up (Clarke-Stewart and Hevey, 1981). This is compatible with the suggestion that apparent discontinuities may be related to changes in important relationships in the children's lives.

The nature of the variables

A major difficulty in studying continuity/discontinuity arises from the fact that a given measure of behaviour may reflect different psychological mechanisms at different ages: apparent discontinuities could thus depend upon changes in the significance of the behaviour under study. For example, the rank order of 'time spent on mother' by rhesus monkey infants shows only moderate consistency from month to month. This could be taken as implying a degree of discontinuity, but it could also depend upon a change in the factors determining the time the infant spends on its mother. Suppose these factors are related to the need for food early on, which is later expressed in active foraging off the mother, and to a need for protection later. The influence of the need for protection on time on the mother might be swamped by the need for food early on, but become predominant later. Thus an apparent discontinuity signalled by a change in rank order in time on the mother could conceal continuity in individual differences in the strengths of 'food' and 'seeking for protection' motivation. Conversely, apparent continuity could conceal major changes in underlying mechanisms.

More closely related to practical problems, a much discussed issue amongst developmental psychologists concerns continuity in the 'difficultness' of children. Assessed in terms of temperamental characteristics of the child, continuity may be relatively low, and correlations of particular symptoms (e.g. perceived 'lack of sootheability, restlessness') are also often low. However, if attention is focused on what matters to the mother, a different picture emerges. Engfer (1986a) found that at

4 months lack of sootheability, at 18 months frequent crying and restlessness, and at 43 months aggressive non-compliance, were the most important constituents of child difficultness. Furthermore restlessness at 18 months was related to perceived lack of sootheability at 4 months ($r = .49$) rather better than to restlessness at 4 months ($r = .34$, difference not significant), and restlessness at 18 months was related to perceived difficultness at 43 months more strongly ($r = .49$) than to restlessness at 43 months ($r = .28$, difference $p < .10$).

Coherence

In such cases the same behavioural propensity may be revealed in different ways at different ages. For instance, Engfer (1986a) interprets the above changes in the bases of child difficultness as a change in the manifestation of behaviour problems with age.

Again, the effects of an experience at one age may be manifest at a later age in behaviour that is apparently unrelated to the experience but is actually causally connected to it. It has thus been suggested that we should seek not for continuity in behaviour (or other psychological measures) over time, but rather for 'coherence across transformations' or causal connections between experiences at one age and their subsequent psychological or behavioural outcomes (Sroufe et al., 1985). Thus children who experience sensitive mothering become 'securely attached' to their mothers (Ainsworth et al., 1978) and then show a wide variety of positive sequelae in school and other contexts subsequently (Bretherton, 1985).

Another example is provided by the study by Sroufe et al. (1985) of mothers showing a 'seductive' pattern with their two-year-old sons. 'Seductive' is used here to refer not to behaviour intended to lead to frank sexual contact, but to behaviour involving physical contact, sensual teasing, or promises of affection that were motivated by the mother's needs rather than being responsive to the needs of the child. Mothers showing this pattern to their sons tended to show hostility (in the form of derision) to their daughters. Thus although the seductive pattern could be identified from 24 to at least 42 months, and was thus a stable aspect of the mother's behaviour, it could not be viewed in maternal trait terms, but only as depending critically on the relationship. However, the mother–son/mother–daughter difference was understandable in terms of psychological processes in the mothers. It was related to a history of emotional exploitation by their own fathers. Sroufe et al. suggest that the mothers behaved seductively to their sons because their own needs of nurturance had not been met and because they had learned in childhood that parents may attempt to meet their emotional needs through their children. However, the mothers' childhoods were reflected in a different way in relationships with daughters. The distance these mothers had felt from their own mothers led to feelings of self-depreciation and, Sroufe suggests, in depreciating their daughters they reconstructed a relationship pattern with which they were already familiar (see below).

Sequential effects

A special type of coherence occurs when effects at one stage in the life cycle are related to earlier experiences not directly but through intervening experiences that the individuals concerned have created or to which they have acquired an enhanced liability. For example, it has been suggested that childhood adversity may lead to difficult behaviour, creating poor relationships and thus exacerbating the difficulties (e.g. Clarke and Clarke, 1976). Again, in a study of the effects of institutional rearing Rutter *et al.* (1983) found that the strongest effect on the women's parental styles was provided by the characteristics of the women's spouses. This, however, could be seen as an indirect effect of the institutional rearing: over half of the institution-reared women married men with psychosocial problems, as compared with 13% in the general population comparison group. Thus the childhood experiences influenced the choice of spouse, and the spouse affected the quality of parenting. A difficult childhood can enhance the risk of psychosocial difficulties in adulthood even though none are apparent at the time (Quinton and Rutter, 1988): a number of other examples are given elsewhere in this volume (e.g. chapters 9, 11 and 17).

A somewhat different type of case involves sequential effects within one dyad. Engfer (1986a) found that child difficultness at 4 and 18 months as perceived by the mother was associated more with a lack of maternal sensitivity at 0 and 8 months respectively than with characteristics of the baby. Perceived difficultness at 18 months was significantly associated with crying and restlessness at this age, the behaviour problems that the mothers then found most difficult. In turn, perceived difficultness at 18 months was related to lack of co-operativeness in the developmental testing situation at 33 months, and this in turn to perceived child difficultness at 43 months. Since at this age maternal characteristics predicted child difficultness only weakly, Engfer (1986b) deduced that some sort of chaining had taken place: 'initially maternal lack of sensitivity made the babies look more difficult to the mothers at 4 and 18 months. But later on these children displayed observable characteristics substantiating these maternal perceptions and thereby stabilizing the maternal view that their children in fact *are* difficult' (see also Maccoby *et al.*, 1984; and Belsky *et al.*, 1984).

Long-term continuity and cross-situation consistency

Such cases suggest that one should not be too hasty in concluding that apparent discontinuities in behaviour indicate a lack of causal relations between behaviour at one time and that shown later, for the connections may be subtle and indirect. Just because every behavioural act depends upon numerous capacities, motivational propensities and aspects of the current environmental context, and especially the social situation, the effects of a given experience on behaviour in either the short term or the long term are not always easily predictable. This is not merely an attempt to seek refuge from the task of understanding behavioural development by an appeal to complexity. Continuities are sometimes obvious, but their apparent absence is not in itself a reason for abandoning the search for causal sequences underlying the changes that occur.

In any case the identification of continuities, coherence or discontinuity in development must be regarded as only a first step: it must lead to an investigation of process. Here, however, as mentioned already, longitudinal studies face a double problem, for changes in behaviour may be due to changes in subjects, situation, or both. A possible research strategy, therefore, is to seek to understand the processes underlying consistency/ inconsistency in behaviour across contemporaneous situations and then to use that knowledge in studies of continuity/discontinuity over time.

It is in fact well established that even quite young children behave differently according to whom they are with. For instance, an infant labelled as 'securely attached' on the basis of behaviour in the Ainsworth Strange Situation with the mother present may behave quite differently with the father (Main and Weston, 1981), and Dunn and Kendrick (1982) found that first-born girls who had difficult relationships with their mothers tended to have positive relationships with their younger siblings. As another example, four-year-olds behave differently to teachers and to peers (Hinde *et al.*, 1983), and adjust the language that they use according to whom they are with (Gelman and Shatz, 1977; Shatz and Gelman, 1973; Snow, 1972).

That older individuals behave differently according to whom they are with is, of course, familiar enough to the student of interpersonal relationships. The issue is implicit in the symbolic interactionists' description of individuals as having a number of 'role identities' which, though emerging as a consequence of interaction with a particular other, also provide both plans for action and the criteria by which action is evaluated (e.g. Goffman, 1959; and McCall, 1970; 1974). Or, to take a different theoretical perspective, the interdependence theorist's insistence that the course of a relationship depends on rewards and costs, and the expectations of rewards and costs, accruing in the course of each interaction (e.g. Kelley, 1979) implies that every relationship is, in part, a product of its own history and anticipated future, and is thereby differentiated from other relationships.

Such a view is also entirely in harmony with current trends in the study of personality. The earlier view that individual differences in behaviour could be ascribed to individual differences in a number of trait dimensions was criticized because of the relatively low cross-situational consistency of the traits (Mischel, 1968). This led to an emphasis on situational determinants and an excessive neglect of person variables (Block, 1977). However, debate about the relative importance of person and situation variables is inevitably sterile (Mischel, 1973); and studies evaluating the contributions of person, situation, and person × situation interaction to the variance in behaviour indicate the importance of the latter (e.g. Endler and Magnusson, 1976a; 1976b). One approach has been to search for 'moderator variables' that affect the relations between the variables under study, or, more specifically, that allow for the way in which supposed basic dispositions might be affected by age, sex, or by other individual characteristics and by aspects of the situation (Alker, 1972); this approach, however, has encountered methodological, statistical and conceptual difficulties (e.g. Wallach and Leggett, 1972; Zedeck, 1971). But if all people are not consistent some of the time about some things, at least some of the people are consistent some of the time about some things (Bem and Allen, 1974; Bem and Funder, 1978; Kendrick and Stringfield, 1980). And where they appear to be inconsistent, analyses of the psychological processes involved may lead to an understanding of underlying coherence.

A first step towards the understanding of process in cross-situational consistency/inconsistency may be to look for coherence across individuals in the manner in which a given characteristic affects behaviour in two situations.

For example, in a study of the behaviour of preschoolers at school and at home, correlations between similar measures in the two situations were seldom significant (Hinde and Tamplin, 1983). Children who interacted much with their mothers did not necessarily interact much with teachers or peers, and children whose interactions with their mothers were often positive did not necessarily tend to have positive interactions in school. Cross-situational consistency was thus low. Furthermore, in a later study assessments of children's temperamental characteristics at home and at school showed very low intercorrelations (Hinde and Tobin, 1986). However, there were meaningful *patterns* of correlations between the two situations: for instance, infrequent warm intercourse with the mother was correlated with greater overall sociability in school, but the interactions tended to be negative in character, involving hostile and controlling behaviour to adults and peers (Hinde and Tamplin, 1983).

In seeking to interpret such findings, one must seek to understand the bases of the observed differences between home and school behaviour:

1. It is essential first that measures of behaviour, and to a lesser extent measures of temperament, be seen as in part measures of relationships, and not directly of individual characteristics. Thus the nature of mother-

child interaction depends on both mother and child, and children in preschool behave differently towards teachers and peers (Hinde and Stevenson-Hinde, 1987).

2. In some cases, linear correlational techniques give a misleading picture, and other methods must be found. For example, in a recent study of preschoolers, the most aggressive boys had mothers who exercised little control at home, moderately aggressive ones tended to have controlling mothers, and unaggressive boys were again subject to little control at home (Hinde and Dennis, 1986).

3. Temperamental characteristics may be expressed differently at home and at school. Interpretation of such differences is sometimes aided by considering boys and girls separately. For example, in the above study girls assessed as assertive on the basis of maternal descriptions of their behaviour at home tended to have poor relationships with teachers, whilst assertive boys tended to interact seldom with teachers but often with peers (Hinde *et al.*, 1985).

4. The relations between home and school behaviour can sometimes be understood better by considering patterns of home variables, rather than individual ones. Thus maternal warmth coupled with moderate control at home is associated with least aggression in school (Baumrind, 1967; 1971). And the above findings on the correlates of warm intercourse with the mother can be partially understood in terms of combinations of child characteristics. Children high on the temperamental characteristics 'active' and 'moody' tended to have few positive interactions with their mothers at home, but moody children tended to interact frequently with peers in school, and active children to have a high proportion of interactions involving hostility. It is a reasonable supposition that the lack of positive interactions at home was a consequence of a tense mother–child relationship induced in part by the child's characteristics, and that those characteristics were expressed in a different way in school (Hinde, 1985; Baumrind, 1967, 1971; Hinde and Tamplin, 1983).

5. In our more recent work we are using additional measures to assess the psychological dynamics of the home–school transition. These include interviewing the children at home about school and at school about home. The emphasis on understanding the processes involved in cross-situational consistency/inconsistency is of course intended primarily as a step towards the more important goal of understanding longitudinal issues.

Mechanisms

The identification of continuities/discontinuities is a first step towards the analysis of process. Further analyses at the behavioural level may then be revealing. Rutter's demonstration that choice of spouse mediates between institutional upbringing and parental dysfunction is a case in point. As another example, Engfer (1986b) classified children as 'difficult' or 'easy' by dividing their scores on a measure of perceived 'difficultness' at the median. Twenty-five mothers found their babies consistently one or the other from 4 to 18 months, but six babies initially perceived as 'easy' were subsequently perceived as 'difficult', and for four the reverse was the case. The discontinuities in the latter cases could be accounted for in terms of other variables. The 'easy–difficult' mothers had few problems with their babies at first, but they did have marital problems. These apparently subsequently reduced their satisfaction with their relationship with their babies. The 'difficult–easy' group, by contrast, had a high proportion of primiparous mothers and a high incidence of obstetrical complications. Apparently these strains influenced their perceptions of their children at first, but subsequently lost their potency as the mothers acquired competence.

Given such a behavioural analysis, the underlying psychological mechanisms must be teased apart. It is implicit in the preceding discussion that these are likely to be diverse, and discussion here is limited to the general issue of the level of analysis at which explanations may be sought.

The mechanisms invoked to explain continuity/discontinuity can be grouped into three categories:

(a) Physiological mechanisms

Some long-term effects of experience may be carried by identifiable changes in physiological mechanisms. In some cases, such as the effects of early stressors on the hypothalamic–adrenal cortex system, or aspects of cardiac functioning (Kagan *et al.*, 1985) these are directly measurable. In others they are imputed on the basis of indirect evidence, as with the effects of prenatal androgenization on gender role determination. In both cases, the physiological change may subsequently involve other mechanisms – as when the effect of prenatal androgenization operates through assigned gender (Adkins, 1980).

(b) Mid-level psychological mechanisms

Some cases of continuity/discontinuity are explained in terms of psychological variables known to be useful in other contexts, either emotional (e.g. Lipsitt, 1983) or cognitive (e.g. Kagan, 1980). For instance, consistent individual differences in aspects of children's behaviour may be described as involving consistent differences in dimensions of personality or temperament. There is a danger of circularity here, because personality and temperamental differences are (or perhaps were – see Goldsmith *et al.*, 1987) often *defined* as having continuity and thus cannot by their nature explain either continuities or discontinuities. By contrast, other psychological constructs are applicable primarily to discontinuities (e.g.

learning). However, in both cases, the explanatory concepts used are susceptible to reasonably tight definition, with relations to independent and/or dependent variables specified.

(c) Complex cognitive mechanisms

The more complex the psychological mechanism postulated, the more difficult the task of precise definition, and an explanatory concept inadequately defined cannot be falsified. It may still have a heuristic value and be useful also in integrating otherwise apparently unrelated facts, but it is necessary to be aware of its dangers.

A case in point is the 'working model' of attachment theorists. Bowlby (1982; see also Craik, 1943) postulated that children construct increasingly complex internal working models (IWM) of the world, and of significant persons in it. He used this concept to explain how a child's early relationship with an attachment figure develops and how it can influence subsequent behaviour in other situations, and thus how consistent differences between children could be explained in terms of differences in their early attachment relationships. Bowlby's discussion of working models is based in large measure on the sort of mechanisms that must be postulated in order to account for the observed behaviour: 'First, the model must be built in accordance with such data as are or can be made available. Secondly, if the model is to be of use in novel situations, it must be extended imaginatively to cover potential realities as well as experienced ones' (Bowlby, 1982, p. 81). Drawing on a wealth of clinical experience, he describes IWMs as 'none other than the "internal worlds" of traditional psychoanalytic theory seen in a new perspective' (p. 82). Such a concept can have, and has had, enormous heuristic value in synthesizing and making sense of data. Bretherton (1985) refers to the IWM as a 'conceptual metaphor', noting that the term 'working' emphasizes the dynamic aspects of representation, and the term 'model' implies construction and modifiability.

However, in the very power of such a model lies a trap: it can too easily explain anything. Main et al. (1985, p. 68) define the IWM as 'a mental representation of an aspect of the world, others, self, or relationships to others that is of special relevance to the individual', and elsewhere (p. 92) as 'a set of conscious and/or unconscious rules for the organization of information relevant to attachment and for obtaining or limiting access to that information'. In this and other papers (Bretherton and Waters, 1985), a number of other properties are attributed to the IWM. For instance, functionally, the IWM is seen both as filtering input from the outside world and as directing motor activity. It is seen as self-perpetuating and resistant to dramatic change, but nevertheless modifiable, the modifications taking place either as a result of interaction with the other individual or through cognitive processes in his/her absence. The IWM is sometimes seen as a model of another individual, and sometimes as a model of a relationship. Furthermore, Sroufe and Fleeson (1986) imply that children can act out both sides of the IWM of a relationship, and thereby explain how abused children may become abusing parents. An individual may have two IWMs of the same person, the discrepancies between them sometimes giving rise to psychopathology.

The IWM is seen as itself consisting of a hierarchical network of representations of increasing specificity, and IWMs are seen as themselves hierarchically organized, that of the mother, for instance, being more potent in influencing subsequent attachment-related behaviour than that of the father. IWMs can exist only in a limited number of types, but further types may remain to be discovered.

It is difficult to avoid the conclusion that properties are added to the working model as new phenomena require explanation, and that at least some of the new properties are isomorphic with the phenomena they purport to explain. At the risk of being repetitious, at this point it might be as well to emphasize that the IWM concept, used (in Bretherton's terms) as a 'conceptual metaphor', certainly has heuristic value and certainly integrates diverse facts. Whether the IWM concept as used by these authors actually explains anything that could not more parsimoniously be explained in terms of concepts well tried in other contexts (see (b) above) is at present an open issue.

Certainly, a more detailed specification of the nature *and limitations* of the IWM in terms of component or ancillary mechanisms would seem to be necessary before much progress can be made (cf. Zivin (1986) for a comparable attempt with expressive behaviour). Work by others who have been concerned with the internalization of social experience must be taken into account. For instance, Forgas (1982) has reached conclusions similar in many ways to those of attachment theorists, and Stern's (1985) concept of the RIG (representation of interactions that have been generalized) is of special interest. Stern supposes that memories of each category of interactive episode (e.g. peck-a-boo with mother) are laid down, the RIG being modifiable by each episode but becoming increasingly conservative as more are experienced. Any attribute of the RIG can serve as a cue to reactivate the lived experience. Stern sees the RIG as a possible component of the attachment theorist's working model. It certainly seems likely that the latter would be more valuable if it were fleshed out with components of a lower degree of complexity.

Conclusion

Very often, as science progresses, yesterday's fierce debate comes to seem like a storm in a teacup, irrelevant to current issues or indeed to real life. But that does not mean that the debate has been fruitless. The continuity/

discontinuity discussion has led to recognition that the phenomena of continuity and discontinuity are themselves heterogeneous, and to clarification of the relevance of different sources of evidence. More importantly, it has facilitated progress, through the classical developmental psychologists' concentration on the description of behaviour or psychological characteristics to an attack on the *processes* of development. The concept of 'discontinuity', like the old concept of instinct, could block the way for further research: by contrast, putting the spotlight on process is bound to open further alleys towards a full understanding of the nature of development. Of course such an enterprise must be based in part on the faith that coherence must be there to be found if only we can understand how it all works, but such an undisprovable assumption is no bad starting point. Be that as it may, it is suggested in this chapter that a new discussion may now be necessary: are the conceptual tools that served so well for description sharp enough for the attack on process?

References

Adkins, E. K. (1980) Genes, hormones, sex and gender. In Barlow, G. W. and Silverberg, J. (eds.) *Sociobiology: beyond nature/nurture.* Boulder, Colorado: Westview, pp. 385–415.

Ainsworth, M. D., Salter., Blehar, M. C., Waters, E. and Wall, S. (1978) *Patterns of attachment,* Hillsdale, NJ: Erlbaum.

Alker, H. A. (1972) Is personality situationally specific or intrapsychically consistent? *Journal of Personality,* 40, 1–16.

Barrett, P. and Bateson, P. (1978) The development of play in cats. *Behaviour,* 66, 106–20.

Bateson, P. P. G. (1978) How does behavior develop? In Bateson, P. P. G. and Klopfer, P. H. (eds.) *Perspectives in ethology,* vol. 3. New York: Plenum Press, pp. 55–66.

Baumrind, D. (1967) Child care practices anteceding three patterns of preschool behaviour. *Genetic Psychology Monographs,* 75, 43–88.

(1971) Current patterns of parental authority. *Developmental Monographs,* 4 (1), part 2, 1–103.

Belsky, J., Rovine, M. and Taylor, D. G. (1984) The Pennsylvania Infant and Family Development Project, III: the origins of individual differences in infant/mother attachment: maternal and infant contributions. *Child Development,* 55, 718–28.

Bem, D. J. and Allen, A. (1974) On predicting some of the people some of the time: the search for cross-situational consistencies in behaviour. *Psychological Review,* 81, 506–20.

Bem, D. J. and Funder, D. C. (1978) Predicting more of the people more of the time. *Psychological Review,* 85, 484–501.

Block, J. (1977) Advancing the psychology of personality: paradigmatic shift or improving the quality of research? In Magnusson, D. and Endler, N. S. (eds.) *Psychology at the crossroads: current issues in interactional psychology.* Hillsdale, NJ: Erlbaum, pp. 37–63.

(1981) Some enduring and consequential structures of personality. In Rabin, A., Aronoff, J., Barclay, A. M. and Zucker, R. A. (eds.) *Further explanations in personality.* New York: Wiley.

Bowlby, J. (1982) *Attachment and loss*, vol. 1, *Attachment*, 2nd edn. London: Hogarth.

Bretherton, I. (1985) Attachment theory: retrospect and prospect. In Bretherton, I. and Waters, E. (eds.) *Growing points of attachment theory and research*. Monographs of the Society for Research in Child Development, vol. 50, nos. 1–2, pp. 3–38.

Bretherton, I. and Waters, E. (1985) *Growing points of attachment theory and research*. Monographs of the Society for Research in Child Development, vol. 50, nos. 1–2.

Clarke, A. M. and Clarke, A. D. B. (1976) *Early experience: myth and evidence*. London: Open Books.

(1982) Intervention and sleeper effects: a reply to Victoria Seitz. *Developmental Review*, 2, 76–86.

Clarke-Stewart, K. A. and Fein, G. G. (1983) Early childhood programs. In Haith, M. M. and Campos, J. J. (eds.) *Infancy and developmental psychobiology, Handbook of child psychology*, ed. P. Mussen, vol. 2, 4th edn. New York: Wiley, pp. 917–99.

Clarke-Stewart, K. A. and Hevey, C. (1981) Longitudinal relations in repeated observations of mother–child interaction from 1 to 2½ years. *Developmental Psychology*, 17, 127–45.

Craik, K. (1943) *The nature of explanation*. Cambridge: Cambridge University Press.

Dunn, J. and Kendrick, C. (1982) *Siblings, love, envy and understanding*. London: Grant McIntyre.

Dunn, J., Plomin, R. and Nettles, M. (1985) Consistency of mothers' behavior towards infant siblings. *Developmental Psychology*, 21, 1188–95.

Emmerich, W. (1964) Continuity and stability in early social development. *Child Development*, 35, 311–22.

Endler, N. S. and Magnusson, D. (1976a) Toward an interactional psychology of personality. *Psychological Bulletin*, 83, 956–74.

(1976b) *Interactional psychology and personality*. New York: Wiley.

Engfer, A. (1986a) Antecedents of perceived behaviour problems in children 4 and 18 months of age – a longitudinal study. In Kohnstam, D. (ed.) *Temperament discussed*. Lisse: Swets and Zeitlinger, pp. 165–80.

(1986b) Stability and change in perceived characteristics of children 4 to 43 months of age. Paper presented at the Second European Conference on Developmental Psychology, Rome.

Forgas, J. P. (1982) Episode cognition: internal representations of interaction routines. *Advances in Experimental and Social Psychology*, vol. 15. New York: Academic Press.

Gelman, R. and Shatz, M. (1977) Speech adjustments in talk to 2-year-olds. In Lewis, M. and Rosenblum, L. A. (eds.) *Interaction, conversation and the development of language*. New York: Academic Press, pp. 27–61.

Gloag, D. (1980) Risks of low-level radiation – the evidence of epidemiology. *British Medical Journal*, 281, 1479–82.

Goffman, E. (1959) *The presentation of self in everyday life*. New York: Doubleday-Anchor.

Goldsmith, H., Buss, A. H., Plomin, R., Rothbart, M. K., Thomas, A., Chess, S., Hinde, R. A. and McCall, R. B. (1987) What is temperament? Four approaches. *Child Development*, 58: 2, 505–30.

Hinde, R. A. (1985) Home correlates of aggressive behavior in preschool. In Ramirez, J. M. and Brain, P. F. (eds.) *Aggression: functions and causes*. Madrid: CICA and PWPA.

Hinde, R. A. and Bateson, P. P. G. (1984) Discontinuities versus continuities in behavioural development and the neglect of process. *International Journal of Behavioral Development*, 7, 129–43.

Hinde, R. A. and Dennis, A. (1986) Categorizing individuals: an alternative to linear analysis. *International Journal of Behavioral Development*, 9, 105–19.

Hinde, R. A. and Spencer-Booth, Y. (1971) Effects of brief separation from mother on rhesus monkeys. *Science*, 773, 111–18.

Hinde, R. A. and Stevenson-Hinde, J. (1987) Interpersonal relationships and child development. *Developmental Review*, 7, 1–21.

Hinde, R. A. and Tamplin, A. (1983) Relations between mother–child interaction and behaviour in preschool. *British Journal of Developmental Psychology*, 1, 231–57.

Hinde, R. A. and Tobin, C. (1986) Temperament at home and behaviour at preschool. In Kohnstamm, D. (ed.) *Temperament discussed*. Lisse: Swets and Zeitlinger.

Hinde, R. A., Leighton-Shapiro, M. E. and McGinnis, L. (1978) Effects of various types of separation experience on rhesus monkeys 5 months later. *Journal of Child Psychology and Psychiatry*, 19, 199–211.

Hinde, R. A., Easton, D. F., Meller, R. E. and Tamplin, A. (1983) Nature and determinants of preschoolers' differential behaviour to adults and peers. *British Journal of Developmental Psychology*, 1, 3–19.

Hinde, R. A., Stevenson-Hinde, J. and Tamplin, A. (1985) Characteristics of 3- to 4-year-olds assessed at home and their interactions in preschool. *Developmental Psychology*, 21, 130–40.

Kagan, J. (1978) Continuity and stage in human development. In Bateson, P. P. G. and Klopfer, P. H. (eds.) *Perspectives in ethology*, vol. 3, *Social behavior*. New York: Plenum Press, pp. 67–84.

— (1980) Perspectives on continuity. In Brim, O. and Kagan, J. (eds.) *Constancy and change in human development*. Cambridge, MA: Harvard University Press, pp. 26–74.

Kagan, J., Reznick, J. S. and Snidman, N. (1985) Temperamental inhibition in early childhood. In Plomin, R. and Dunn, J. (eds.) *The study of temperament: changes, continuities and challenges*. Hillsdale, NJ and London: Erlbaum, pp. 53–66.

Kelley, H. H. (1979) *Personal relationships: their structures and processes*. Hillsdale, NJ: Erlbaum

Kendrick, D. T. and Stringfield, D. O. (1980) Personality traits and the eye of the beholder. *Psychological Review*, 87, 88–104.

Lazar, I. and Darlington, R. B. (1982) *Lasting effects of early education*. Monographs of the Society for Research in Child Development 195, vol. 47.

Lipsitt, L. P. (1983) Stress in infancy. In Garmezy, N. and Rutter, M. (eds.) *Stress, coping and development in children*. New York: McGraw-Hill.

McCall, G. J. (1970) The social organization of relationships. In McCall, G. J., McCall, M., Denzin, N. K., Suttles, G. D. and Kurth, S. B. (eds.) *Social relationships*. Chicago: Aldine.

— (1974) A symbolic interactionist approach to attraction. In Huston, T. L. (ed.) *Foundations of interpersonal attraction*. New York: Academic Press, pp. 217–31.

Maccoby, E. E., Snow, M. E. and Jacklin, C. N. (1984) Children's dispositions and mother–child interaction at 12 and 18 months: a short term longitudinal study. *Developmental Psychology*, 20, 459–72.

Main, M. B. and Weston, D. R. (1981) Security of attachment to mother and father: related to conflict behavior and the readiness to establish new relationships. *Child Development*, 52, 932–40.

Main, M., Kaplan, N. and Cassidy, J. (1985) Security in infancy, childhood and adulthood: a move to the level of representation. In Bretherton, I. and Waters, E. (eds.) *Growing points of attachment theory and research.* Monographs of the Society for Research in Child Development, vol. 50, nos. 1–2, pp. 66–104.

Mischel, W. (1968) *Personality and assessment.* New York: Wiley.

(1973) Toward a cognitive social learning reconceptualization of personality. *Psychological Review*, 80, 252–83.

Quinton, D. and Rutter, M. (1988) *Parenting breakdown: making and breaking intergenerational cycles.* Aldershot: Gower.

Rushton, J. P., Brainerd, C. J. and Pressley, M. (1983) Behavioural development and construct validity: the principle of aggregation. *Psychological Bulletin*, 84, 18–38.

Rutter, M. (1987) Continuities and discontinuities from infancy. In Osofsky, J. (ed.) *Handbook of infant development* 2nd edn. New York: Wiley, pp. 1256–96.

Rutter, M., Quinton, D. and Liddle, C. (1983) Parenting in two generations. In Madge, N. (ed.) *Families at risk.* London: Heinemann, pp. 60–98.

Sackett, G. P., Sameroff, A. J., Cairns, R. B. and Suomi, S. (1981) Continuity in behavioral development: theoretical and empirical issues. In Immelmann, K., Barlow, G. W., Petrinovich, L. and Main, M. (eds.) *Behavioral development.* Cambridge: Cambridge University Press, pp. 23–58.

Sameroff, A. J. and Chandler, M. J. (1975) Reproductive risk and the continuum of caretaking casualty. In Horowitz, F. D. (ed.) *Review of child development research*, vol. 4. Chicago: University of Chicago Press, pp. 187–244.

Shatz, M. and Gelman, R. (1973) *The development of communication skills: modifications in the speech of young children as a function of the listener.* Monographs of the Society for Research in Child Development, vol. 38, no. 5.

Snow, C. (1972) Mother's speech to children learning language. *Child Development*, 43, 549–64.

Sroufe, L. A. and Fleeson, J. (1986) Attachment and the construction of relationships. In Hartup, W. W. and Rubin, Z. (eds.) *Relationships and development.* Hillsdale, NJ: Erlbaum, pp. 51–72.

Sroufe, L. A., Jacobwitz, D., Mangelodarf, F., De Angelo, E. and Ward, M. J. (1985) Generational boundary dissolution between mothers and their preschool children: a relationship systems approach. *Child Development*, 56, 317–25.

Stern, D. N. (1985) *The interpersonal world of the infant.* New York: Basic Books.

Stevenson-Hinde, J. (1987) Towards a more open construct. In Kohnstamm, D. (ed.) *Temperament discussed.* Amsterdam: Swets and Zeitlinger, pp. 97–106.

Wallach, M. A. and Leggett, M. I. (1972) Testing the hypothesis that a person will be consistent: stylistic consistency versus situational specificity in size of children's drawings. *Journal of Personality*, 40, 309–30.

Zedeck, S. (1971) Problems with the use of 'moderator' variables. *Psychological Bulletin*, 76, 295–310.

Zivin, G. (1986) Processes of expressive behavior development. *Merrill-Palmer Quarterly*, 32, 103–40.

Index